Batman
DEATH AND THE CITY

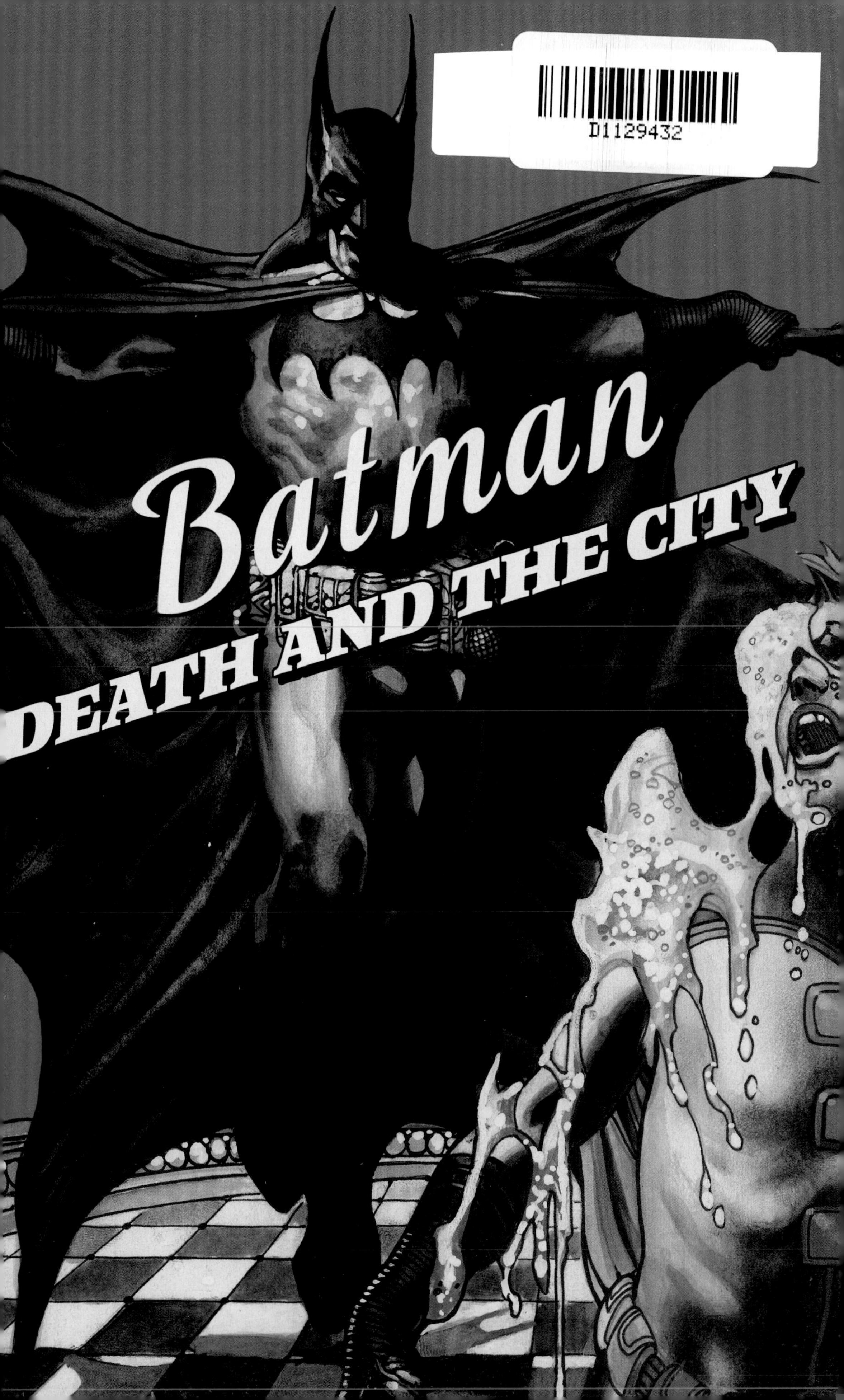

DON KRAMER &
WAYNE FAUCHER
ANDY CLARKE
artists

JOHN KALISZ NATHAN EYRING
JOHN J. HILL TRAVIS LANHAM
colorists

JARED K. FLETCHER JOHN J. HILL
letterers

SIMONE BIANCHI
original covers

BATMAN created by BOB KANE

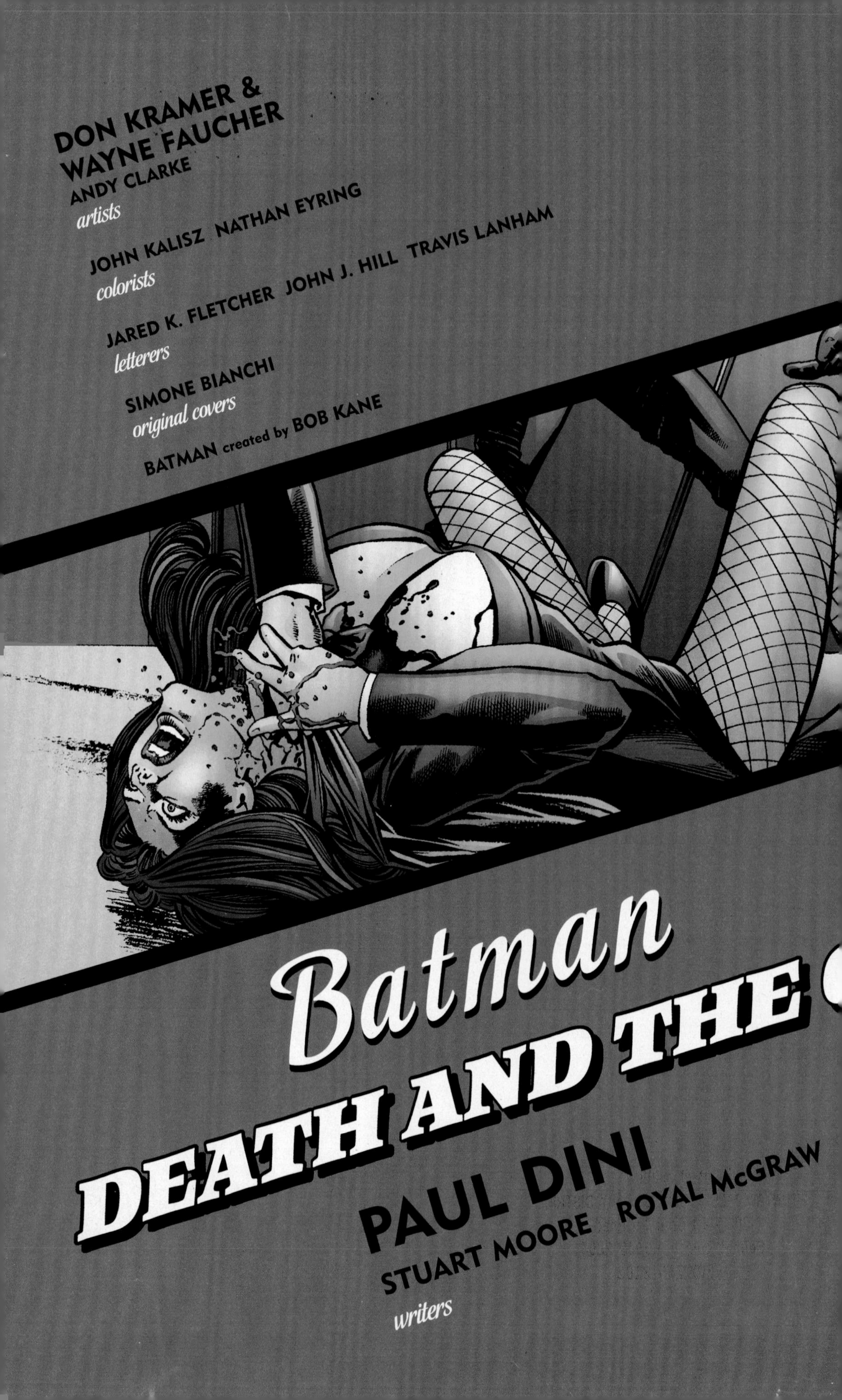

Batman
DEATH AND THE

PAUL DINI
STUART MOORE ROYAL McGRAW
writers

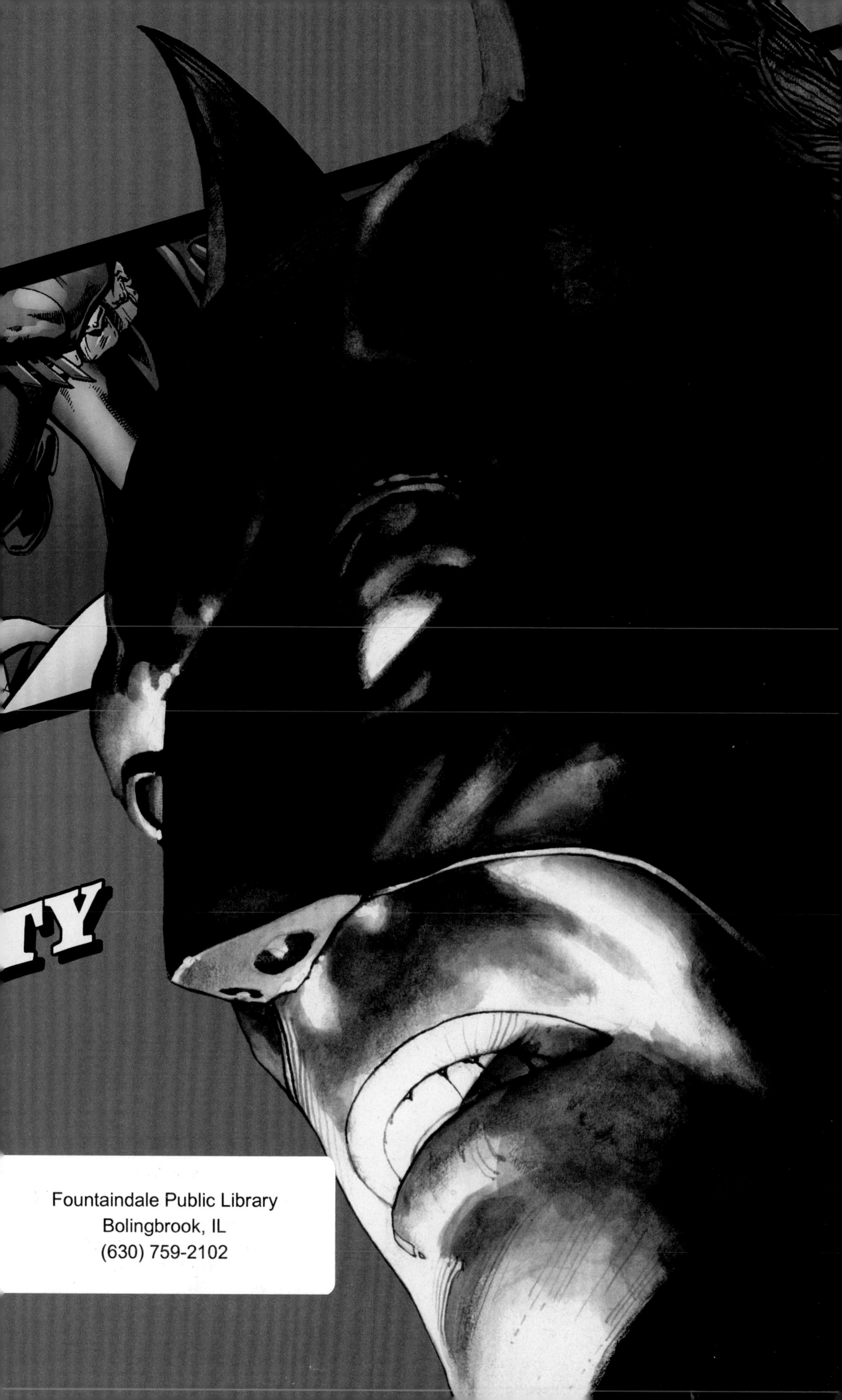
TY

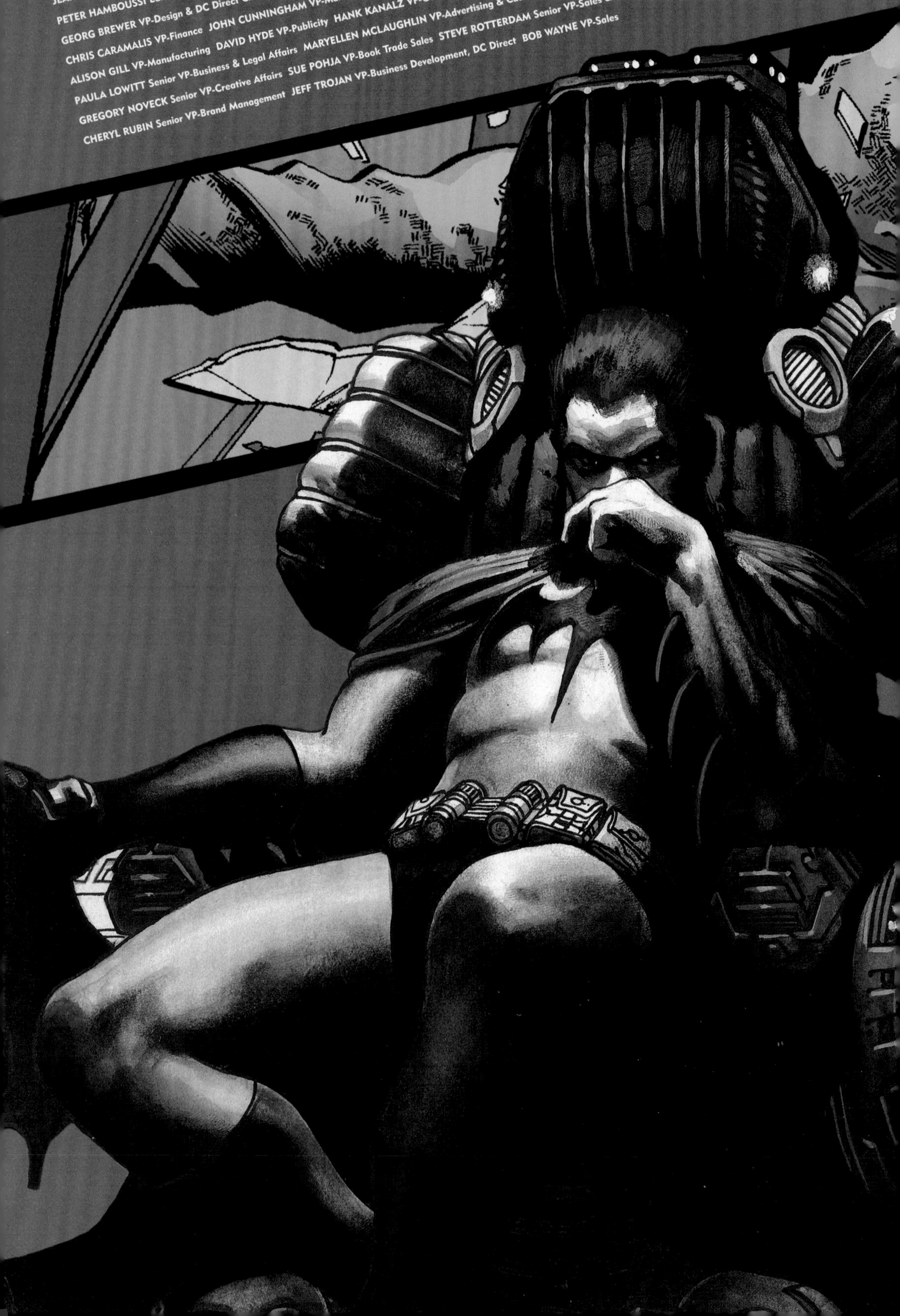

Cover art by Simone Bianchi. Special thanks to Misty Lee for a magical touch.

BATMAN: DEATH AND THE CITY

Published by DC Comics. Cover, text and compilation copyright © 2007 DC Comics. All Rights Reserved.

Originally published in single magazine form in DETECTIVE COMICS #827-834. Copyright © 2007 DC Comics. All Rights Reserved. All characters, their distinctive likenesses and related elements featured in this publication are trademarks of DC Comics. The stories, characters and incidents featured in this publication are entirely fictional. DC Comics does not read or accept unsolicited submissions of ideas, stories or artwork.

DC Comics, 1700 Broadway, New York, NY 10019
A Warner Bros. Entertainment Company Printed in Canada. First Printing.
ISBN: 1-4012-1575-0 ISBN 13: 978-1-4012-1575-0

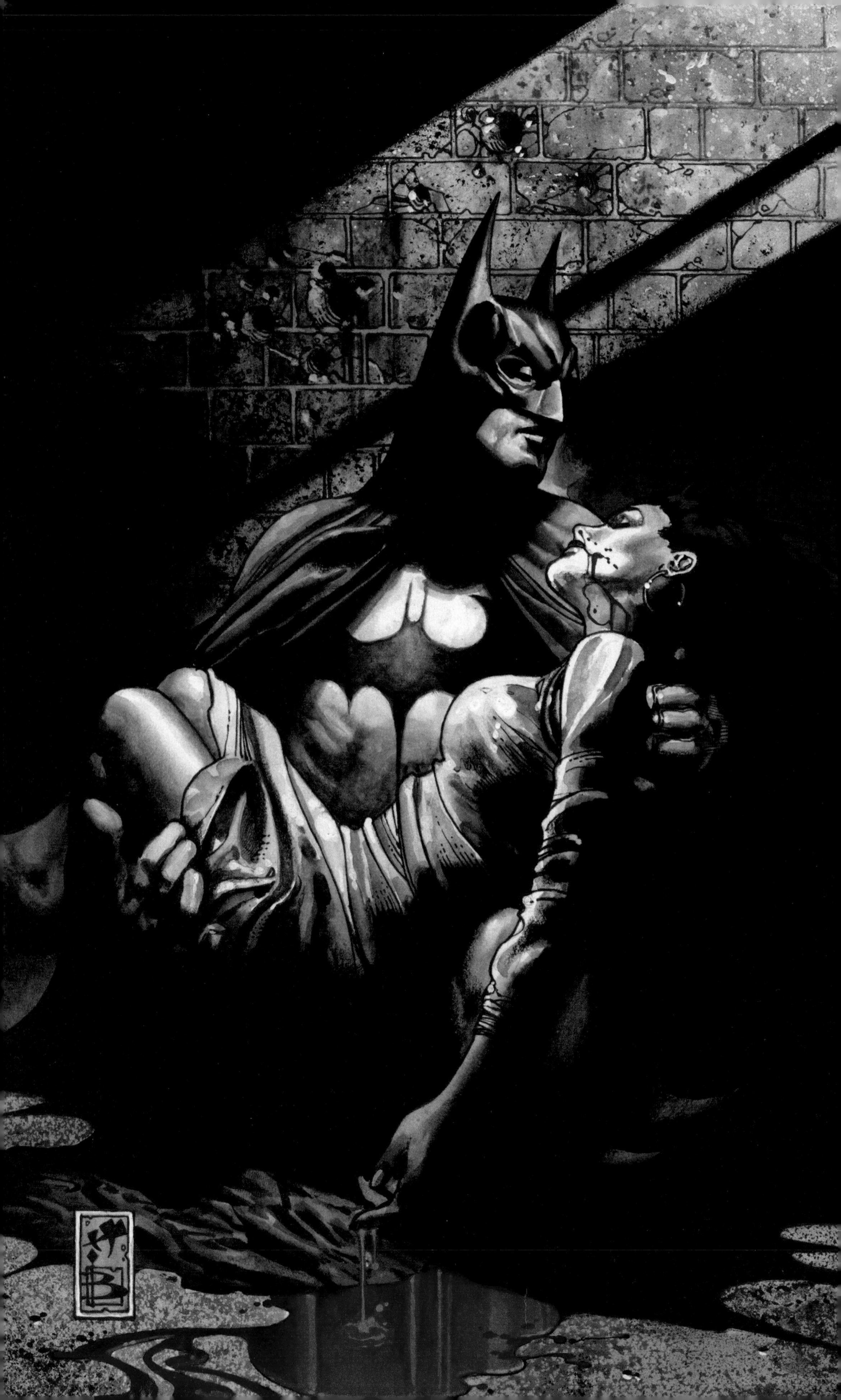

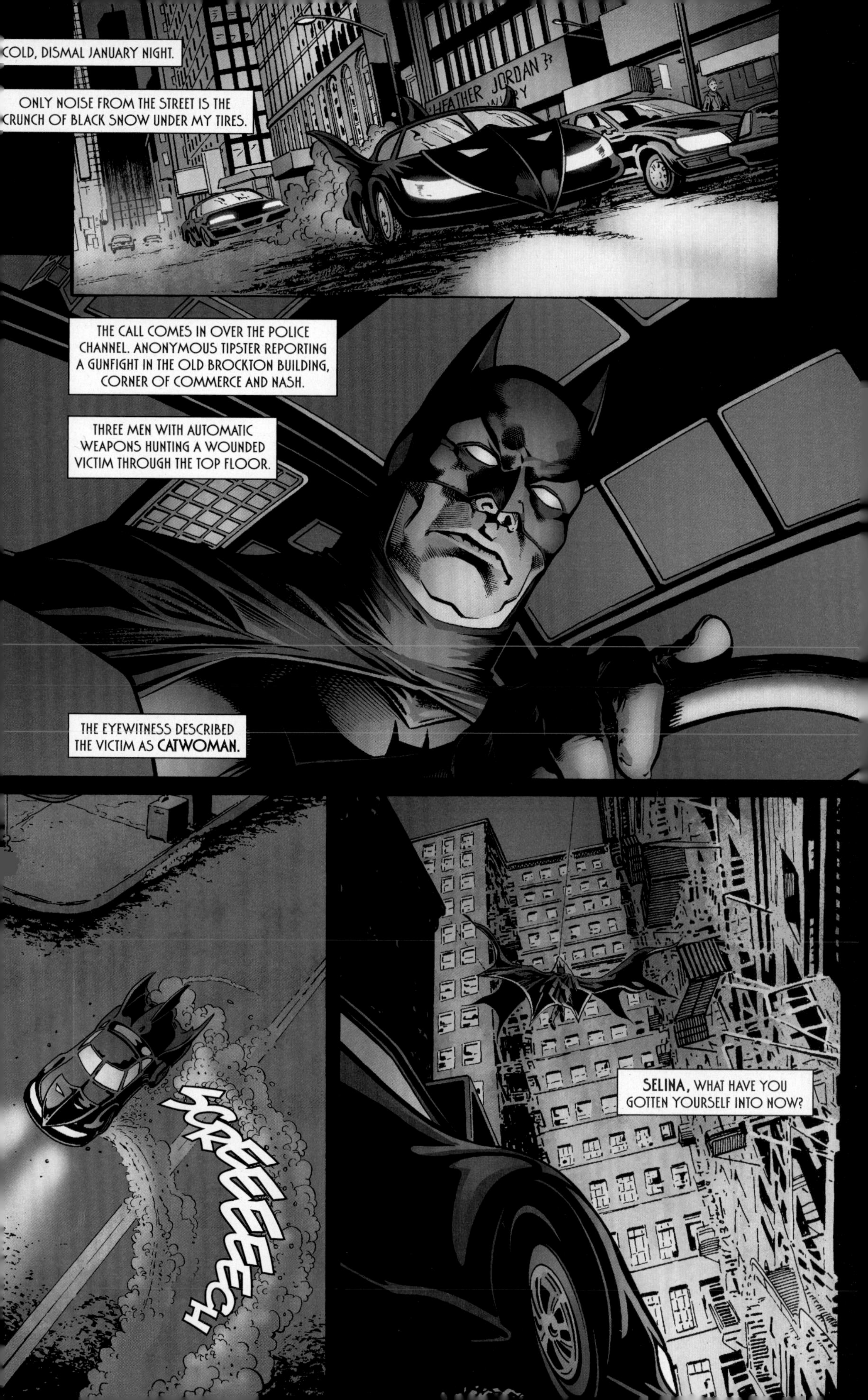
COLD, DISMAL JANUARY NIGHT.
ONLY NOISE FROM THE STREET IS THE CRUNCH OF BLACK SNOW UNDER MY TIRES.
HEATHER JORDAN
THE CALL COMES IN OVER THE POLICE CHANNEL. ANONYMOUS TIPSTER REPORTING A GUNFIGHT IN THE OLD BROCKTON BUILDING, CORNER OF COMMERCE AND NASH.
THREE MEN WITH AUTOMATIC WEAPONS HUNTING A WOUNDED VICTIM THROUGH THE TOP FLOOR.
THE EYEWITNESS DESCRIBED THE VICTIM AS CATWOMAN.
SCREEEEECH
SELINA, WHAT HAVE YOU GOTTEN YOURSELF INTO NOW?

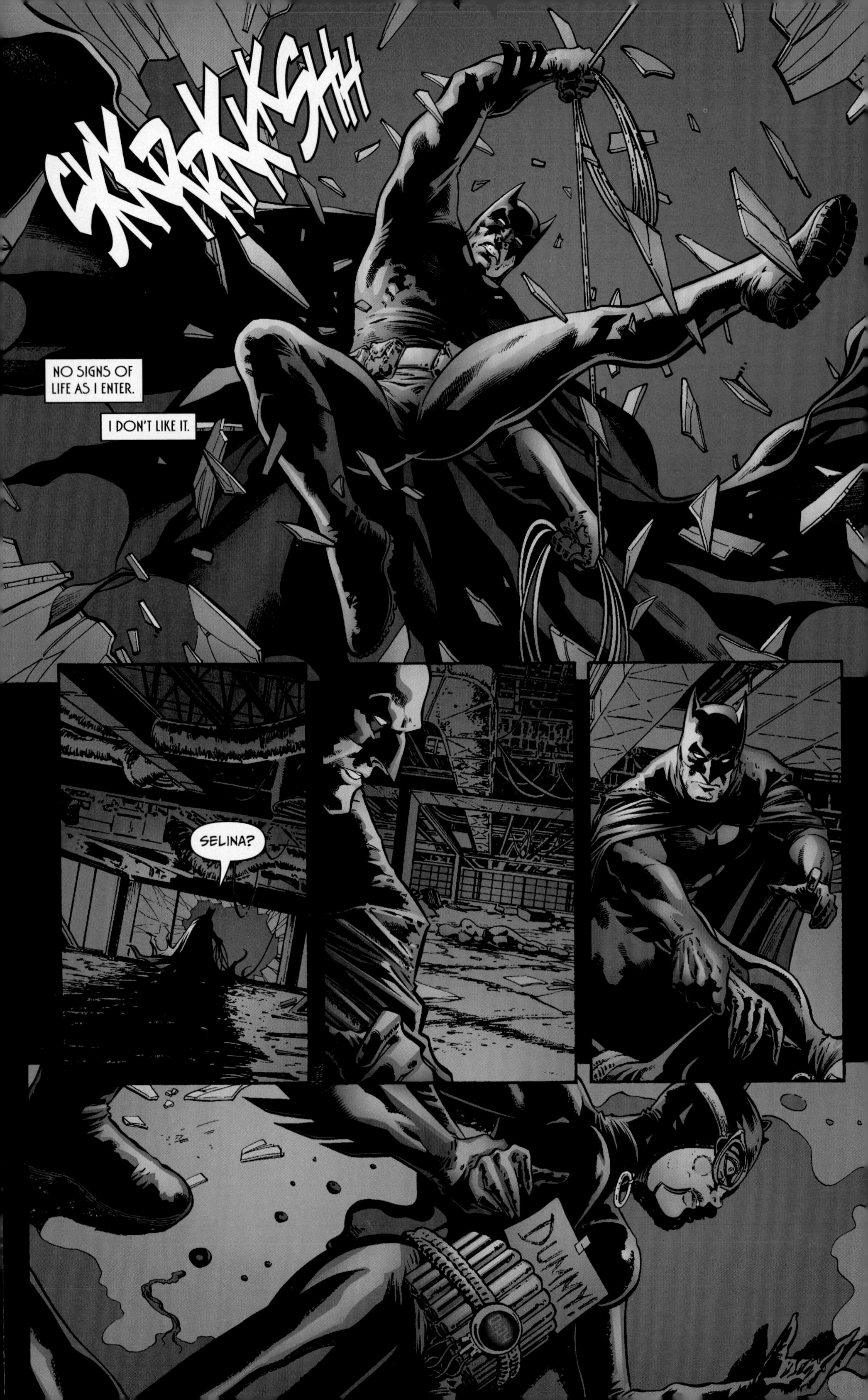
NO SIGNS OF LIFE AS I ENTER.
I DON'T LIKE IT.
SELINA?
DUMMY

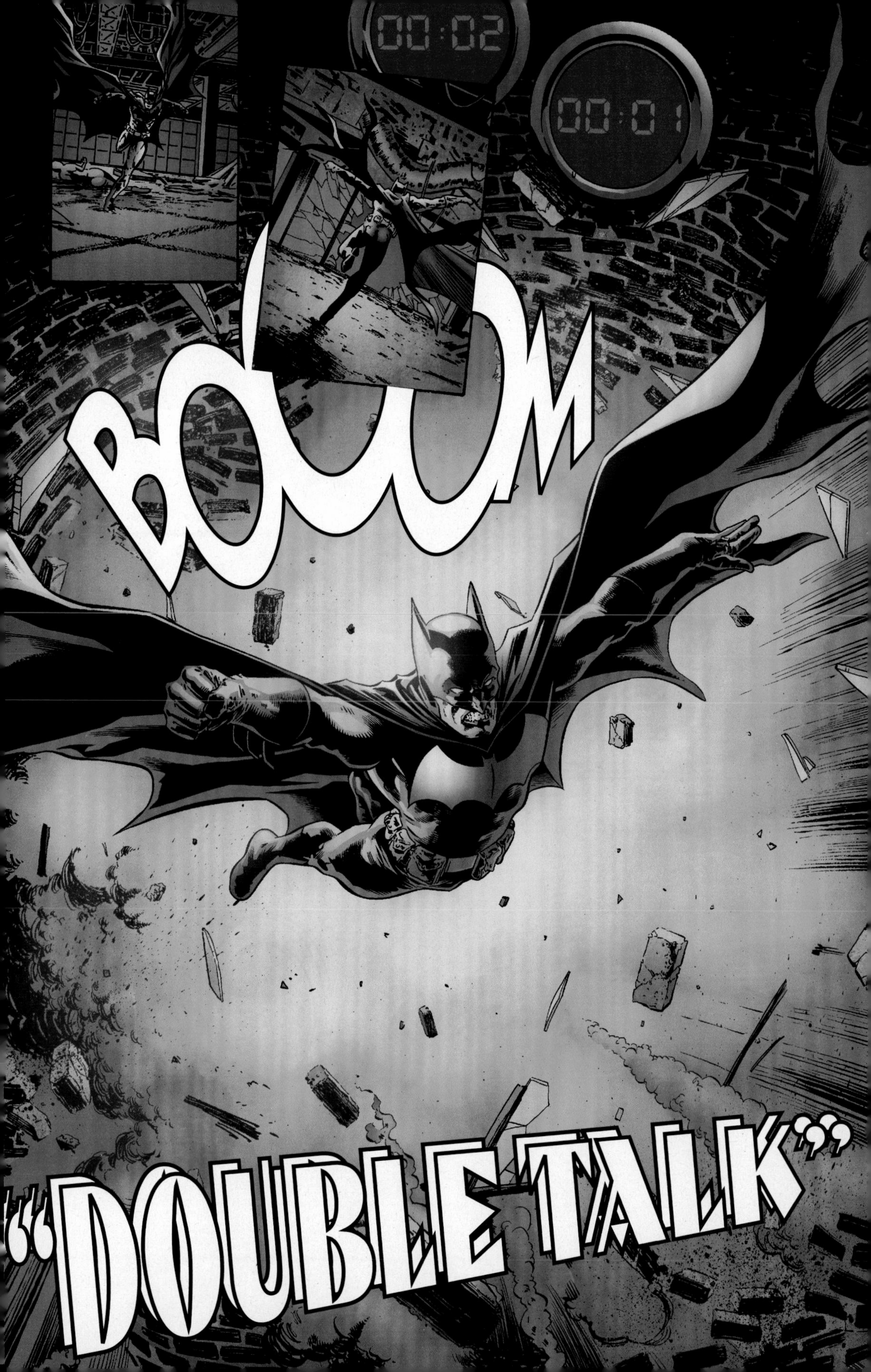
00:02
00:01
BOOOM
"DOUBLE TALK"

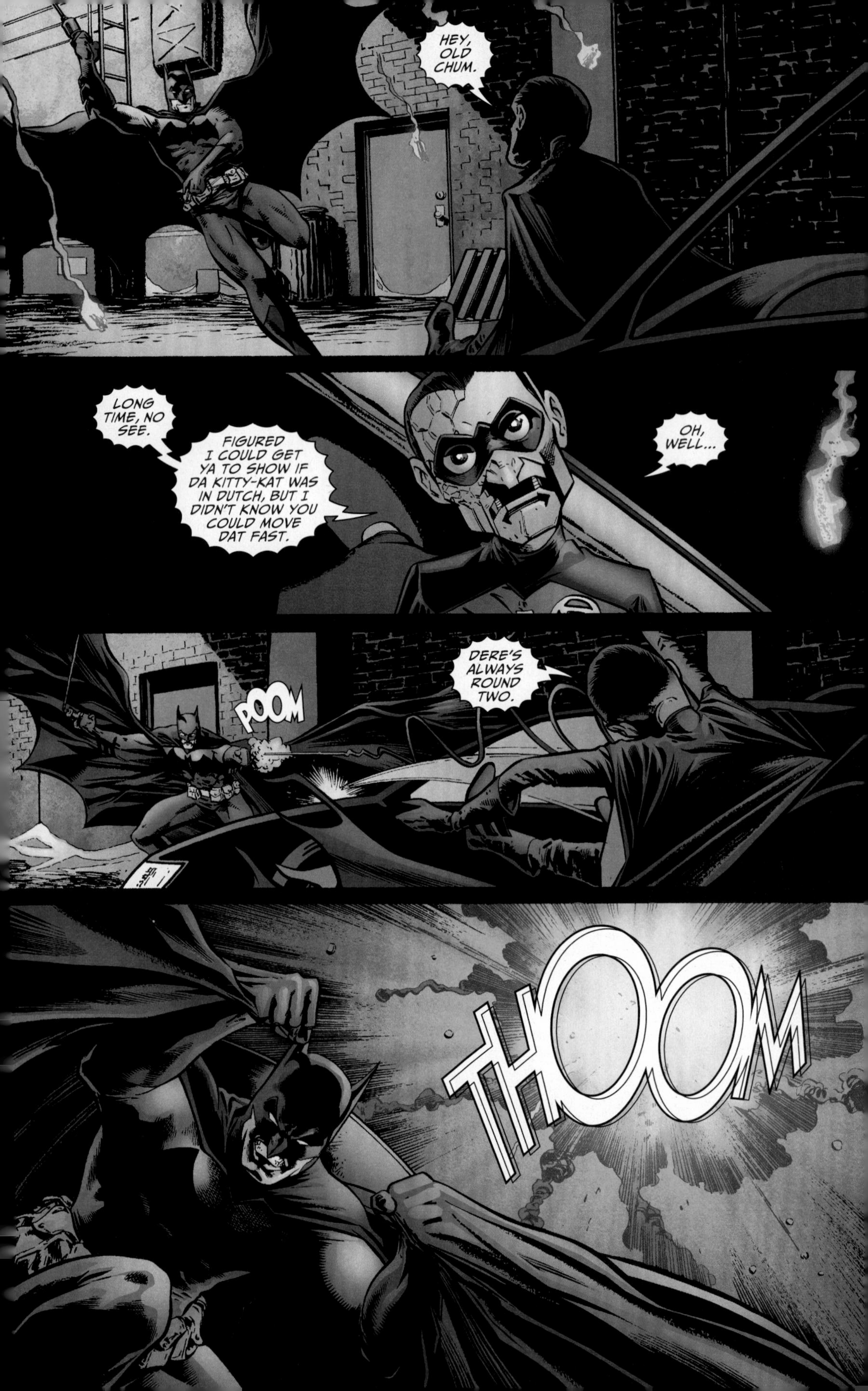
HEY, OLD CHUM.
LONG TIME, NO SEE.
FIGURED I COULD GET YA TO SHOW IF DA KITTY-KAT WAS IN DUTCH, BUT I DIDN'T KNOW YOU COULD MOVE DAT FAST.
OH, WELL...
POOM
DERE'S ALWAYS ROUND TWO.
THOOM

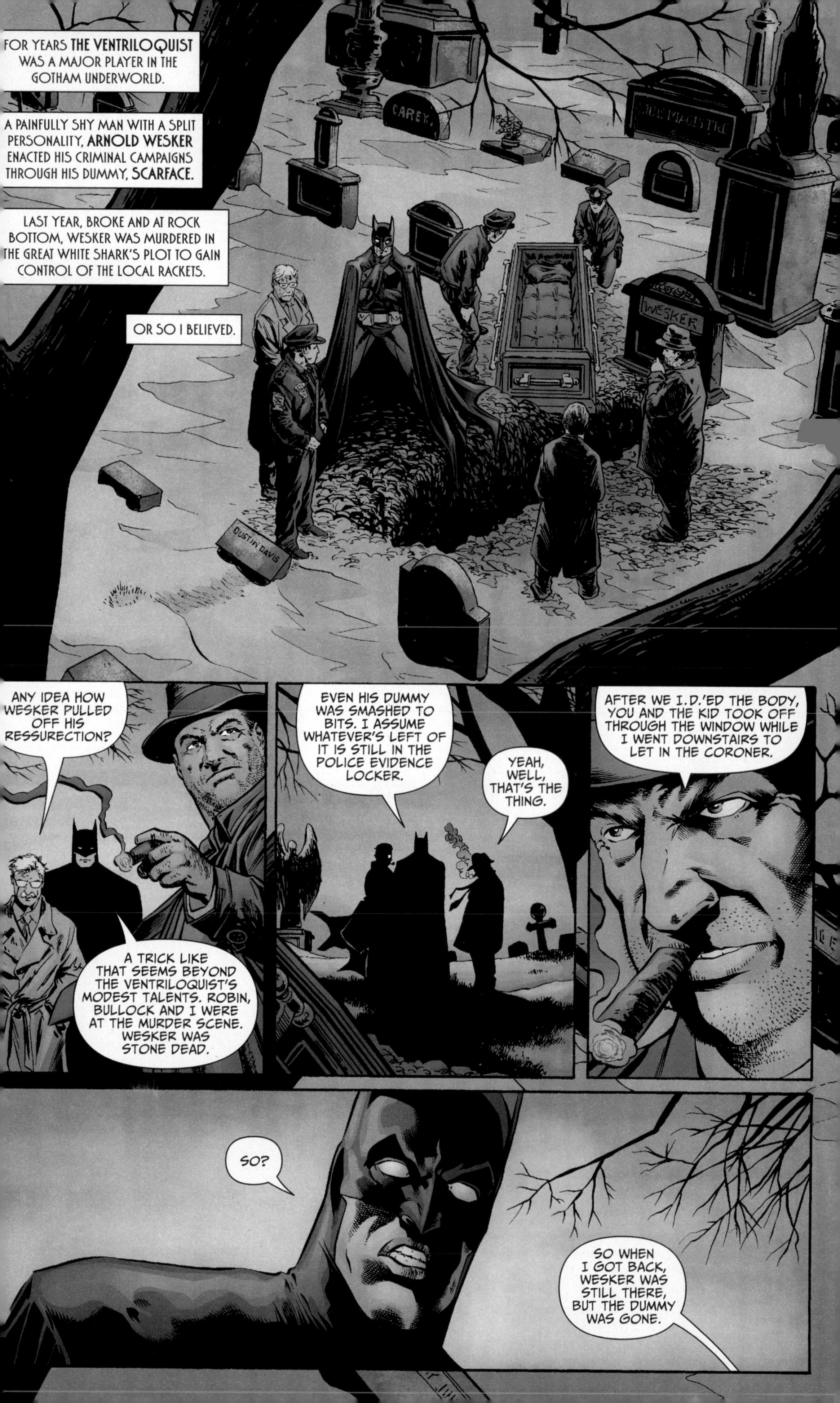

FOR YEARS THE VENTRILOQUIST WAS A MAJOR PLAYER IN THE GOTHAM UNDERWORLD.
A PAINFULLY SHY MAN WITH A SPLIT PERSONALITY, ARNOLD WESKER ENACTED HIS CRIMINAL CAMPAIGNS THROUGH HIS DUMMY, SCARFACE.
LAST YEAR, BROKE AND AT ROCK BOTTOM, WESKER WAS MURDERED IN THE GREAT WHITE SHARK'S PLOT TO GAIN CONTROL OF THE LOCAL RACKETS.
OR SO I BELIEVED.
CAREY
WESKER
DUSTIN DAVIS
ANY IDEA HOW WESKER PULLED OFF HIS RESSURECTION?
A TRICK LIKE THAT SEEMS BEYOND THE VENTRILOQUIST'S MODEST TALENTS. ROBIN, BULLOCK AND I WERE AT THE MURDER SCENE. WESKER WAS STONE DEAD.
EVEN HIS DUMMY WAS SMASHED TO BITS. I ASSUME WHATEVER'S LEFT OF IT IS STILL IN THE POLICE EVIDENCE LOCKER.
YEAH, WELL, THAT'S THE THING.
AFTER WE I.D.'ED THE BODY, YOU AND THE KID TOOK OFF THROUGH THE WINDOW WHILE I WENT DOWNSTAIRS TO LET IN THE CORONER.
SO?
SO WHEN I GOT BACK, WESKER WAS STILL THERE, BUT THE DUMMY WAS GONE.

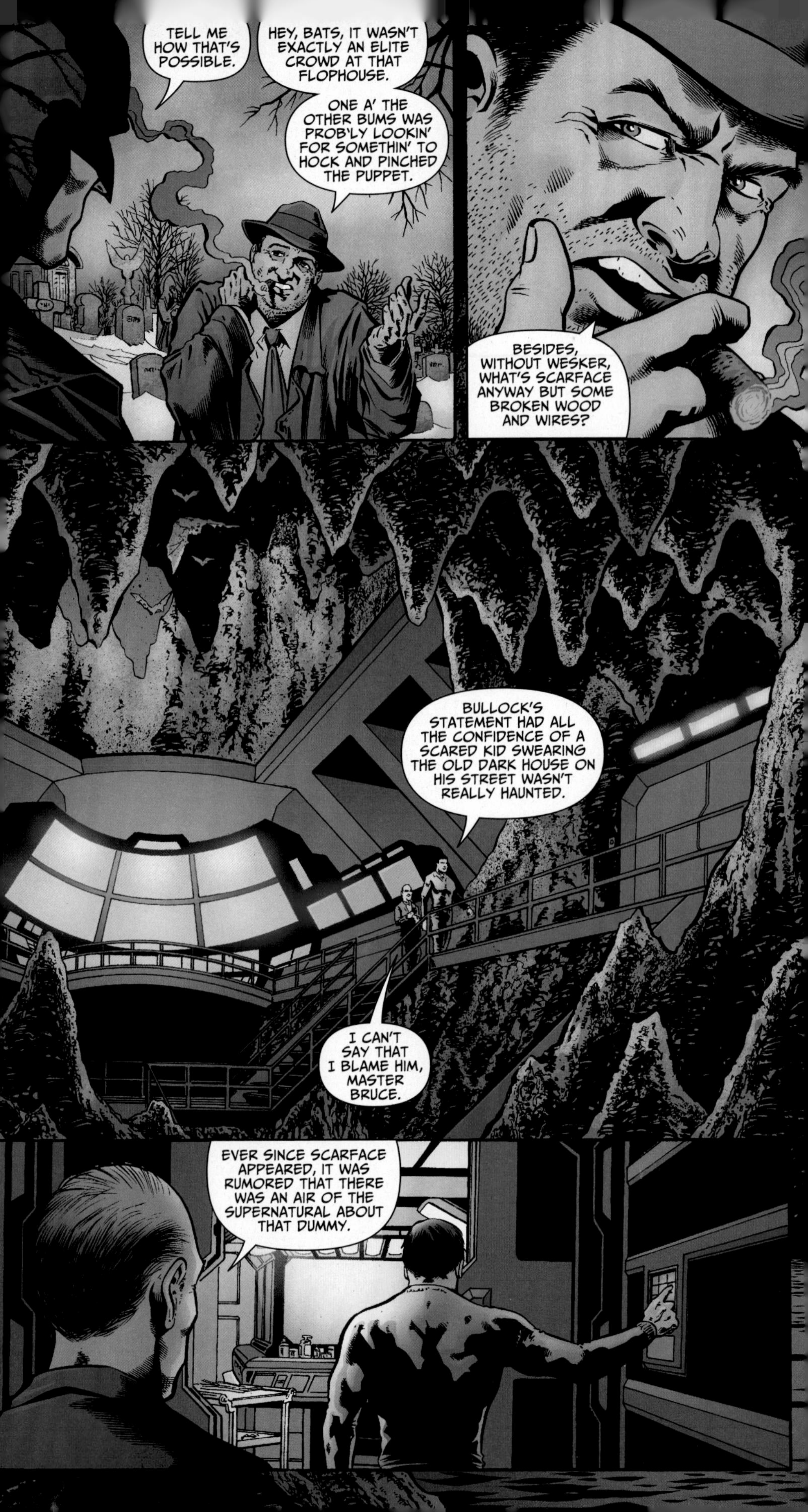
TELL ME HOW THAT'S POSSIBLE.
HEY, BATS, IT WASN'T EXACTLY AN ELITE CROWD AT THAT FLOPHOUSE.
ONE A' THE OTHER BUMS WAS PROB'LY LOOKIN' FOR SOMETHIN' TO HOCK AND PINCHED THE PUPPET.
BESIDES, WITHOUT WESKER, WHAT'S SCARFACE ANYWAY BUT SOME BROKEN WOOD AND WIRES?
BULLOCK'S STATEMENT HAD ALL THE CONFIDENCE OF A SCARED KID SWEARING THE OLD DARK HOUSE ON HIS STREET WASN'T REALLY HAUNTED.
I CAN'T SAY THAT I BLAME HIM, MASTER BRUCE.
EVER SINCE SCARFACE APPEARED, IT WAS RUMORED THAT THERE WAS AN AIR OF THE SUPERNATURAL ABOUT THAT DUMMY.

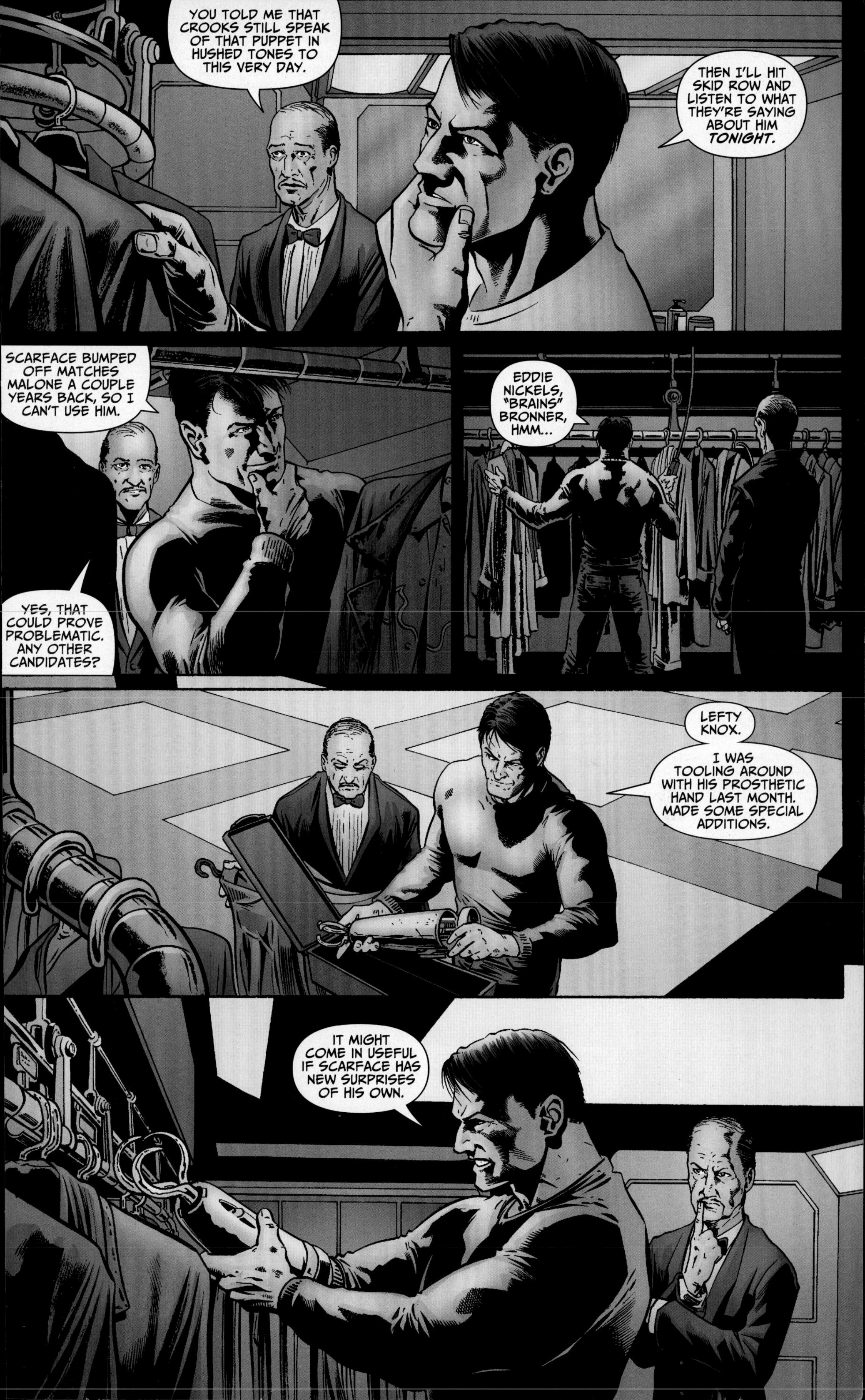
YOU TOLD ME THAT CROOKS STILL SPEAK OF THAT PUPPET IN HUSHED TONES TO THIS VERY DAY.
THEN I'LL HIT SKID ROW AND LISTEN TO WHAT THEY'RE SAYING ABOUT HIM *TONIGHT.*
SCARFACE BUMPED OFF MATCHES MALONE A COUPLE YEARS BACK, SO I CAN'T USE HIM.
YES, THAT COULD PROVE PROBLEMATIC. ANY OTHER CANDIDATES?
EDDIE NICKELS, "BRAINS" BRONNER, HMM...
LEFTY KNOX.
I WAS TOOLING AROUND WITH HIS PROSTHETIC HAND LAST MONTH. MADE SOME SPECIAL ADDITIONS.
IT MIGHT COME IN USEFUL IF SCARFACE HAS NEW SURPRISES OF HIS OWN.

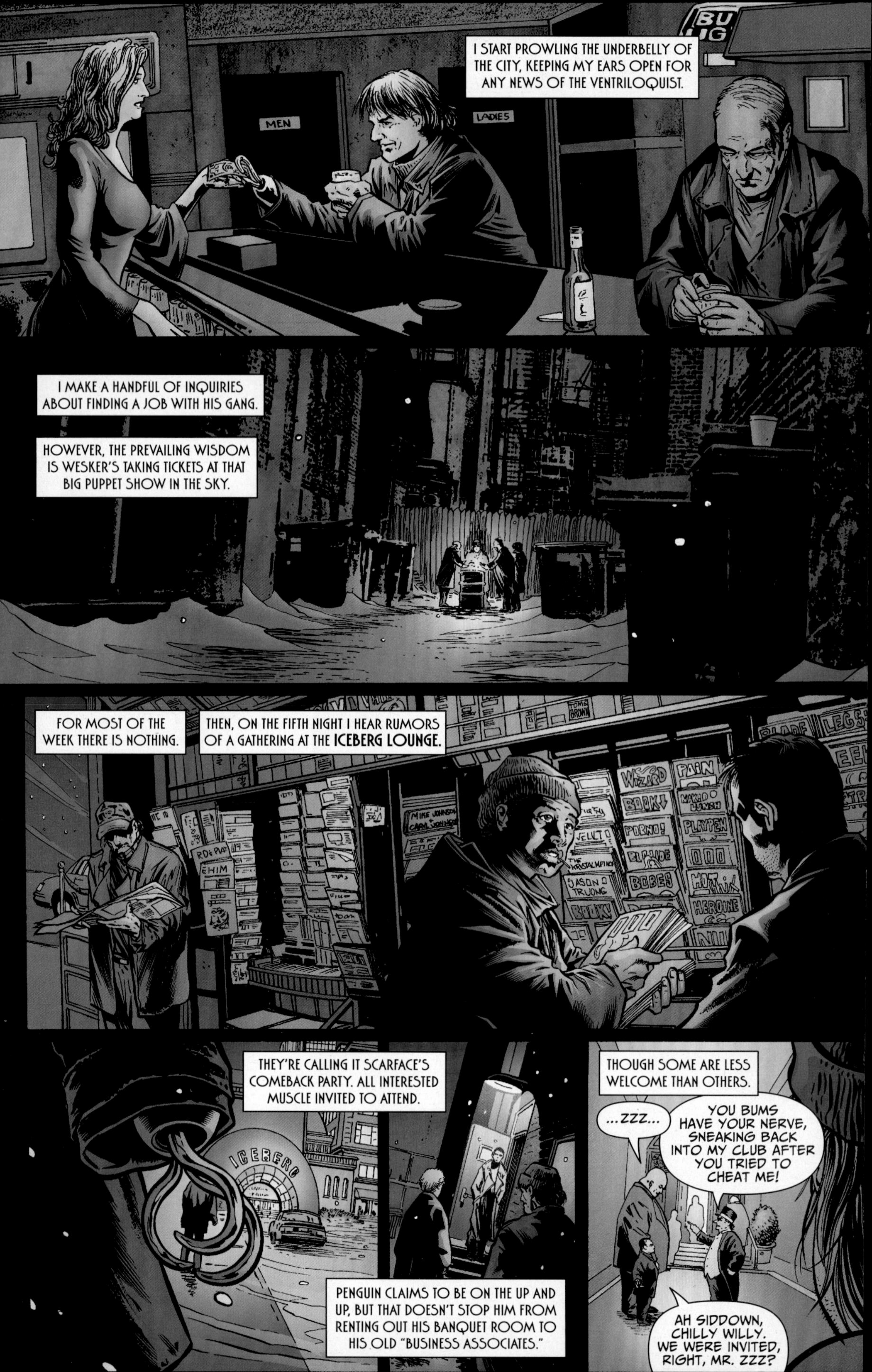
I START PROWLING THE UNDERBELLY OF THE CITY, KEEPING MY EARS OPEN FOR ANY NEWS OF THE VENTRILOQUIST.
MEN
LADIES
I MAKE A HANDFUL OF INQUIRIES ABOUT FINDING A JOB WITH HIS GANG.
HOWEVER, THE PREVAILING WISDOM IS WESKER'S TAKING TICKETS AT THAT BIG PUPPET SHOW IN THE SKY.
FOR MOST OF THE WEEK THERE IS NOTHING.
THEN, ON THE FIFTH NIGHT I HEAR RUMORS OF A GATHERING AT THE **ICEBERG LOUNGE.**
THEY'RE CALLING IT SCARFACE'S COMEBACK PARTY. ALL INTERESTED MUSCLE INVITED TO ATTEND.
ICEBERG
PENGUIN CLAIMS TO BE ON THE UP AND UP, BUT THAT DOESN'T STOP HIM FROM RENTING OUT HIS BANQUET ROOM TO HIS OLD "BUSINESS ASSOCIATES."
THOUGH SOME ARE LESS WELCOME THAN OTHERS.
...ZZZ...
YOU BUMS HAVE YOUR NERVE, SNEAKING BACK INTO MY CLUB AFTER YOU TRIED TO CHEAT ME!
AH SIDDOWN, CHILLY WILLY. WE WERE INVITED, RIGHT, MR. ZZZ?

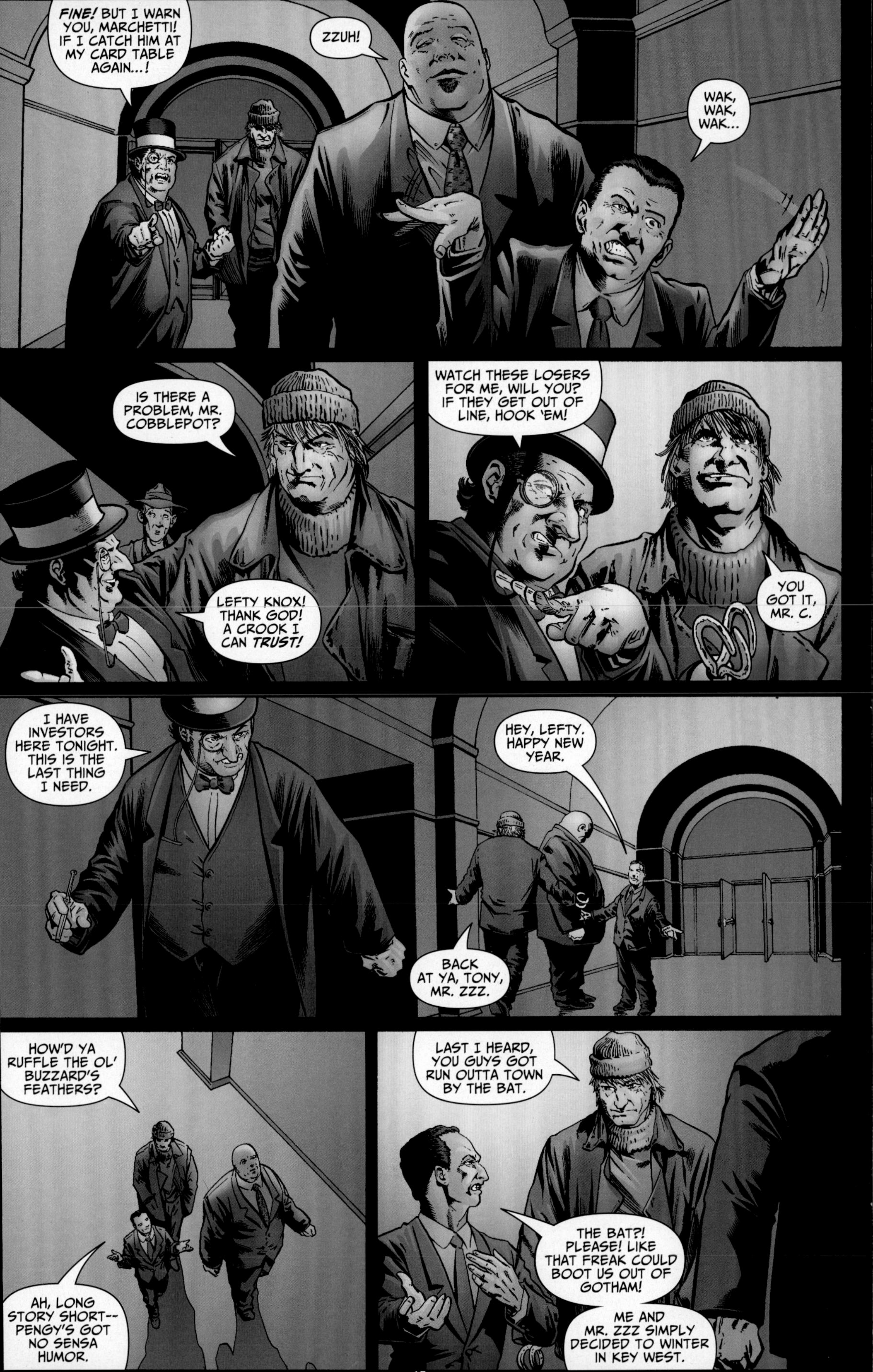
FINE! BUT I WARN YOU, MARCHETTI! IF I CATCH HIM AT MY CARD TABLE AGAIN...!
ZZUH!
WAK, WAK, WAK...
IS THERE A PROBLEM, MR. COBBLEPOT?
LEFTY KNOX! THANK GOD! A CROOK I CAN TRUST!
WATCH THESE LOSERS FOR ME, WILL YOU? IF THEY GET OUT OF LINE, HOOK 'EM!
YOU GOT IT, MR. C.
I HAVE INVESTORS HERE TONIGHT. THIS IS THE LAST THING I NEED.
HEY, LEFTY. HAPPY NEW YEAR.
BACK AT YA, TONY, MR. ZZZ.
HOW'D YA RUFFLE THE OL' BUZZARD'S FEATHERS?
AH, LONG STORY SHORT-- PENGY'S GOT NO SENSA HUMOR.
LAST I HEARD, YOU GUYS GOT RUN OUTTA TOWN BY THE BAT.
THE BAT?! PLEASE! LIKE THAT FREAK COULD BOOT US OUT OF GOTHAM!
ME AND MR. ZZZ SIMPLY DECIDED TO WINTER IN KEY WEST.

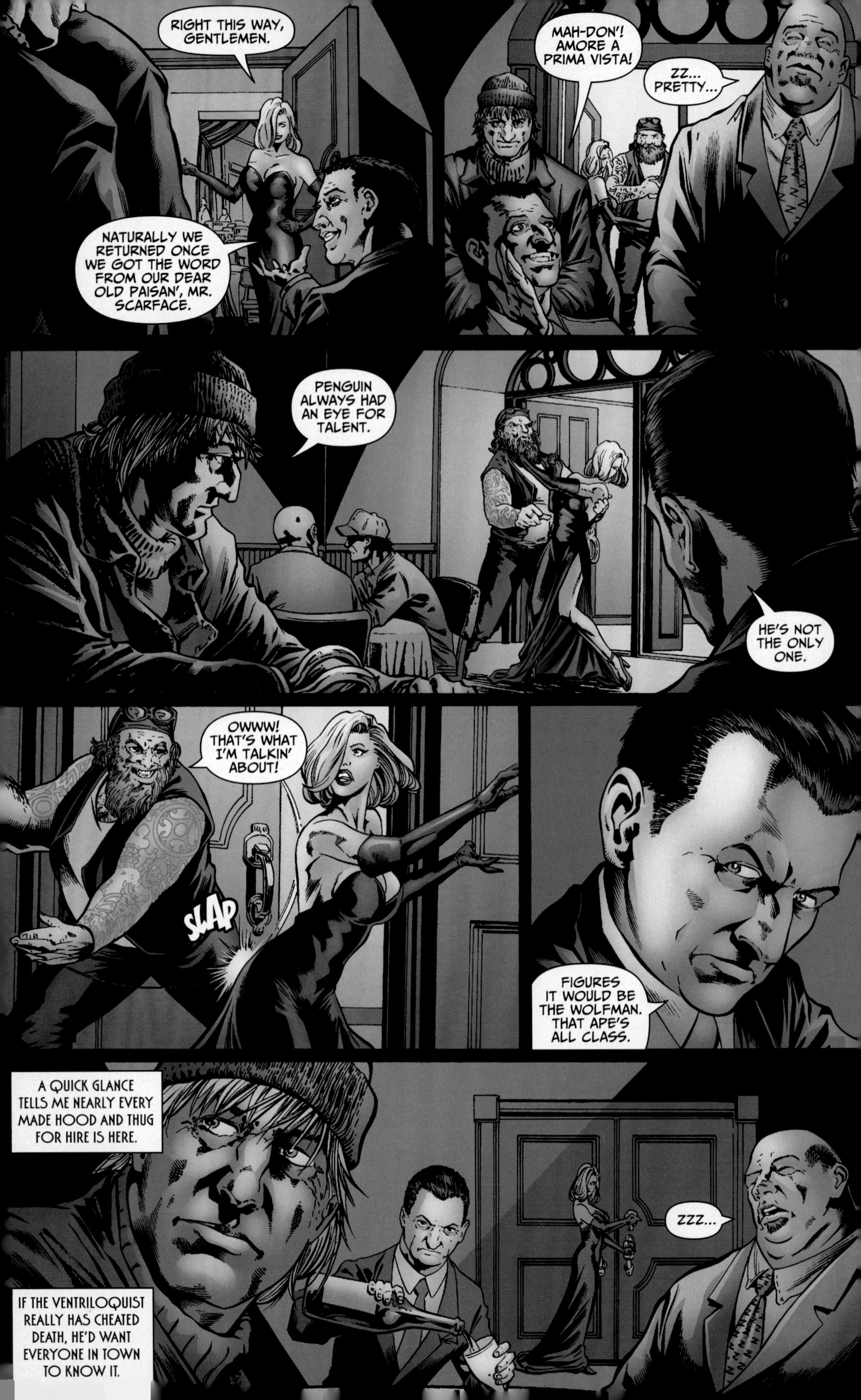
RIGHT THIS WAY, GENTLEMEN.
NATURALLY WE RETURNED ONCE WE GOT THE WORD FROM OUR DEAR OLD PAISAN', MR. SCARFACE.
MAH-DON'! AMORE A PRIMA VISTA!
ZZ... PRETTY...
PENGUIN ALWAYS HAD AN EYE FOR TALENT.
HE'S NOT THE ONLY ONE.
OWWW! THAT'S WHAT I'M TALKIN' ABOUT!
SLAP
FIGURES IT WOULD BE THE WOLFMAN. THAT APE'S ALL CLASS.
A QUICK GLANCE TELLS ME NEARLY EVERY MADE HOOD AND THUG FOR HIRE IS HERE.
ZZZ...
IF THE VENTRILOQUIST REALLY HAS CHEATED DEATH, HE'D WANT EVERYONE IN TOWN TO KNOW IT.

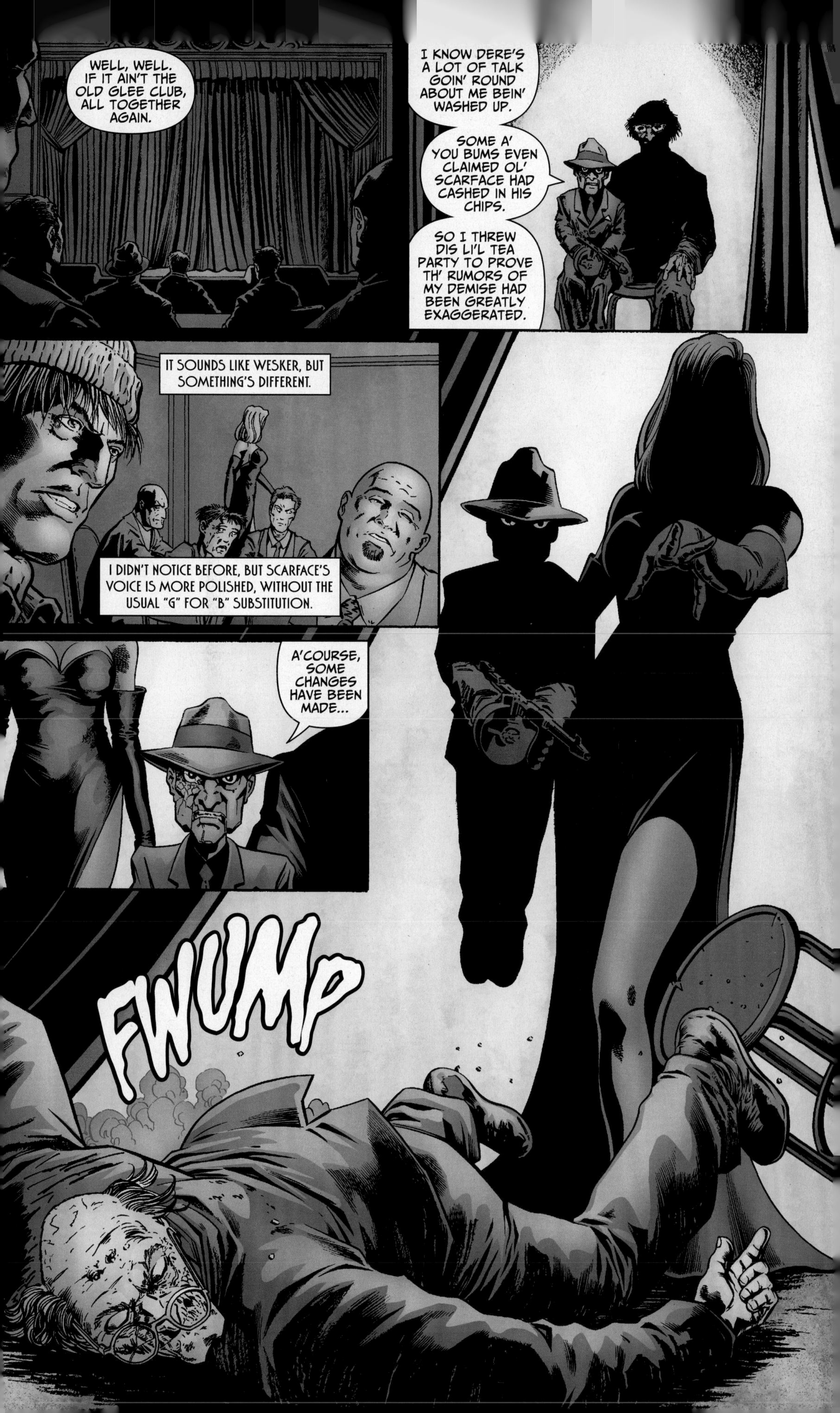
WELL, WELL. IF IT AIN'T THE OLD GLEE CLUB, ALL TOGETHER AGAIN.
I KNOW DERE'S A LOT OF TALK GOIN' ROUND ABOUT ME BEIN' WASHED UP.
SOME A' YOU BUMS EVEN CLAIMED OL' SCARFACE HAD CASHED IN HIS CHIPS.
SO I THREW DIS LI'L TEA PARTY TO PROVE TH' RUMORS OF MY DEMISE HAD BEEN GREATLY EXAGGERATED.
IT SOUNDS LIKE WESKER, BUT SOMETHING'S DIFFERENT.
I DIDN'T NOTICE BEFORE, BUT SCARFACE'S VOICE IS MORE POLISHED, WITHOUT THE USUAL "G" FOR "B" SUBSTITUTION.
A'COURSE, SOME CHANGES HAVE BEEN MADE...
FWUMP

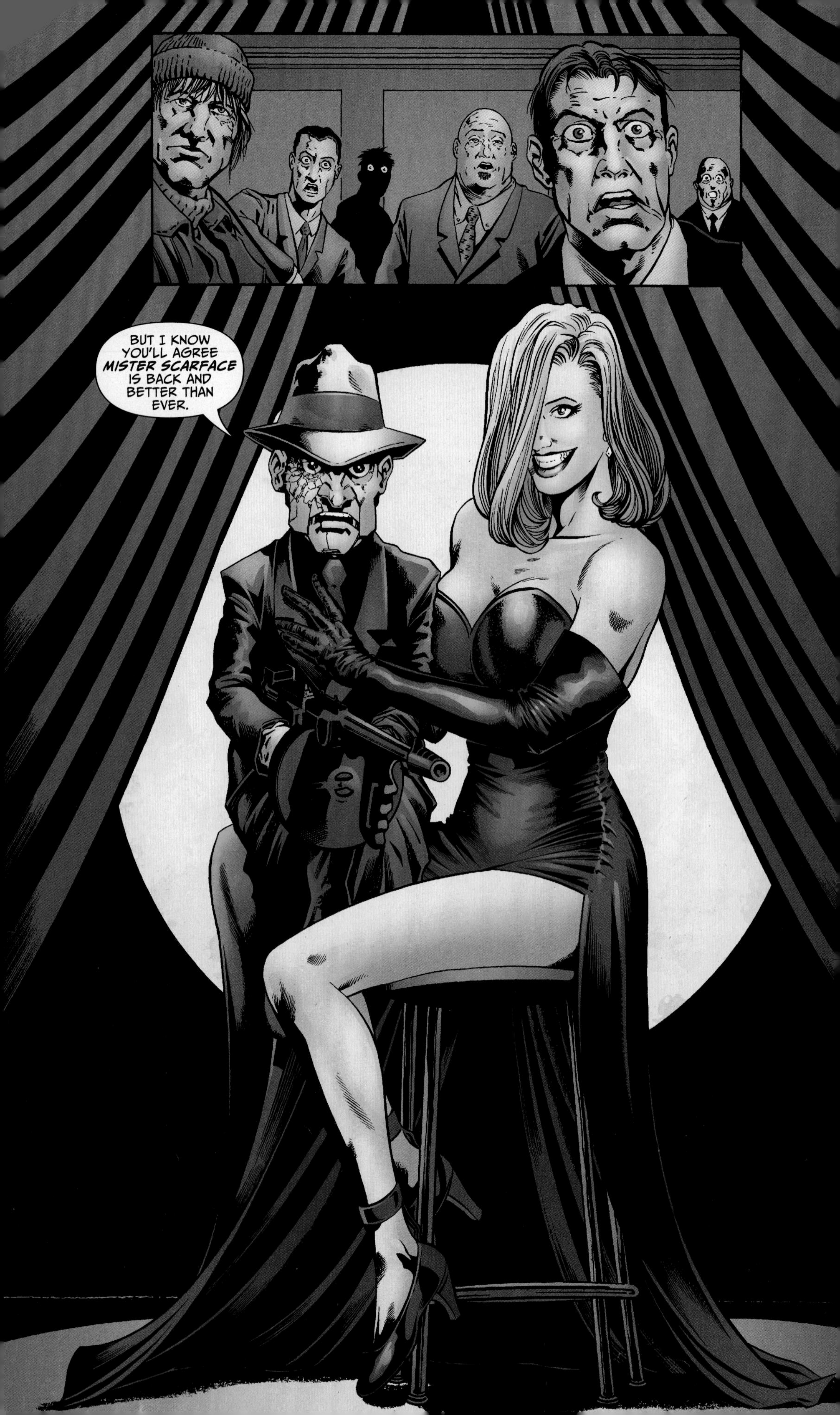
BUT I KNOW YOU'LL AGREE MISTER SCARFACE IS BACK AND BETTER THAN EVER.

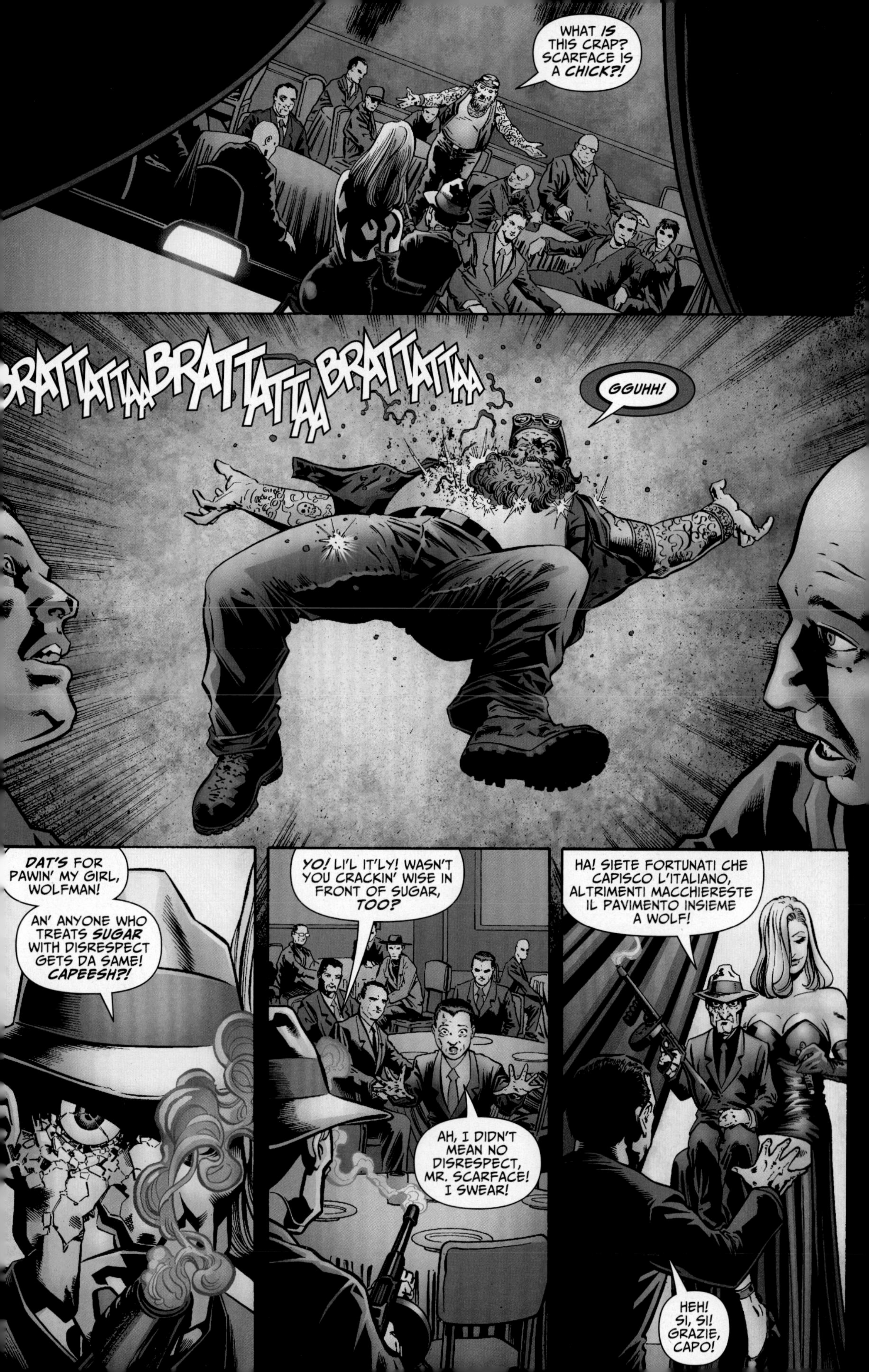
WHAT IS THIS CRAP? SCARFACE IS A CHICK?!
BRATTATTAA BRATTATTAA BRATTATTAA
GGUHH!
DAT'S FOR PAWIN' MY GIRL, WOLFMAN!
AN' ANYONE WHO TREATS SUGAR WITH DISRESPECT GETS DA SAME! CAPEESH?!
YO! LI'L IT'LY! WASN'T YOU CRACKIN' WISE IN FRONT OF SUGAR, TOO?
AH, I DIDN'T MEAN NO DISRESPECT, MR. SCARFACE! I SWEAR!
HA! SIETE FORTUNATI CHE CAPISCO L'ITALIANO, ALTRIMENTI MACCHIERESTE IL PAVIMENTO INSIEME A WOLF!
HEH! SI, SI! GRAZIE, CAPO!

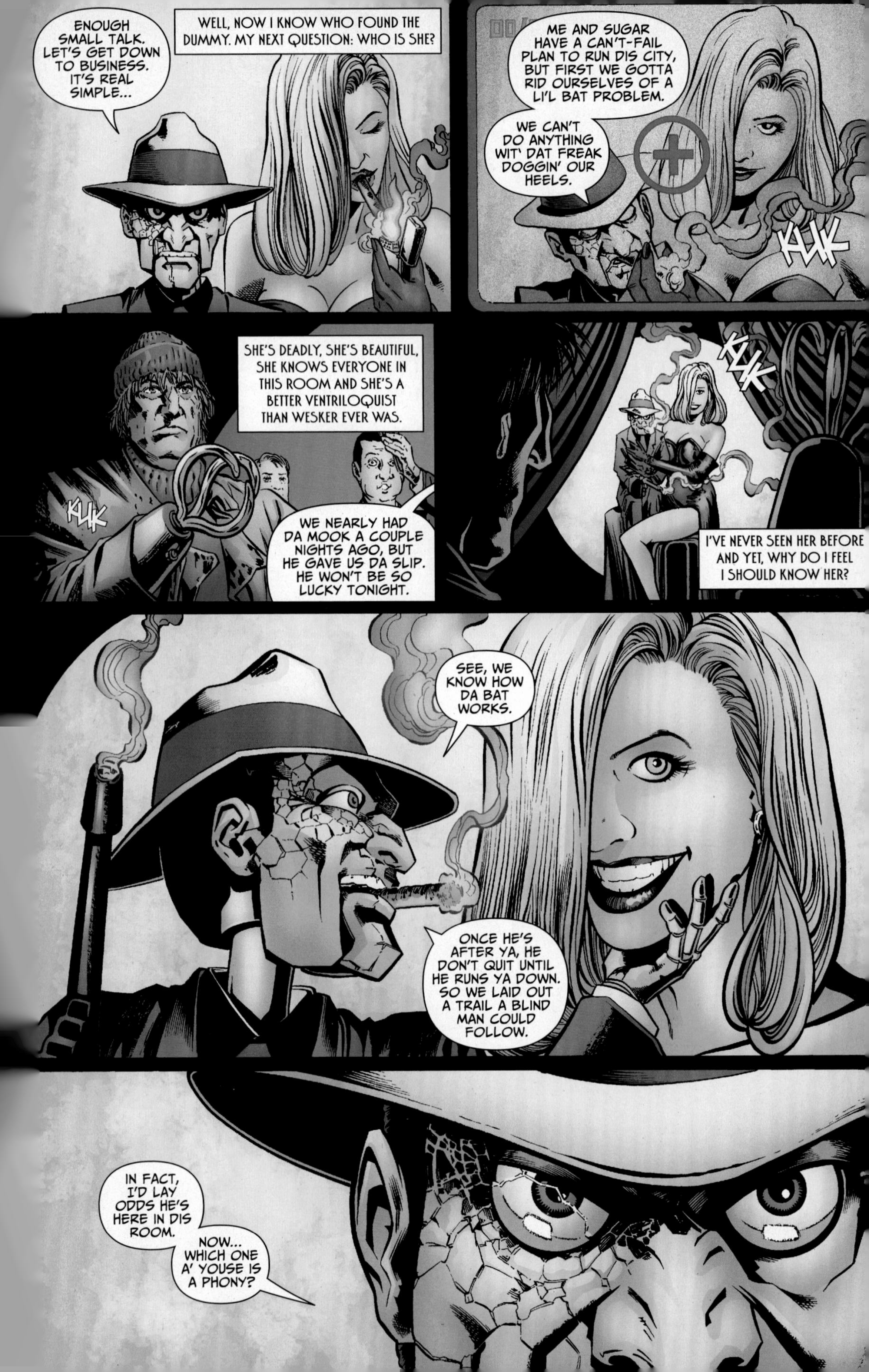
ENOUGH SMALL TALK. LET'S GET DOWN TO BUSINESS. IT'S REAL SIMPLE...
WELL, NOW I KNOW WHO FOUND THE DUMMY. MY NEXT QUESTION: WHO IS SHE?
ME AND SUGAR HAVE A CAN'T-FAIL PLAN TO RUN DIS CITY, BUT FIRST WE GOTTA RID OURSELVES OF A LI'L BAT PROBLEM.
WE CAN'T DO ANYTHING WIT' DAT FREAK DOGGIN' OUR HEELS.
KUK
SHE'S DEADLY, SHE'S BEAUTIFUL, SHE KNOWS EVERYONE IN THIS ROOM AND SHE'S A BETTER VENTRILOQUIST THAN WESKER EVER WAS.
KUK
WE NEARLY HAD DA MOOK A COUPLE NIGHTS AGO, BUT HE GAVE US DA SLIP. HE WON'T BE SO LUCKY TONIGHT.
KUK
I'VE NEVER SEEN HER BEFORE AND YET, WHY DO I FEEL I SHOULD KNOW HER?
SEE, WE KNOW HOW DA BAT WORKS.
ONCE HE'S AFTER YA, HE DON'T QUIT UNTIL HE RUNS YA DOWN. SO WE LAID OUT A TRAIL A BLIND MAN COULD FOLLOW.
IN FACT, I'D LAY ODDS HE'S HERE IN DIS ROOM.
NOW... WHICH ONE A' YOUSE IS A PHONY?

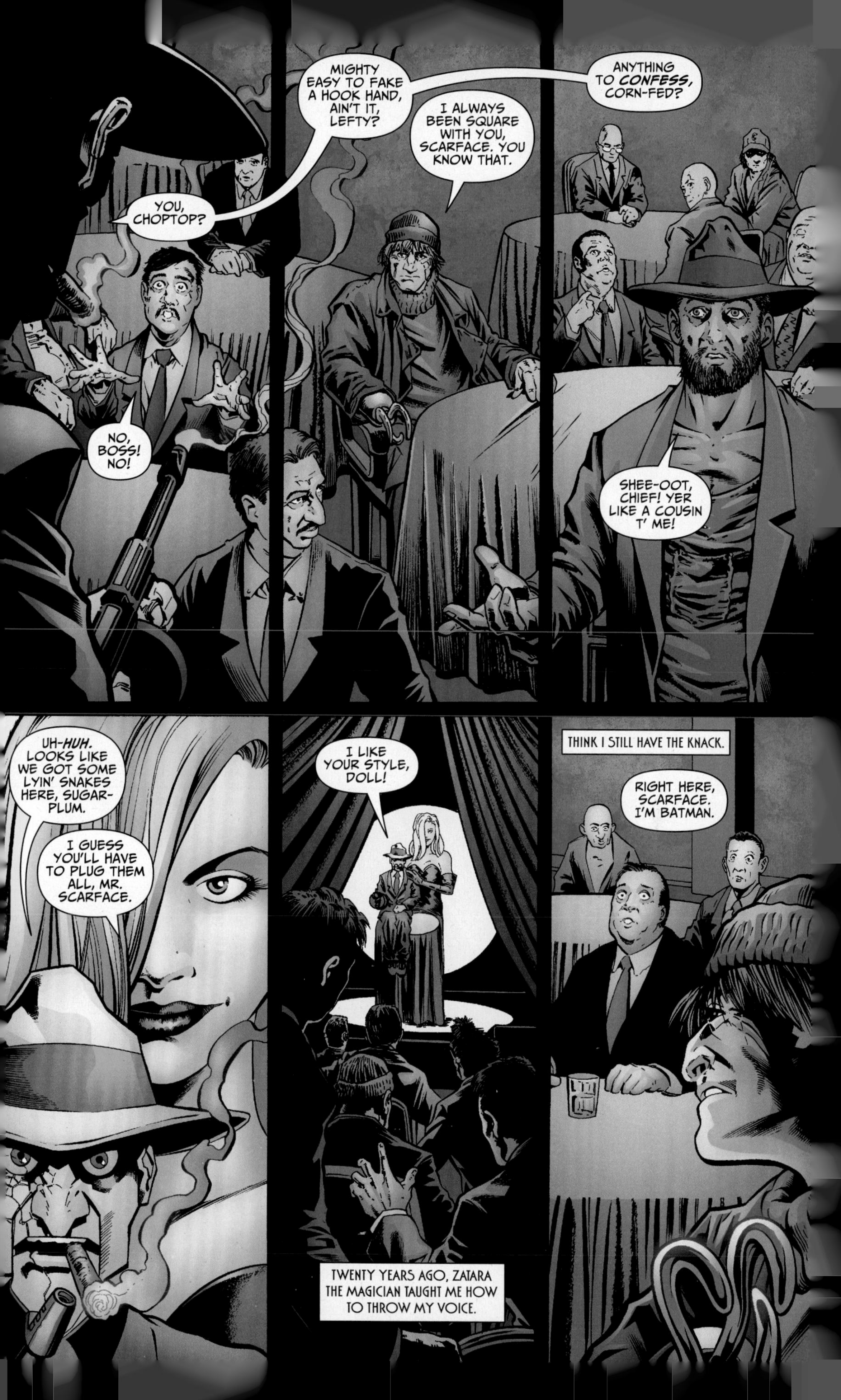

YOU, CHOPTOP?
NO, BOSS! NO!
MIGHTY EASY TO FAKE A HOOK HAND, AIN'T IT, LEFTY?
I ALWAYS BEEN SQUARE WITH YOU, SCARFACE. YOU KNOW THAT.
ANYTHING TO CONFESS, CORN-FED?
SHEE-OOT, CHIEF! YER LIKE A COUSIN T' ME!
UH-HUH. LOOKS LIKE WE GOT SOME LYIN' SNAKES HERE, SUGAR-PLUM.
I GUESS YOU'LL HAVE TO PLUG THEM ALL, MR. SCARFACE.
I LIKE YOUR STYLE, DOLL!
TWENTY YEARS AGO, ZATARA THE MAGICIAN TAUGHT ME HOW TO THROW MY VOICE.
THINK I STILL HAVE THE KNACK.
RIGHT HERE, SCARFACE. I'M BATMAN.

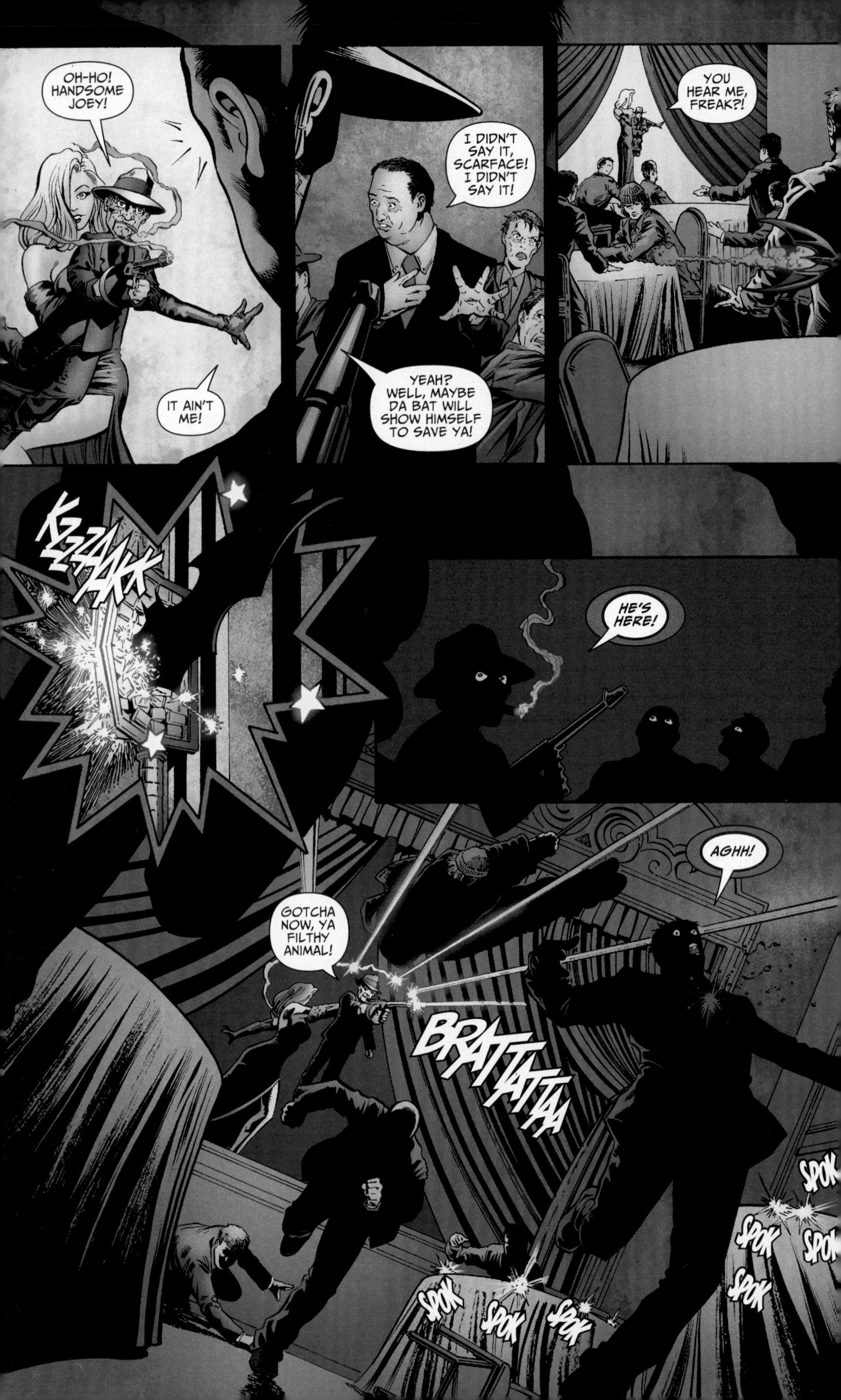
OH-HO! HANDSOME JOEY!
IT AIN'T ME!
I DIDN'T SAY IT, SCARFACE! I DIDN'T SAY IT!
YEAH? WELL, MAYBE DA BAT WILL SHOW HIMSELF TO SAVE YA!
YOU HEAR ME, FREAK?!
KZZZAAKK
HE'S HERE!
GOTCHA NOW, YA FILTHY ANIMAL!
AGHH!
BRATTATTAA
SPOK
SPOK
SPOK
SPOK
SPOK
SPOK
SPOK

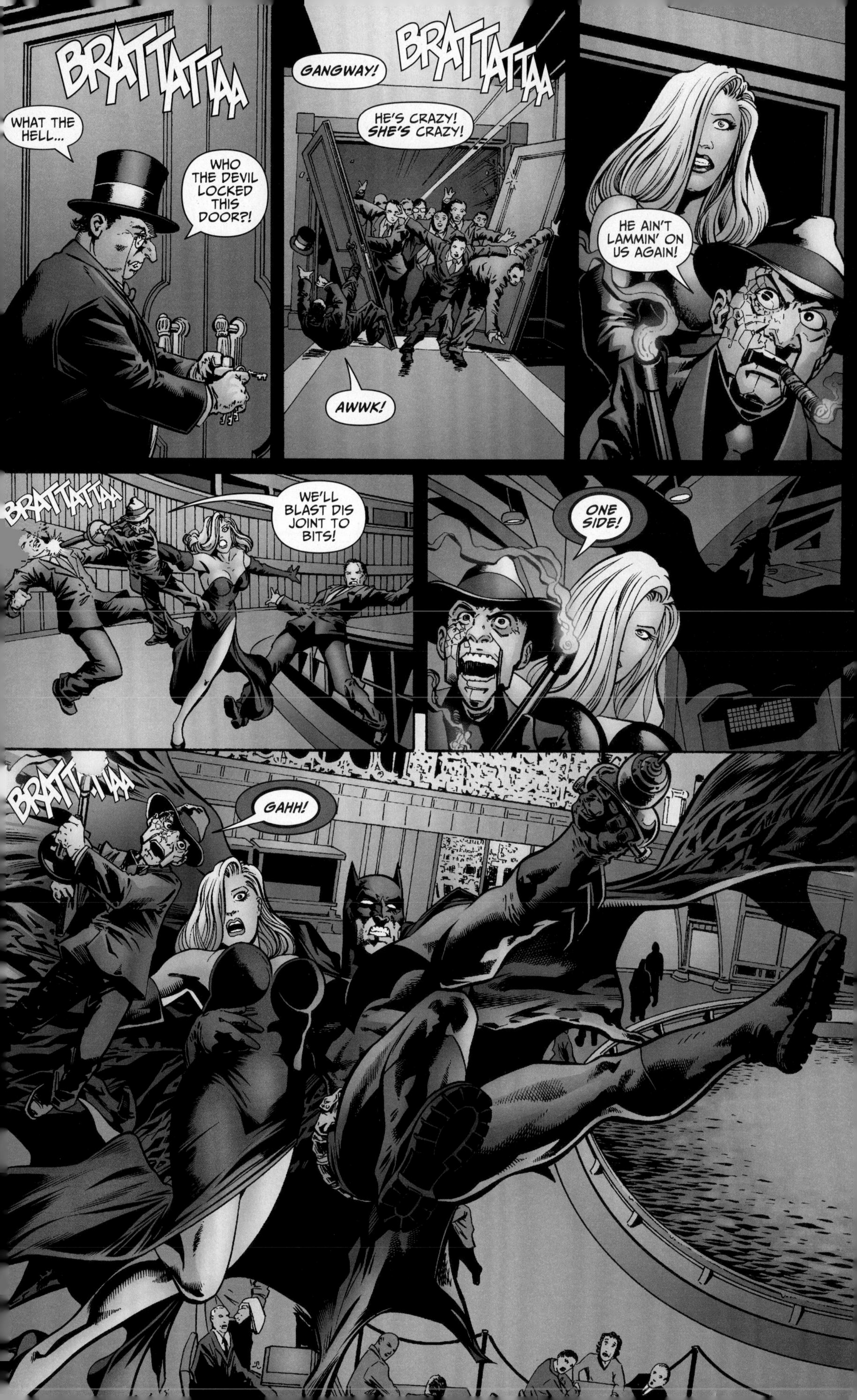
BRATTATTAA
WHAT THE HELL...
WHO THE DEVIL LOCKED THIS DOOR?!
GANGWAY!
BRATTATTAA
HE'S CRAZY! SHE'S CRAZY!
AWWK!
HE AIN'T LAMMIN' ON US AGAIN!
BRATTATTAA
WE'LL BLAST DIS JOINT TO BITS!
ONE SIDE!
GAHH!

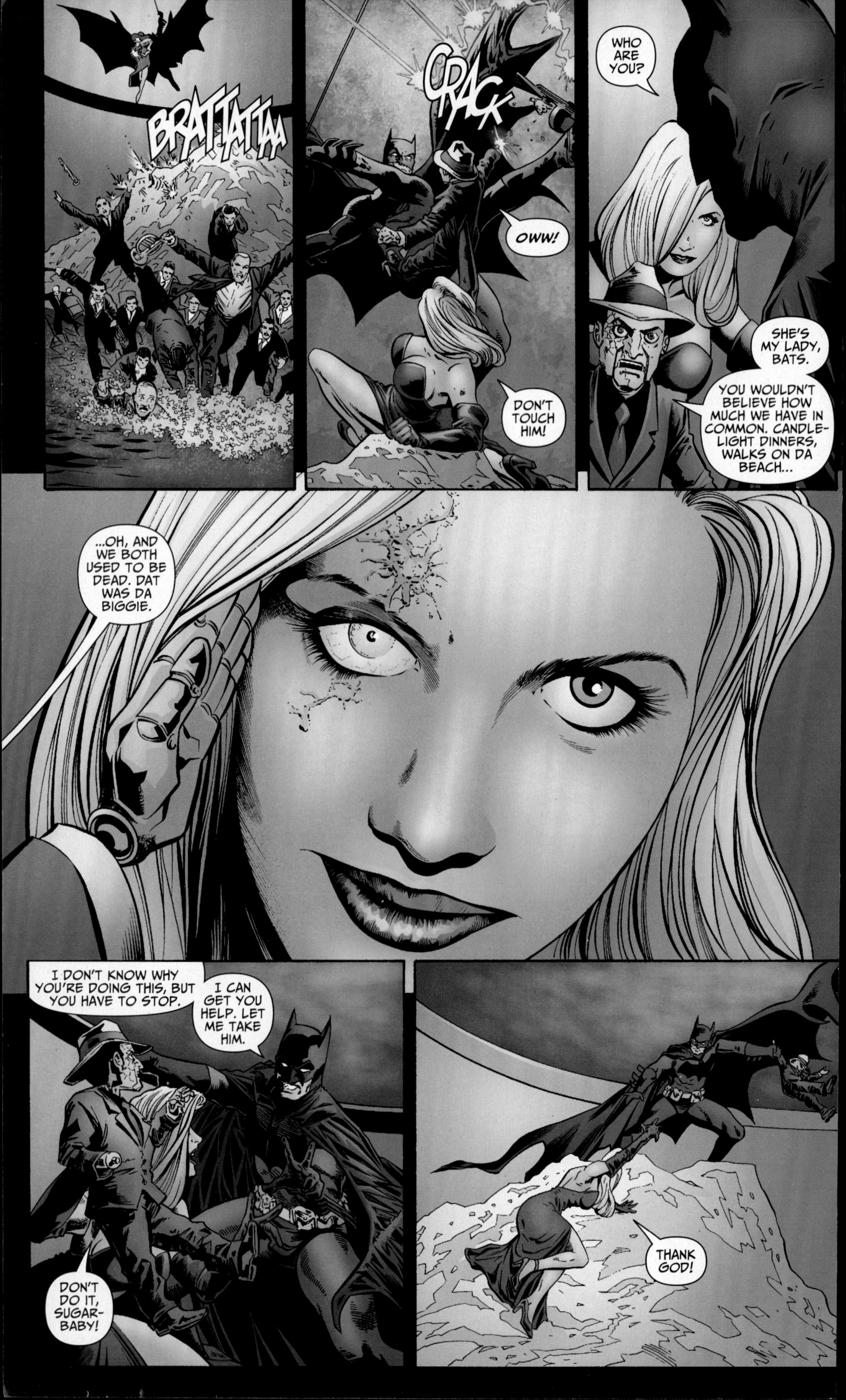
BRATTATTAA
CRACK
OWW!
DON'T TOUCH HIM!
WHO ARE YOU?
SHE'S MY LADY, BATS.
YOU WOULDN'T BELIEVE HOW MUCH WE HAVE IN COMMON. CANDLE-LIGHT DINNERS, WALKS ON DA BEACH...
...OH, AND WE BOTH USED TO BE DEAD. DAT WAS DA BIGGIE.
I DON'T KNOW WHY YOU'RE DOING THIS, BUT YOU HAVE TO STOP.
I CAN GET YOU HELP. LET ME TAKE HIM.
DON'T DO IT, SUGAR-BABY!
THANK GOD!

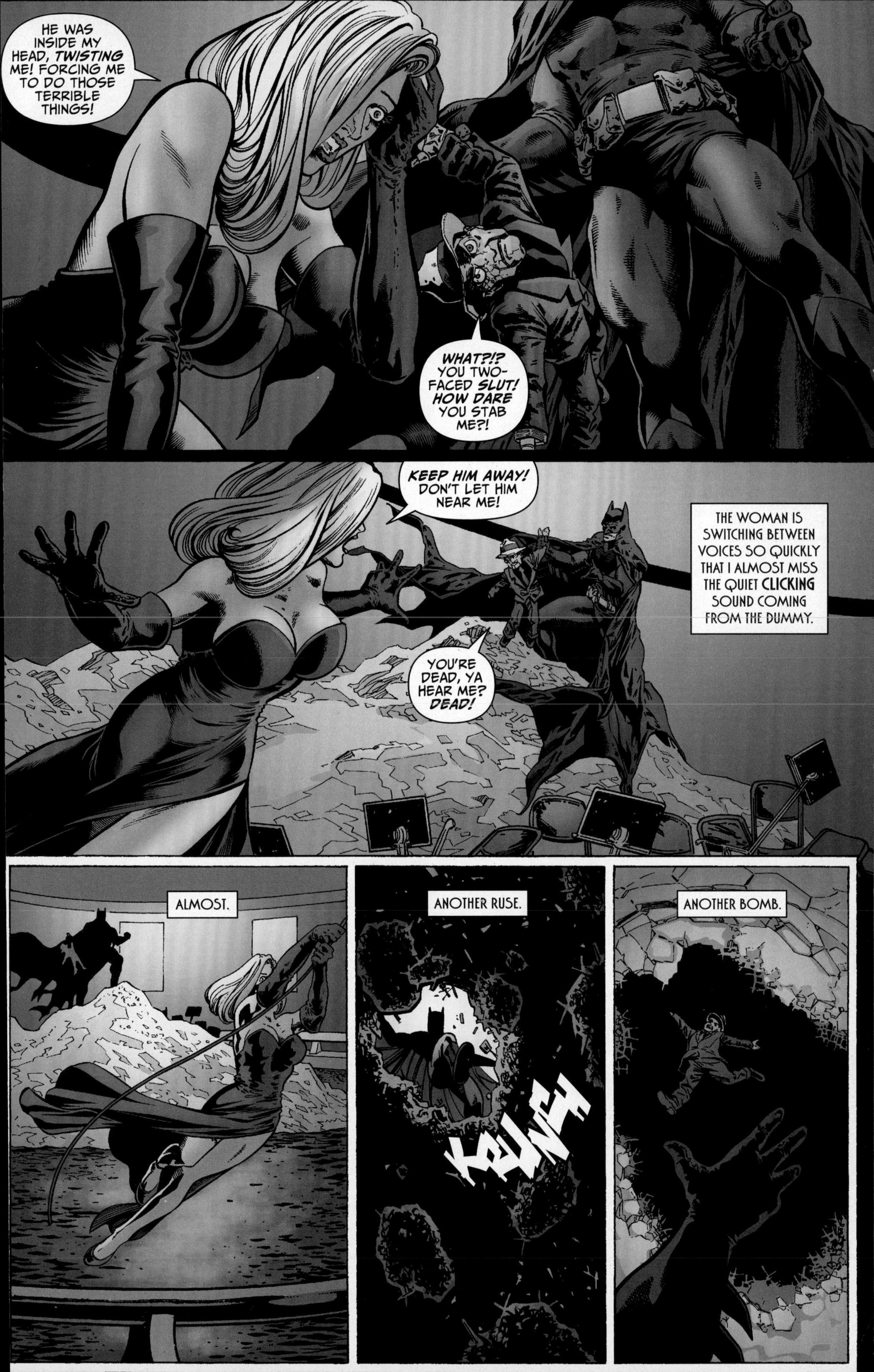
HE WAS INSIDE MY HEAD, TWISTING ME! FORCING ME TO DO THOSE TERRIBLE THINGS!
WHAT?!? YOU TWO-FACED SLUT! HOW DARE YOU STAB ME?!
KEEP HIM AWAY! DON'T LET HIM NEAR ME!
THE WOMAN IS SWITCHING BETWEEN VOICES SO QUICKLY THAT I ALMOST MISS THE QUIET CLICKING SOUND COMING FROM THE DUMMY.
YOU'RE DEAD, YA HEAR ME? DEAD!
ALMOST.
ANOTHER RUSE.
KRUNCH
ANOTHER BOMB.

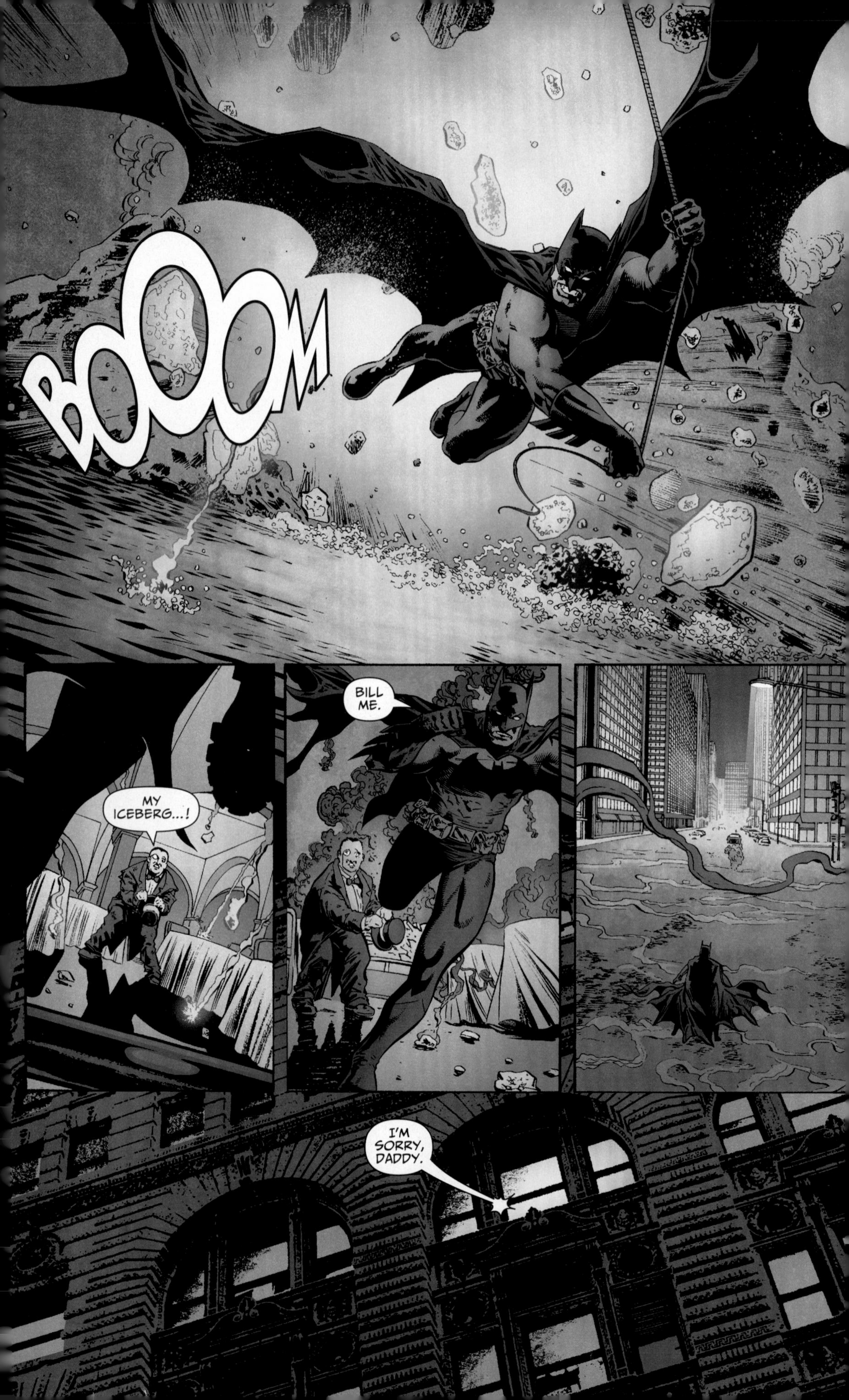
BOOOM!
MY ICEBERG...!
BILL ME.
I'M SORRY, DADDY.

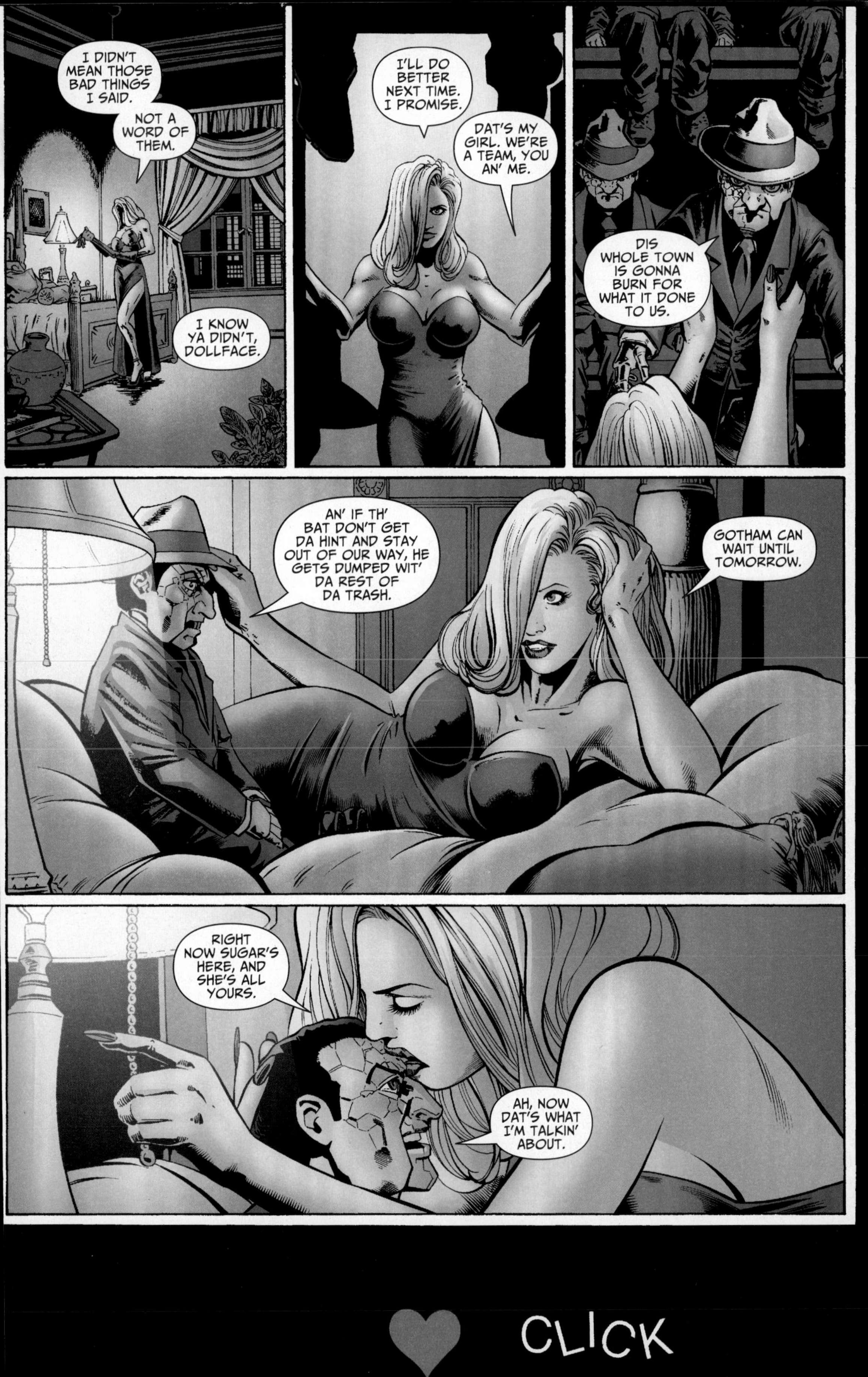
I DIDN'T MEAN THOSE BAD THINGS I SAID.
NOT A WORD OF THEM.
I KNOW YA DIDN'T, DOLLFACE.
I'LL DO BETTER NEXT TIME. I PROMISE.
DAT'S MY GIRL. WE'RE A TEAM, YOU AN' ME.
DIS WHOLE TOWN IS GONNA BURN FOR WHAT IT DONE TO US.
AN' IF TH' BAT DON'T GET DA HINT AND STAY OUT OF OUR WAY, HE GETS DUMPED WIT' DA REST OF DA TRASH.
GOTHAM CAN WAIT UNTIL TOMORROW.
RIGHT NOW SUGAR'S HERE, AND SHE'S ALL YOURS.
AH, NOW DAT'S WHAT I'M TALKIN' ABOUT.
CLICK

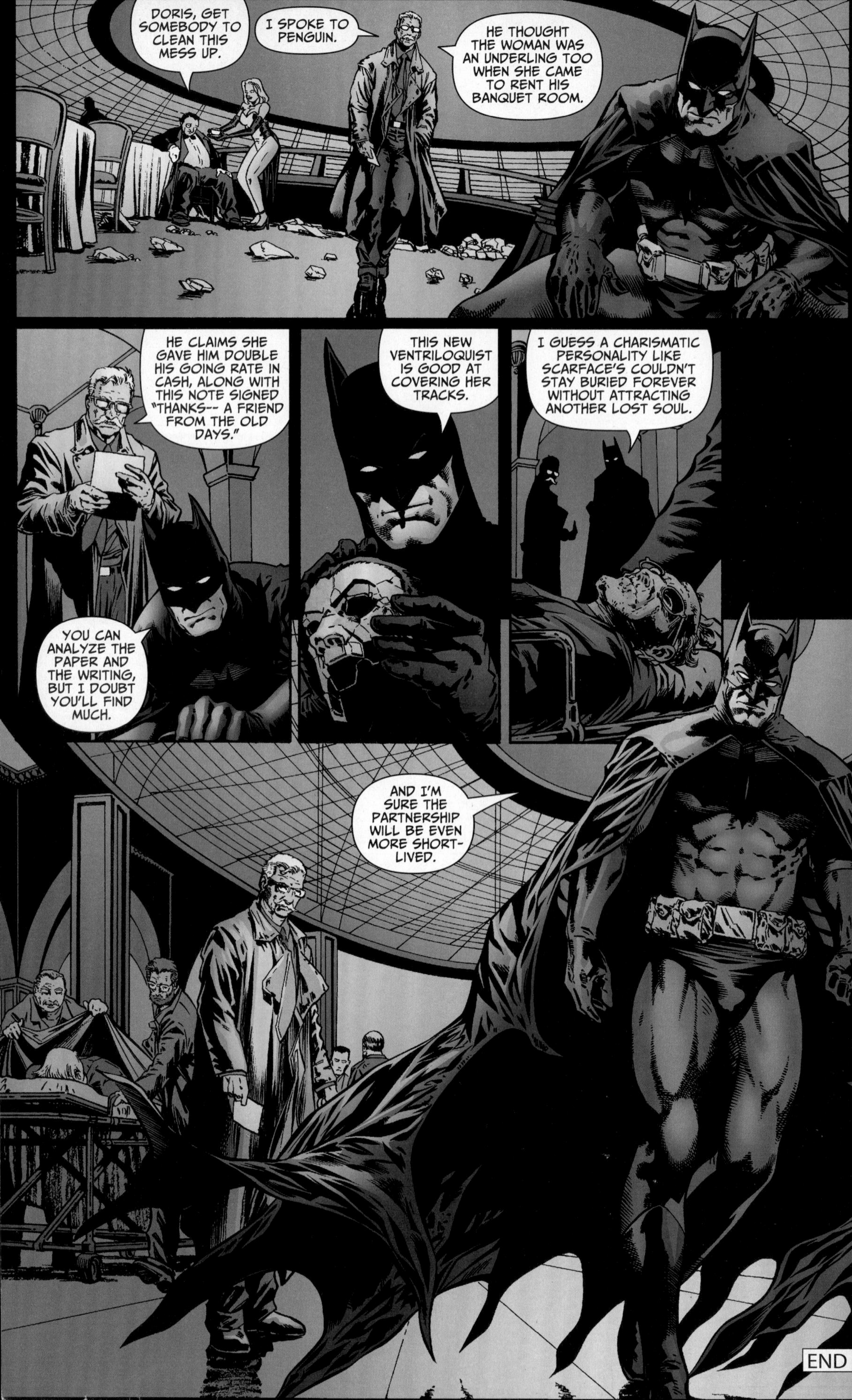
DORIS, GET SOMEBODY TO CLEAN THIS MESS UP.
I SPOKE TO PENGUIN.
HE THOUGHT THE WOMAN WAS AN UNDERLING TOO WHEN SHE CAME TO RENT HIS BANQUET ROOM.
HE CLAIMS SHE GAVE HIM DOUBLE HIS GOING RATE IN CASH, ALONG WITH THIS NOTE SIGNED "THANKS-- A FRIEND FROM THE OLD DAYS."
YOU CAN ANALYZE THE PAPER AND THE WRITING, BUT I DOUBT YOU'LL FIND MUCH.
THIS NEW VENTRILOQUIST IS GOOD AT COVERING HER TRACKS.
I GUESS A CHARISMATIC PERSONALITY LIKE SCARFACE'S COULDN'T STAY BURIED FOREVER WITHOUT ATTRACTING ANOTHER LOST SOUL.
AND I'M SURE THE PARTNERSHIP WILL BE EVEN MORE SHORT-LIVED.
END

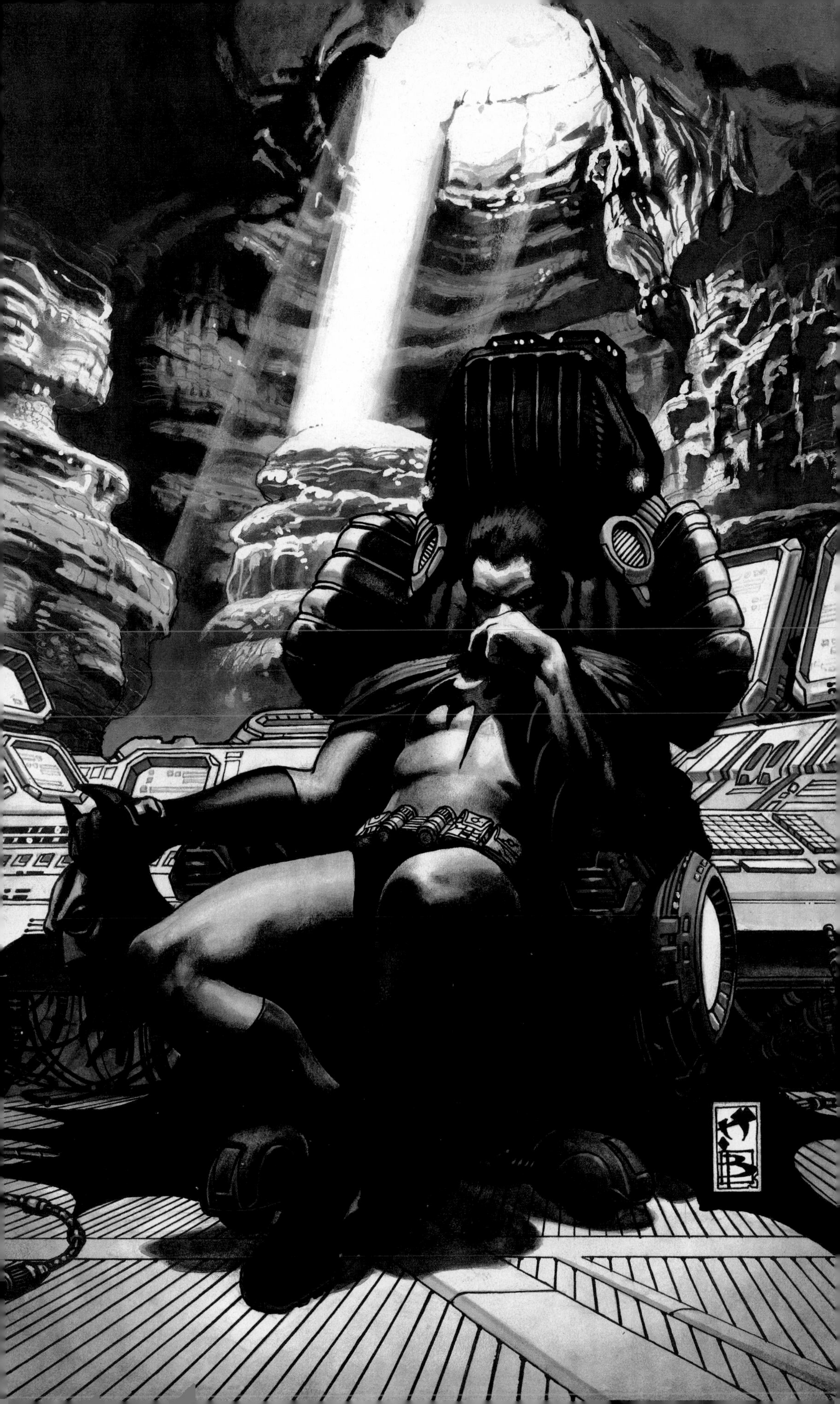

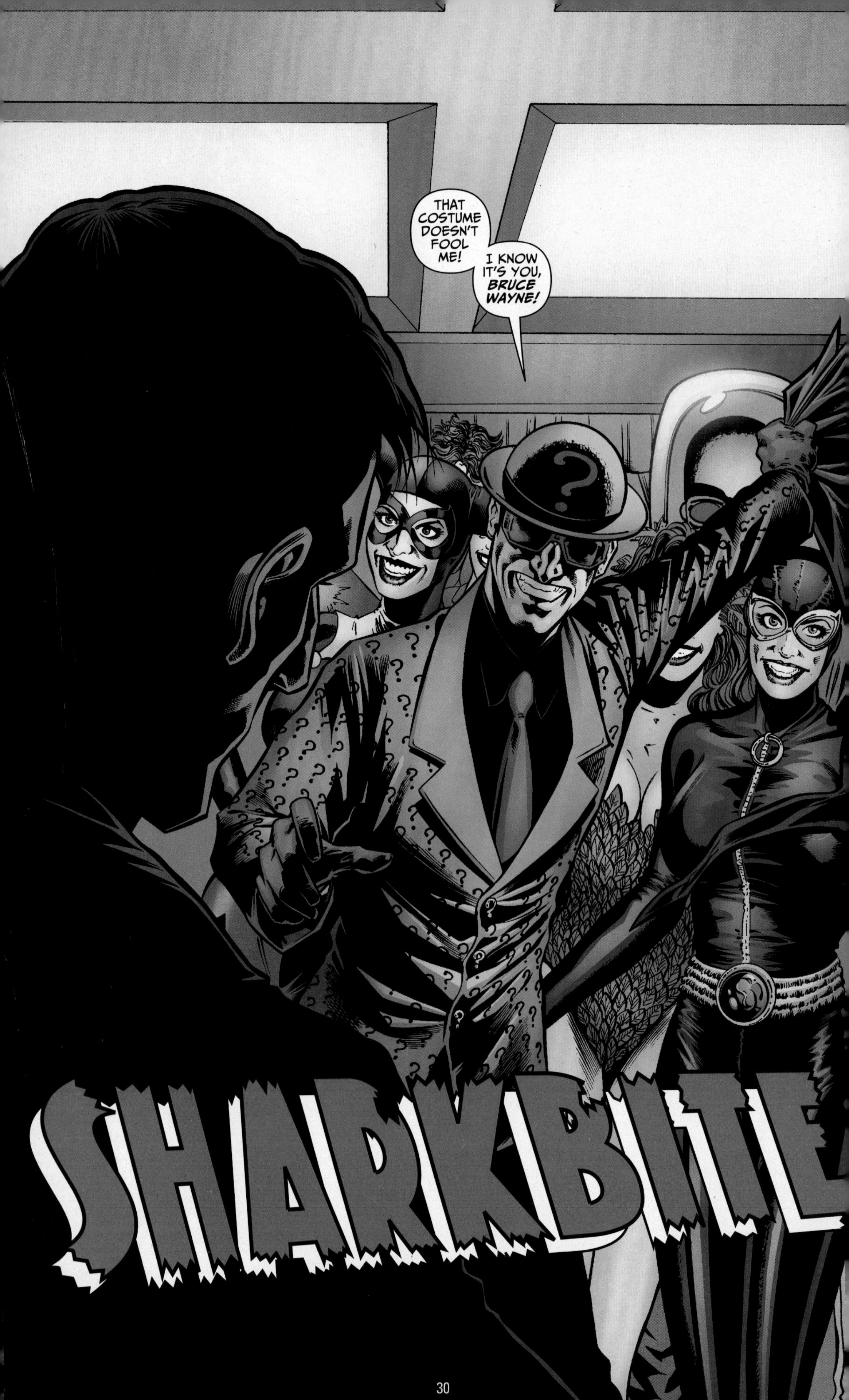
THAT COSTUME DOESN'T FOOL ME!
I KNOW IT'S YOU, BRUCE WAYNE!
SHARKBITE

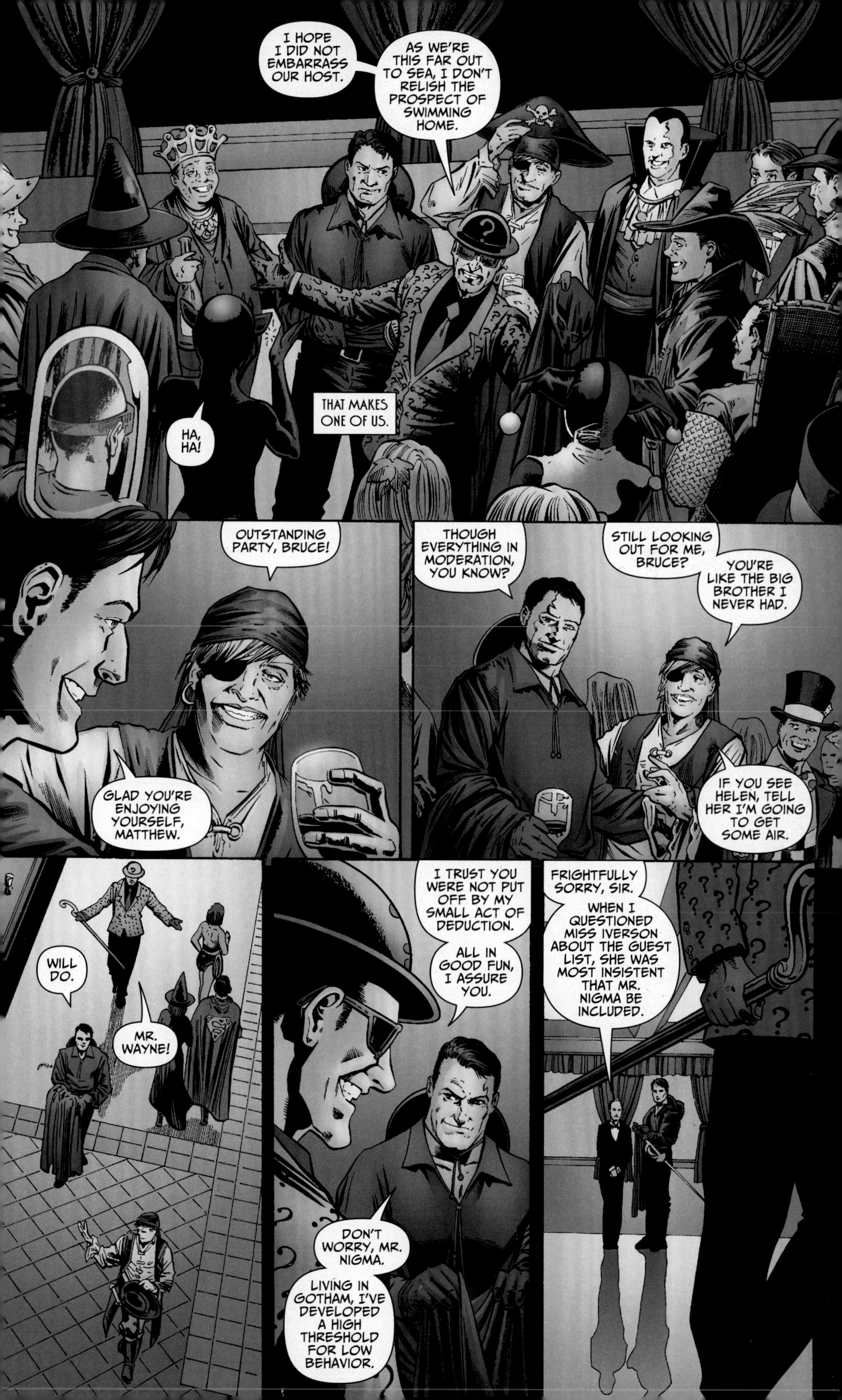
I HOPE I DID NOT EMBARRASS OUR HOST.
AS WE'RE THIS FAR OUT TO SEA, I DON'T RELISH THE PROSPECT OF SWIMMING HOME.
HA, HA!
THAT MAKES ONE OF US.
OUTSTANDING PARTY, BRUCE!
GLAD YOU'RE ENJOYING YOURSELF, MATTHEW.
THOUGH EVERYTHING IN MODERATION, YOU KNOW?
STILL LOOKING OUT FOR ME, BRUCE?
YOU'RE LIKE THE BIG BROTHER I NEVER HAD.
IF YOU SEE HELEN, TELL HER I'M GOING TO GET SOME AIR.
WILL DO.
MR. WAYNE!
I TRUST YOU WERE NOT PUT OFF BY MY SMALL ACT OF DEDUCTION.
ALL IN GOOD FUN, I ASSURE YOU.
DON'T WORRY, MR. NIGMA.
LIVING IN GOTHAM, I'VE DEVELOPED A HIGH THRESHOLD FOR LOW BEHAVIOR.
FRIGHTFULLY SORRY, SIR.
WHEN I QUESTIONED MISS IVERSON ABOUT THE GUEST LIST, SHE WAS MOST INSISTENT THAT MR. NIGMA BE INCLUDED.

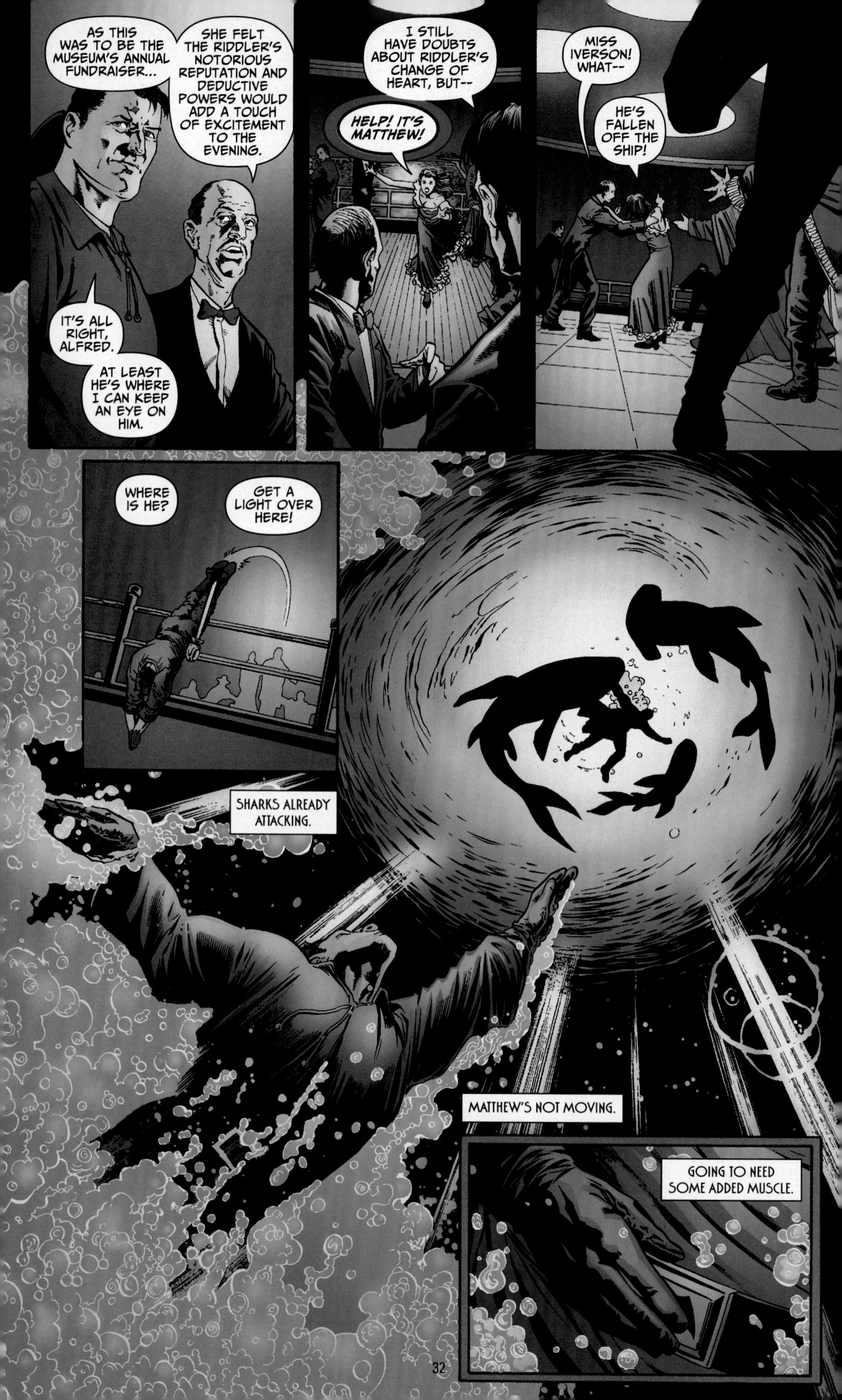
AS THIS WAS TO BE THE MUSEUM'S ANNUAL FUNDRAISER...
SHE FELT THE RIDDLER'S NOTORIOUS REPUTATION AND DEDUCTIVE POWERS WOULD ADD A TOUCH OF EXCITEMENT TO THE EVENING.
IT'S ALL RIGHT, ALFRED.
AT LEAST HE'S WHERE I CAN KEEP AN EYE ON HIM.
I STILL HAVE DOUBTS ABOUT RIDDLER'S CHANGE OF HEART, BUT--
HELP! IT'S MATTHEW!
MISS IVERSON! WHAT--
HE'S FALLEN OFF THE SHIP!
WHERE IS HE?
GET A LIGHT OVER HERE!
SHARKS ALREADY ATTACKING.
MATTHEW'S NOT MOVING.
GOING TO NEED SOME ADDED MUSCLE.

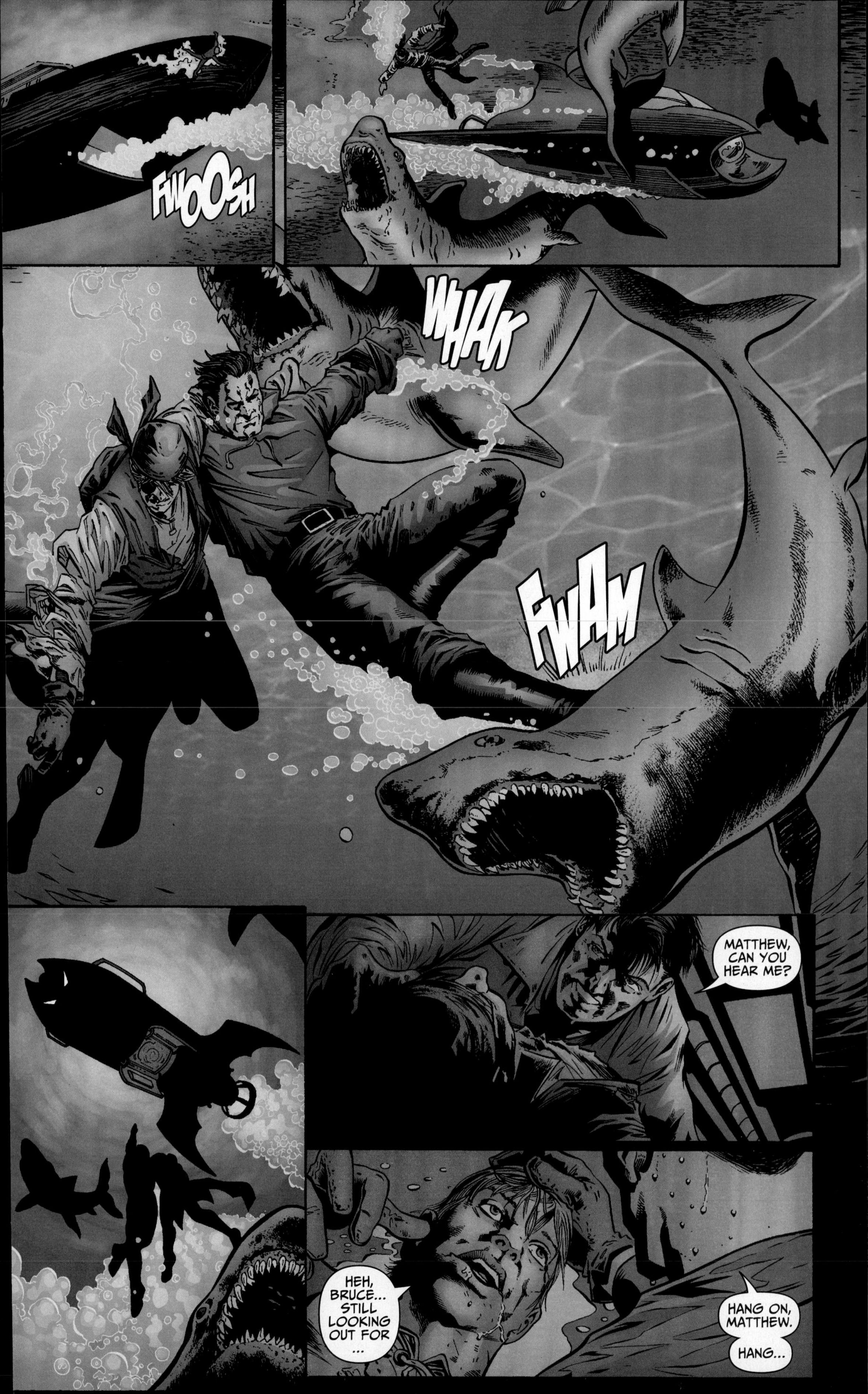
FWOOSH
WHAK
FWAM
MATTHEW, CAN YOU HEAR ME?
HEH, BRUCE... STILL LOOKING OUT FOR ...
HANG ON, MATTHEW.
HANG...

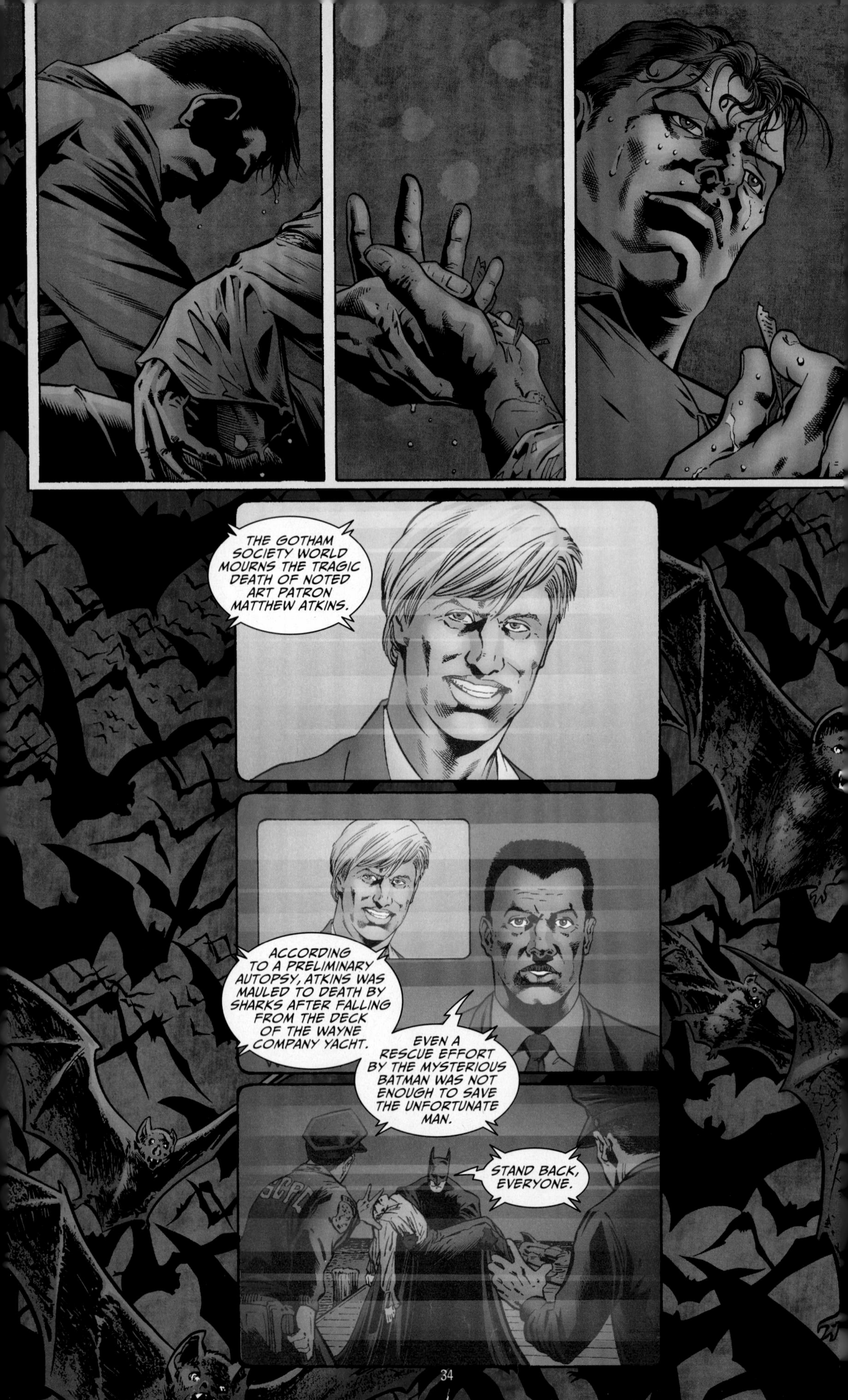
THE GOTHAM SOCIETY WORLD MOURNS THE TRAGIC DEATH OF NOTED ART PATRON MATTHEW ATKINS.
ACCORDING TO A PRELIMINARY AUTOPSY, ATKINS WAS MAULED TO DEATH BY SHARKS AFTER FALLING FROM THE DECK OF THE WAYNE COMPANY YACHT.
EVEN A RESCUE EFFORT BY THE MYSTERIOUS BATMAN WAS NOT ENOUGH TO SAVE THE UNFORTUNATE MAN.
STAND BACK, EVERYONE.
GCPD

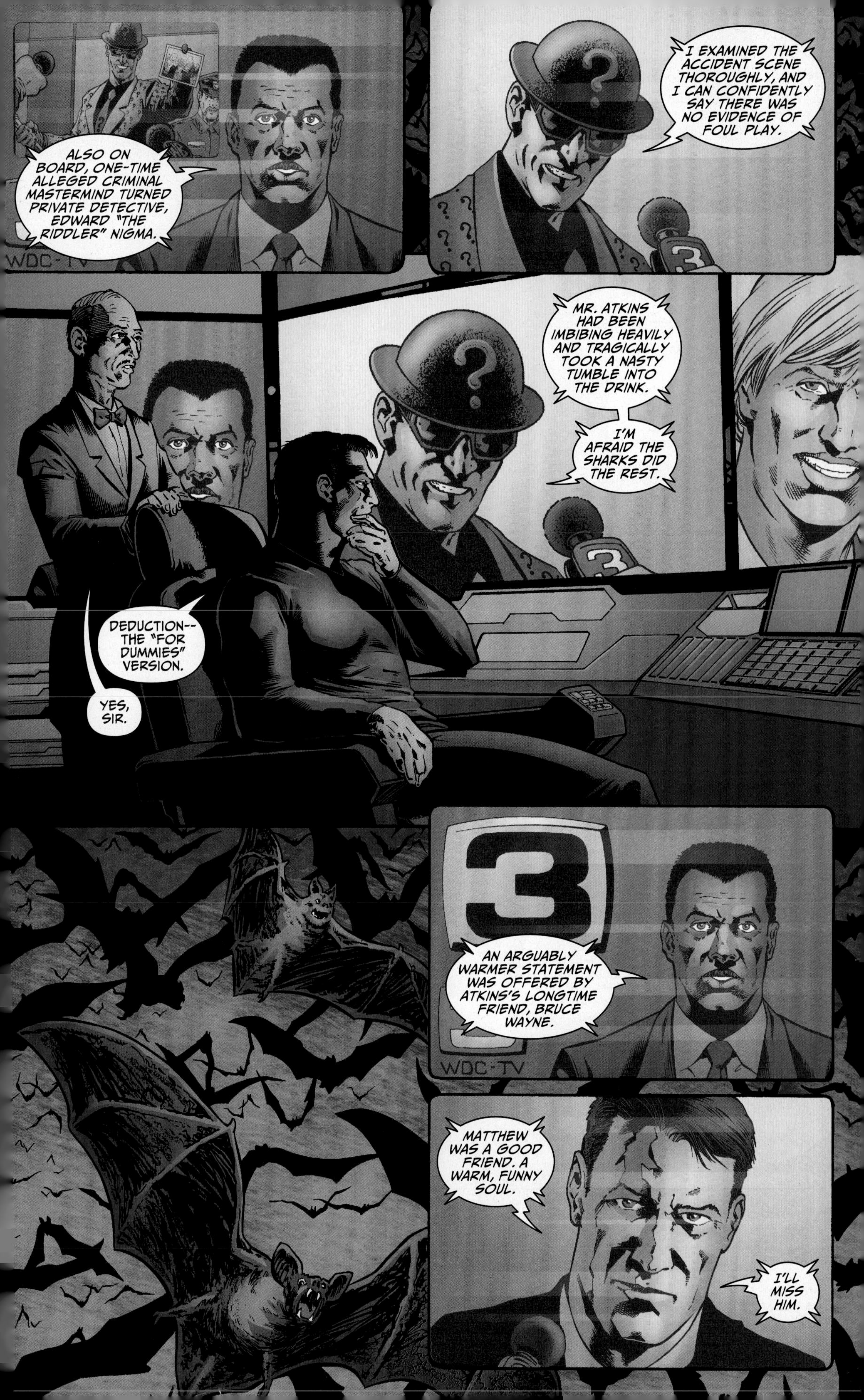
ALSO ON BOARD, ONE-TIME ALLEGED CRIMINAL MASTERMIND TURNED PRIVATE DETECTIVE, EDWARD "THE RIDDLER" NIGMA.
WDC-TV
I EXAMINED THE ACCIDENT SCENE THOROUGHLY, AND I CAN CONFIDENTLY SAY THERE WAS NO EVIDENCE OF FOUL PLAY.
MR. ATKINS HAD BEEN IMBIBING HEAVILY AND TRAGICALLY TOOK A NASTY TUMBLE INTO THE DRINK.
I'M AFRAID THE SHARKS DID THE REST.
DEDUCTION--THE "FOR DUMMIES" VERSION.
YES, SIR.
AN ARGUABLY WARMER STATEMENT WAS OFFERED BY ATKINS'S LONGTIME FRIEND, BRUCE WAYNE.
WDC-TV
MATTHEW WAS A GOOD FRIEND. A WARM, FUNNY SOUL.
I'LL MISS HIM.

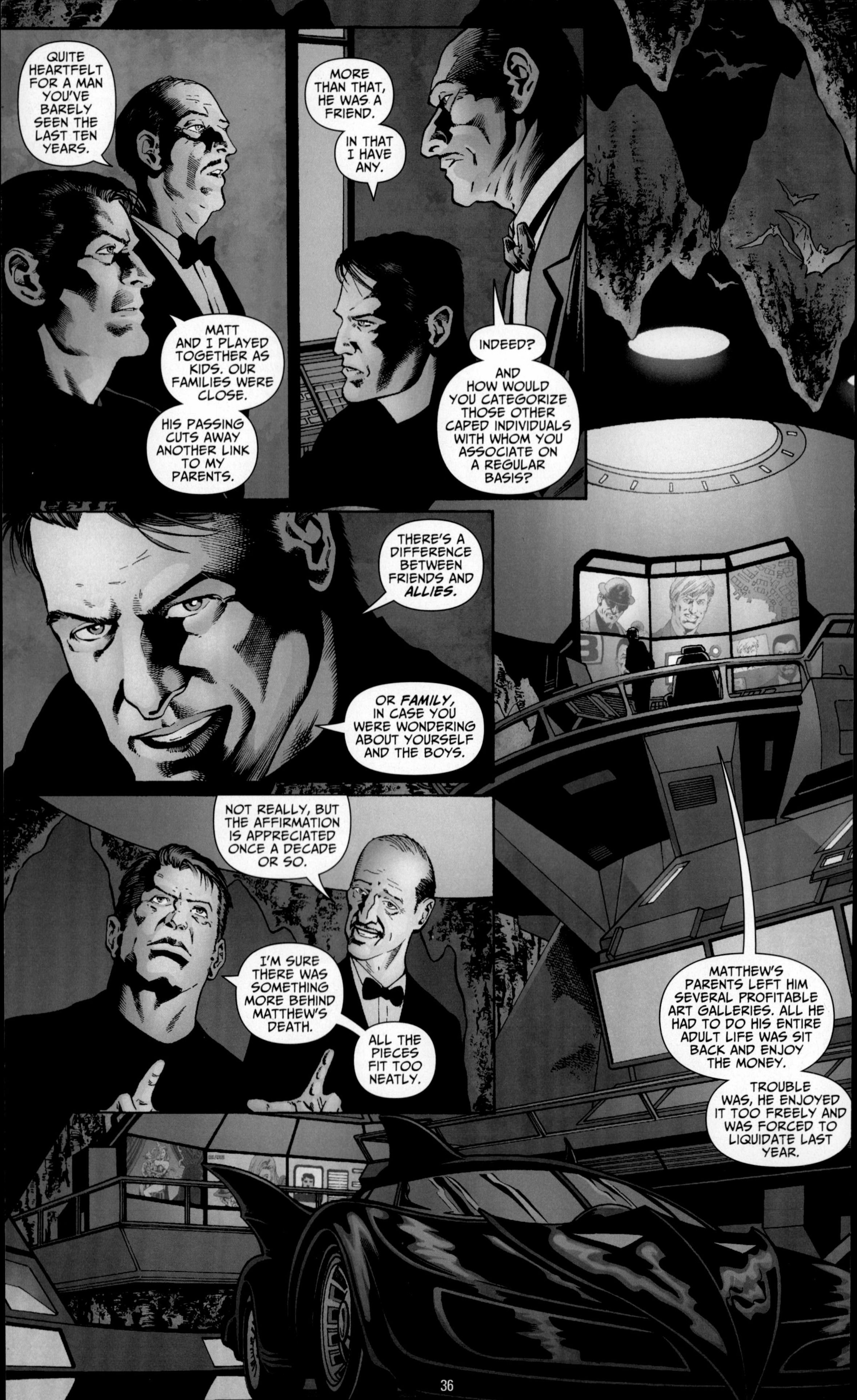
QUITE HEARTFELT FOR A MAN YOU'VE BARELY SEEN THE LAST TEN YEARS.
MATT AND I PLAYED TOGETHER AS KIDS. OUR FAMILIES WERE CLOSE.
HIS PASSING CUTS AWAY ANOTHER LINK TO MY PARENTS.
MORE THAN THAT, HE WAS A FRIEND.
IN THAT I HAVE ANY.
INDEED?
AND HOW WOULD YOU CATEGORIZE THOSE OTHER CAPED INDIVIDUALS WITH WHOM YOU ASSOCIATE ON A REGULAR BASIS?
THERE'S A DIFFERENCE BETWEEN FRIENDS AND ALLIES.
OR FAMILY, IN CASE YOU WERE WONDERING ABOUT YOURSELF AND THE BOYS.
NOT REALLY, BUT THE AFFIRMATION IS APPRECIATED ONCE A DECADE OR SO.
I'M SURE THERE WAS SOMETHING MORE BEHIND MATTHEW'S DEATH.
ALL THE PIECES FIT TOO NEATLY.
MATTHEW'S PARENTS LEFT HIM SEVERAL PROFITABLE ART GALLERIES. ALL HE HAD TO DO HIS ENTIRE ADULT LIFE WAS SIT BACK AND ENJOY THE MONEY.
TROUBLE WAS, HE ENJOYED IT TOO FREELY AND WAS FORCED TO LIQUIDATE LAST YEAR.

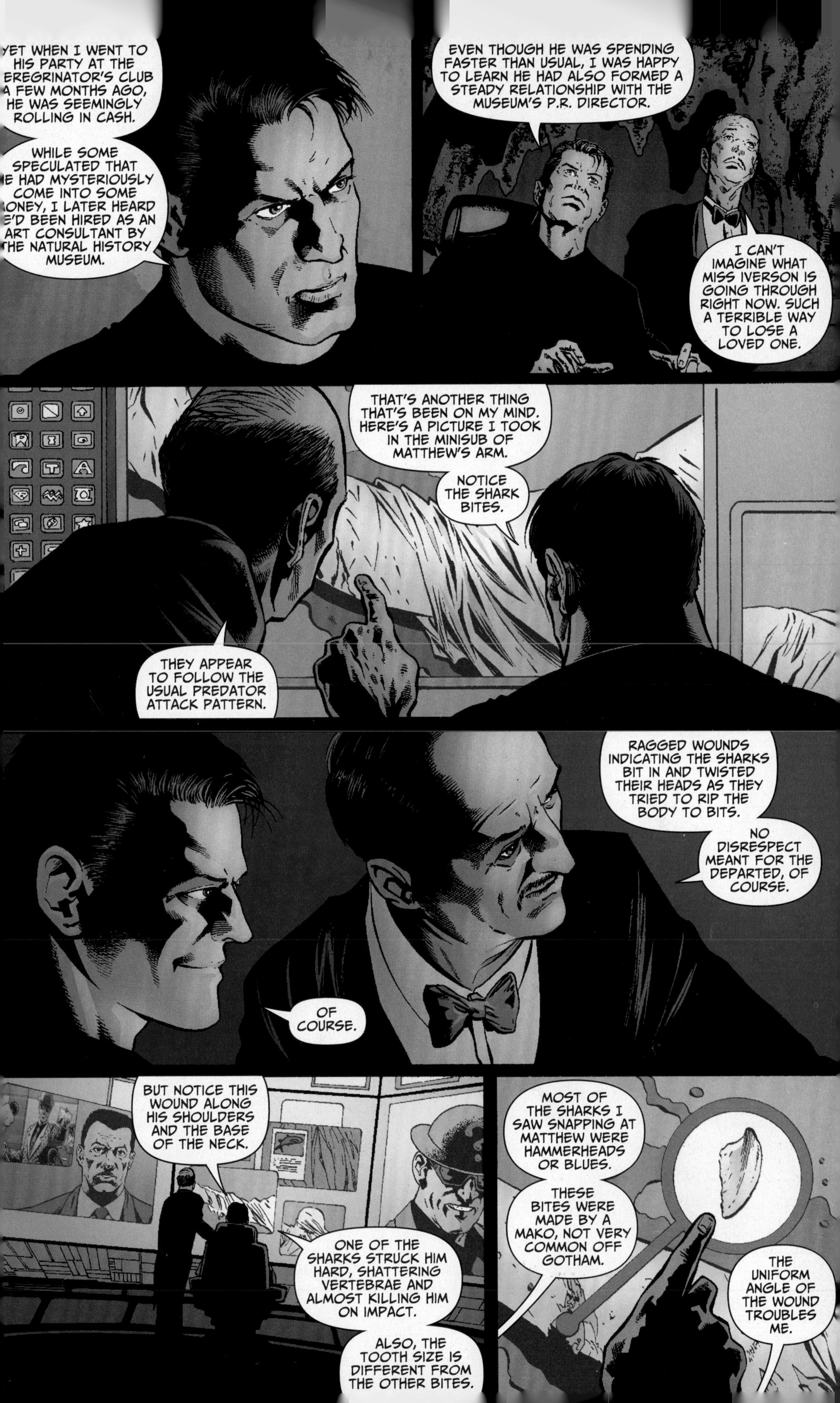

YET WHEN I WENT TO HIS PARTY AT THE EREGRINATOR'S CLUB A FEW MONTHS AGO, HE WAS SEEMINGLY ROLLING IN CASH.
WHILE SOME SPECULATED THAT E HAD MYSTERIOUSLY COME INTO SOME ONEY, I LATER HEARD E'D BEEN HIRED AS AN ART CONSULTANT BY THE NATURAL HISTORY MUSEUM.
EVEN THOUGH HE WAS SPENDING FASTER THAN USUAL, I WAS HAPPY TO LEARN HE HAD ALSO FORMED A STEADY RELATIONSHIP WITH THE MUSEUM'S P.R. DIRECTOR.
I CAN'T IMAGINE WHAT MISS IVERSON IS GOING THROUGH RIGHT NOW. SUCH A TERRIBLE WAY TO LOSE A LOVED ONE.
THAT'S ANOTHER THING THAT'S BEEN ON MY MIND. HERE'S A PICTURE I TOOK IN THE MINISUB OF MATTHEW'S ARM.
NOTICE THE SHARK BITES.
THEY APPEAR TO FOLLOW THE USUAL PREDATOR ATTACK PATTERN.
RAGGED WOUNDS INDICATING THE SHARKS BIT IN AND TWISTED THEIR HEADS AS THEY TRIED TO RIP THE BODY TO BITS.
NO DISRESPECT MEANT FOR THE DEPARTED, OF COURSE.
OF COURSE.
BUT NOTICE THIS WOUND ALONG HIS SHOULDERS AND THE BASE OF THE NECK.
ONE OF THE SHARKS STRUCK HIM HARD, SHATTERING VERTEBRAE AND ALMOST KILLING HIM ON IMPACT.
ALSO, THE TOOTH SIZE IS DIFFERENT FROM THE OTHER BITES.
MOST OF THE SHARKS I SAW SNAPPING AT MATTHEW WERE HAMMERHEADS OR BLUES.
THESE BITES WERE MADE BY A MAKO, NOT VERY COMMON OFF GOTHAM.
THE UNIFORM ANGLE OF THE WOUND TROUBLES ME.

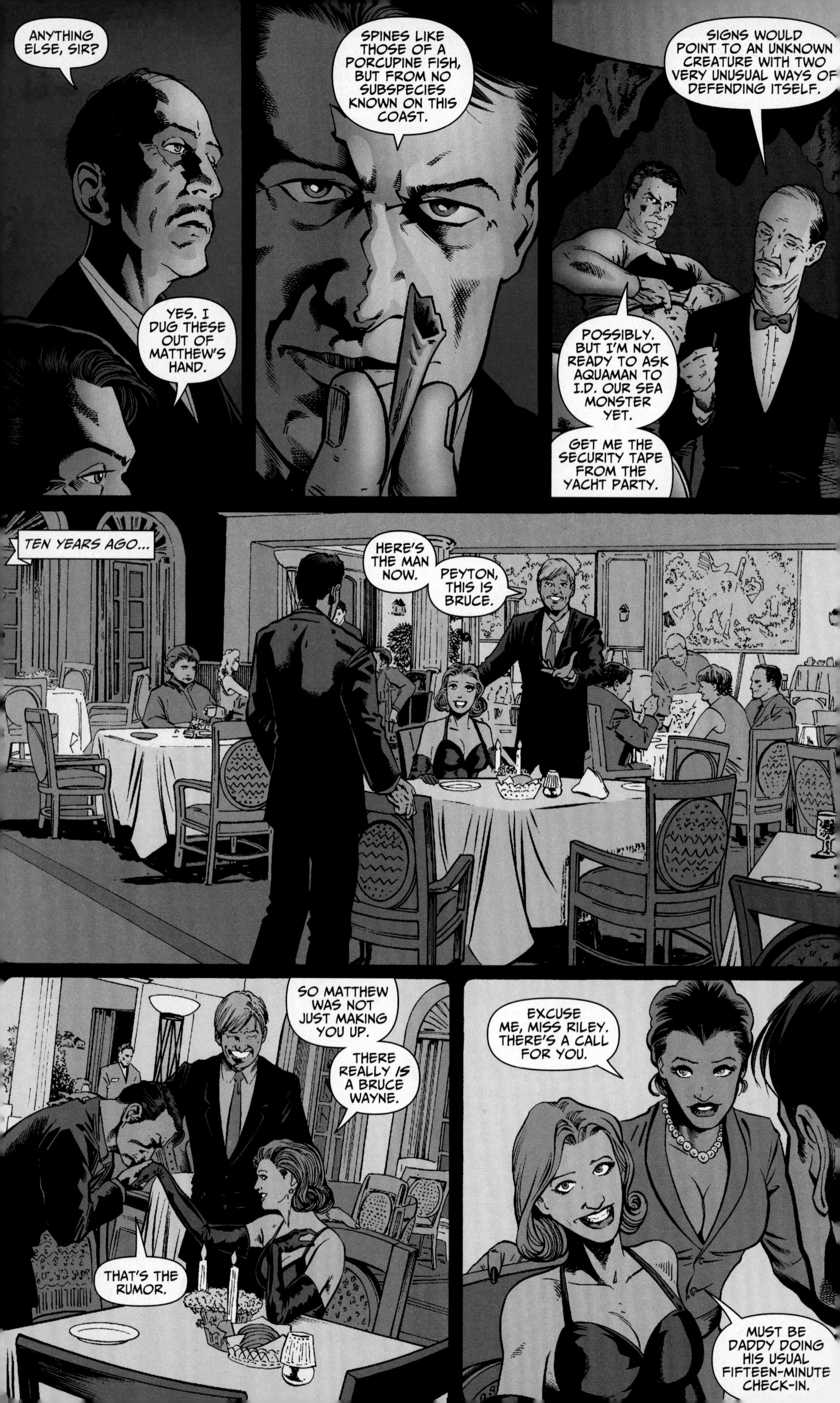

ANYTHING ELSE, SIR?
YES. I DUG THESE OUT OF MATTHEW'S HAND.
SPINES LIKE THOSE OF A PORCUPINE FISH, BUT FROM NO SUBSPECIES KNOWN ON THIS COAST.
SIGNS WOULD POINT TO AN UNKNOWN CREATURE WITH TWO VERY UNUSUAL WAYS OF DEFENDING ITSELF.
POSSIBLY. BUT I'M NOT READY TO ASK AQUAMAN TO I.D. OUR SEA MONSTER YET.
GET ME THE SECURITY TAPE FROM THE YACHT PARTY.
TEN YEARS AGO...
HERE'S THE MAN NOW.
PEYTON, THIS IS BRUCE.
SO MATTHEW WAS NOT JUST MAKING YOU UP.
THERE REALLY *IS* A BRUCE WAYNE.
THAT'S THE RUMOR.
EXCUSE ME, MISS RILEY. THERE'S A CALL FOR YOU.
MUST BE DADDY DOING HIS USUAL FIFTEEN-MINUTE CHECK-IN.

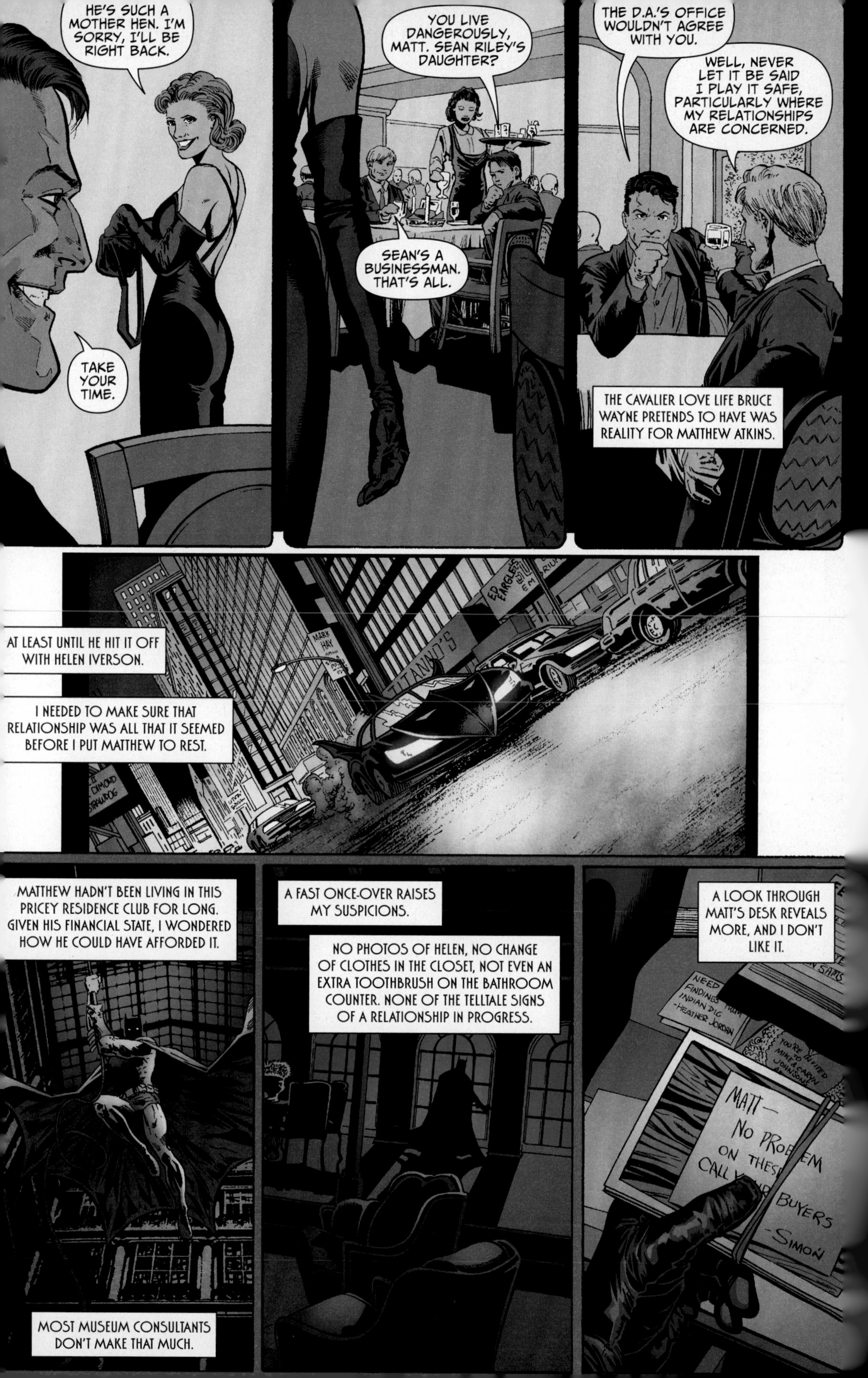
HE'S SUCH A MOTHER HEN. I'M SORRY, I'LL BE RIGHT BACK.
TAKE YOUR TIME.
YOU LIVE DANGEROUSLY, MATT. SEAN RILEY'S DAUGHTER?
SEAN'S A BUSINESSMAN. THAT'S ALL.
THE D.A.'S OFFICE WOULDN'T AGREE WITH YOU.
WELL, NEVER LET IT BE SAID I PLAY IT SAFE, PARTICULARLY WHERE MY RELATIONSHIPS ARE CONCERNED.
THE CAVALIER LOVE LIFE BRUCE WAYNE PRETENDS TO HAVE WAS REALITY FOR MATTHEW ATKINS.
AT LEAST UNTIL HE HIT IT OFF WITH HELEN IVERSON.
I NEEDED TO MAKE SURE THAT RELATIONSHIP WAS ALL THAT IT SEEMED BEFORE I PUT MATTHEW TO REST.
MATTHEW HADN'T BEEN LIVING IN THIS PRICEY RESIDENCE CLUB FOR LONG. GIVEN HIS FINANCIAL STATE, I WONDERED HOW HE COULD HAVE AFFORDED IT.
MOST MUSEUM CONSULTANTS DON'T MAKE THAT MUCH.
A FAST ONCE-OVER RAISES MY SUSPICIONS.
NO PHOTOS OF HELEN, NO CHANGE OF CLOTHES IN THE CLOSET, NOT EVEN AN EXTRA TOOTHBRUSH ON THE BATHROOM COUNTER. NONE OF THE TELLTALE SIGNS OF A RELATIONSHIP IN PROGRESS.
A LOOK THROUGH MATT'S DESK REVEALS MORE, AND I DON'T LIKE IT.
NEED FINDINGS FROM INDIAN DIG -HEATHER JORDAN

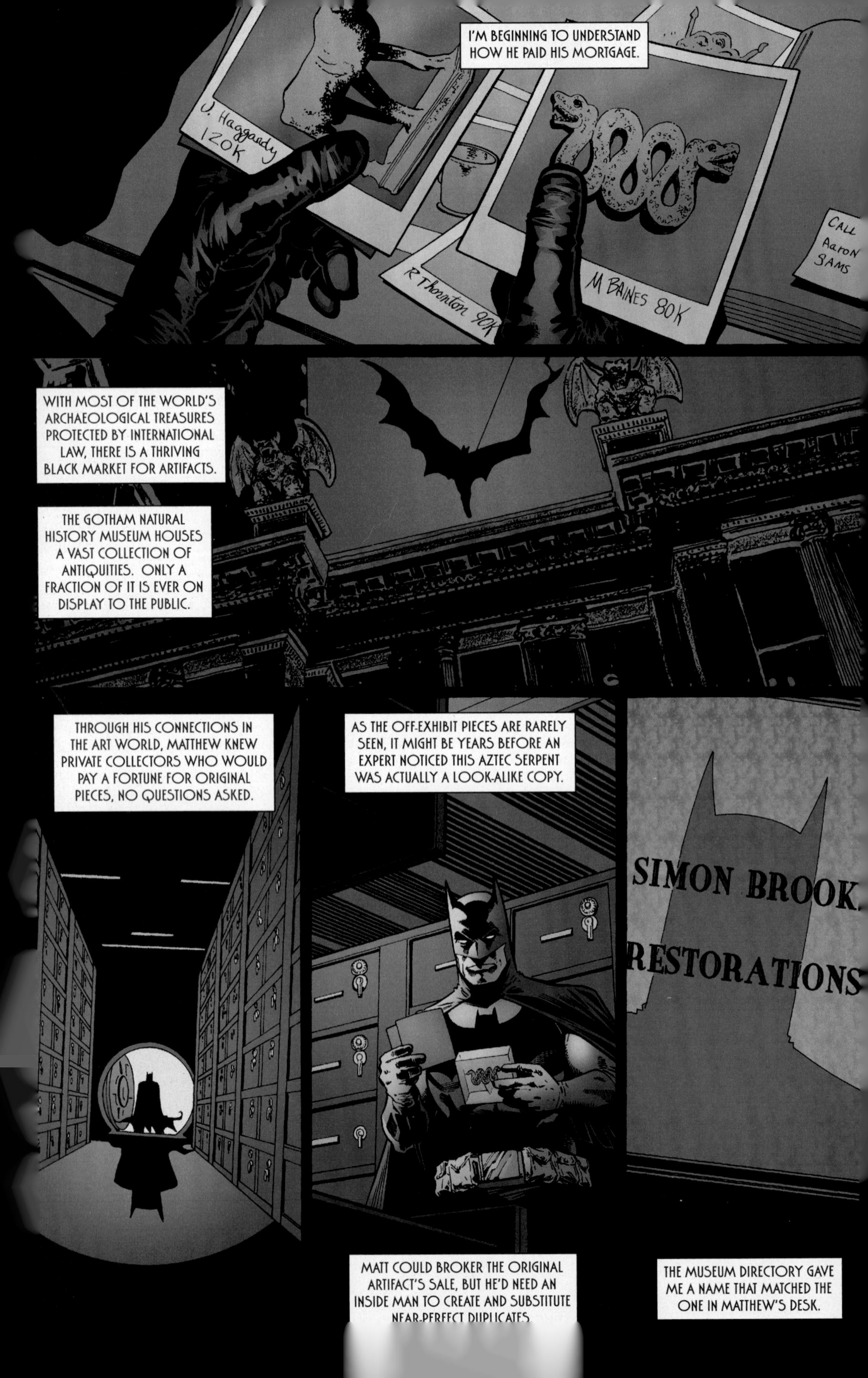
I'M BEGINNING TO UNDERSTAND HOW HE PAID HIS MORTGAGE.
J. Haggardy 120K
R Thornton 90K
M BAINES 80K
CALL Aaron SAMS
WITH MOST OF THE WORLD'S ARCHAEOLOGICAL TREASURES PROTECTED BY INTERNATIONAL LAW, THERE IS A THRIVING BLACK MARKET FOR ARTIFACTS.
THE GOTHAM NATURAL HISTORY MUSEUM HOUSES A VAST COLLECTION OF ANTIQUITIES. ONLY A FRACTION OF IT IS EVER ON DISPLAY TO THE PUBLIC.
THROUGH HIS CONNECTIONS IN THE ART WORLD, MATTHEW KNEW PRIVATE COLLECTORS WHO WOULD PAY A FORTUNE FOR ORIGINAL PIECES, NO QUESTIONS ASKED.
AS THE OFF-EXHIBIT PIECES ARE RARELY SEEN, IT MIGHT BE YEARS BEFORE AN EXPERT NOTICED THIS AZTEC SERPENT WAS ACTUALLY A LOOK-ALIKE COPY.
MATT COULD BROKER THE ORIGINAL ARTIFACT'S SALE, BUT HE'D NEED AN INSIDE MAN TO CREATE AND SUBSTITUTE NEAR-PERFECT DUPLICATES.
SIMON BROOK RESTORATIONS
THE MUSEUM DIRECTORY GAVE ME A NAME THAT MATCHED THE ONE IN MATTHEW'S DESK.

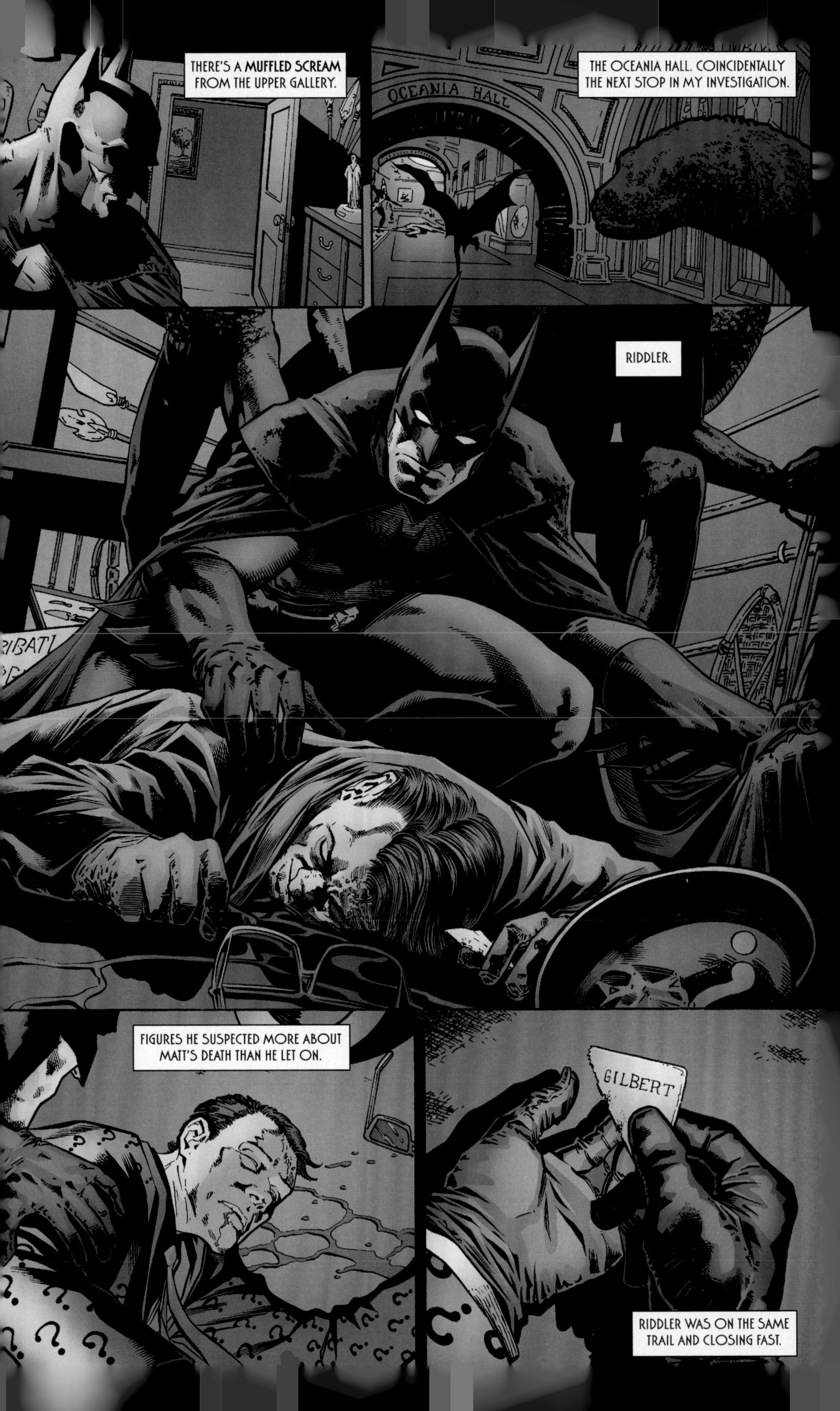
THERE'S A MUFFLED SCREAM FROM THE UPPER GALLERY.
THE OCEANIA HALL. COINCIDENTALLY THE NEXT STOP IN MY INVESTIGATION.
OCEANIA HALL
RIDDLER.
FIGURES HE SUSPECTED MORE ABOUT MATT'S DEATH THAN HE LET ON.
GILBERT
RIDDLER WAS ON THE SAME TRAIL AND CLOSING FAST.

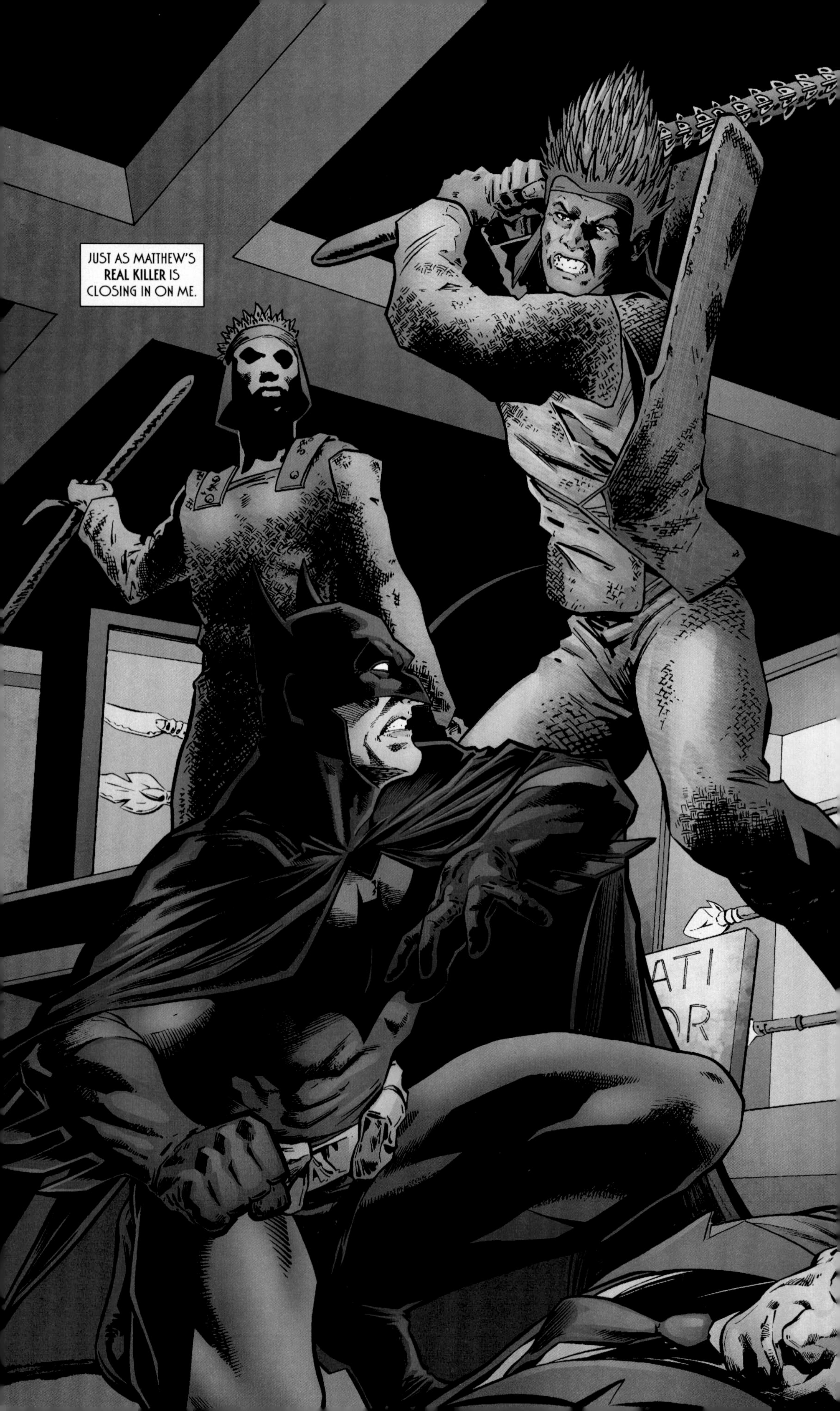
JUST AS MATTHEW'S REAL KILLER IS CLOSING IN ON ME.

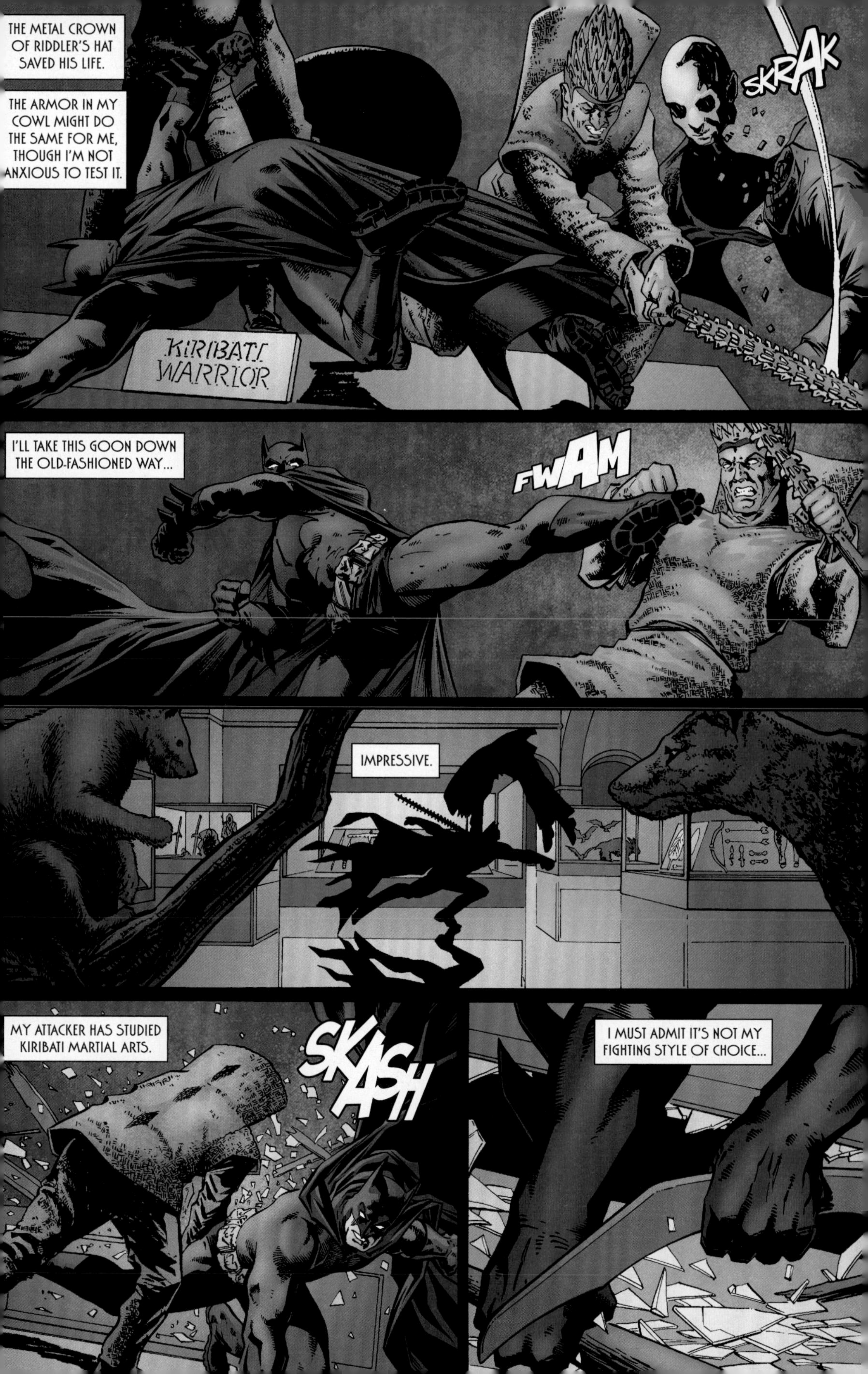
THE METAL CROWN OF RIDDLER'S HAT SAVED HIS LIFE.
THE ARMOR IN MY COWL MIGHT DO THE SAME FOR ME, THOUGH I'M NOT ANXIOUS TO TEST IT.
SKRAK
KIRIBATI WARRIOR
I'LL TAKE THIS GOON DOWN THE OLD-FASHIONED WAY...
FWAM
IMPRESSIVE.
MY ATTACKER HAS STUDIED KIRIBATI MARTIAL ARTS.
SKASH
I MUST ADMIT IT'S NOT MY FIGHTING STYLE OF CHOICE...

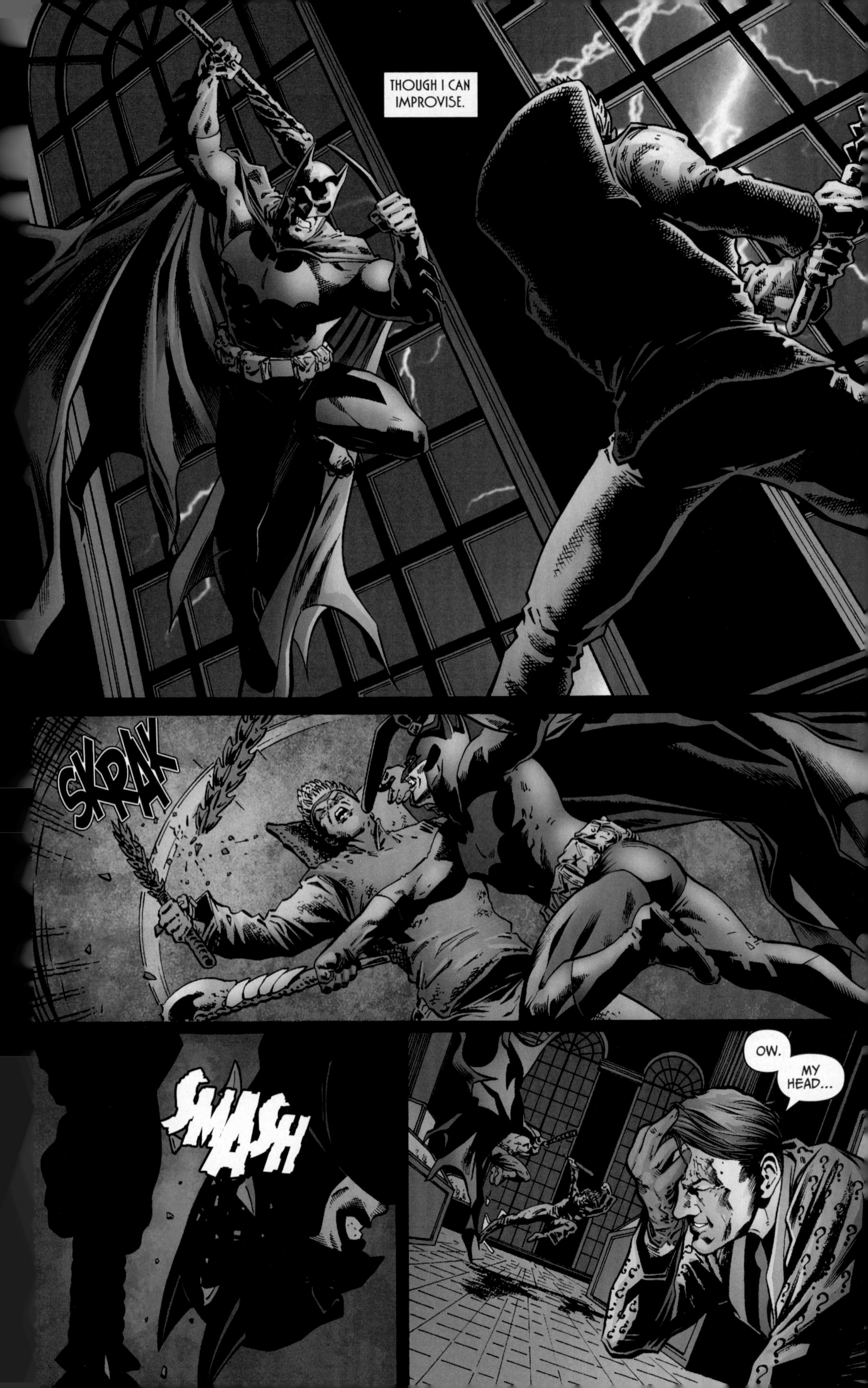
THOUGH I CAN IMPROVISE.
SKRAK
SMASH
OW.
MY HEAD...

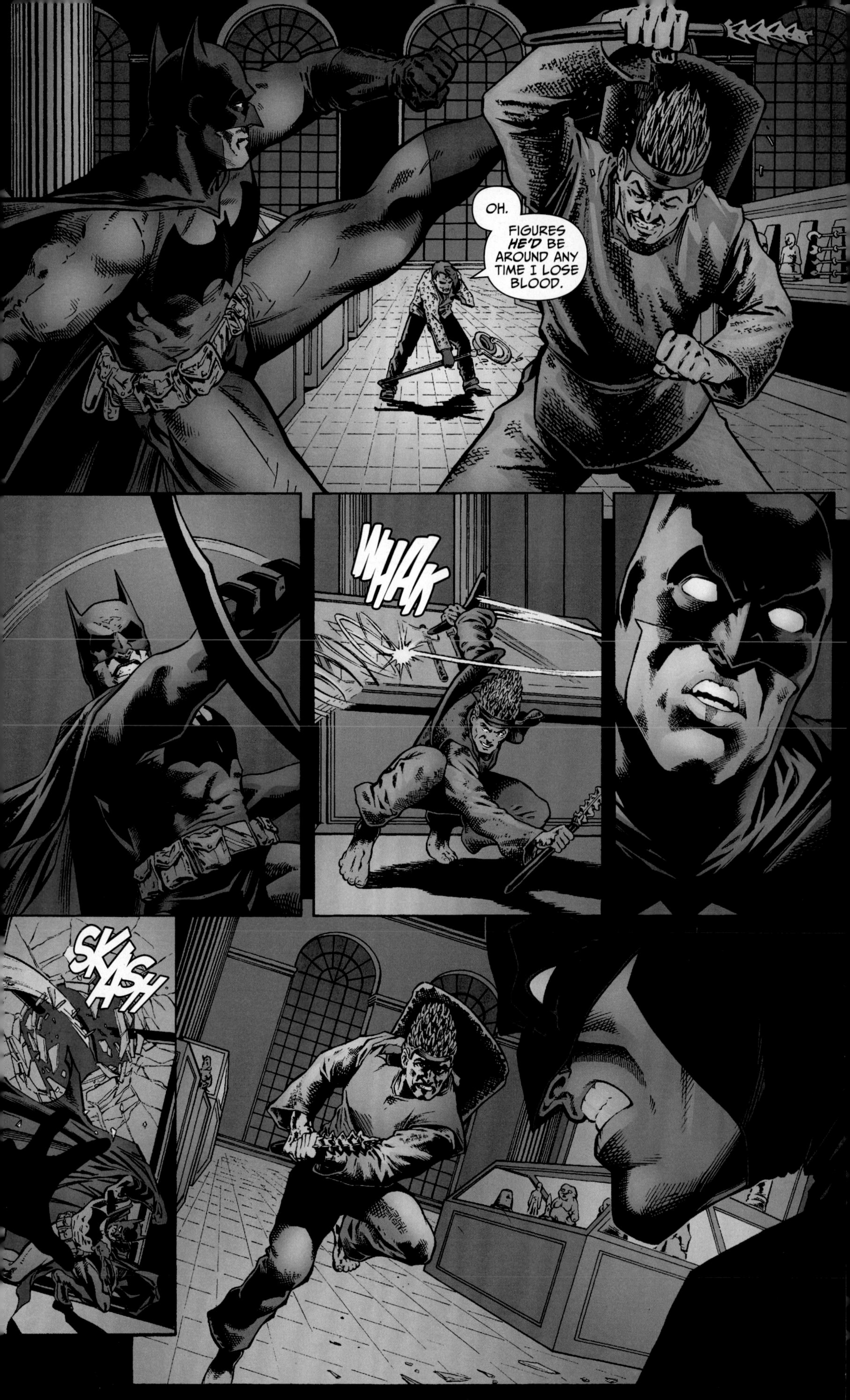
OH.
FIGURES HE'D BE AROUND ANY TIME I LOSE BLOOD.
WHAK
SKASH

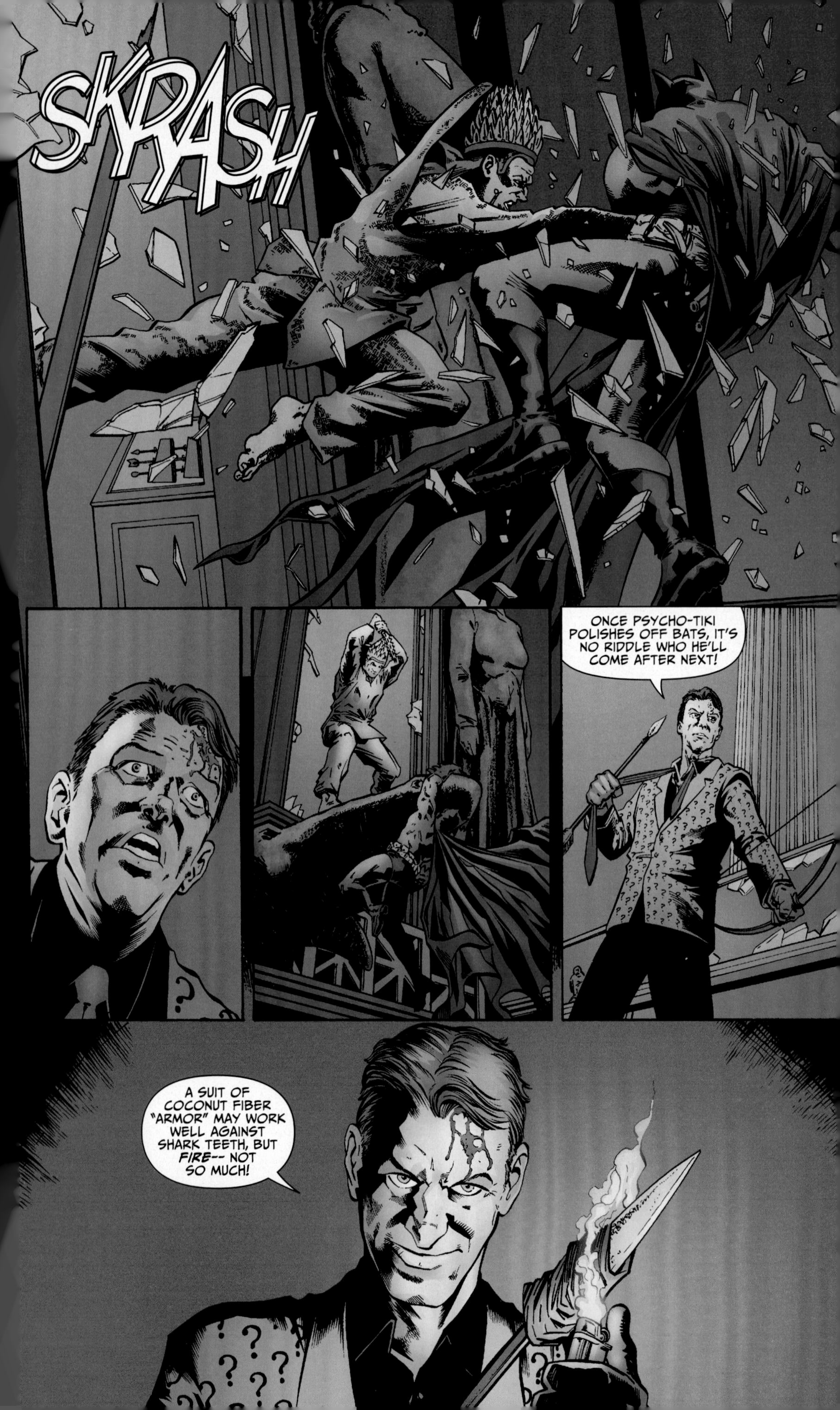
SKRASH
ONCE PSYCHO-TIKI POLISHES OFF BATS, IT'S NO RIDDLE WHO HE'LL COME AFTER NEXT!
A SUIT OF COCONUT FIBER "ARMOR" MAY WORK WELL AGAINST SHARK TEETH, BUT FIRE-- NOT SO MUCH!

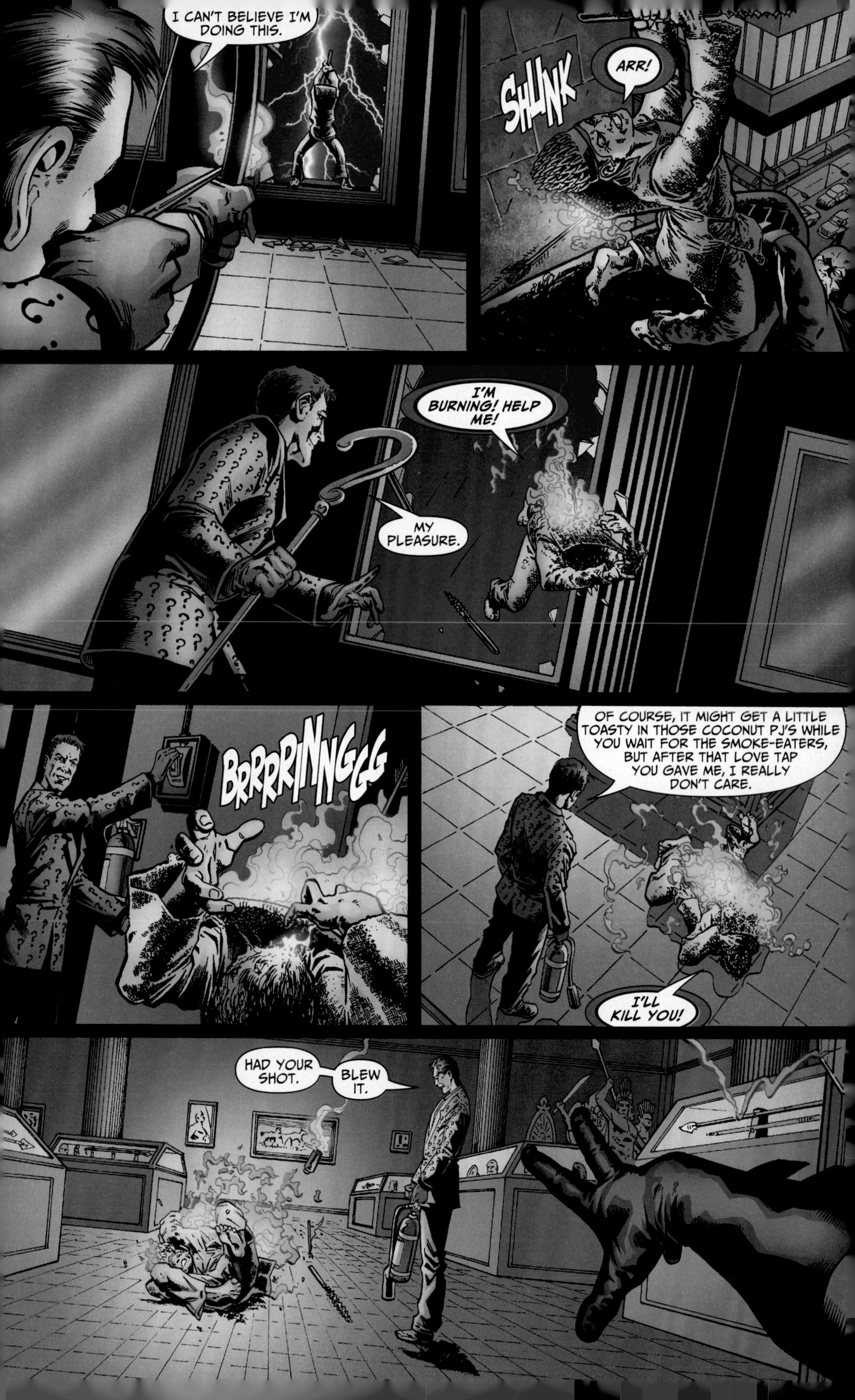
I CAN'T BELIEVE I'M DOING THIS.
SHUNK
ARR!
I'M BURNING! HELP ME!
MY PLEASURE.
BRRRRINNGGG
OF COURSE, IT MIGHT GET A LITTLE TOASTY IN THOSE COCONUT PJ'S WHILE YOU WAIT FOR THE SMOKE-EATERS, BUT AFTER THAT LOVE TAP YOU GAVE ME, I REALLY DON'T CARE.
I'LL KILL YOU!
HAD YOUR SHOT.
BLEW IT.

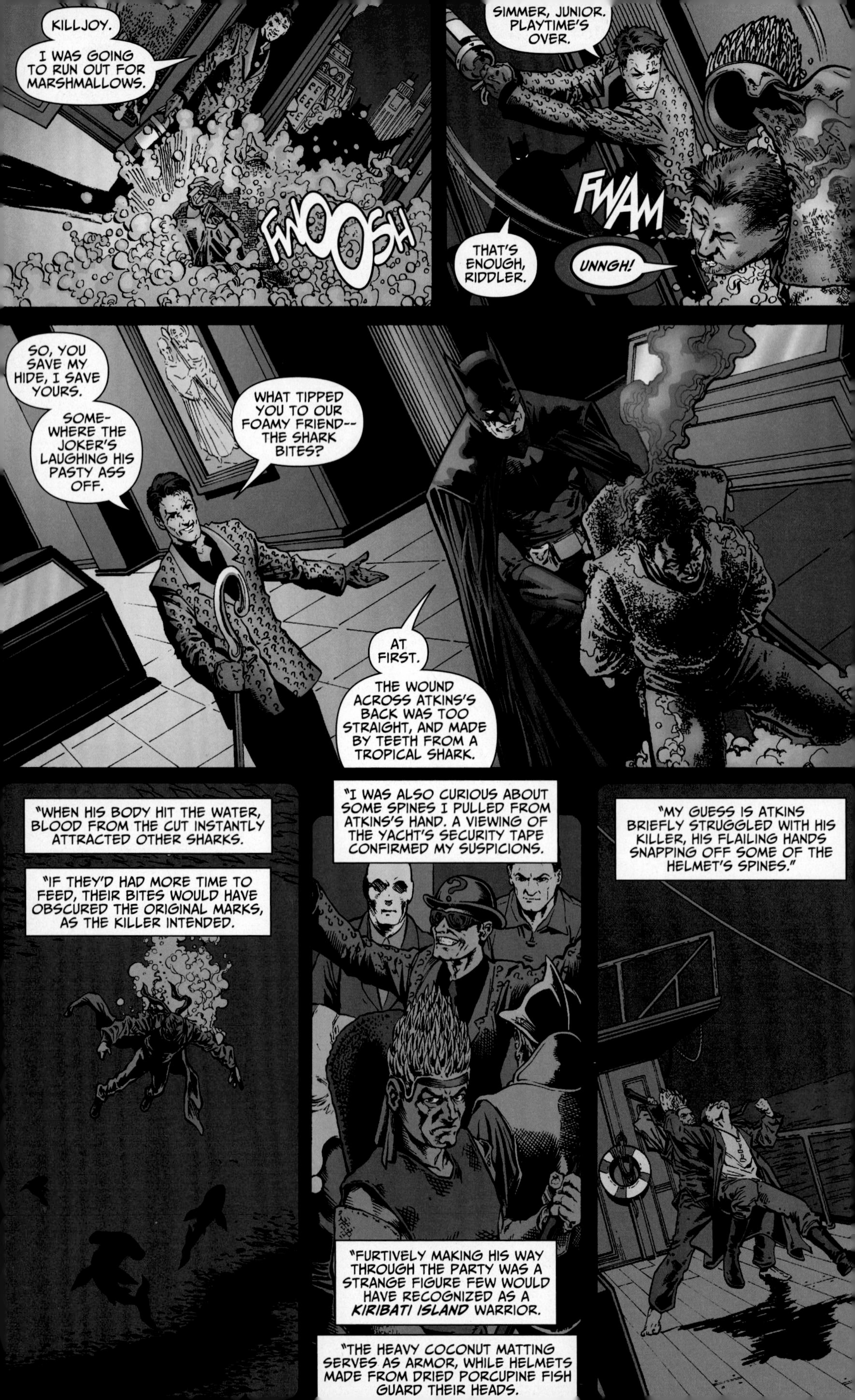
KILLJOY.
I WAS GOING TO RUN OUT FOR MARSHMALLOWS.
FWOOOSH
SIMMER, JUNIOR. PLAYTIME'S OVER.
FWAM
THAT'S ENOUGH, RIDDLER.
UNNGH!
SO, YOU SAVE MY HIDE, I SAVE YOURS.
SOME-WHERE THE JOKER'S LAUGHING HIS PASTY ASS OFF.
WHAT TIPPED YOU TO OUR FOAMY FRIEND-- THE SHARK BITES?
AT FIRST.
THE WOUND ACROSS ATKINS'S BACK WAS TOO STRAIGHT, AND MADE BY TEETH FROM A TROPICAL SHARK.
"WHEN HIS BODY HIT THE WATER, BLOOD FROM THE CUT INSTANTLY ATTRACTED OTHER SHARKS.
"IF THEY'D HAD MORE TIME TO FEED, THEIR BITES WOULD HAVE OBSCURED THE ORIGINAL MARKS, AS THE KILLER INTENDED.
"I WAS ALSO CURIOUS ABOUT SOME SPINES I PULLED FROM ATKINS'S HAND. A VIEWING OF THE YACHT'S SECURITY TAPE CONFIRMED MY SUSPICIONS.
"FURTIVELY MAKING HIS WAY THROUGH THE PARTY WAS A STRANGE FIGURE FEW WOULD HAVE RECOGNIZED AS A *KIRIBATI ISLAND* WARRIOR.
"THE HEAVY COCONUT MATTING SERVES AS ARMOR, WHILE HELMETS MADE FROM DRIED PORCUPINE FISH GUARD THEIR HEADS.
"MY GUESS IS ATKINS BRIEFLY STRUGGLED WITH HIS KILLER, HIS FLAILING HANDS SNAPPING OFF SOME OF THE HELMET'S SPINES."

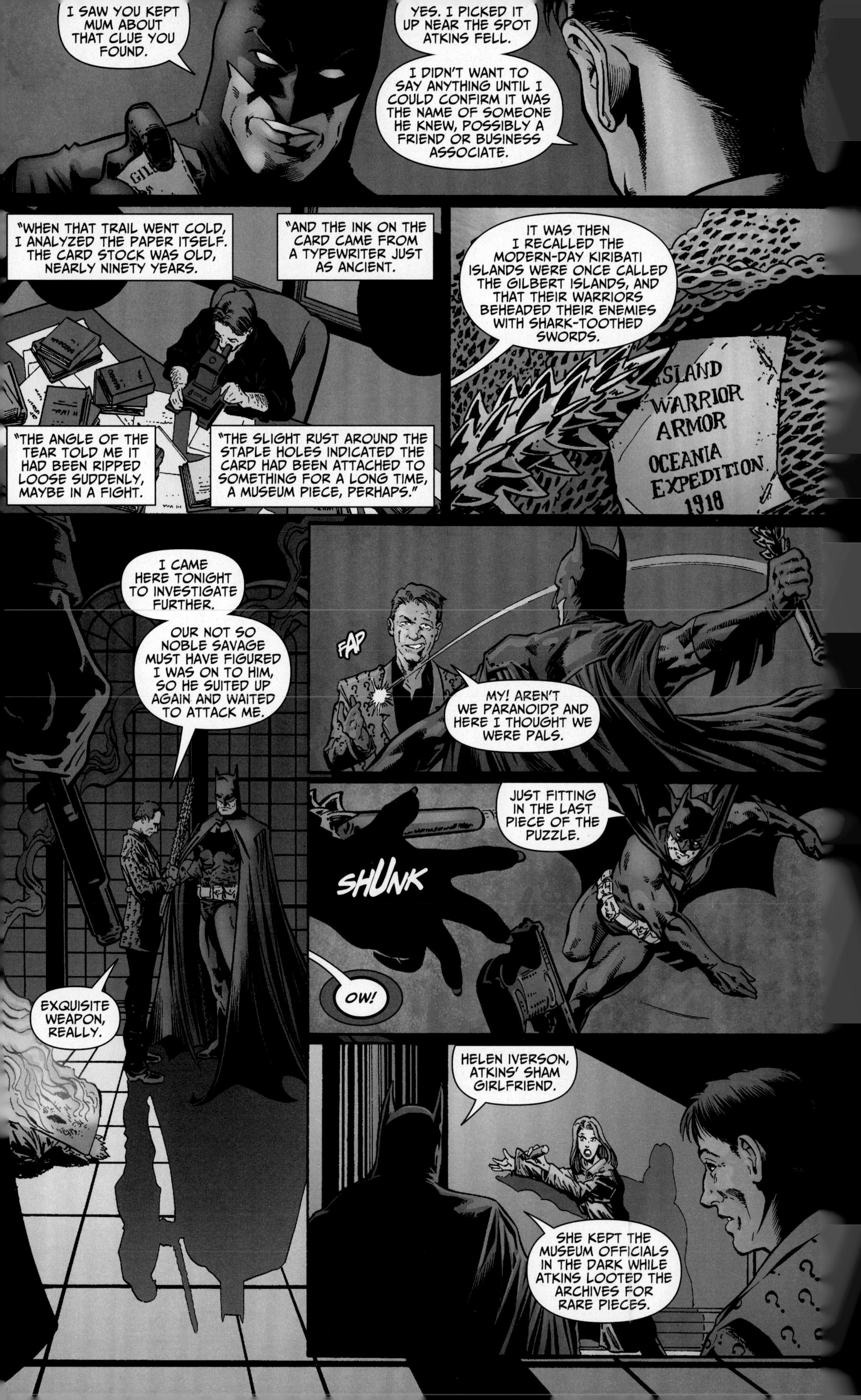
I SAW YOU KEPT MUM ABOUT THAT CLUE YOU FOUND.
YES. I PICKED IT UP NEAR THE SPOT ATKINS FELL.
I DIDN'T WANT TO SAY ANYTHING UNTIL I COULD CONFIRM IT WAS THE NAME OF SOMEONE HE KNEW, POSSIBLY A FRIEND OR BUSINESS ASSOCIATE.
"WHEN THAT TRAIL WENT COLD, I ANALYZED THE PAPER ITSELF. THE CARD STOCK WAS OLD, NEARLY NINETY YEARS.
"AND THE INK ON THE CARD CAME FROM A TYPEWRITER JUST AS ANCIENT.
"THE ANGLE OF THE TEAR TOLD ME IT HAD BEEN RIPPED LOOSE SUDDENLY, MAYBE IN A FIGHT.
"THE SLIGHT RUST AROUND THE STAPLE HOLES INDICATED THE CARD HAD BEEN ATTACHED TO SOMETHING FOR A LONG TIME, A MUSEUM PIECE, PERHAPS."
IT WAS THEN I RECALLED THE MODERN-DAY KIRIBATI ISLANDS WERE ONCE CALLED THE GILBERT ISLANDS, AND THAT THEIR WARRIORS BEHEADED THEIR ENEMIES WITH SHARK-TOOTHED SWORDS.
SLAND WARRIOR ARMOR OCEANIA EXPEDITION 1918
I CAME HERE TONIGHT TO INVESTIGATE FURTHER.
OUR NOT SO NOBLE SAVAGE MUST HAVE FIGURED I WAS ON TO HIM, SO HE SUITED UP AGAIN AND WAITED TO ATTACK ME.
EXQUISITE WEAPON, REALLY.
FAP
MY! AREN'T WE PARANOID? AND HERE I THOUGHT WE WERE PALS.
JUST FITTING IN THE LAST PIECE OF THE PUZZLE.
SHUNK
OW!
HELEN IVERSON, ATKINS' SHAM GIRLFRIEND.
SHE KEPT THE MUSEUM OFFICIALS IN THE DARK WHILE ATKINS LOOTED THE ARCHIVES FOR RARE PIECES.

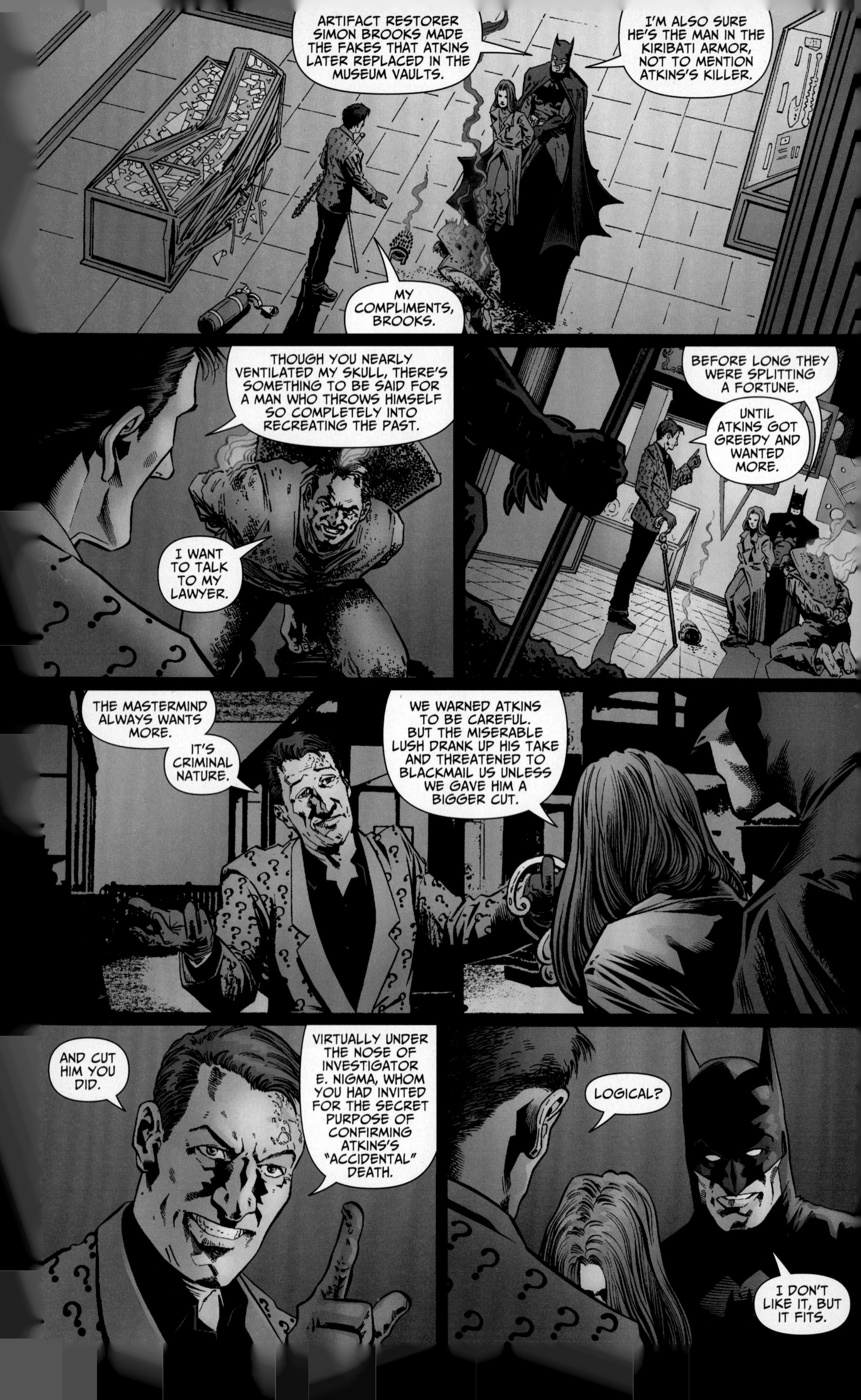
ARTIFACT RESTORER SIMON BROOKS MADE THE FAKES THAT ATKINS LATER REPLACED IN THE MUSEUM VAULTS.
I'M ALSO SURE HE'S THE MAN IN THE KIRIBATI ARMOR, NOT TO MENTION ATKINS'S KILLER.
MY COMPLIMENTS, BROOKS.
THOUGH YOU NEARLY VENTILATED MY SKULL, THERE'S SOMETHING TO BE SAID FOR A MAN WHO THROWS HIMSELF SO COMPLETELY INTO RECREATING THE PAST.
I WANT TO TALK TO MY LAWYER.
BEFORE LONG THEY WERE SPLITTING A FORTUNE.
UNTIL ATKINS GOT GREEDY AND WANTED MORE.
THE MASTERMIND ALWAYS WANTS MORE.
IT'S CRIMINAL NATURE.
WE WARNED ATKINS TO BE CAREFUL. BUT THE MISERABLE LUSH DRANK UP HIS TAKE AND THREATENED TO BLACKMAIL US UNLESS WE GAVE HIM A BIGGER CUT.
AND CUT HIM YOU DID.
VIRTUALLY UNDER THE NOSE OF INVESTIGATOR E. NIGMA, WHOM YOU HAD INVITED FOR THE SECRET PURPOSE OF CONFIRMING ATKINS'S "ACCIDENTAL" DEATH.
LOGICAL?
I DON'T LIKE IT, BUT IT FITS.

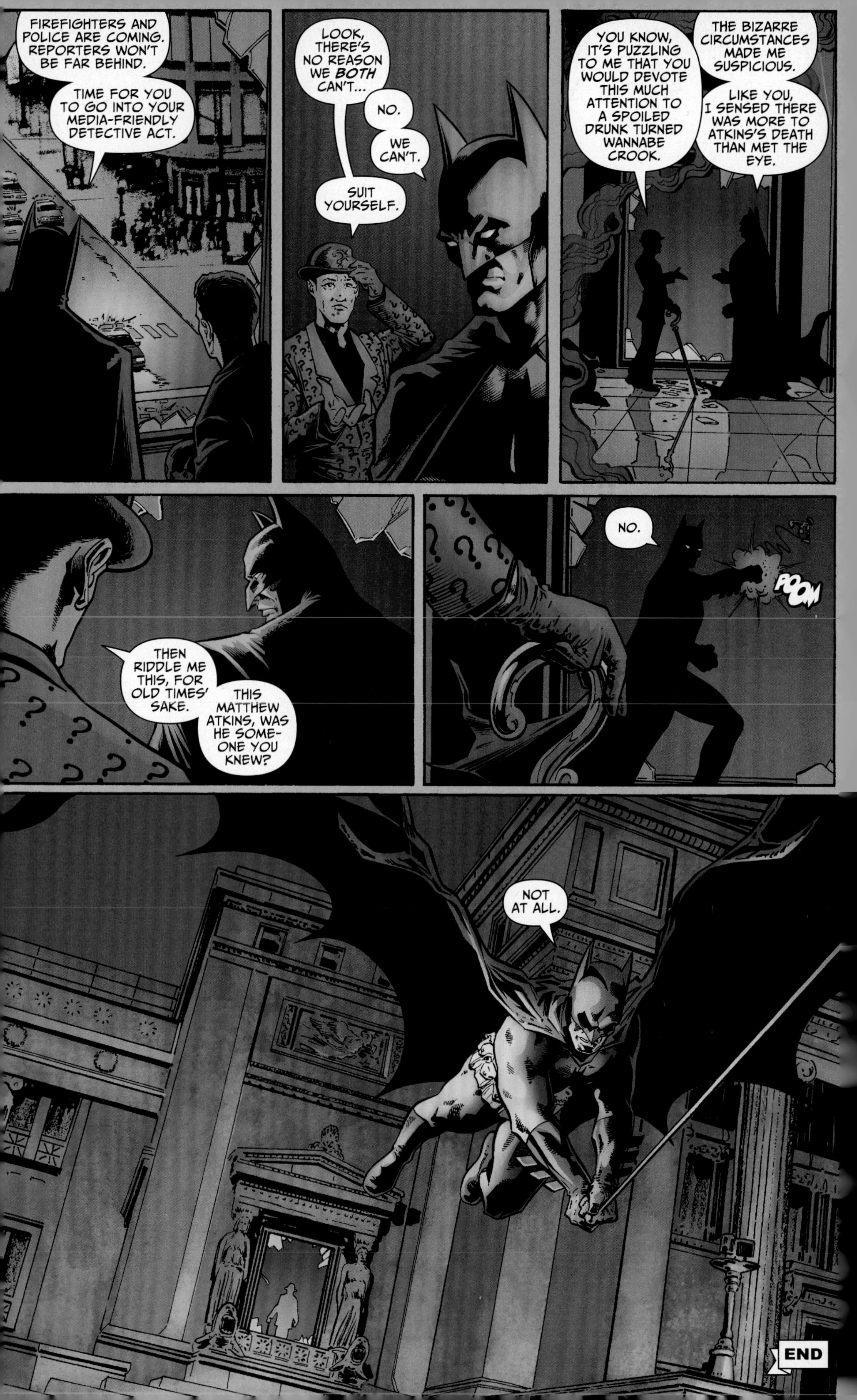
FIREFIGHTERS AND POLICE ARE COMING. REPORTERS WON'T BE FAR BEHIND.
TIME FOR YOU TO GO INTO YOUR MEDIA-FRIENDLY DETECTIVE ACT.
LOOK, THERE'S NO REASON WE *BOTH* CAN'T...
NO.
WE CAN'T.
SUIT YOURSELF.
YOU KNOW, IT'S PUZZLING TO ME THAT YOU WOULD DEVOTE THIS MUCH ATTENTION TO A SPOILED DRUNK TURNED WANNABE CROOK.
THE BIZARRE CIRCUMSTANCES MADE ME SUSPICIOUS.
LIKE YOU, I SENSED THERE WAS MORE TO ATKINS'S DEATH THAN MET THE EYE.
THEN RIDDLE ME THIS, FOR OLD TIMES' SAKE.
THIS MATTHEW ATKINS, WAS HE SOME-ONE YOU KNEW?
NO.
POOM
NOT AT ALL.
END

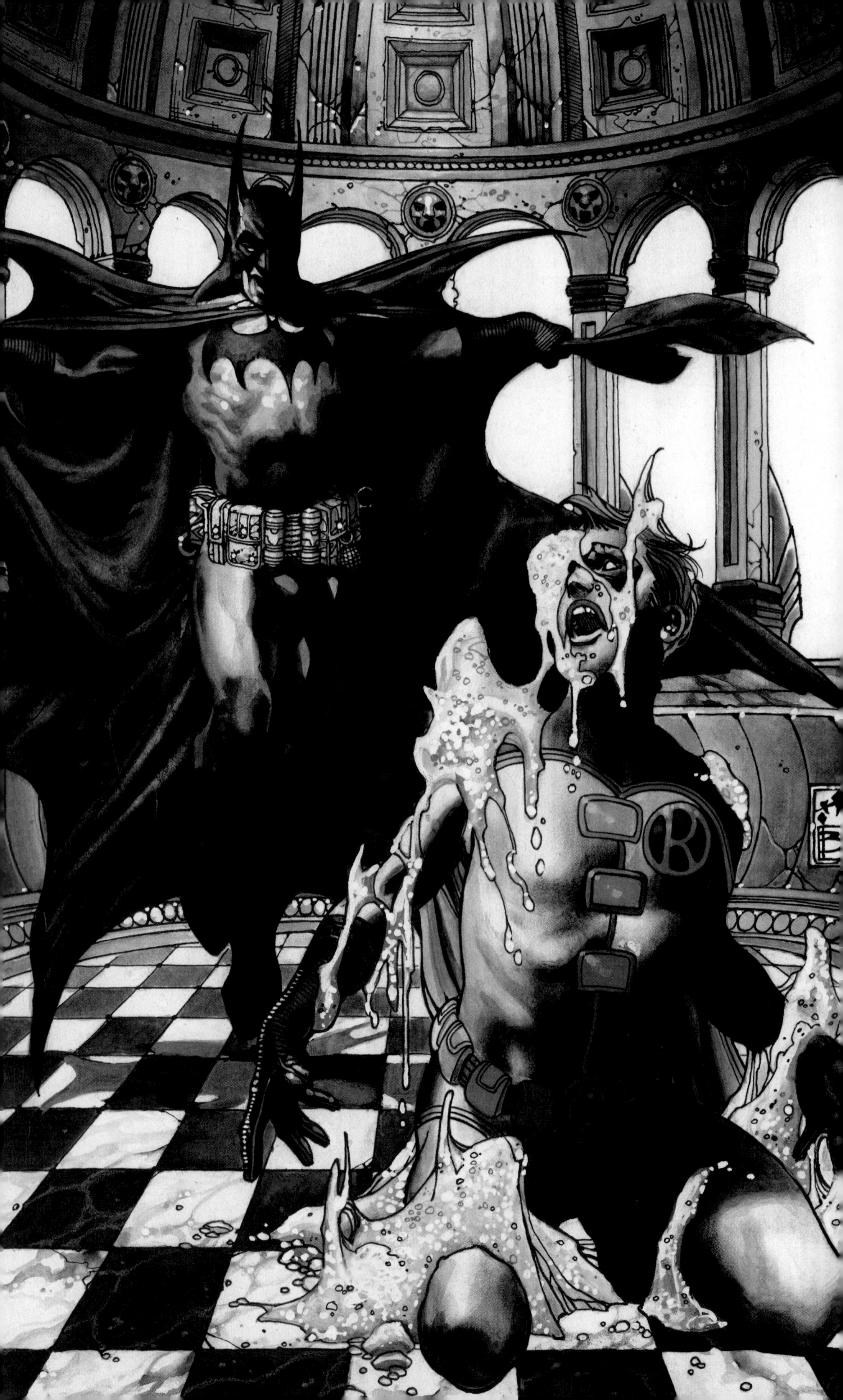

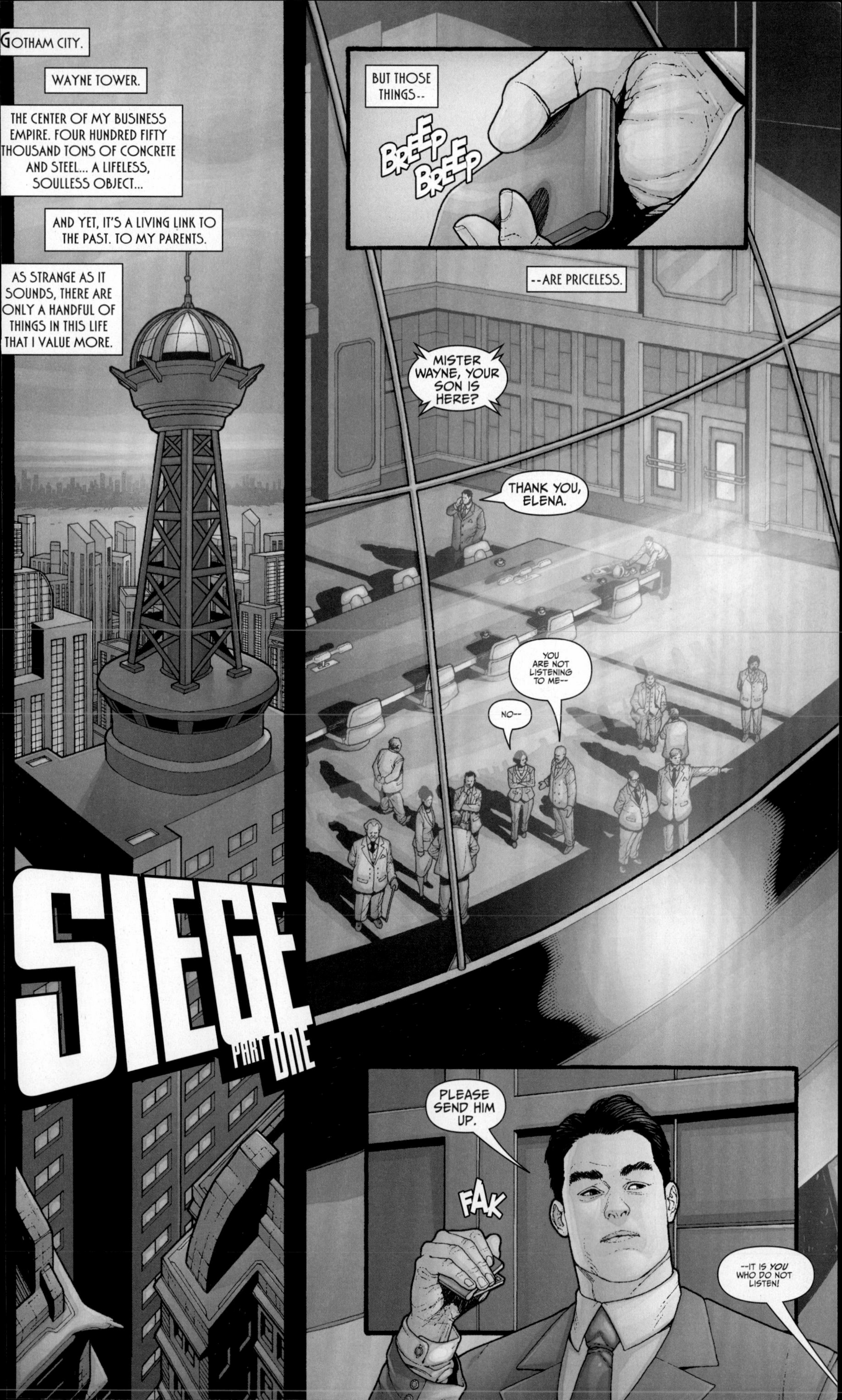
GOTHAM CITY.
WAYNE TOWER.
THE CENTER OF MY BUSINESS EMPIRE. FOUR HUNDRED FIFTY THOUSAND TONS OF CONCRETE AND STEEL... A LIFELESS, SOULLESS OBJECT...
AND YET, IT'S A LIVING LINK TO THE PAST. TO MY PARENTS.
AS STRANGE AS IT SOUNDS, THERE ARE ONLY A HANDFUL OF THINGS IN THIS LIFE THAT I VALUE MORE.
SIEGE PART ONE
BUT THOSE THINGS--
BREEP BREEP
--ARE PRICELESS.
MISTER WAYNE, YOUR SON IS HERE?
THANK YOU, ELENA.
YOU ARE NOT LISTENING TO ME--
NO--
PLEASE SEND HIM UP.
FAK
--IT IS YOU WHO DO NOT LISTEN!

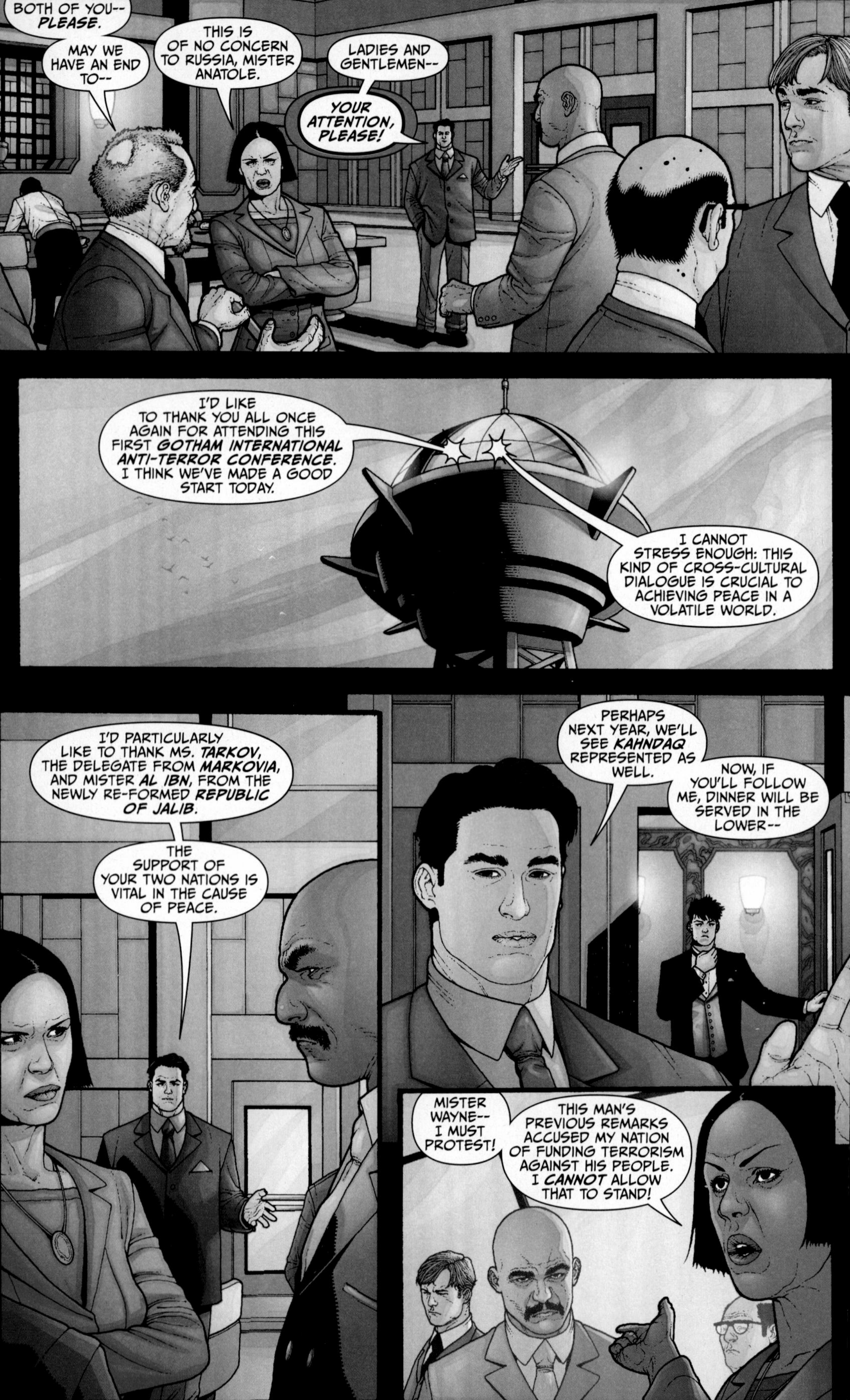
BOTH OF YOU-- PLEASE.
MAY WE HAVE AN END TO--
THIS IS OF NO CONCERN TO RUSSIA, MISTER ANATOLE.
LADIES AND GENTLEMEN--
YOUR ATTENTION, PLEASE!
I'D LIKE TO THANK YOU ALL ONCE AGAIN FOR ATTENDING THIS FIRST GOTHAM INTERNATIONAL ANTI-TERROR CONFERENCE. I THINK WE'VE MADE A GOOD START TODAY.
I CANNOT STRESS ENOUGH: THIS KIND OF CROSS-CULTURAL DIALOGUE IS CRUCIAL TO ACHIEVING PEACE IN A VOLATILE WORLD.
I'D PARTICULARLY LIKE TO THANK MS. TARKOV, THE DELEGATE FROM MARKOVIA, AND MISTER AL IBN, FROM THE NEWLY RE-FORMED REPUBLIC OF JALIB.
THE SUPPORT OF YOUR TWO NATIONS IS VITAL IN THE CAUSE OF PEACE.
PERHAPS NEXT YEAR, WE'LL SEE KAHNDAQ REPRESENTED AS WELL.
NOW, IF YOU'LL FOLLOW ME, DINNER WILL BE SERVED IN THE LOWER--
MISTER WAYNE-- I MUST PROTEST!
THIS MAN'S PREVIOUS REMARKS ACCUSED MY NATION OF FUNDING TERRORISM AGAINST HIS PEOPLE. I CANNOT ALLOW THAT TO STAND!

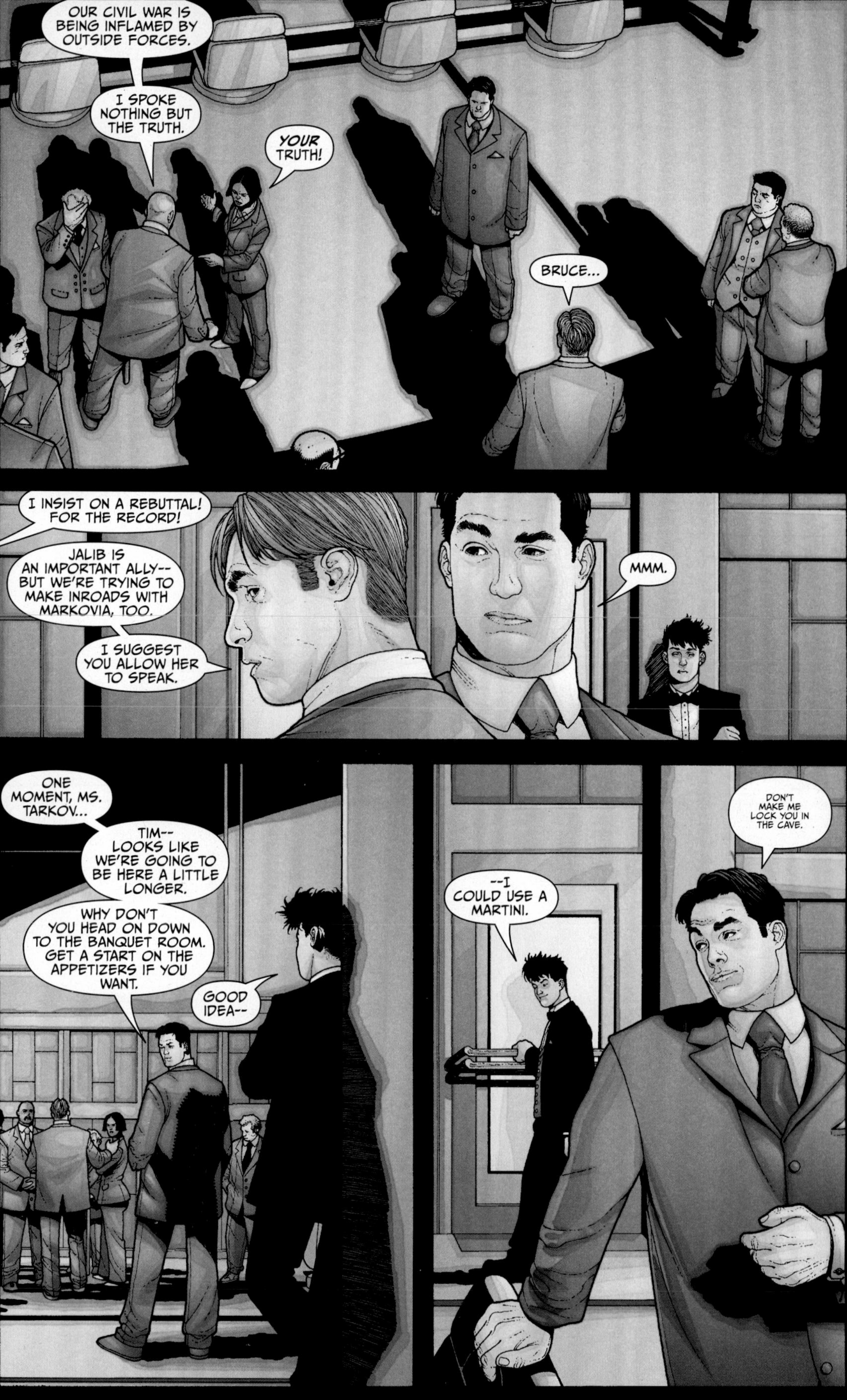
OUR CIVIL WAR IS BEING INFLAMED BY OUTSIDE FORCES.
I SPOKE NOTHING BUT THE TRUTH.
YOUR TRUTH!
BRUCE...
I INSIST ON A REBUTTAL! FOR THE RECORD!
JALIB IS AN IMPORTANT ALLY-- BUT WE'RE TRYING TO MAKE INROADS WITH MARKOVIA, TOO.
I SUGGEST YOU ALLOW HER TO SPEAK.
MMM.
ONE MOMENT, MS. TARKOV...
TIM-- LOOKS LIKE WE'RE GOING TO BE HERE A LITTLE LONGER.
WHY DON'T YOU HEAD ON DOWN TO THE BANQUET ROOM. GET A START ON THE APPETIZERS IF YOU WANT.
GOOD IDEA--
--I COULD USE A MARTINI.
DON'T MAKE ME LOCK YOU IN THE CAVE.

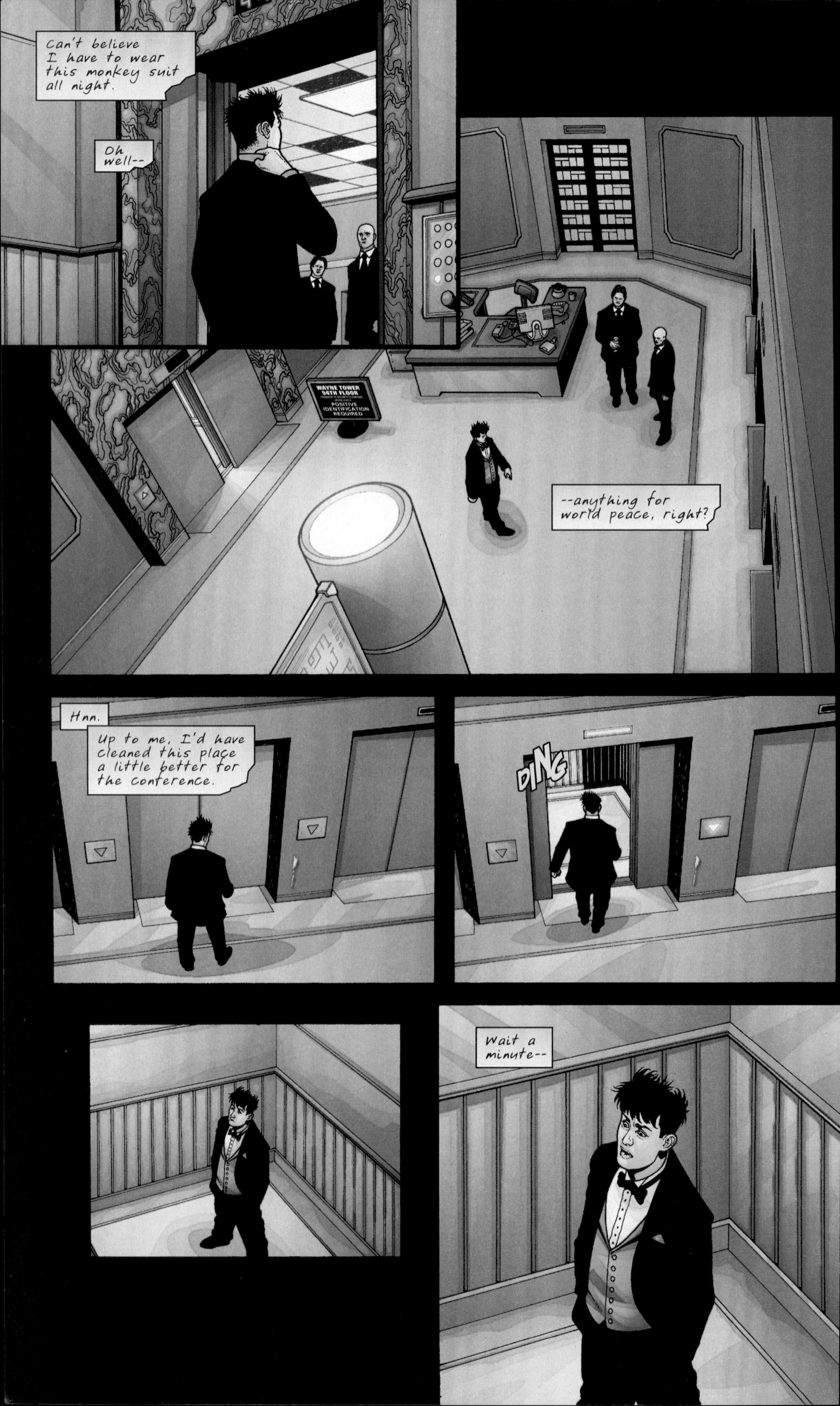
Can't believe I have to wear this monkey suit all night.
Oh well--
WAYNE TOWER 94TH FLOOR
POSITIVE IDENTIFICATION REQUIRED
--anything for world peace, right?
Hnn.
Up to me, I'd have cleaned this place a little better for the conference.
DING
Wait a minute--

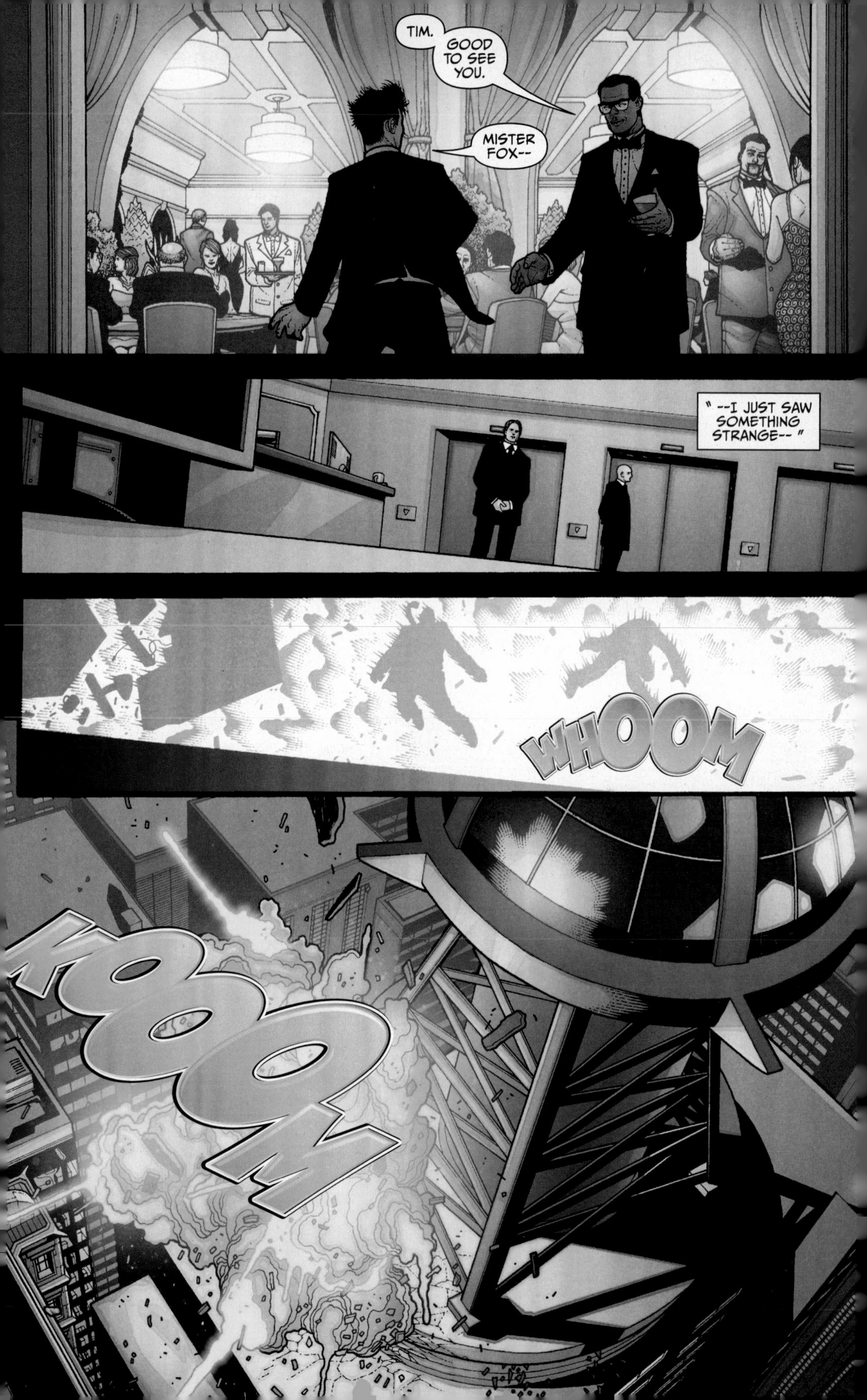
TIM.
GOOD TO SEE YOU.
MISTER FOX--
" --I JUST SAW SOMETHING STRANGE-- "
WHOOM
KOOOM

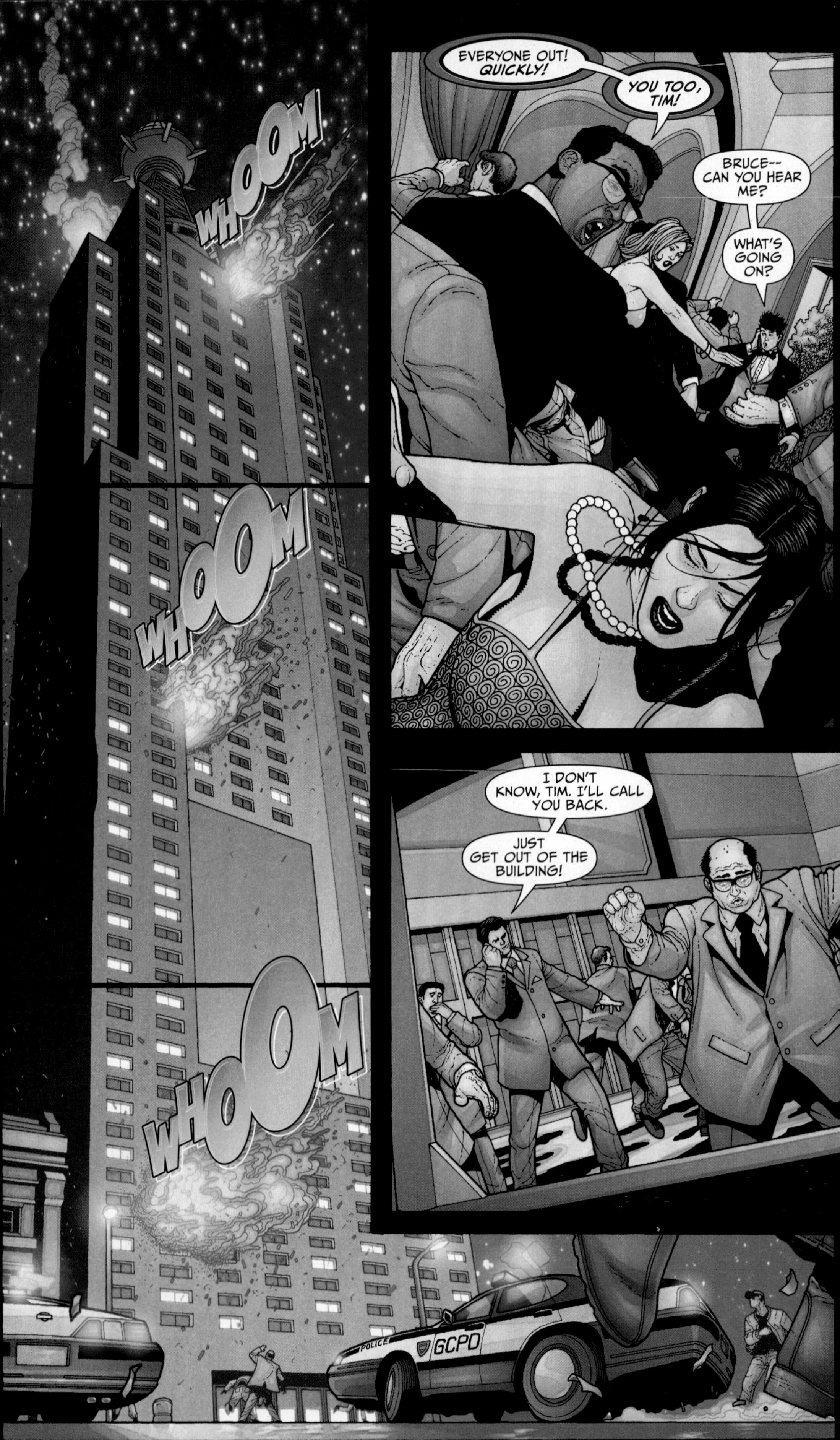
WHOOM
WHOOM
WHOOM
EVERYONE OUT! QUICKLY!
YOU TOO, TIM!
BRUCE-- CAN YOU HEAR ME?
WHAT'S GOING ON?
I DON'T KNOW, TIM. I'LL CALL YOU BACK.
JUST GET OUT OF THE BUILDING!
POLICE
GCPD

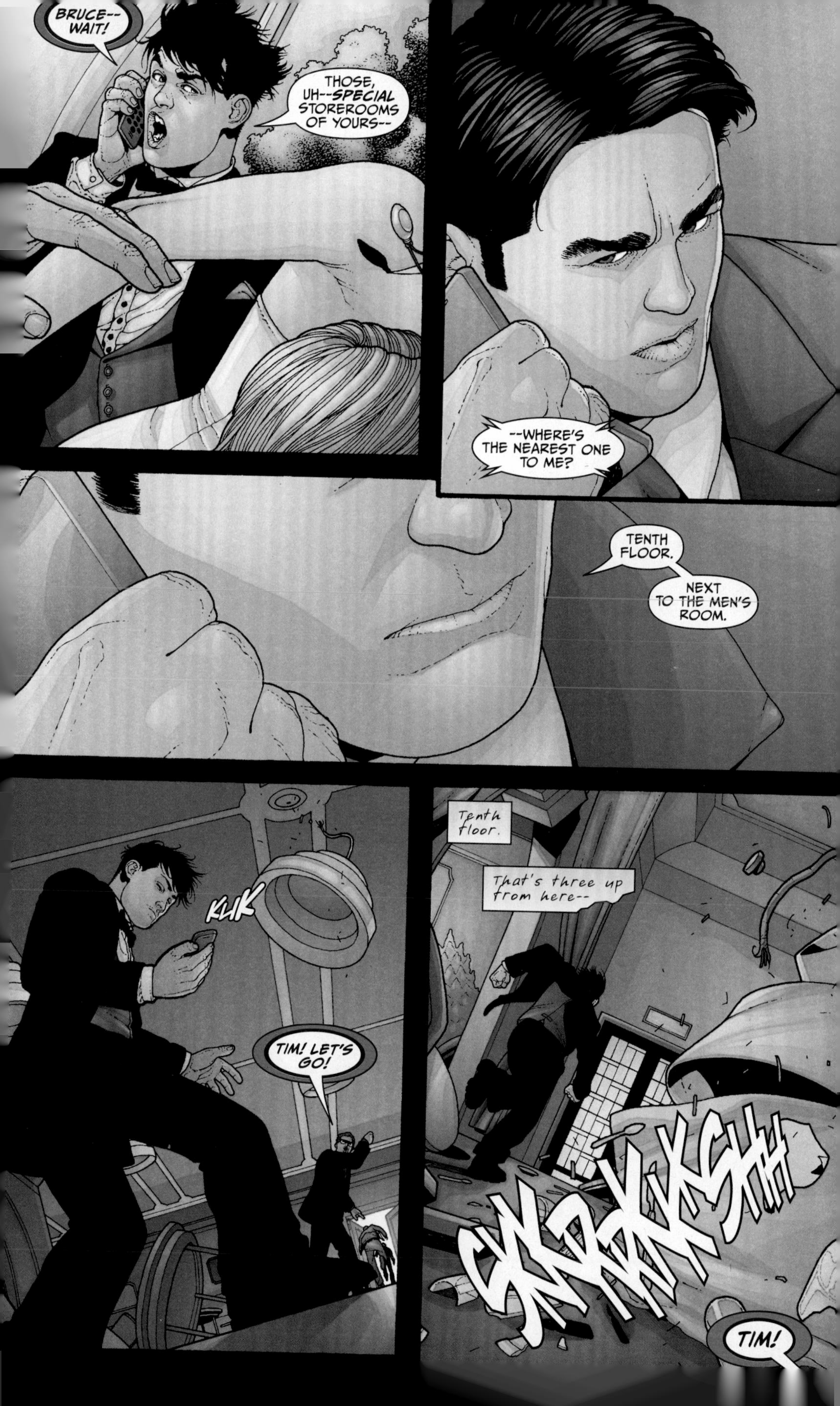
BRUCE--
WAIT!
THOSE,
UH--SPECIAL
STOREROOMS
OF YOURS--
--WHERE'S
THE NEAREST ONE
TO ME?
TENTH
FLOOR.
NEXT
TO THE MEN'S
ROOM.
KLIK
TIM! LET'S
GO!
Tenth
floor.
That's three up
from here--
CKRAKKSHH
TIM!

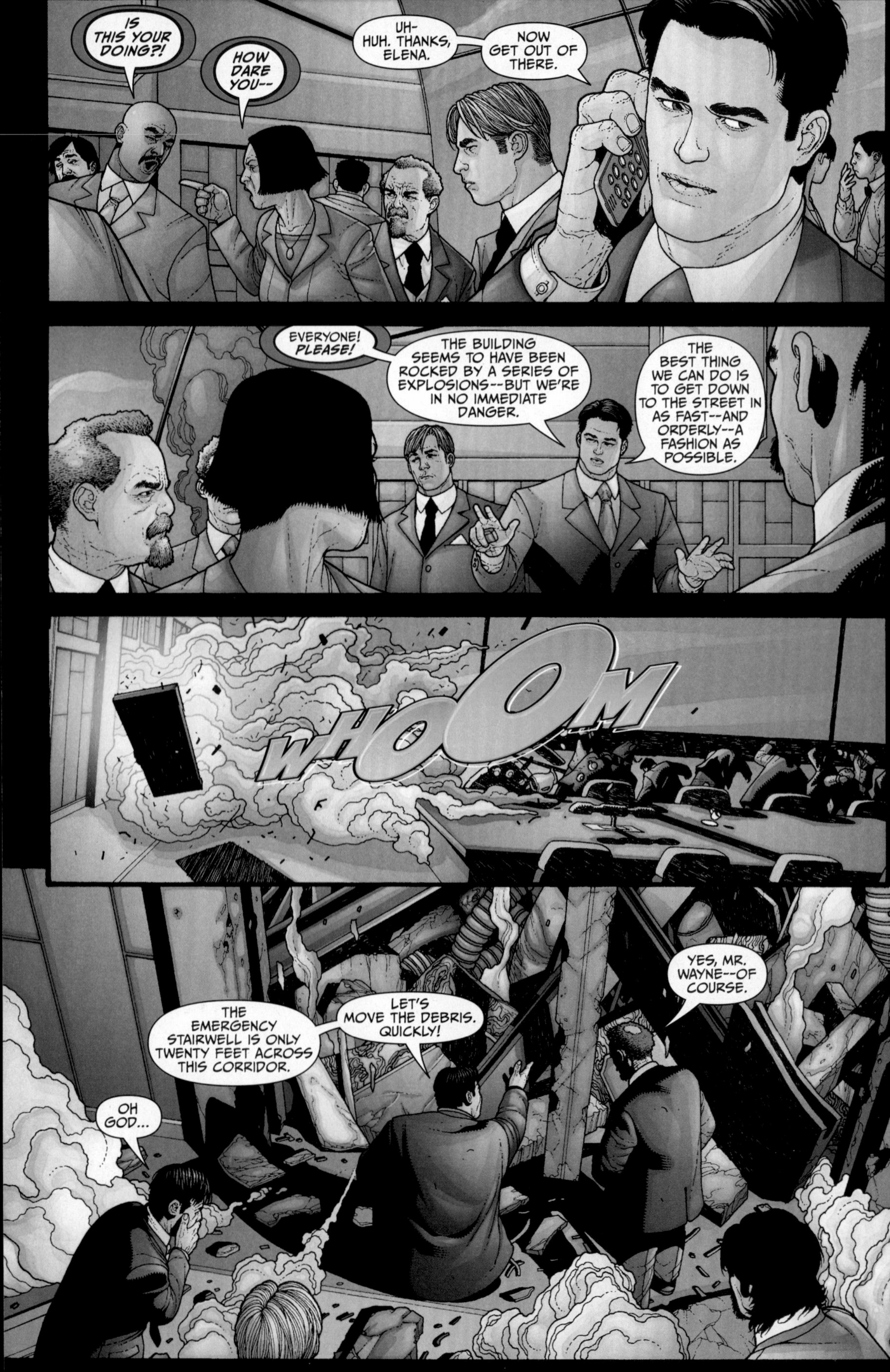

IS THIS YOUR DOING?!
HOW DARE YOU--
UH-HUH. THANKS, ELENA.
NOW GET OUT OF THERE.
EVERYONE! PLEASE!
THE BUILDING SEEMS TO HAVE BEEN ROCKED BY A SERIES OF EXPLOSIONS--BUT WE'RE IN NO IMMEDIATE DANGER.
THE BEST THING WE CAN DO IS TO GET DOWN TO THE STREET IN AS FAST--AND ORDERLY--A FASHION AS POSSIBLE.
WHOOOM
THE EMERGENCY STAIRWELL IS ONLY TWENTY FEET ACROSS THIS CORRIDOR.
LET'S MOVE THE DEBRIS. QUICKLY!
YES, MR. WAYNE--OF COURSE.
OH GOD...

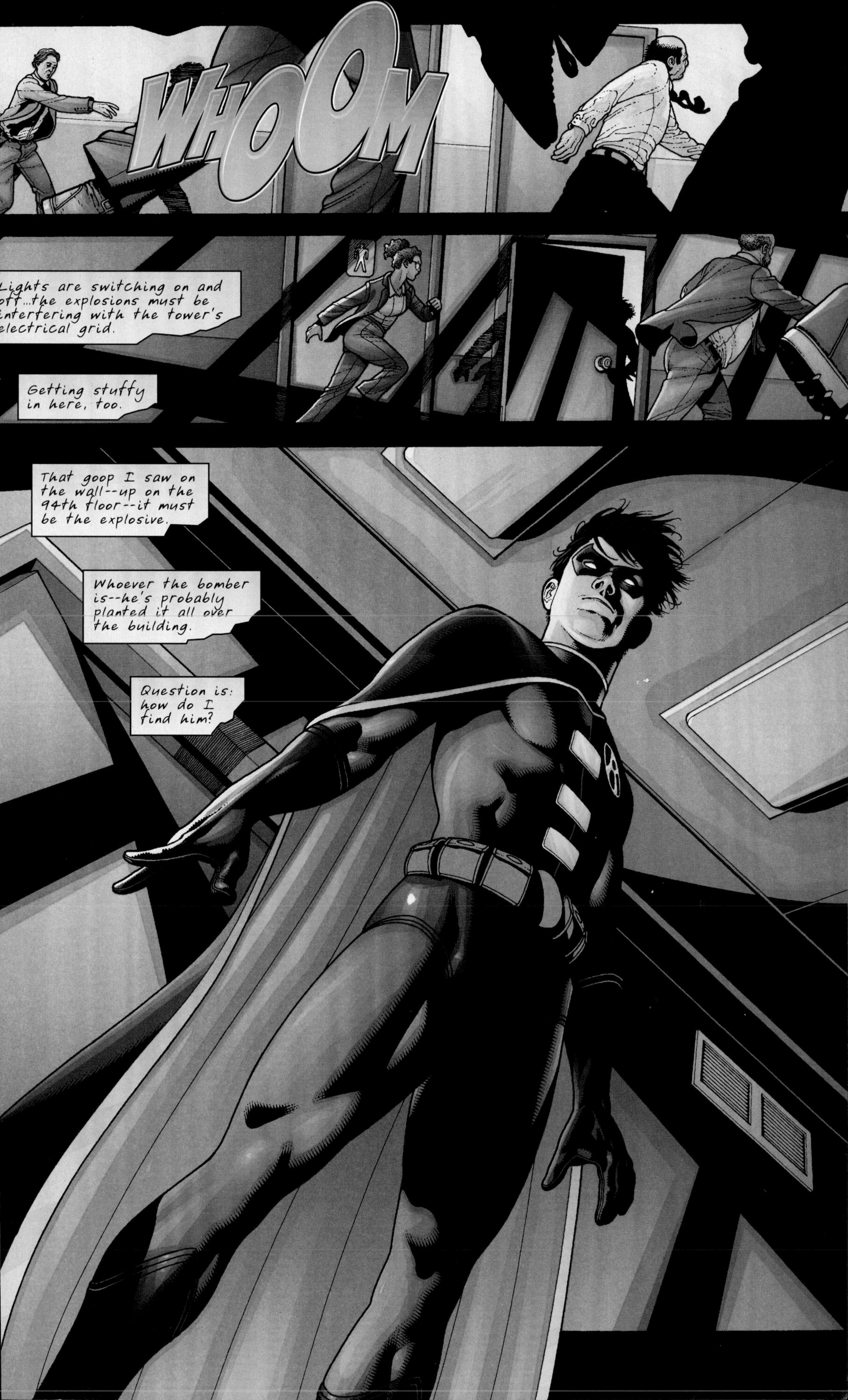
WHOOM
Lights are switching on and off...the explosions must be interfering with the tower's electrical grid.
Getting stuffy in here, too.
That goop I saw on the wall--up on the 94th floor--it must be the explosive.
Whoever the bomber is--he's probably planted it all over the building.
Question is: how do I find him?

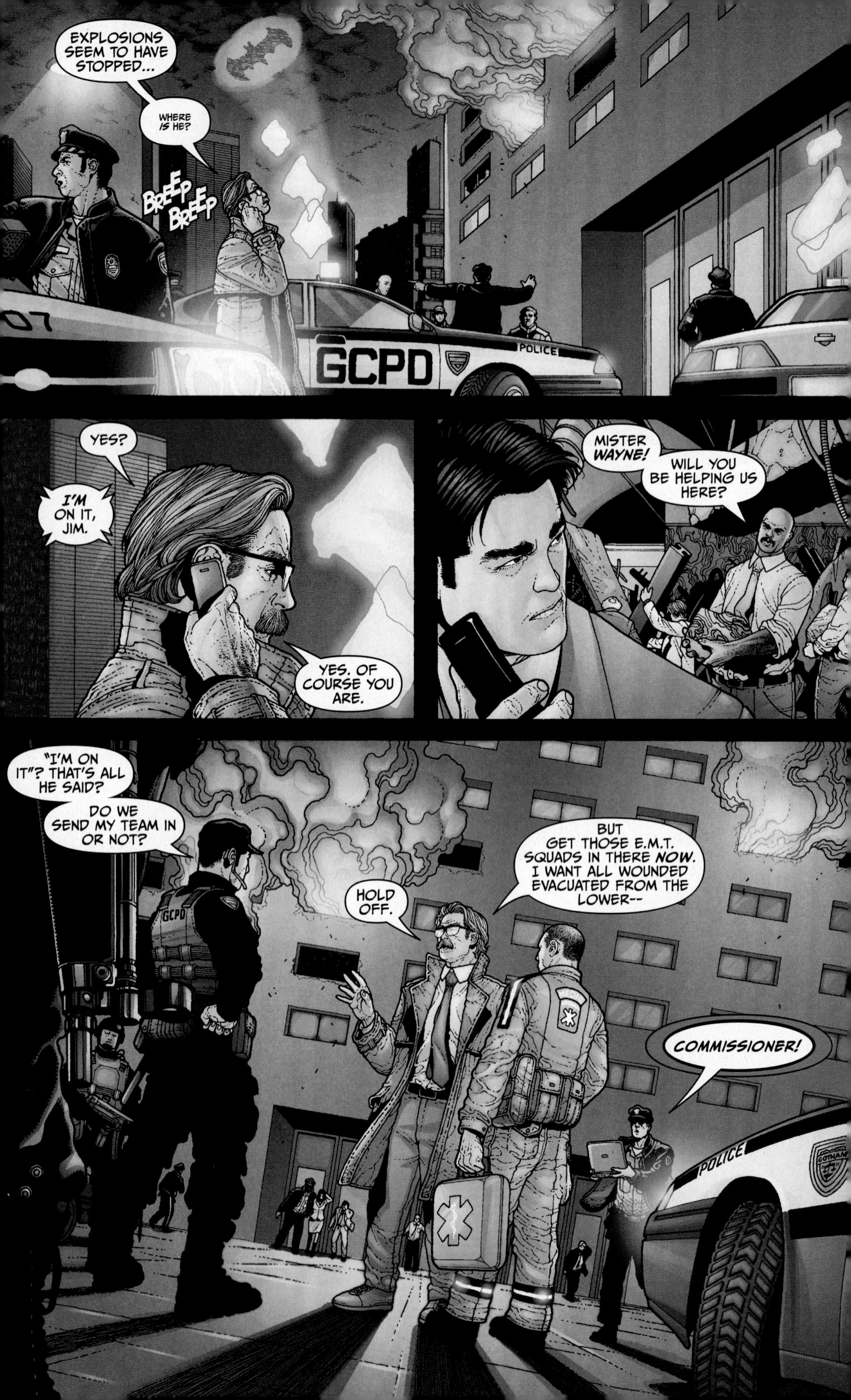
EXPLOSIONS SEEM TO HAVE STOPPED...
WHERE IS HE?
BREEP BREEP
GCPD
POLICE
YES?
I'M ON IT, JIM.
YES. OF COURSE YOU ARE.
MISTER WAYNE!
WILL YOU BE HELPING US HERE?
"I'M ON IT"? THAT'S ALL HE SAID?
DO WE SEND MY TEAM IN OR NOT?
HOLD OFF.
BUT GET THOSE E.M.T. SQUADS IN THERE NOW. I WANT ALL WOUNDED EVACUATED FROM THE LOWER--
COMMISSIONER!
POLICE

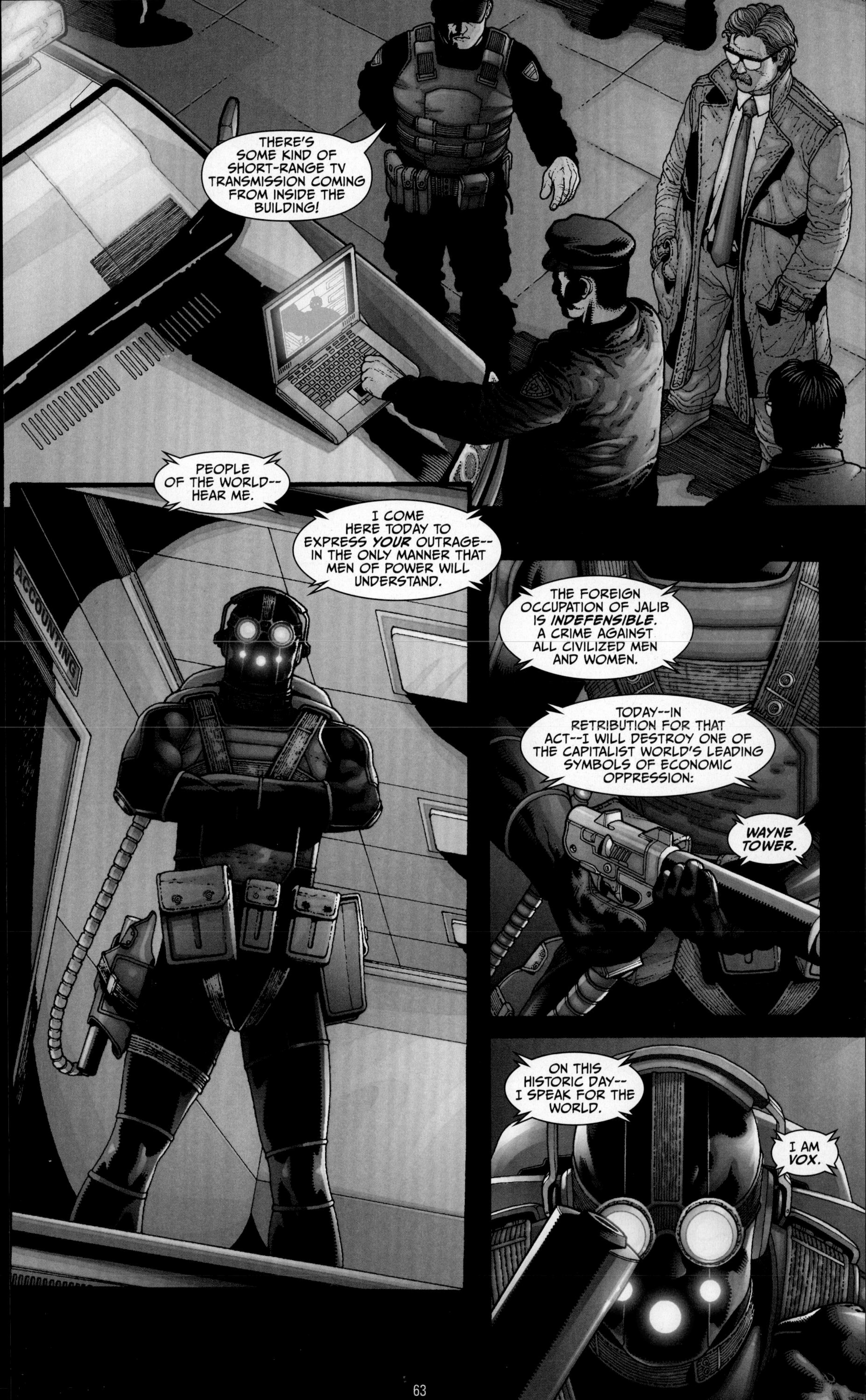
THERE'S SOME KIND OF SHORT-RANGE TV TRANSMISSION COMING FROM INSIDE THE BUILDING!
PEOPLE OF THE WORLD-- HEAR ME.
I COME HERE TODAY TO EXPRESS YOUR OUTRAGE-- IN THE ONLY MANNER THAT MEN OF POWER WILL UNDERSTAND.
ACCOUNTING
THE FOREIGN OCCUPATION OF JALIB IS INDEFENSIBLE. A CRIME AGAINST ALL CIVILIZED MEN AND WOMEN.
TODAY--IN RETRIBUTION FOR THAT ACT--I WILL DESTROY ONE OF THE CAPITALIST WORLD'S LEADING SYMBOLS OF ECONOMIC OPPRESSION:
WAYNE TOWER.
ON THIS HISTORIC DAY-- I SPEAK FOR THE WORLD.
I AM VOX.

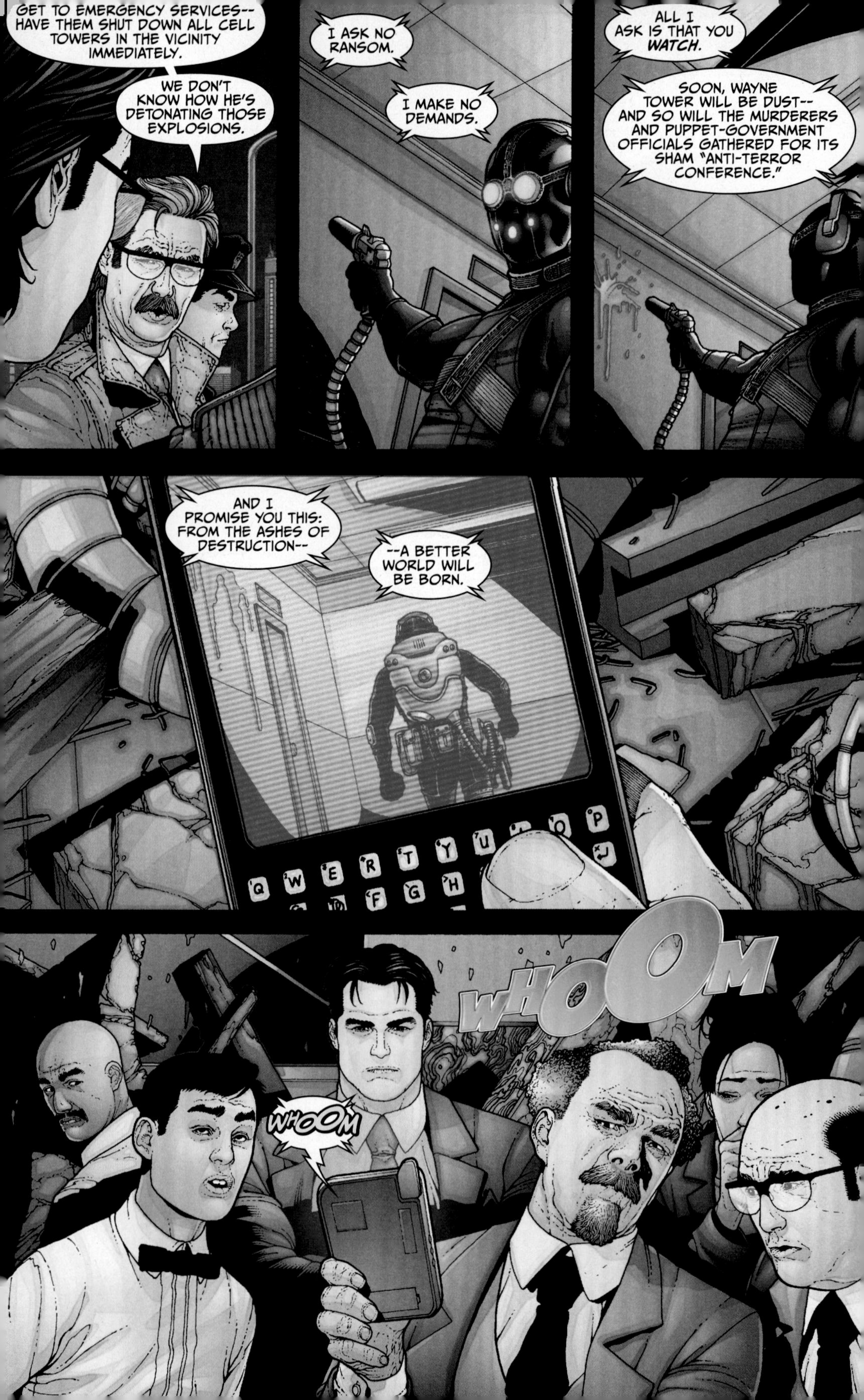
GET TO EMERGENCY SERVICES-- HAVE THEM SHUT DOWN ALL CELL TOWERS IN THE VICINITY IMMEDIATELY.
WE DON'T KNOW HOW HE'S DETONATING THOSE EXPLOSIONS.
I ASK NO RANSOM.
I MAKE NO DEMANDS.
ALL I ASK IS THAT YOU *WATCH*.
SOON, WAYNE TOWER WILL BE DUST-- AND SO WILL THE MURDERERS AND PUPPET-GOVERNMENT OFFICIALS GATHERED FOR ITS SHAM "ANTI-TERROR CONFERENCE."
AND I PROMISE YOU THIS: FROM THE ASHES OF DESTRUCTION--
--A BETTER WORLD WILL BE BORN.
WHOOOM
WHOOM

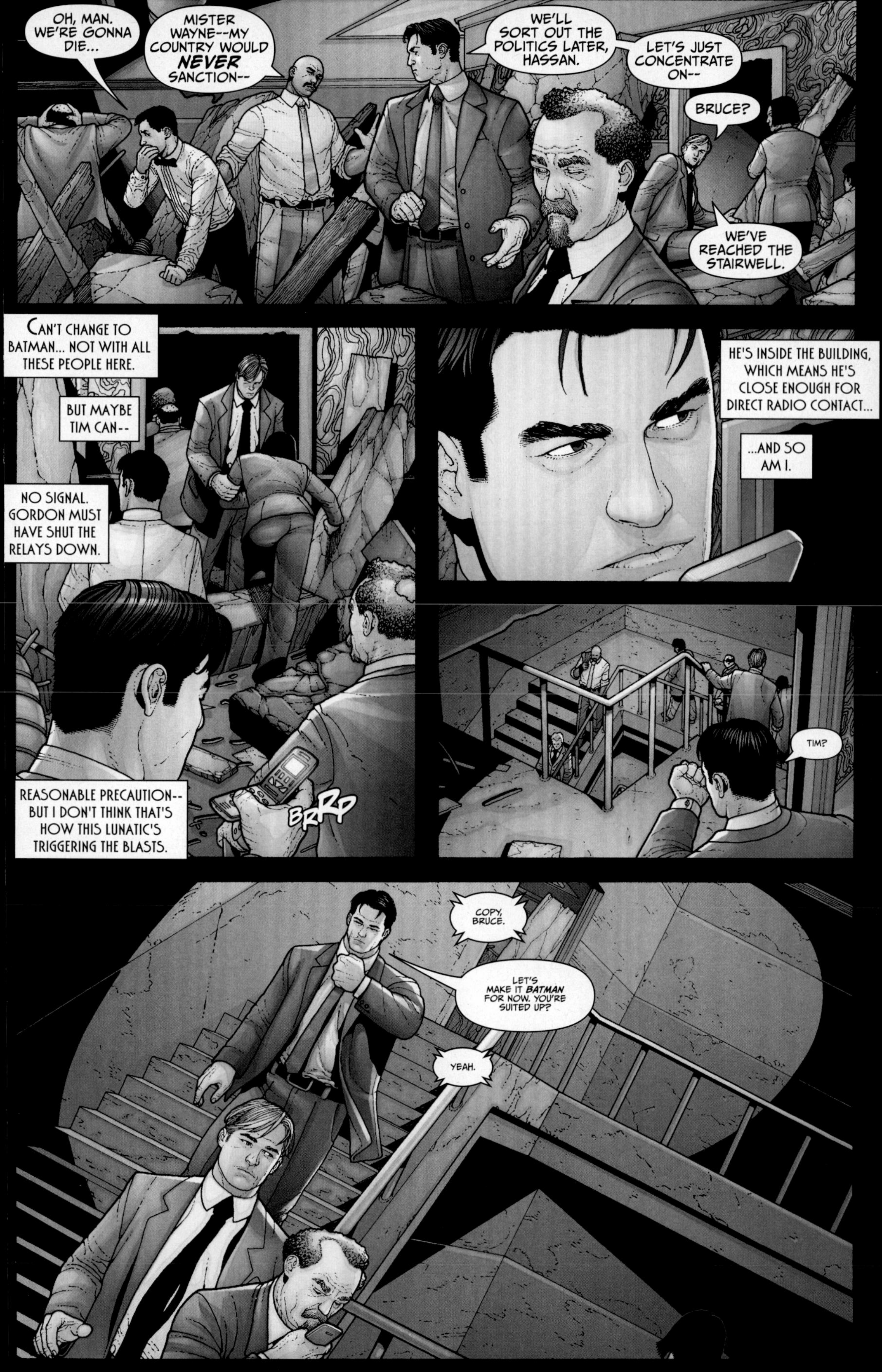
OH, MAN. WE'RE GONNA DIE...
MISTER WAYNE--MY COUNTRY WOULD NEVER SANCTION--
WE'LL SORT OUT THE POLITICS LATER, HASSAN.
LET'S JUST CONCENTRATE ON--
BRUCE?
WE'VE REACHED THE STAIRWELL.
CAN'T CHANGE TO BATMAN... NOT WITH ALL THESE PEOPLE HERE.
BUT MAYBE TIM CAN--
NO SIGNAL. GORDON MUST HAVE SHUT THE RELAYS DOWN.
REASONABLE PRECAUTION--BUT I DON'T THINK THAT'S HOW THIS LUNATIC'S TRIGGERING THE BLASTS.
BRRP
HE'S INSIDE THE BUILDING, WHICH MEANS HE'S CLOSE ENOUGH FOR DIRECT RADIO CONTACT...
...AND SO AM I.
TIM?
COPY, BRUCE.
LET'S MAKE IT BATMAN FOR NOW. YOU'RE SUITED UP?
YEAH.

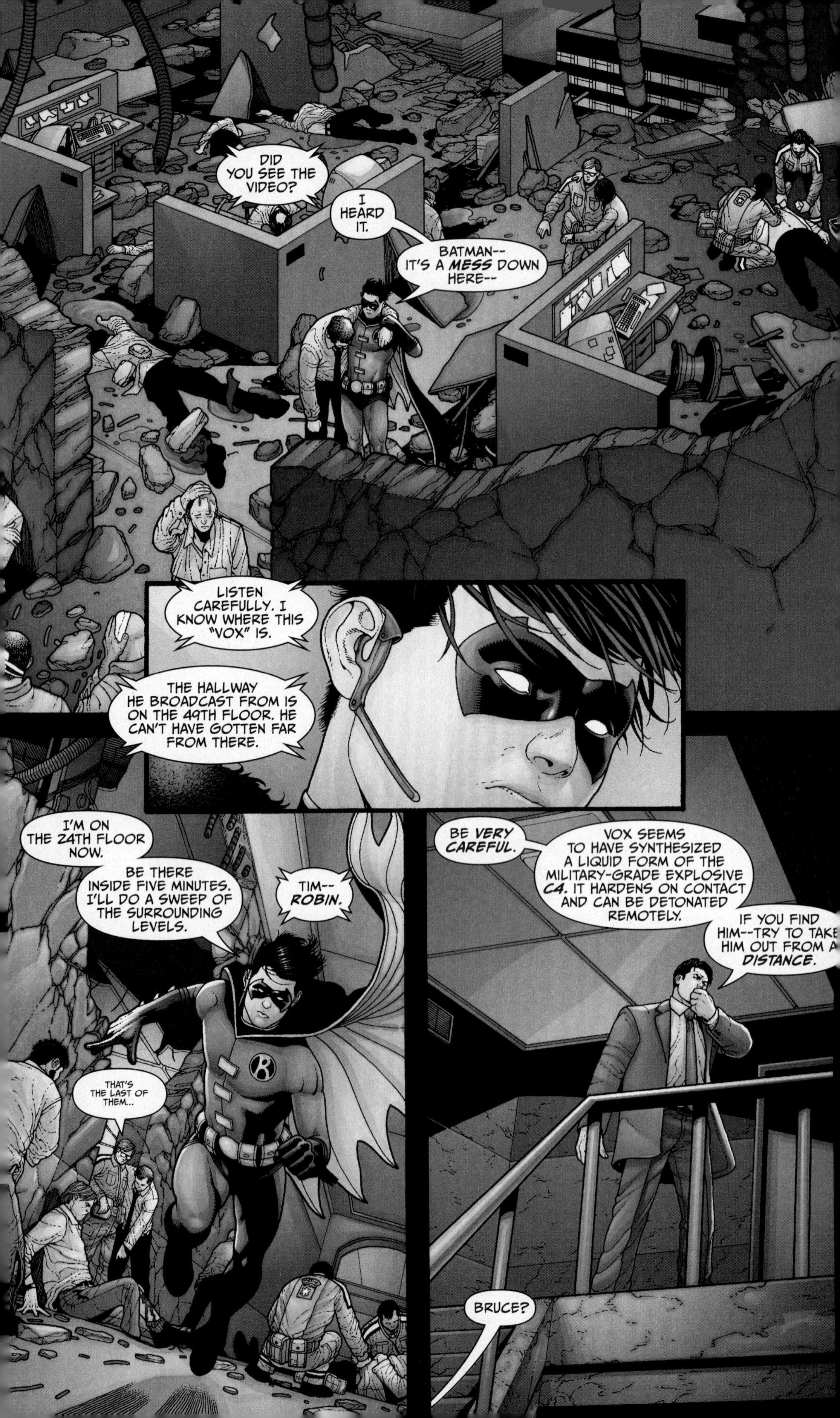
DID YOU SEE THE VIDEO?
I HEARD IT.
BATMAN-- IT'S A MESS DOWN HERE--
LISTEN CAREFULLY. I KNOW WHERE THIS "VOX" IS.
THE HALLWAY HE BROADCAST FROM IS ON THE 49TH FLOOR. HE CAN'T HAVE GOTTEN FAR FROM THERE.
I'M ON THE 24TH FLOOR NOW.
BE THERE INSIDE FIVE MINUTES. I'LL DO A SWEEP OF THE SURROUNDING LEVELS.
TIM-- ROBIN.
THAT'S THE LAST OF THEM...
BE VERY CAREFUL.
VOX SEEMS TO HAVE SYNTHESIZED A LIQUID FORM OF THE MILITARY-GRADE EXPLOSIVE C4. IT HARDENS ON CONTACT AND CAN BE DETONATED REMOTELY.
IF YOU FIND HIM--TRY TO TAKE HIM OUT FROM A DISTANCE.
BRUCE?

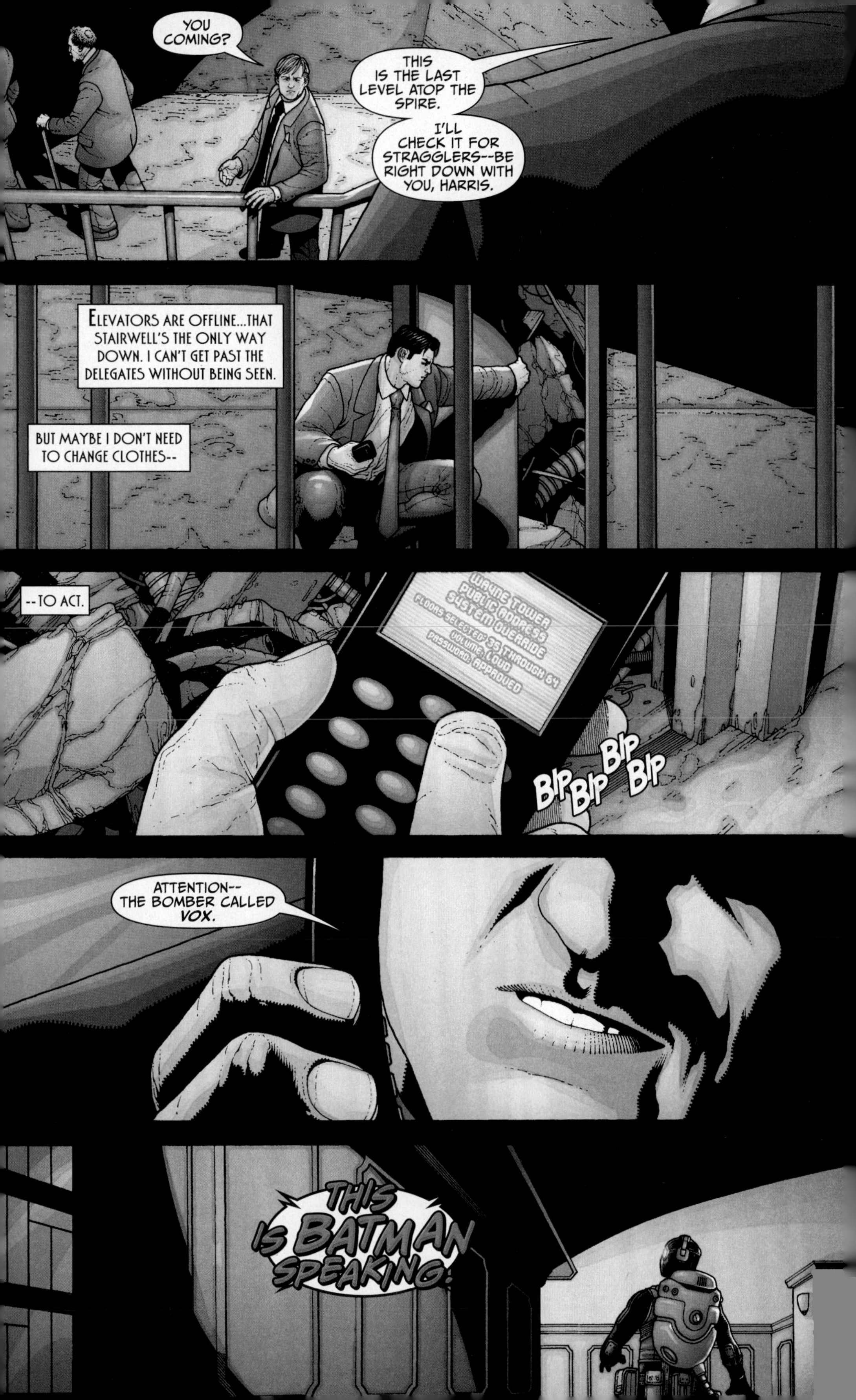
YOU COMING?
THIS IS THE LAST LEVEL ATOP THE SPIRE.
I'LL CHECK IT FOR STRAGGLERS--BE RIGHT DOWN WITH YOU, HARRIS.
ELEVATORS ARE OFFLINE...THAT STAIRWELL'S THE ONLY WAY DOWN. I CAN'T GET PAST THE DELEGATES WITHOUT BEING SEEN.
BUT MAYBE I DON'T NEED TO CHANGE CLOTHES--
--TO ACT.
WAYNE TOWER
PUBLIC ADDRESS
SYSTEM OVERRIDE
FLOORS SELECTED: 35 THROUGH 64
VOLUME: LOUD
PASSWORD: APPROVED
BIP BIP BIP BIP
ATTENTION-- THE BOMBER CALLED VOX.
THIS IS BATMAN SPEAKING!

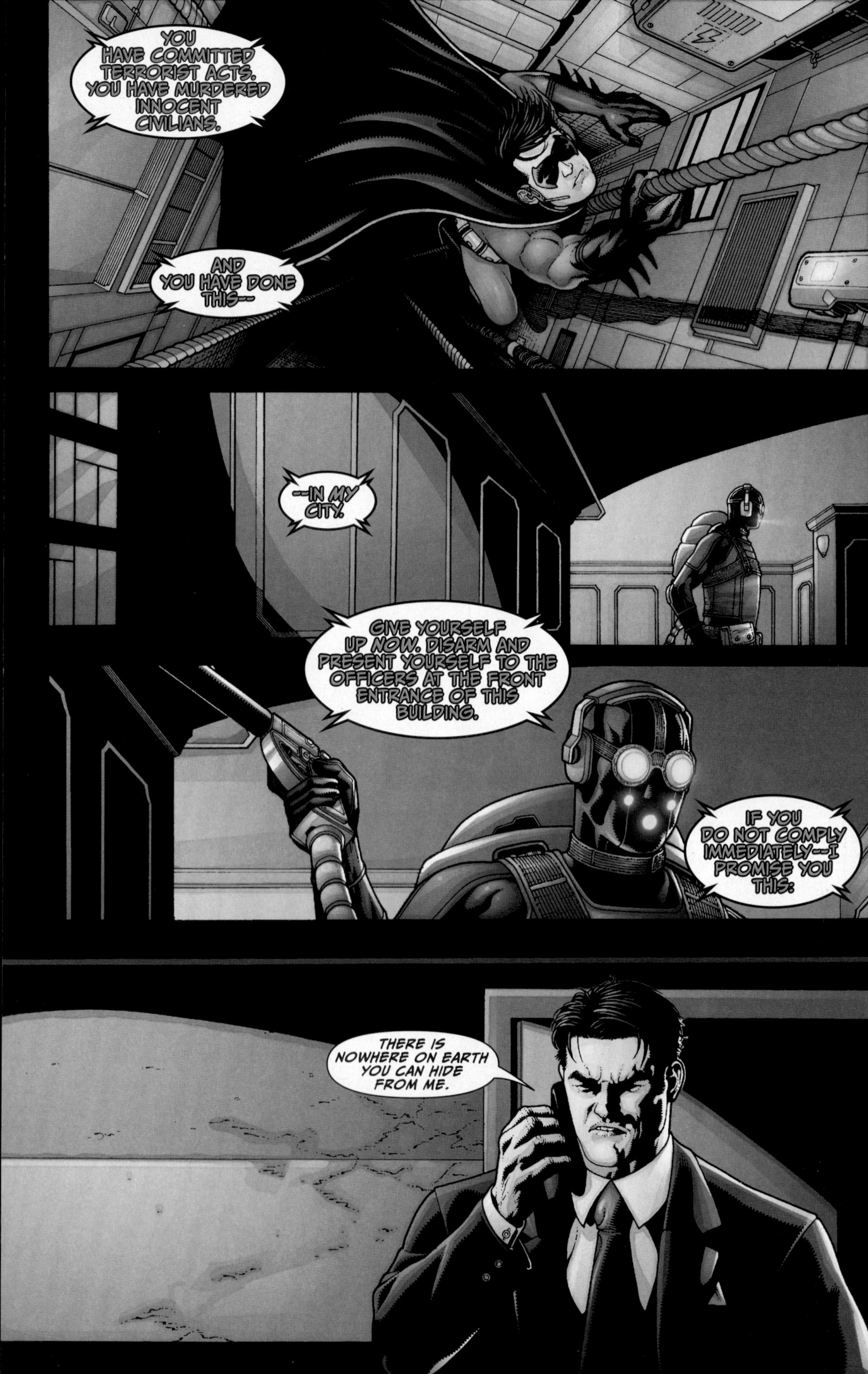
YOU HAVE COMMITTED TERRORIST ACTS. YOU HAVE MURDERED INNOCENT CIVILIANS.
AND YOU HAVE DONE THIS--
--IN MY CITY.
GIVE YOURSELF UP NOW. DISARM AND PRESENT YOURSELF TO THE OFFICERS AT THE FRONT ENTRANCE OF THIS BUILDING.
IF YOU DO NOT COMPLY IMMEDIATELY--I PROMISE YOU THIS:
THERE IS NOWHERE ON EARTH YOU CAN HIDE FROM ME.

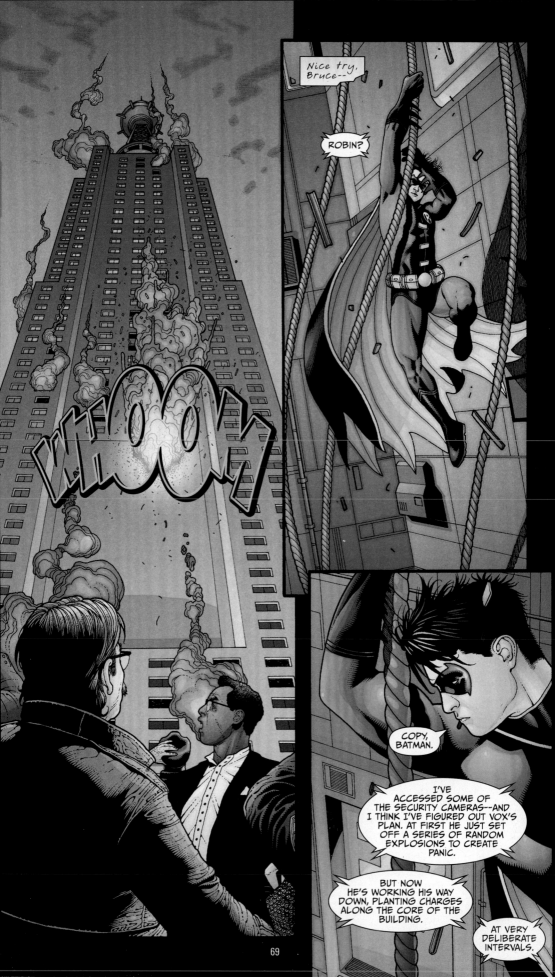

Nice try, Bruce--

ROBIN?

WHOOM!

COPY, BATMAN.

I'VE ACCESSED SOME OF THE SECURITY CAMERAS--AND I THINK I'VE FIGURED OUT VOX'S PLAN. AT FIRST HE JUST SET OFF A SERIES OF RANDOM EXPLOSIONS TO CREATE PANIC.

BUT NOW HE'S WORKING HIS WAY DOWN, PLANTING CHARGES ALONG THE CORE OF THE BUILDING.

AT VERY DELIBERATE INTERVALS.

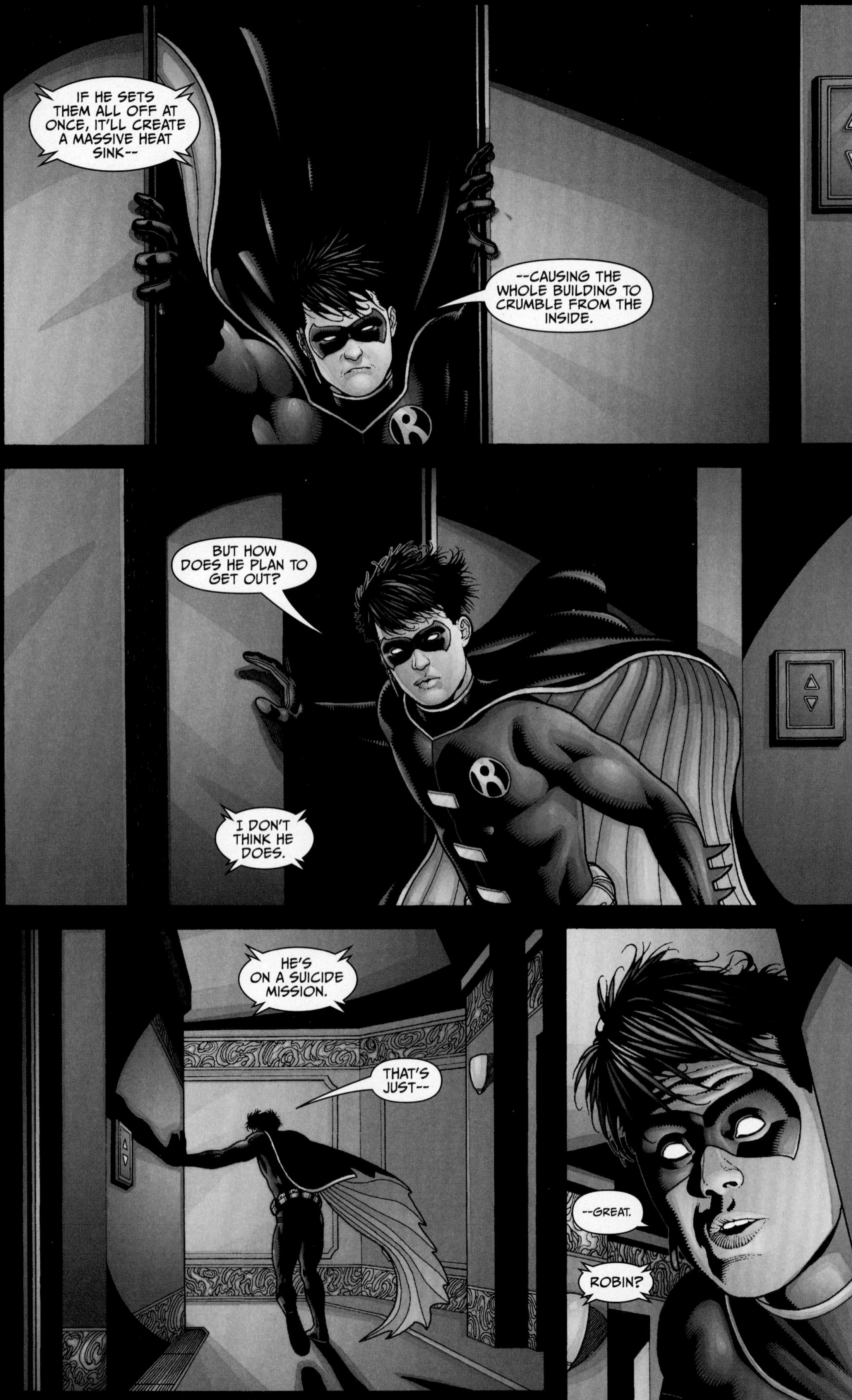
IF HE SETS THEM ALL OFF AT ONCE, IT'LL CREATE A MASSIVE HEAT SINK--
--CAUSING THE WHOLE BUILDING TO CRUMBLE FROM THE INSIDE.
BUT HOW DOES HE PLAN TO GET OUT?
I DON'T THINK HE DOES.
HE'S ON A SUICIDE MISSION.
THAT'S JUST--
--GREAT.
ROBIN?

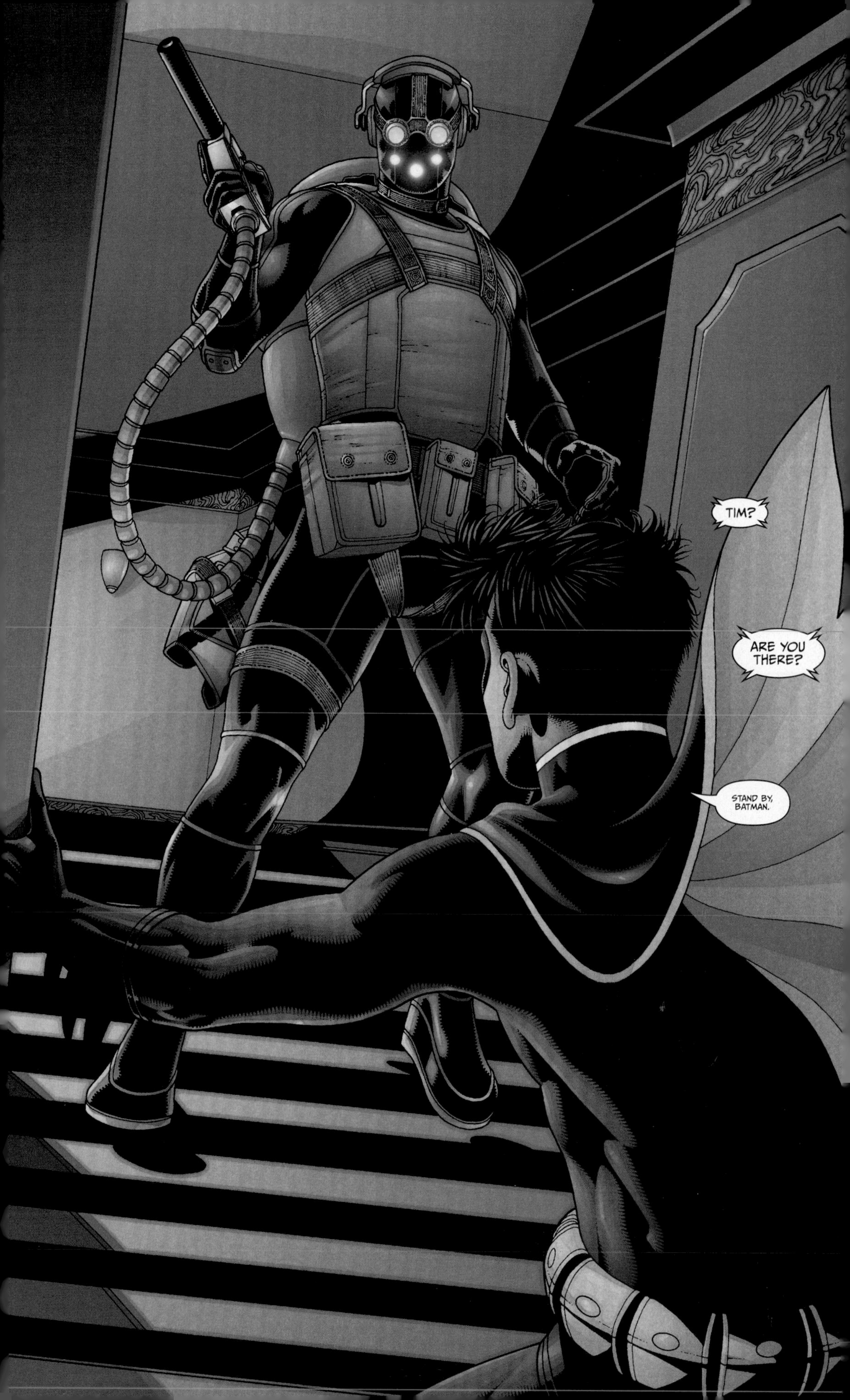
TIM?
ARE YOU THERE?
STAND BY, BATMAN.

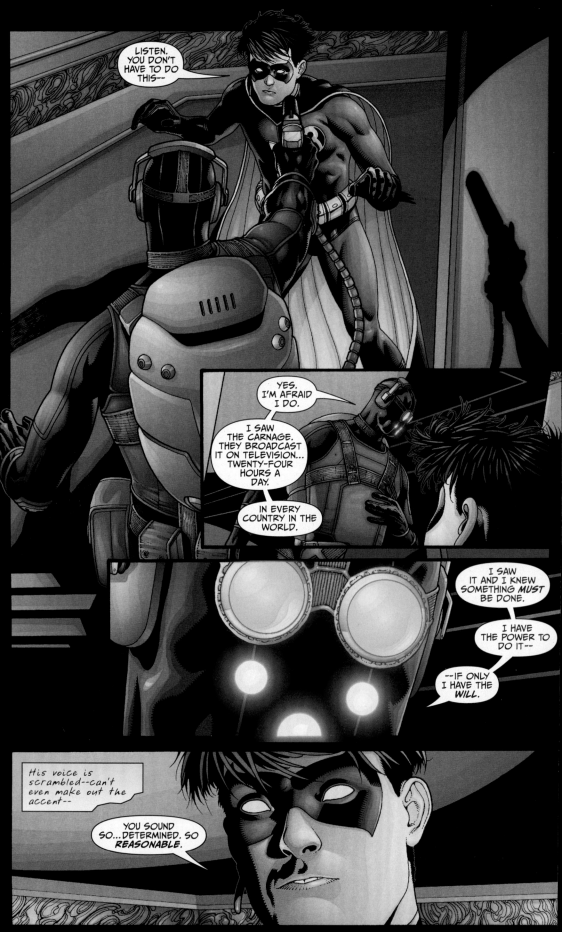

LISTEN. YOU DON'T HAVE TO DO THIS--

YES. I'M AFRAID I DO.

I SAW THE CARNAGE. THEY BROADCAST IT ON TELEVISION... TWENTY-FOUR HOURS A DAY.

IN EVERY COUNTRY IN THE WORLD.

I SAW IT AND I KNEW SOMETHING *MUST* BE DONE.

I HAVE THE POWER TO DO IT--

--IF ONLY I HAVE THE *WILL*.

His voice is scrambled--can't even make out the accent--

YOU SOUND SO...DETERMINED. SO *REASONABLE*.

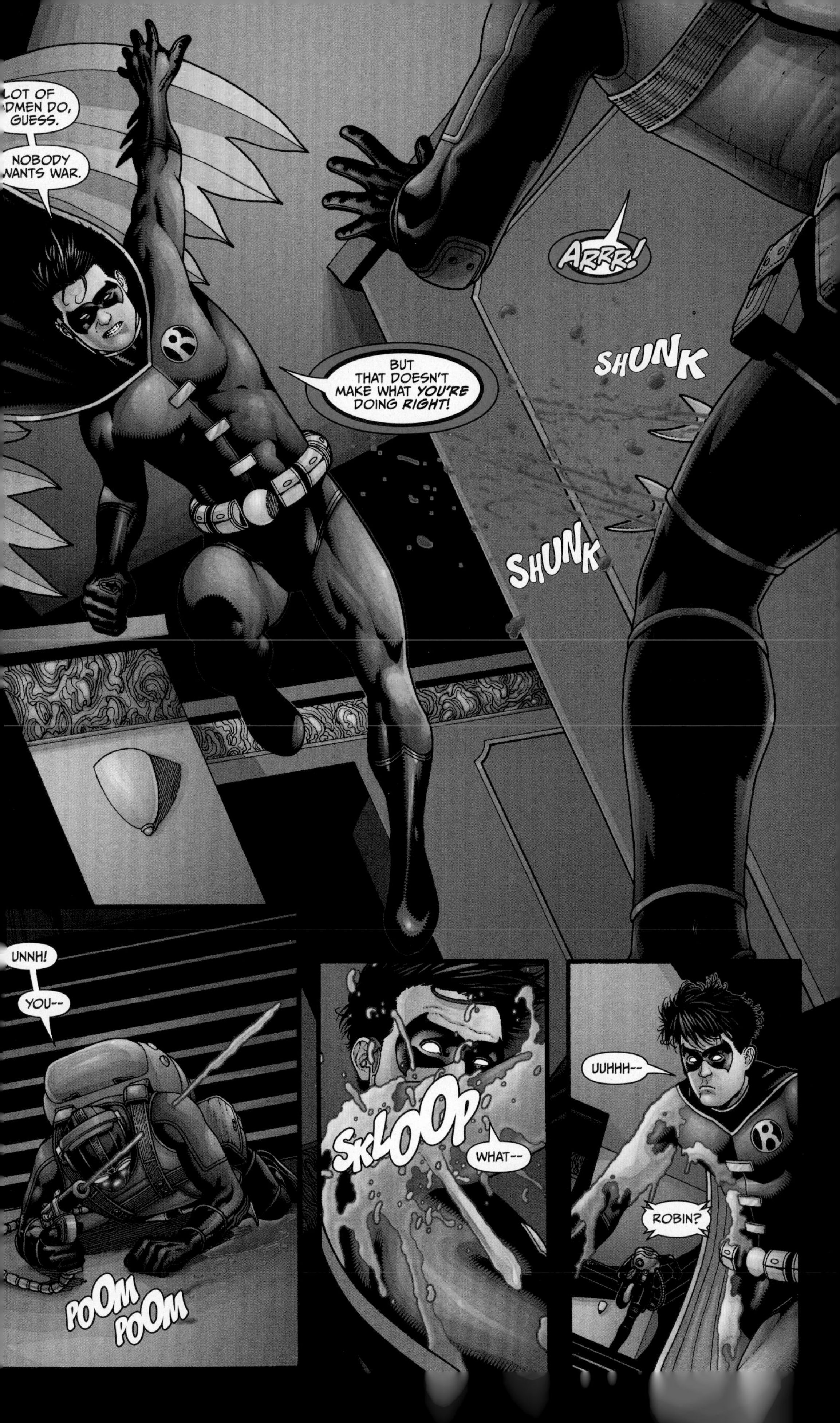
LOT OF
DMEN DO,
GUESS.
NOBODY
WANTS WAR.
BUT THAT DOESN'T MAKE WHAT *YOU'RE* DOING *RIGHT!*
ARRR!
SHUNK
SHUNK
UNNH!
YOU--
POOM POOM
SKLOOP
WHAT--
UUHHH--
ROBIN?

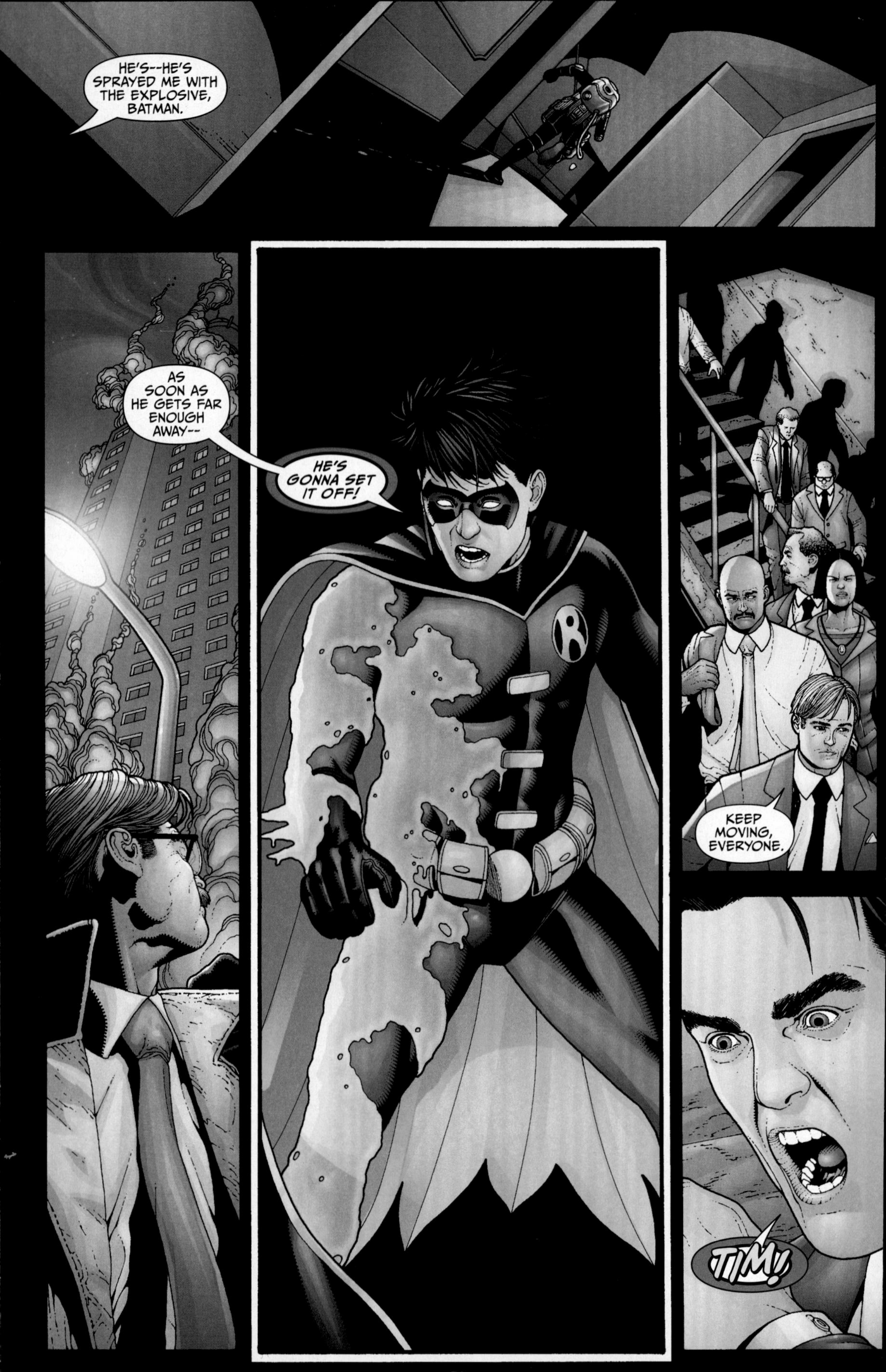
HE'S--HE'S SPRAYED ME WITH THE EXPLOSIVE, BATMAN.
AS SOON AS HE GETS FAR ENOUGH AWAY--
HE'S GONNA SET IT OFF!
KEEP MOVING, EVERYONE.
TIM!

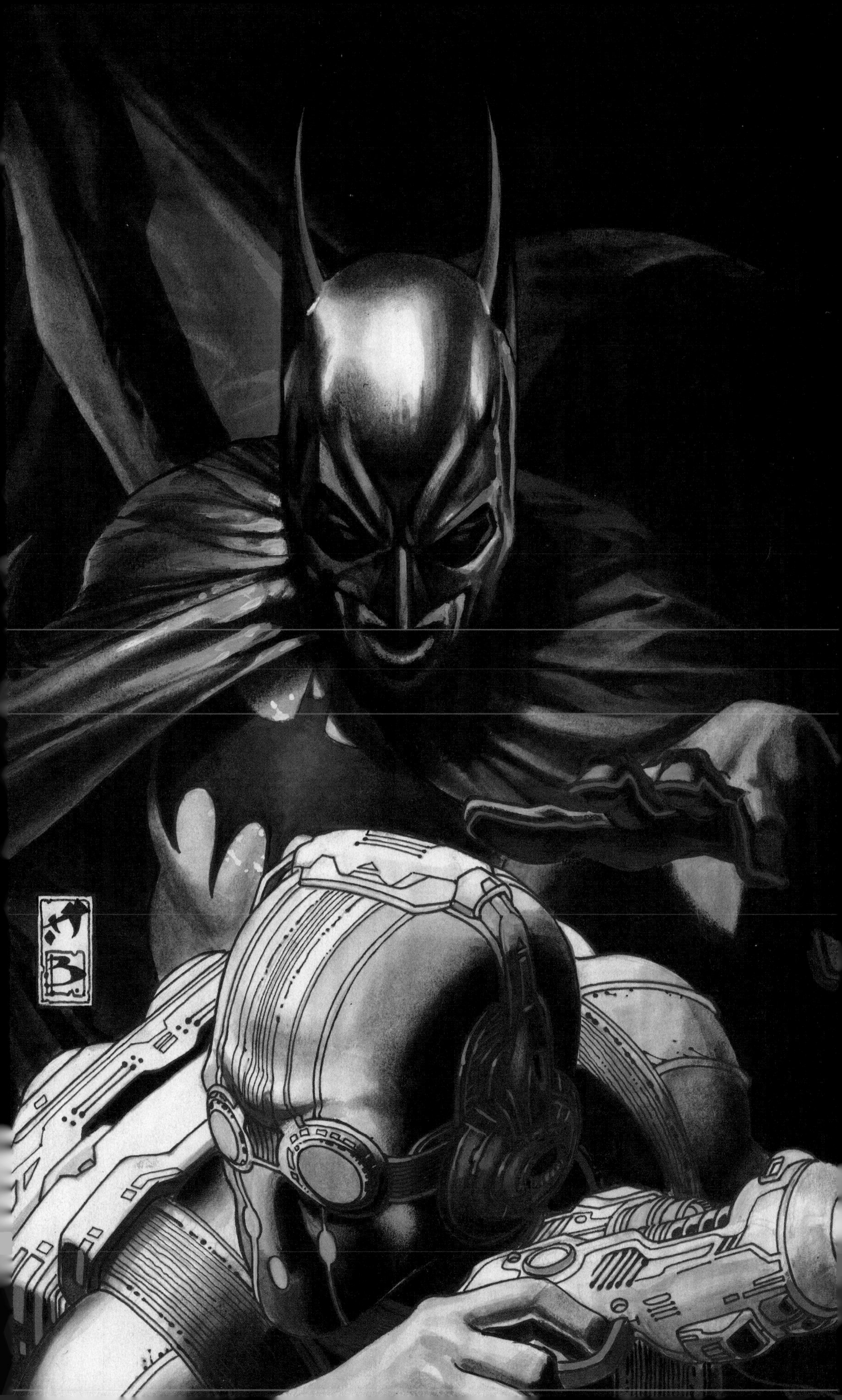

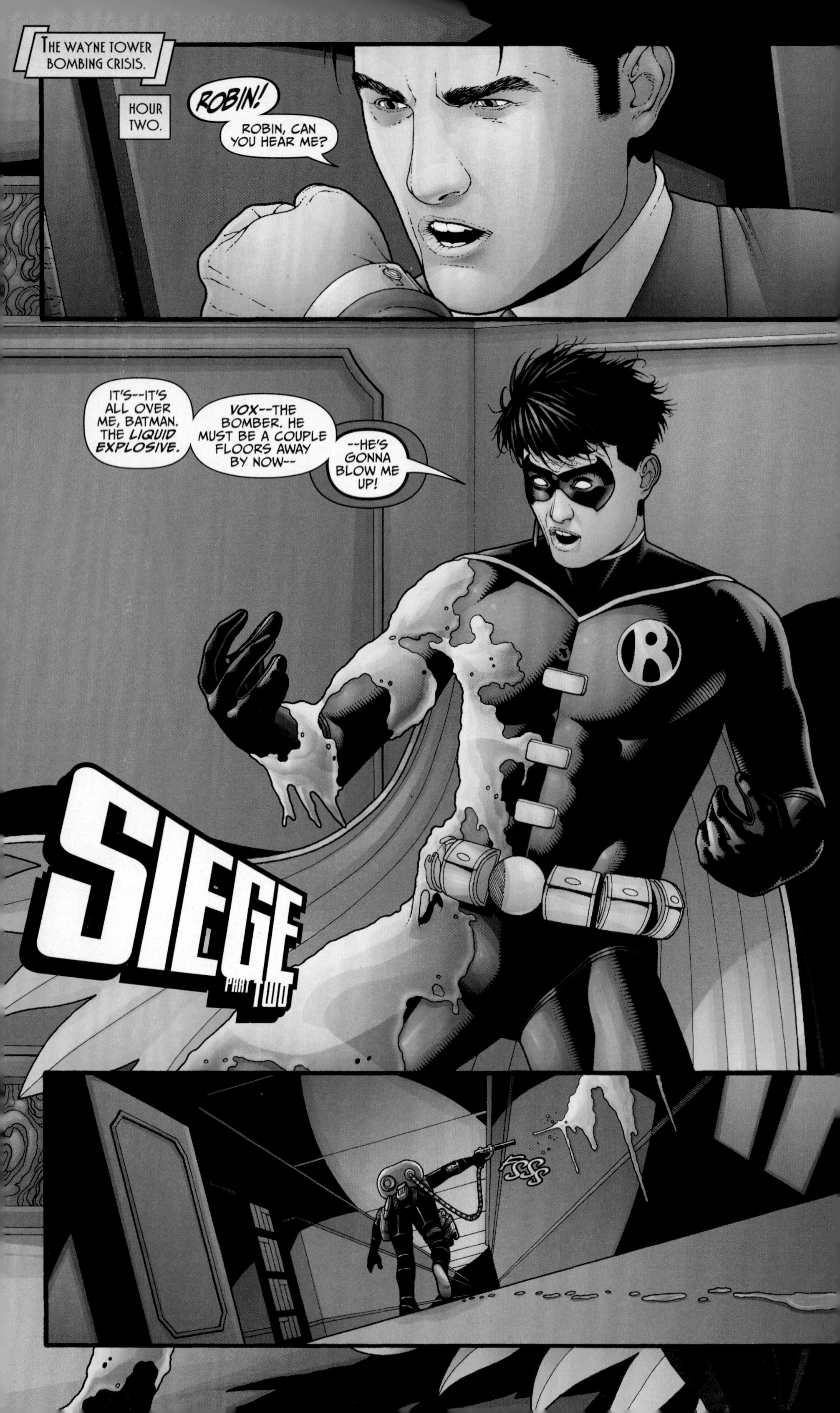

THE WAYNE TOWER BOMBING CRISIS.
HOUR TWO.
ROBIN!
ROBIN, CAN YOU HEAR ME?
IT'S--IT'S ALL OVER ME, BATMAN. THE LIQUID EXPLOSIVE.
VOX--THE BOMBER. HE MUST BE A COUPLE FLOORS AWAY BY NOW--
--HE'S GONNA BLOW ME UP!
SIEGE PART TWO
FSSS

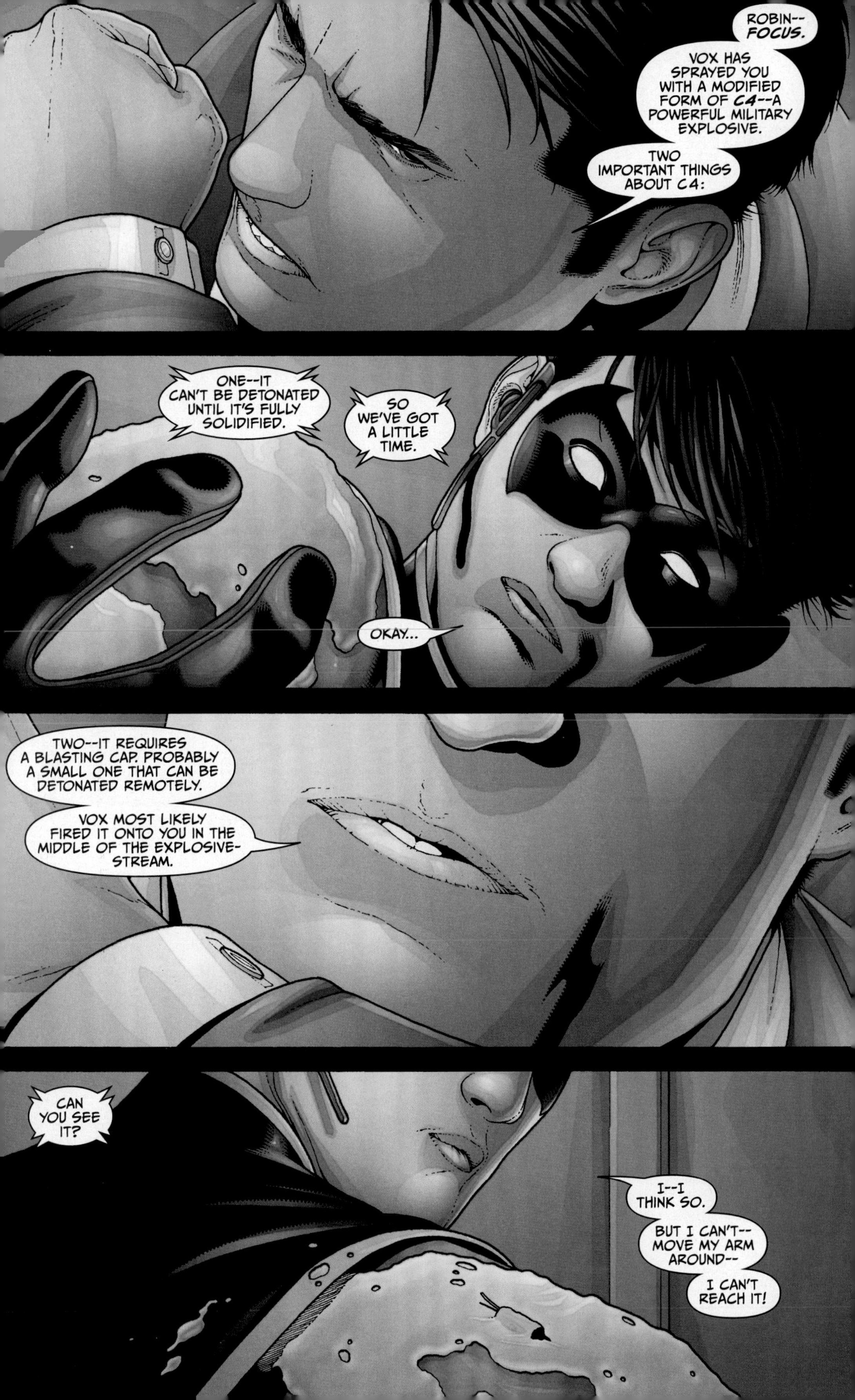
ROBIN-- FOCUS.
VOX HAS SPRAYED YOU WITH A MODIFIED FORM OF C4--A POWERFUL MILITARY EXPLOSIVE.
TWO IMPORTANT THINGS ABOUT C4:
ONE--IT CAN'T BE DETONATED UNTIL IT'S FULLY SOLIDIFIED.
SO WE'VE GOT A LITTLE TIME.
OKAY...
TWO--IT REQUIRES A BLASTING CAP. PROBABLY A SMALL ONE THAT CAN BE DETONATED REMOTELY.
VOX MOST LIKELY FIRED IT ONTO YOU IN THE MIDDLE OF THE EXPLOSIVE-STREAM.
CAN YOU SEE IT?
I--I THINK SO.
BUT I CAN'T-- MOVE MY ARM AROUND--
I CAN'T REACH IT!

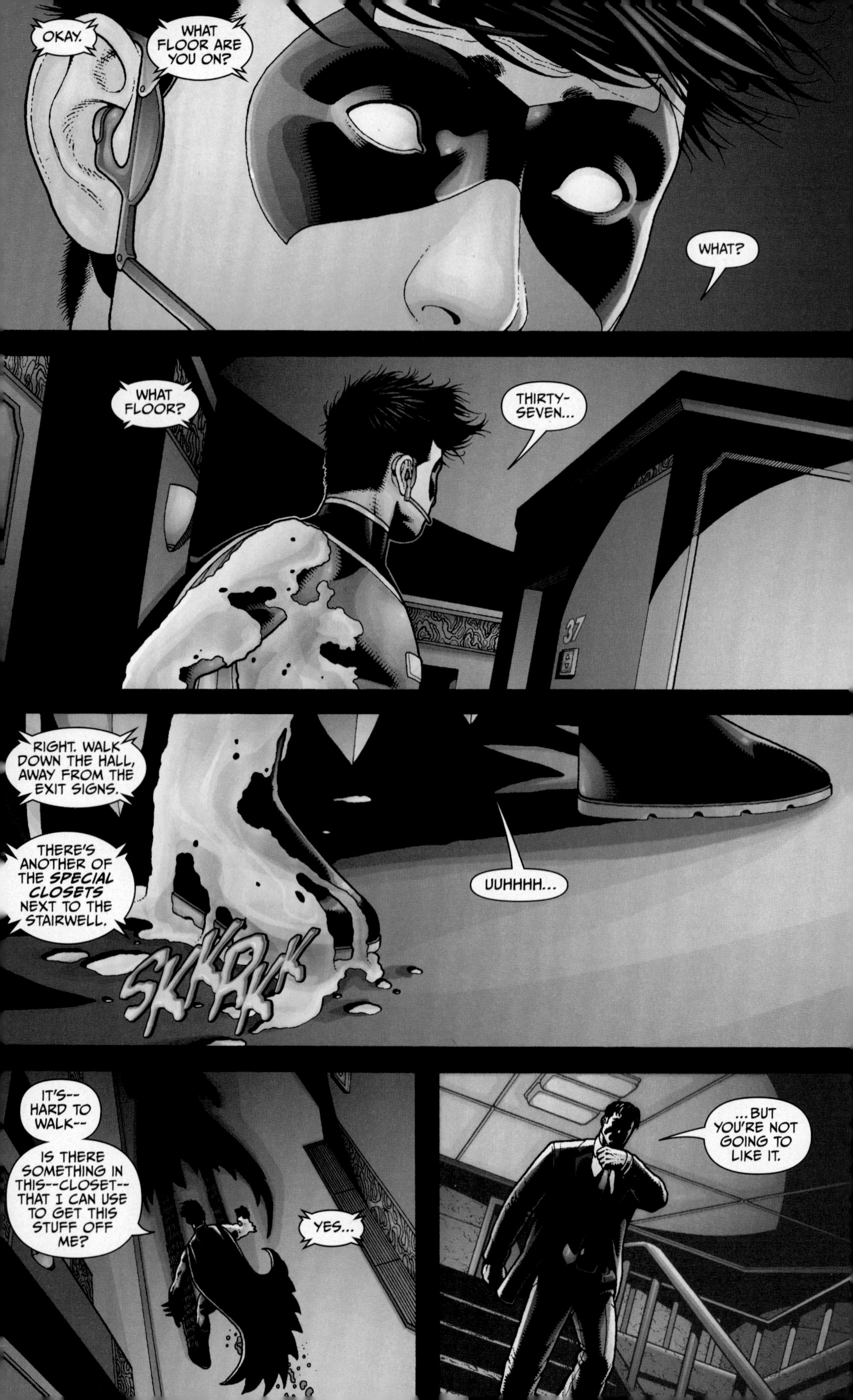
OKAY.
WHAT FLOOR ARE YOU ON?
WHAT?
WHAT FLOOR?
THIRTY-SEVEN...
37
RIGHT. WALK DOWN THE HALL, AWAY FROM THE EXIT SIGNS.
THERE'S ANOTHER OF THE SPECIAL CLOSETS NEXT TO THE STAIRWELL.
UUHHHH...
SKKRKK
IT'S-- HARD TO WALK--
IS THERE SOMETHING IN THIS--CLOSET-- THAT I CAN USE TO GET THIS STUFF OFF ME?
YES...
...BUT YOU'RE NOT GOING TO LIKE IT.

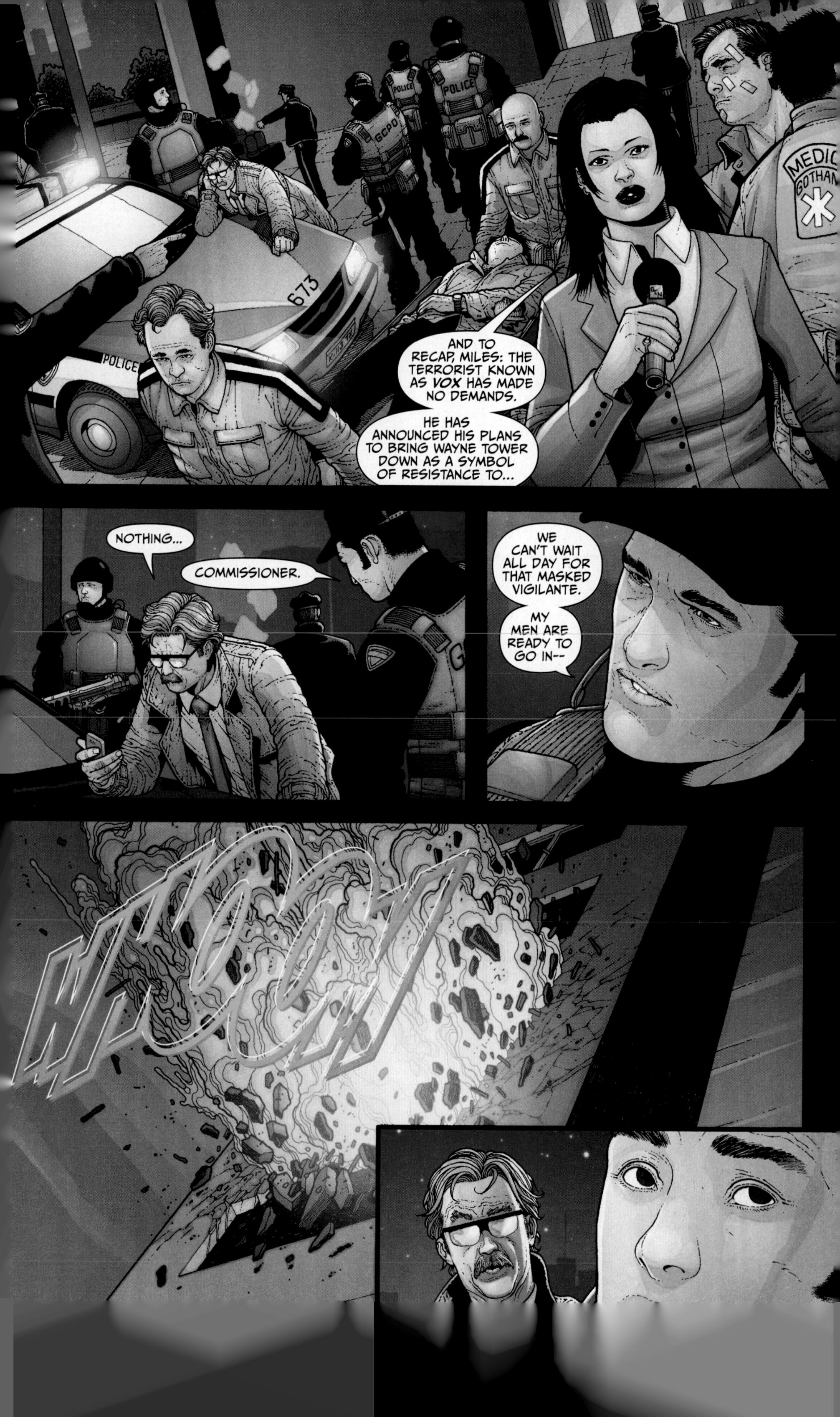

AND TO RECAP, MILES: THE TERRORIST KNOWN AS VOX HAS MADE NO DEMANDS.
HE HAS ANNOUNCED HIS PLANS TO BRING WAYNE TOWER DOWN AS A SYMBOL OF RESISTANCE TO...
NOTHING...
COMMISSIONER.
WE CAN'T WAIT ALL DAY FOR THAT MASKED VIGILANTE.
MY MEN ARE READY TO GO IN--

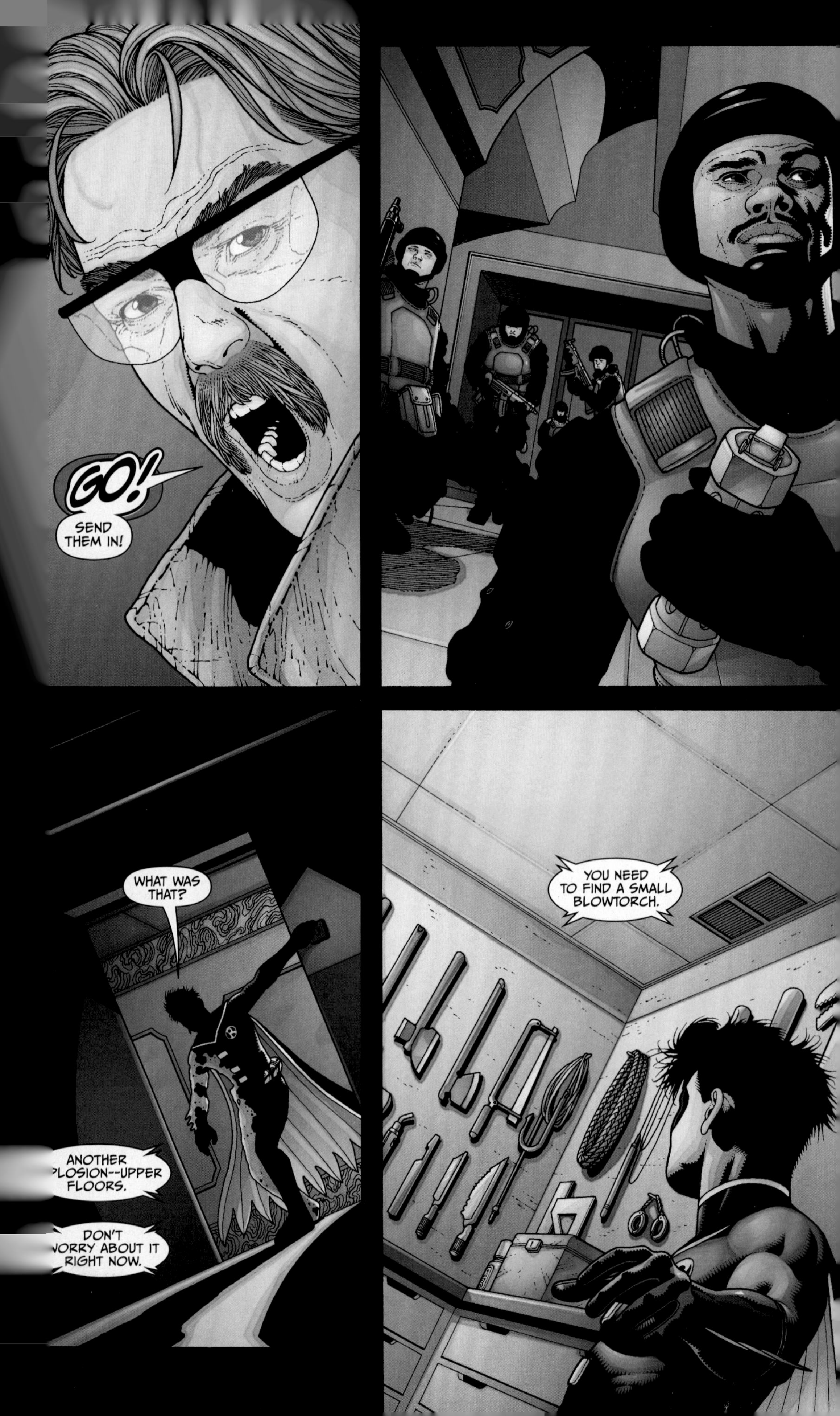
GO!
SEND THEM IN!
WHAT WAS THAT?
ANOTHER PLOSION--UPPER FLOORS.
DON'T WORRY ABOUT IT RIGHT NOW.
YOU NEED TO FIND A SMALL BLOWTORCH.

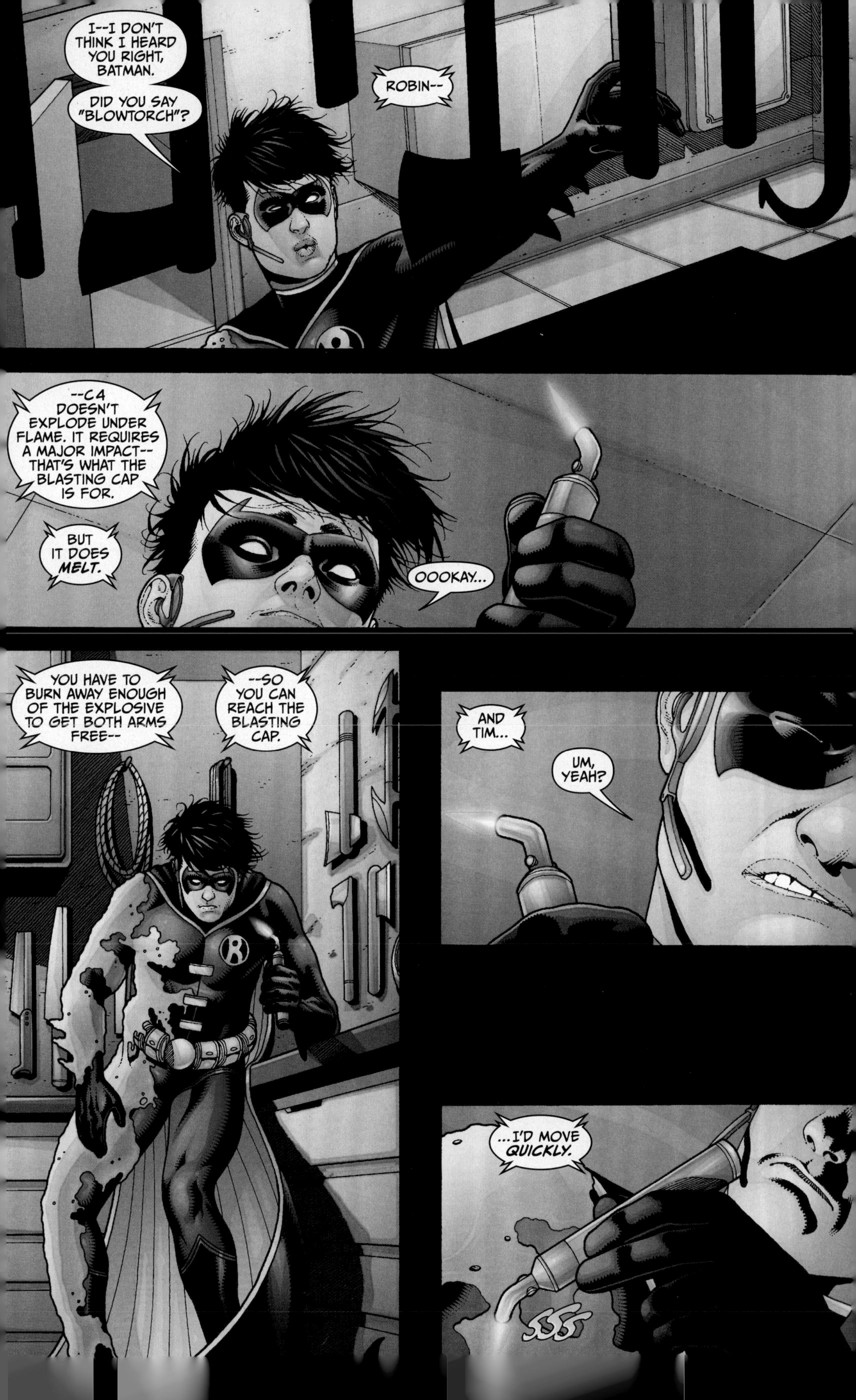
I--I DON'T THINK I HEARD YOU RIGHT, BATMAN.
DID YOU SAY "BLOWTORCH"?
ROBIN--
--C4 DOESN'T EXPLODE UNDER FLAME. IT REQUIRES A MAJOR IMPACT--THAT'S WHAT THE BLASTING CAP IS FOR.
BUT IT DOES MELT.
OOOKAY...
YOU HAVE TO BURN AWAY ENOUGH OF THE EXPLOSIVE TO GET BOTH ARMS FREE--
--SO YOU CAN REACH THE BLASTING CAP.
AND TIM...
UM, YEAH?
...I'D MOVE QUICKLY.
SSSS

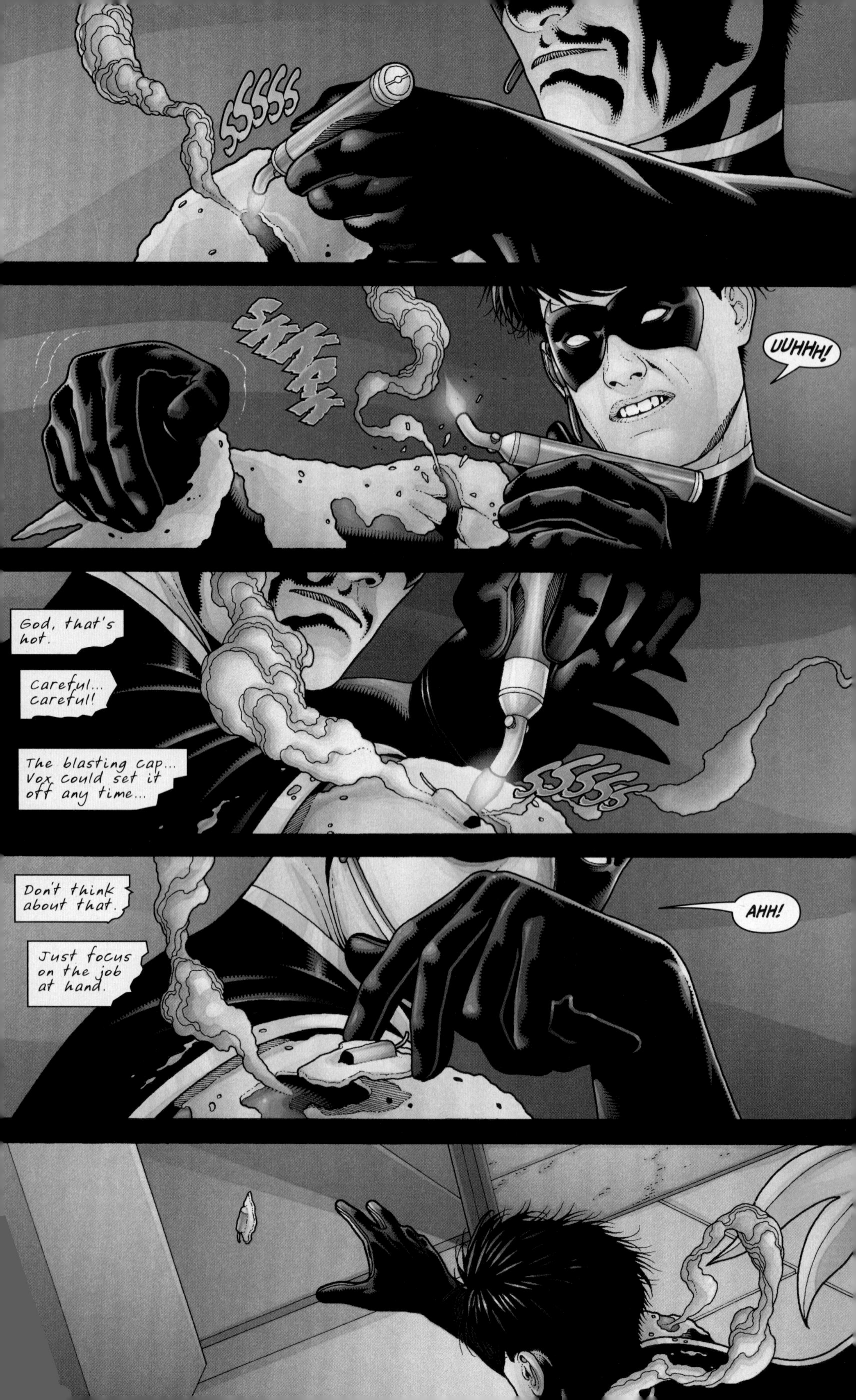
SSSSS
SKKAKK
UUHHH!
God, that's hot.
Careful... careful!
The blasting cap... Vox could set it off any time...
SSSSS
Don't think about that.
AHH!
Just focus on the job at hand.

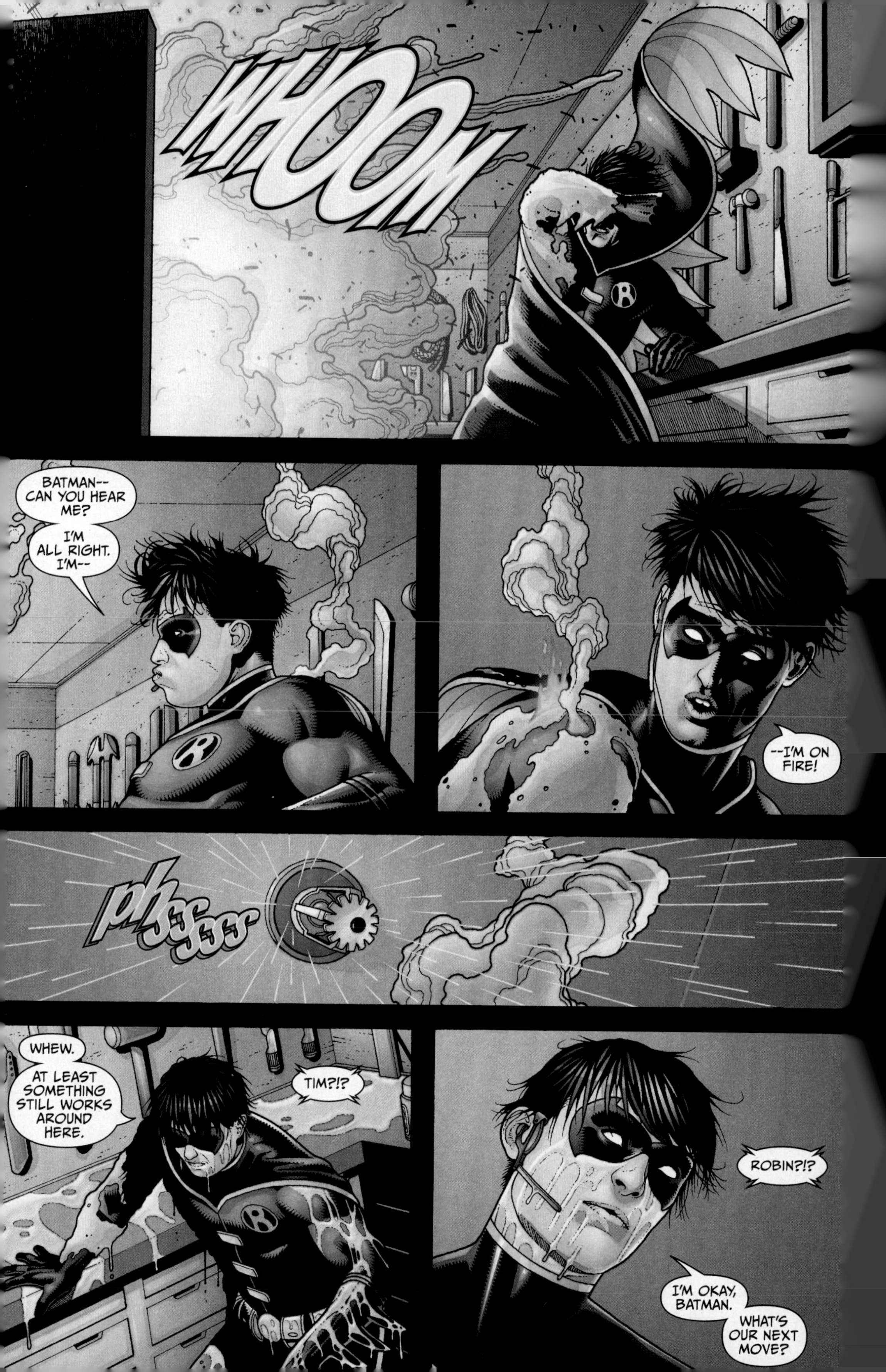
WHOOM
BATMAN-- CAN YOU HEAR ME?
I'M ALL RIGHT. I'M--
--I'M ON FIRE!
phssssss
WHEW.
AT LEAST SOMETHING STILL WORKS AROUND HERE.
TIM?!?
ROBIN?!?
I'M OKAY, BATMAN.
WHAT'S OUR NEXT MOVE?

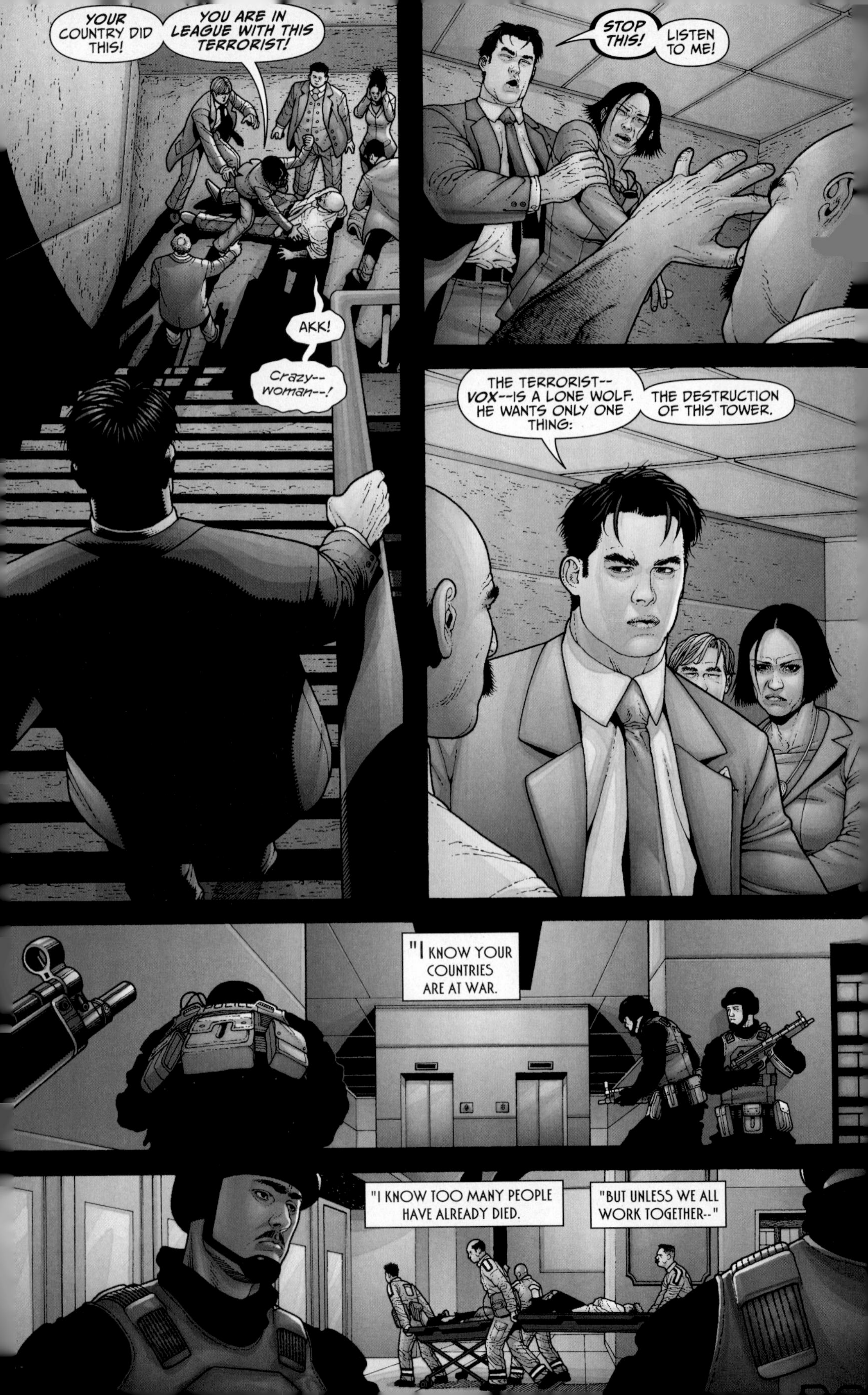
YOUR COUNTRY DID THIS!
YOU ARE IN LEAGUE WITH THIS TERRORIST!
AKK!
Crazy-- woman--!
STOP THIS!
LISTEN TO ME!
THE TERRORIST-- VOX--IS A LONE WOLF. HE WANTS ONLY ONE THING:
THE DESTRUCTION OF THIS TOWER.
"I KNOW YOUR COUNTRIES ARE AT WAR.
"I KNOW TOO MANY PEOPLE HAVE ALREADY DIED.
"BUT UNLESS WE ALL WORK TOGETHER--"

--THERE WILL BE MORE DEAD TODAY.

DO NOT TRUST HER!

DAMN. LOOKS LIKE DIPLOMACY'S FAILED AGAIN.

REMOVE YOUR HANDS FROM ME!

PLEASE! THIS IS MADNESS!

YOU ARE A FOOL!

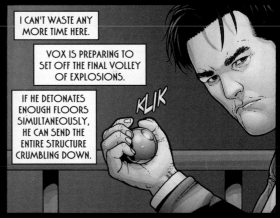

I CAN'T WASTE ANY MORE TIME HERE.

VOX IS PREPARING TO SET OFF THE FINAL VOLLEY OF EXPLOSIONS.

IF HE DETONATES ENOUGH FLOORS SIMULTANEOUSLY, HE CAN SEND THE ENTIRE STRUCTURE CRUMBLING DOWN.

KLIK

SO THAT MEANS--

MUCH AS I HATE THE IDEA--

85

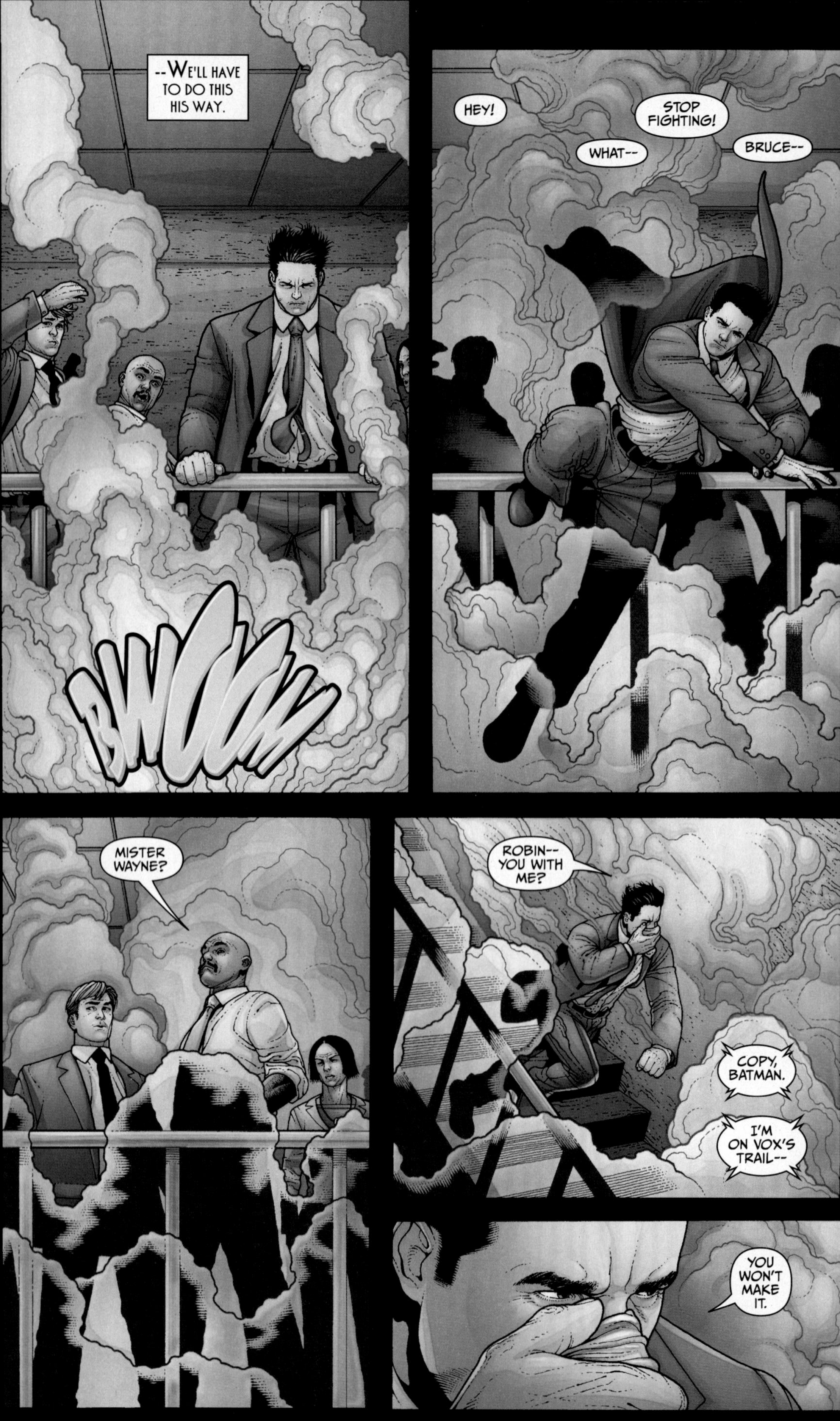
--WE'LL HAVE TO DO THIS HIS WAY.
BWOOOM
HEY!
STOP FIGHTING!
WHAT--
BRUCE--
MISTER WAYNE?
ROBIN-- YOU WITH ME?
COPY, BATMAN.
I'M ON VOX'S TRAIL--
YOU WON'T MAKE IT.

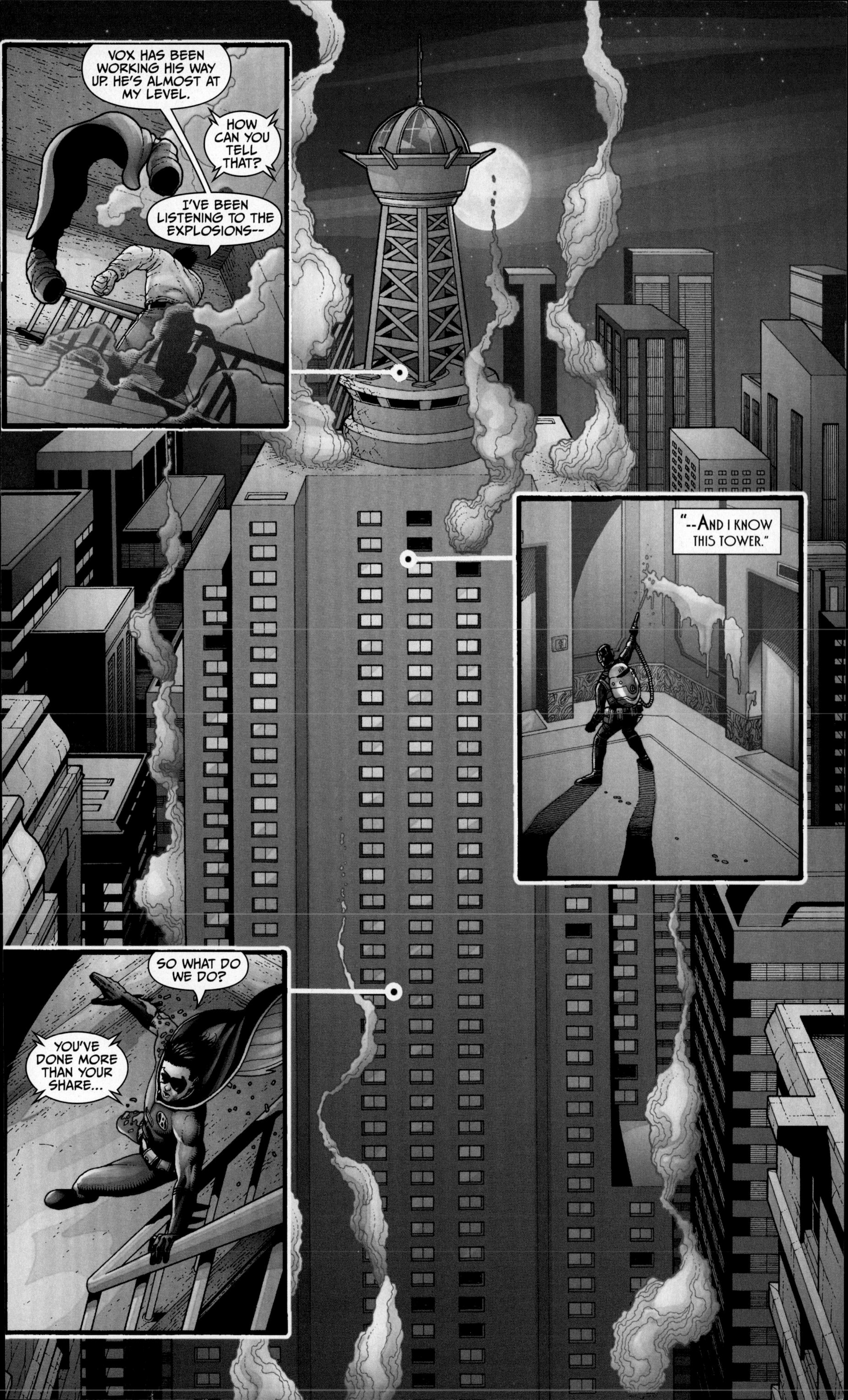
VOX HAS BEEN WORKING HIS WAY UP. HE'S ALMOST AT MY LEVEL.
HOW CAN YOU TELL THAT?
I'VE BEEN LISTENING TO THE EXPLOSIONS--
"--AND I KNOW THIS TOWER."
SO WHAT DO WE DO?
YOU'VE DONE MORE THAN YOUR SHARE...

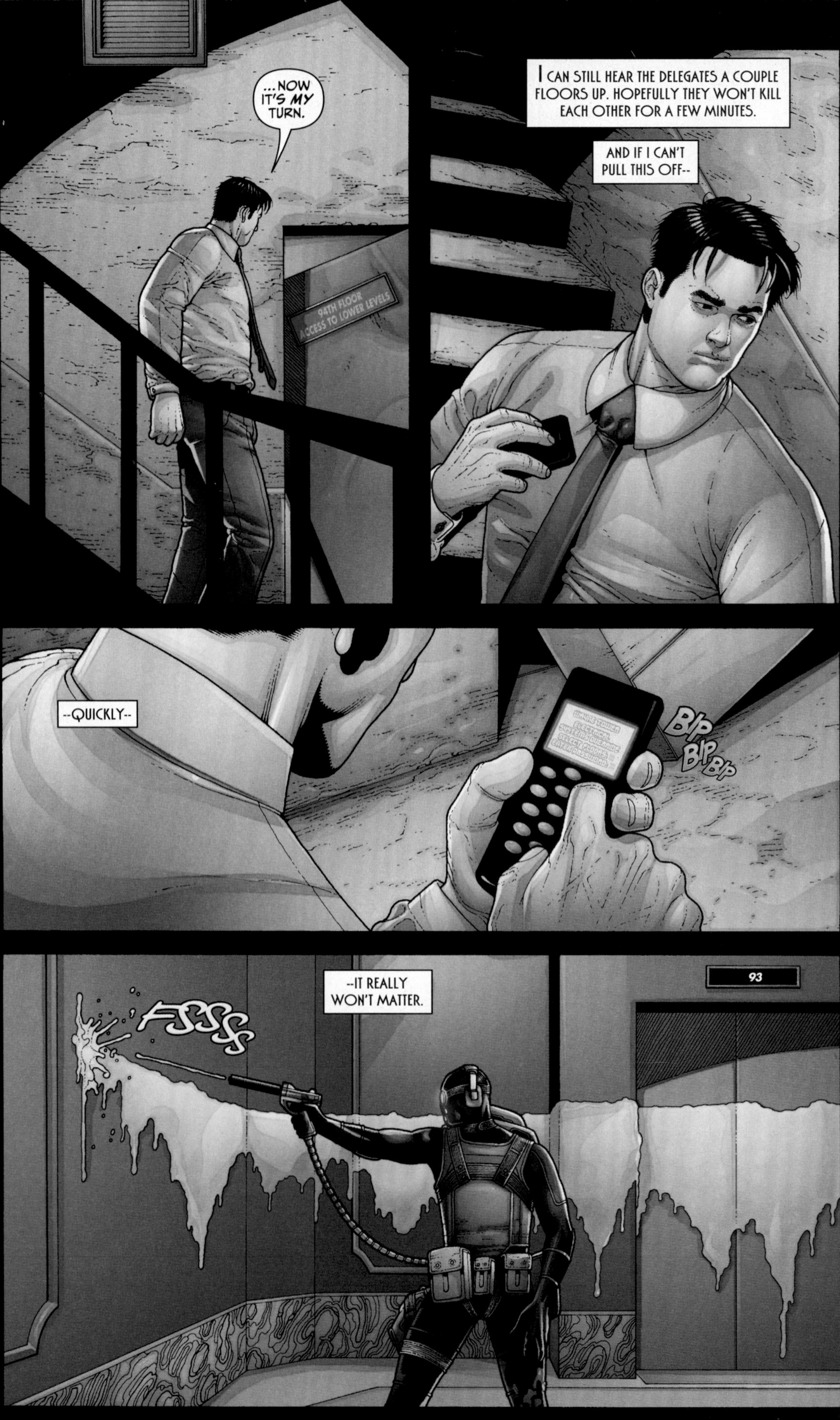
...NOW IT'S *MY* TURN.
94TH FLOOR ACCESS TO LOWER LEVELS
I CAN STILL HEAR THE DELEGATES A COUPLE FLOORS UP. HOPEFULLY THEY WON'T KILL EACH OTHER FOR A FEW MINUTES.
AND IF I CAN'T PULL THIS OFF--
--QUICKLY--
WAYNE TOWER
ELECTRICAL
SYSTEMS OVERRIDE
SELECT FLOORS:
ENTER PASSWORD:
BIP
BIP BIP
--IT REALLY WON'T MATTER.
93
FSSS

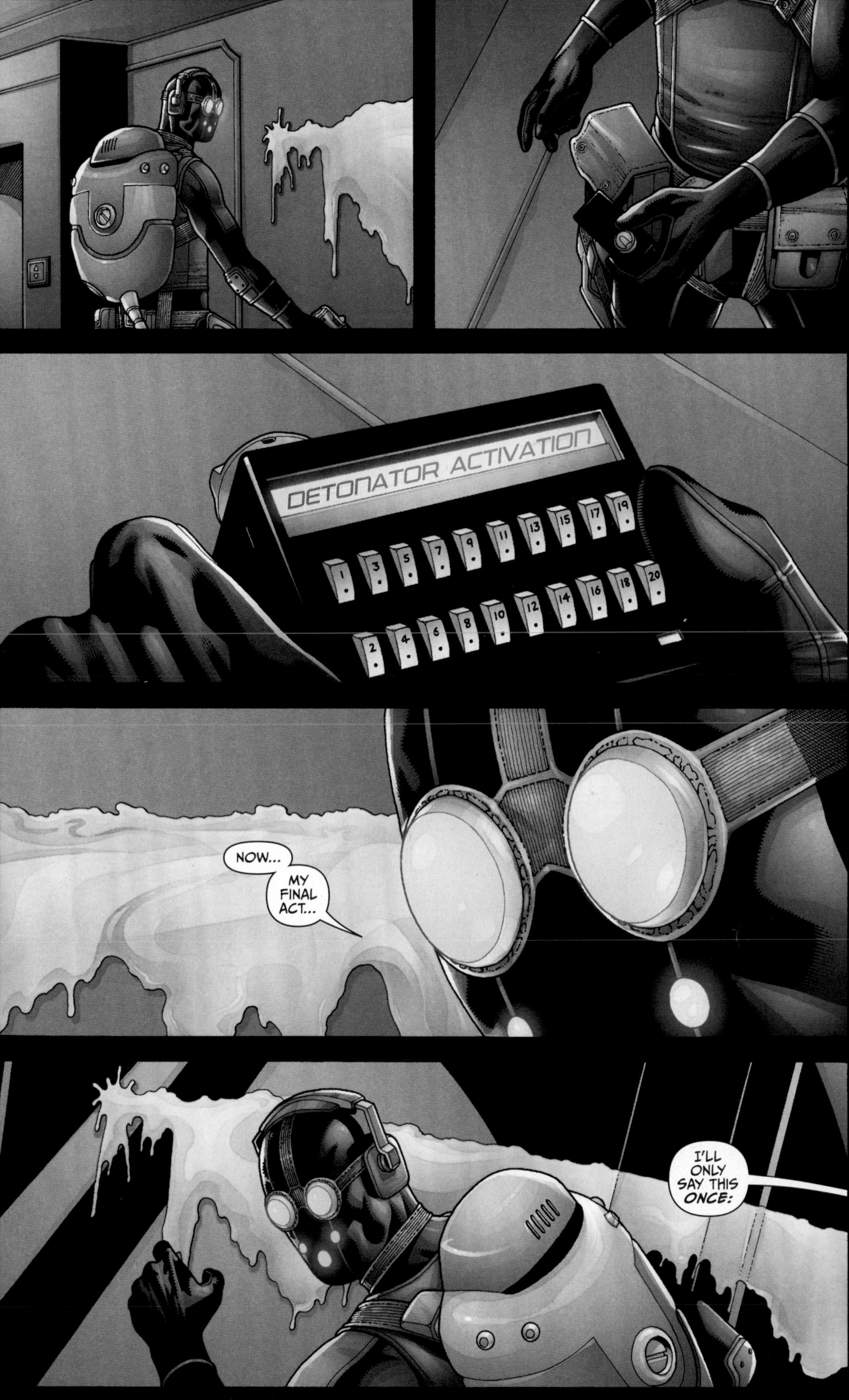
DETONATOR ACTIVATION
1
2
3
4
5
6
7
8
9
10
11
12
13
14
15
16
17
18
19
20
NOW...
MY FINAL ACT...
I'LL ONLY SAY THIS ONCE:

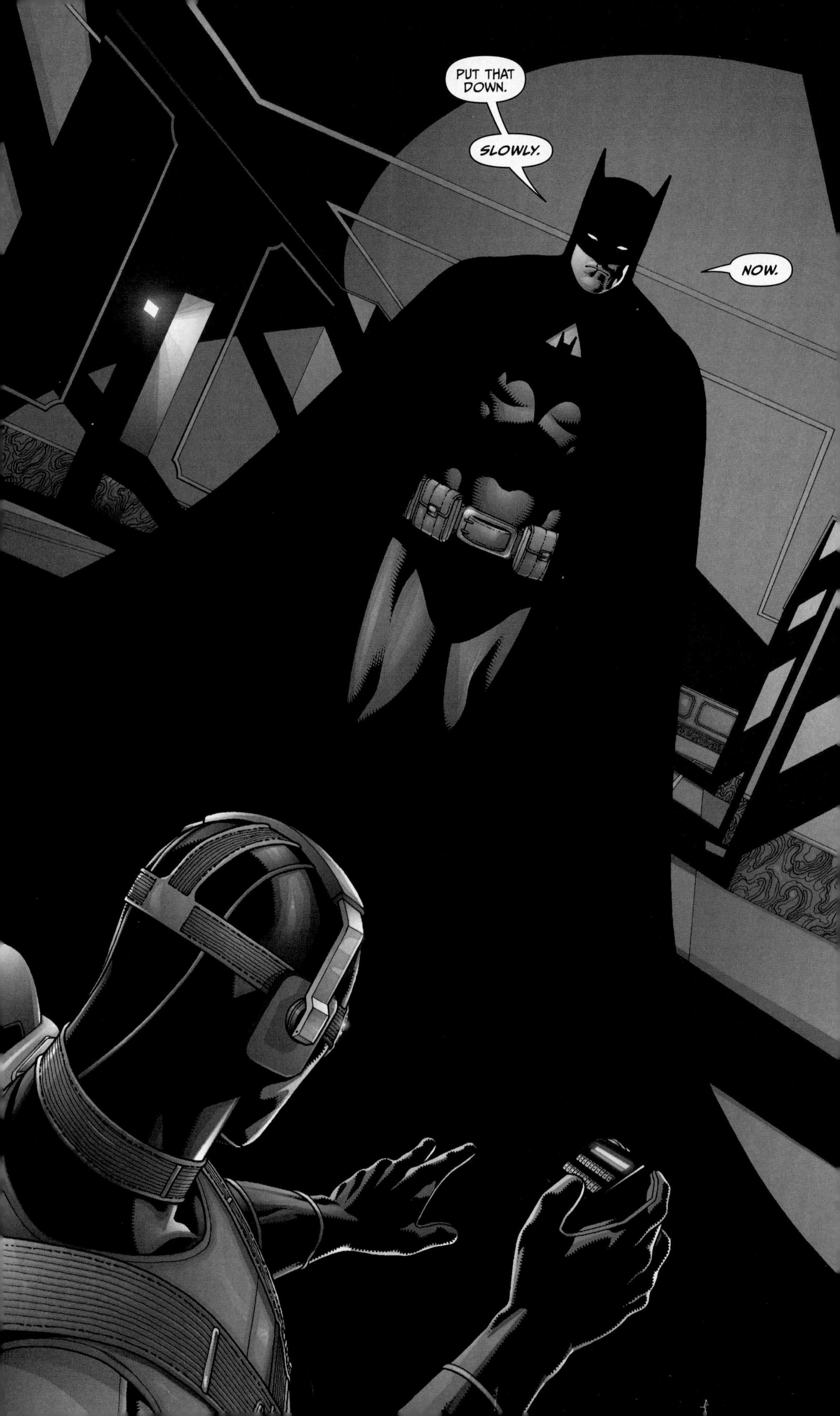
PUT THAT DOWN.
SLOWLY.
NOW.

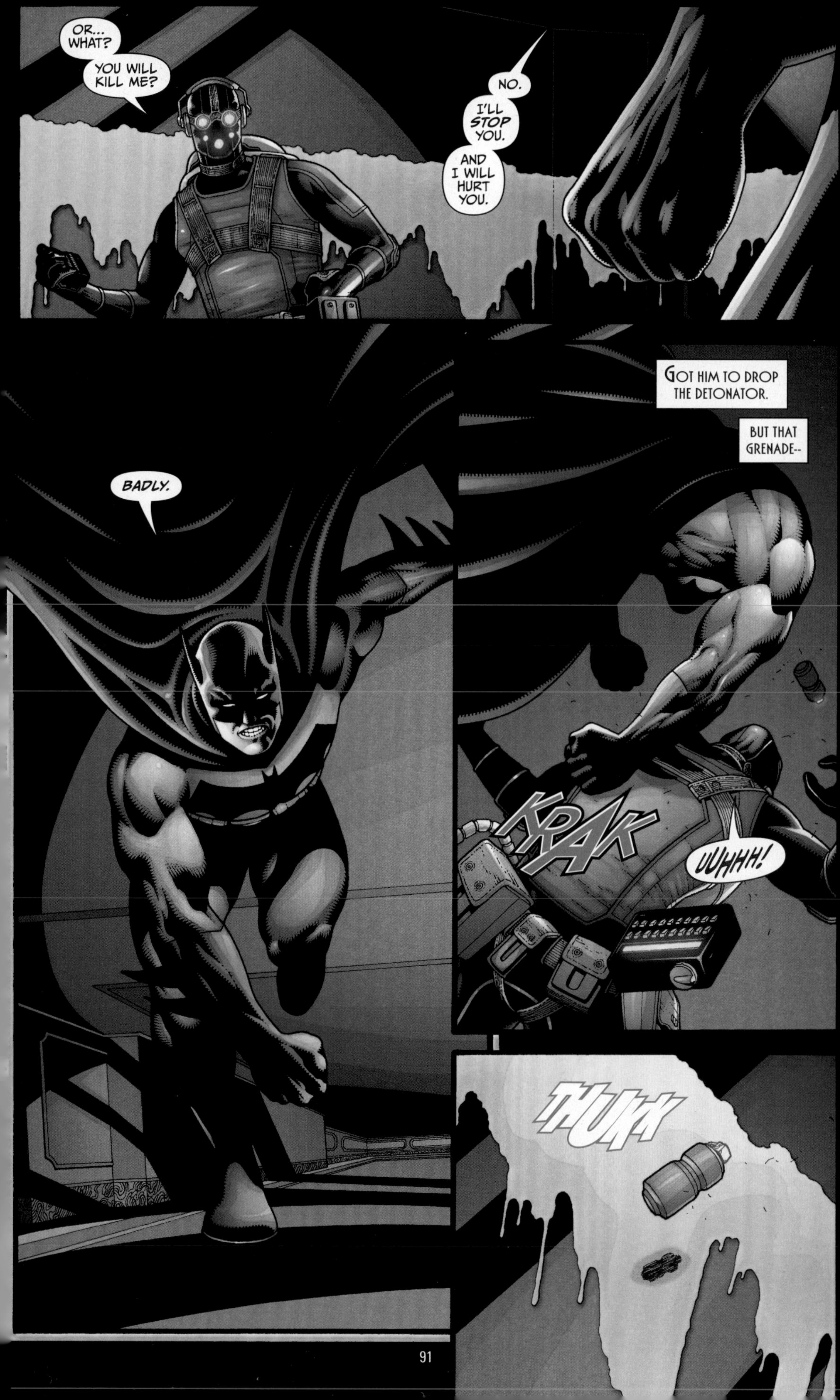

OR... WHAT?
YOU WILL KILL ME?
NO.
I'LL STOP YOU.
AND I WILL HURT YOU.
BADLY.
GOT HIM TO DROP THE DETONATOR.
BUT THAT GRENADE--
KRAK
UUHHH!
THUKK

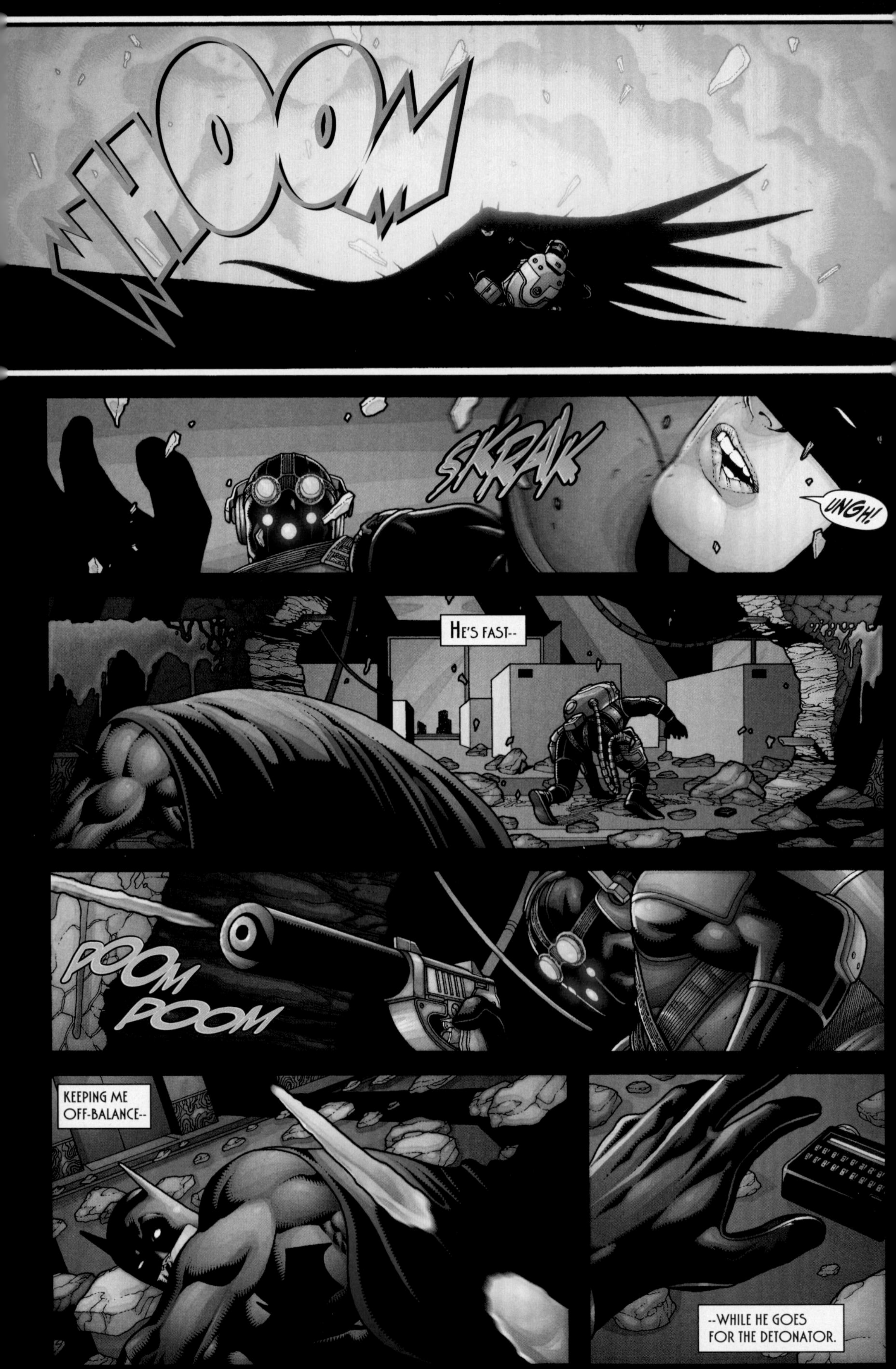
WHOOM
SKRAK
UNGH!
HE'S FAST--
POOM POOM
KEEPING ME OFF-BALANCE--
--WHILE HE GOES FOR THE DETONATOR.

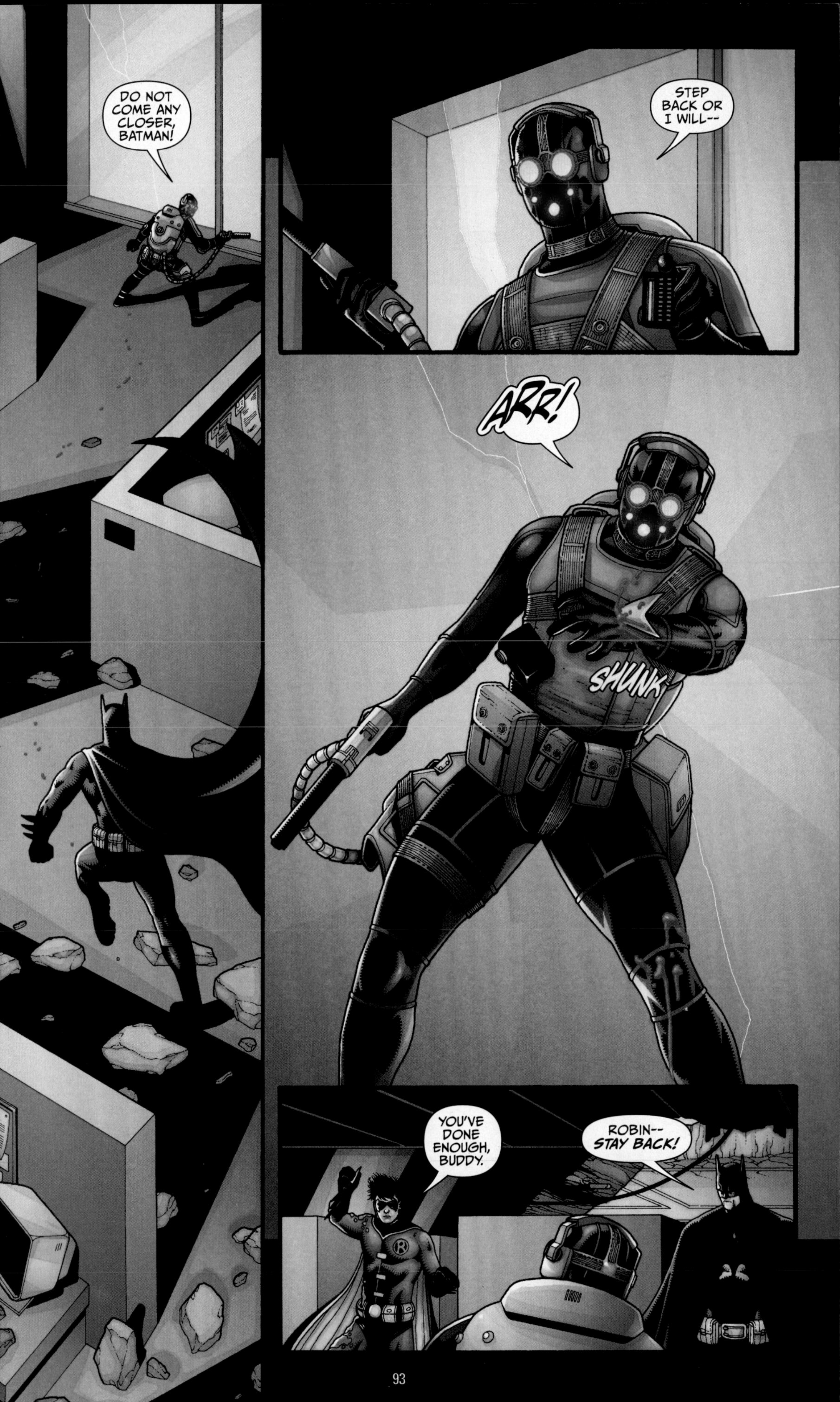
DO NOT COME ANY CLOSER, BATMAN!
STEP BACK OR I WILL--
ARR!
SHUNK
YOU'VE DONE ENOUGH, BUDDY.
ROBIN-- STAY BACK!

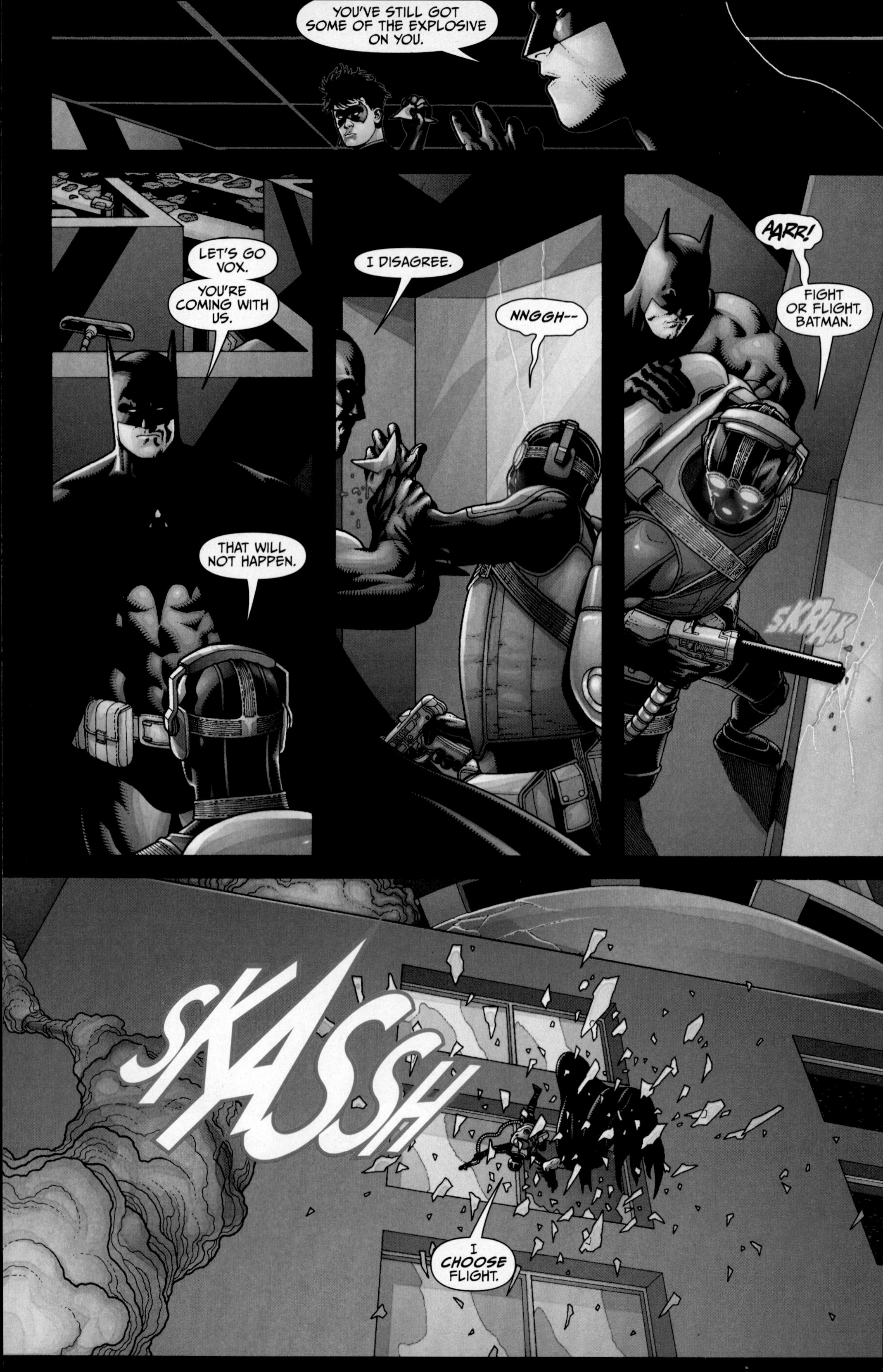

YOU'VE STILL GOT SOME OF THE EXPLOSIVE ON YOU.
LET'S GO VOX.
YOU'RE COMING WITH US.
THAT WILL NOT HAPPEN.
I DISAGREE.
NNGGH--
AARR!
FIGHT OR FLIGHT, BATMAN.
SKRAK
SKASSH
I CHOOSE FLIGHT.

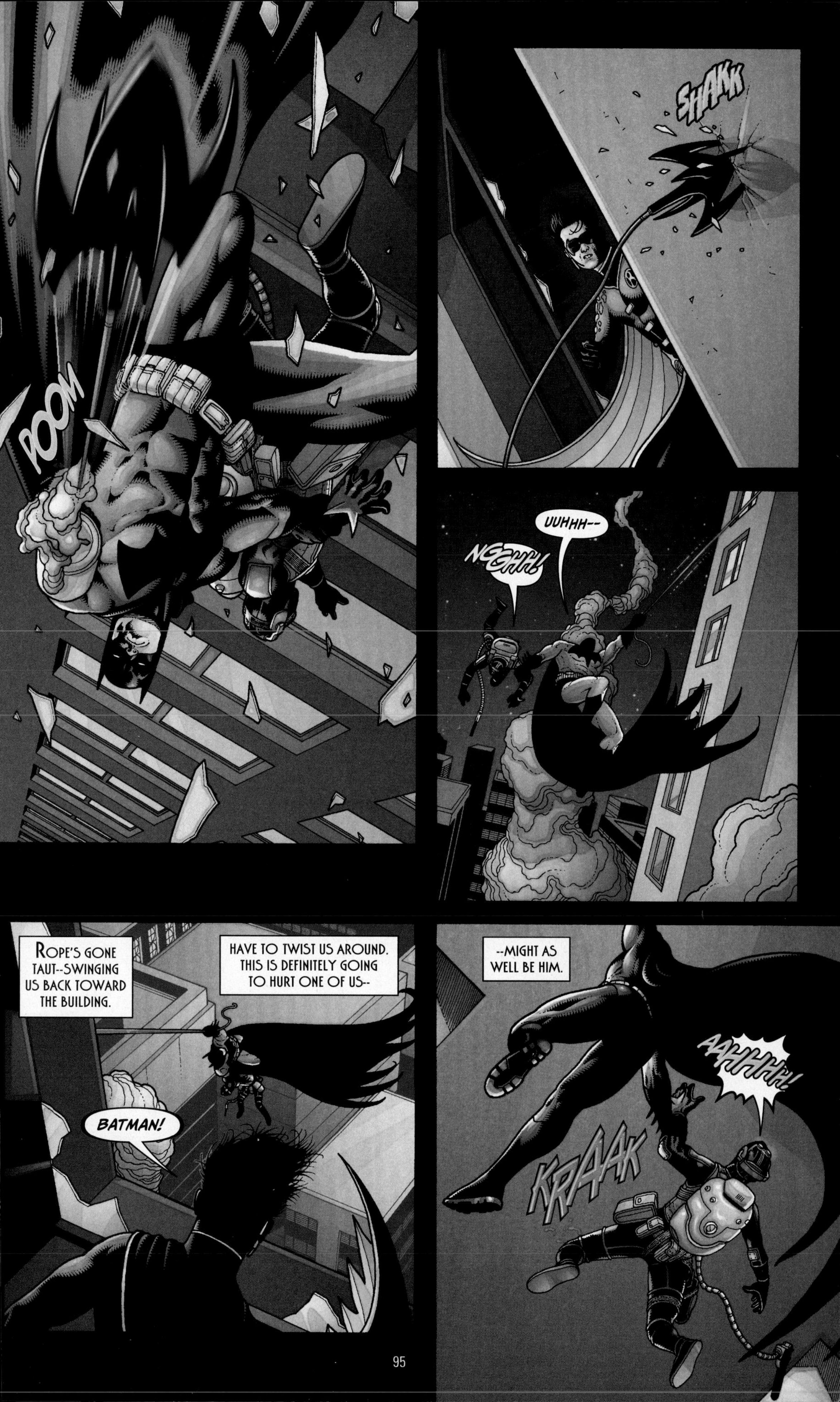
POOM
SHAKK
UUHHH--
NEGHHH!
ROPE'S GONE TAUT--SWINGING US BACK TOWARD THE BUILDING.
HAVE TO TWIST US AROUND. THIS IS DEFINITELY GOING TO HURT ONE OF US--
BATMAN!
--MIGHT AS WELL BE HIM.
AAHHHH!
KRAAK

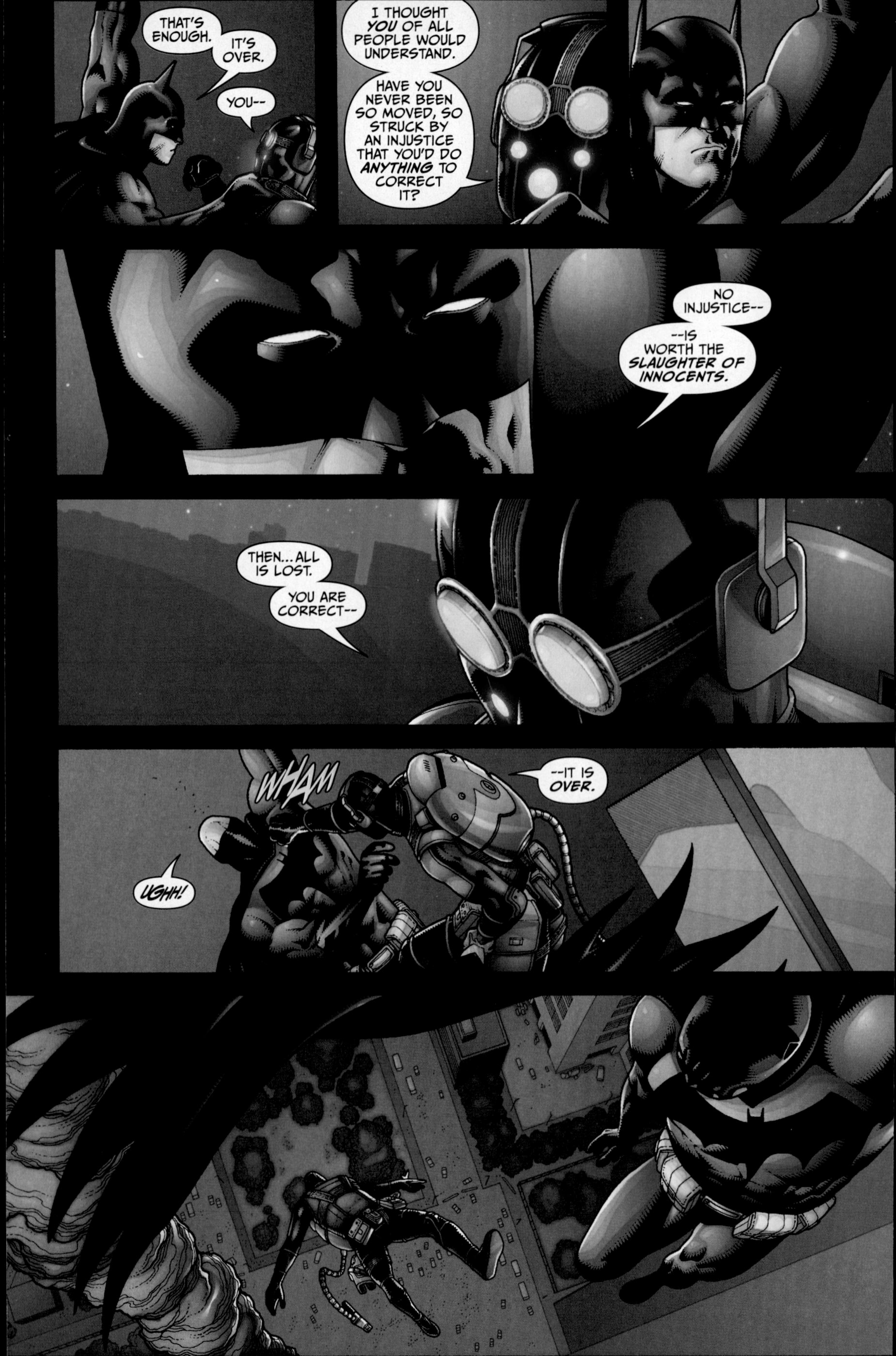
THAT'S ENOUGH.
IT'S OVER.
YOU--
I THOUGHT YOU OF ALL PEOPLE WOULD UNDERSTAND.
HAVE YOU NEVER BEEN SO MOVED, SO STRUCK BY AN INJUSTICE THAT YOU'D DO ANYTHING TO CORRECT IT?
NO INJUSTICE--
--IS WORTH THE SLAUGHTER OF INNOCENTS.
THEN... ALL IS LOST.
YOU ARE CORRECT--
WHAM
--IT IS OVER.
UGHH!

SSHLATCH

YOU OKAY, BATMAN?

YES. YOU?

I FEEL LIKE A TOXIC WASTE SITE. BUT ON THE BRIGHT SIDE--

--AT LEAST I DON'T HAVE TO WEAR THAT *TUX* ALL NIGHT.

THIS IS THE LAST OF THE AFFECTED FLOORS.

BATMAN!

BOMB SQUADS ARE NEUTRALIZING THE EXPLOSIVES RIGHT NOW.

IT WAS JUST THE ONE MAN, RIGHT?

YES.

EXCUSE ME--

HAS ANYONE SEEN *BRUCE WAYNE?*

HE GUIDED US OUT OF THE SPIRE-- SAVED OUR LIVES. THEN THERE WAS ANOTHER EXPLOSION--AND HE DISAPPEARED--

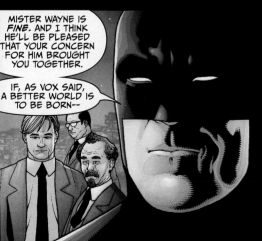

MISTER WAYNE IS *FINE.* AND I THINK HE'LL BE PLEASED THAT YOUR CONCERN FOR HIM BROUGHT YOU TOGETHER.

IF, AS VOX SAID, A BETTER WORLD IS TO BE BORN--

"--MAYBE THAT'S THE *REAL* FIRST STEP."

The End

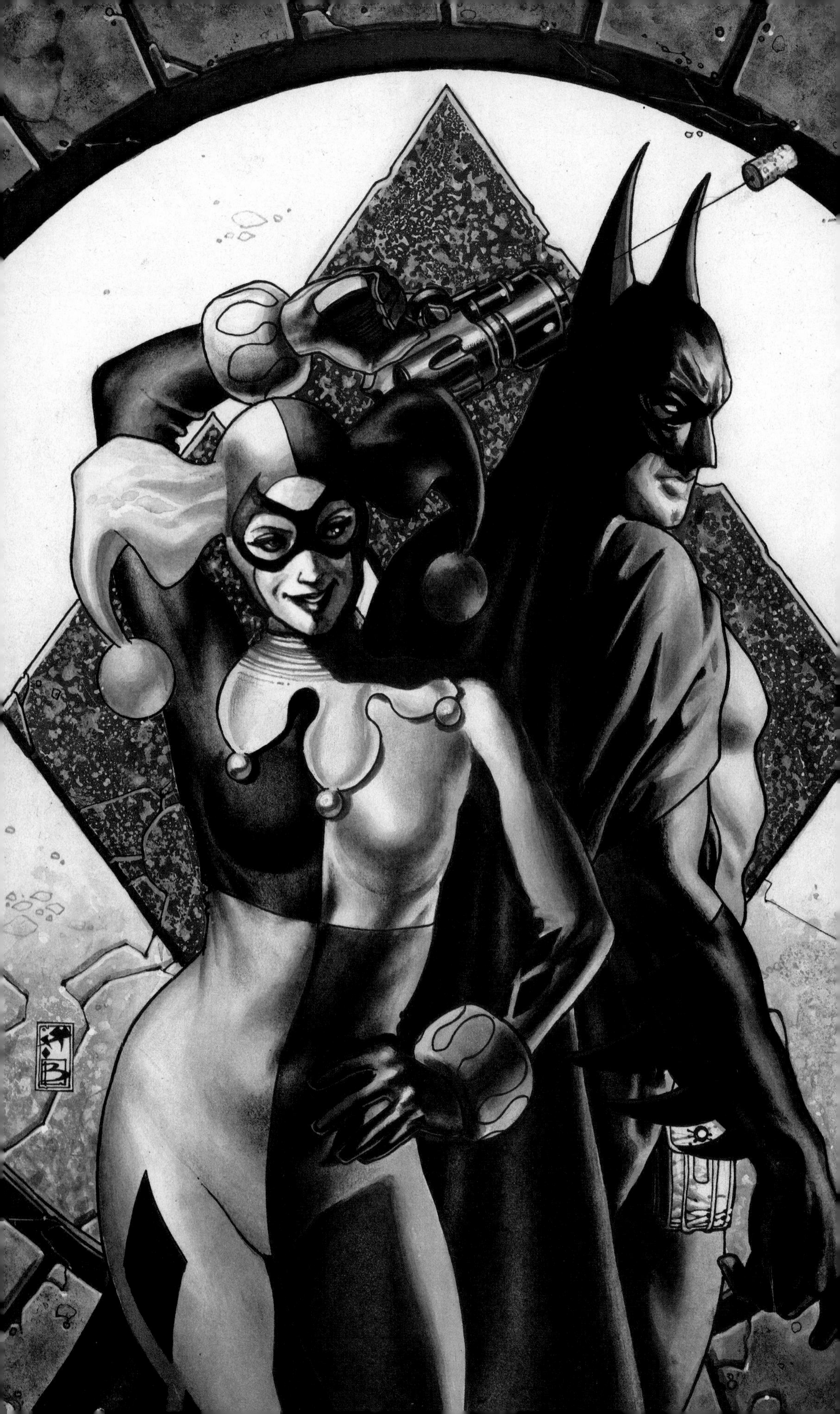

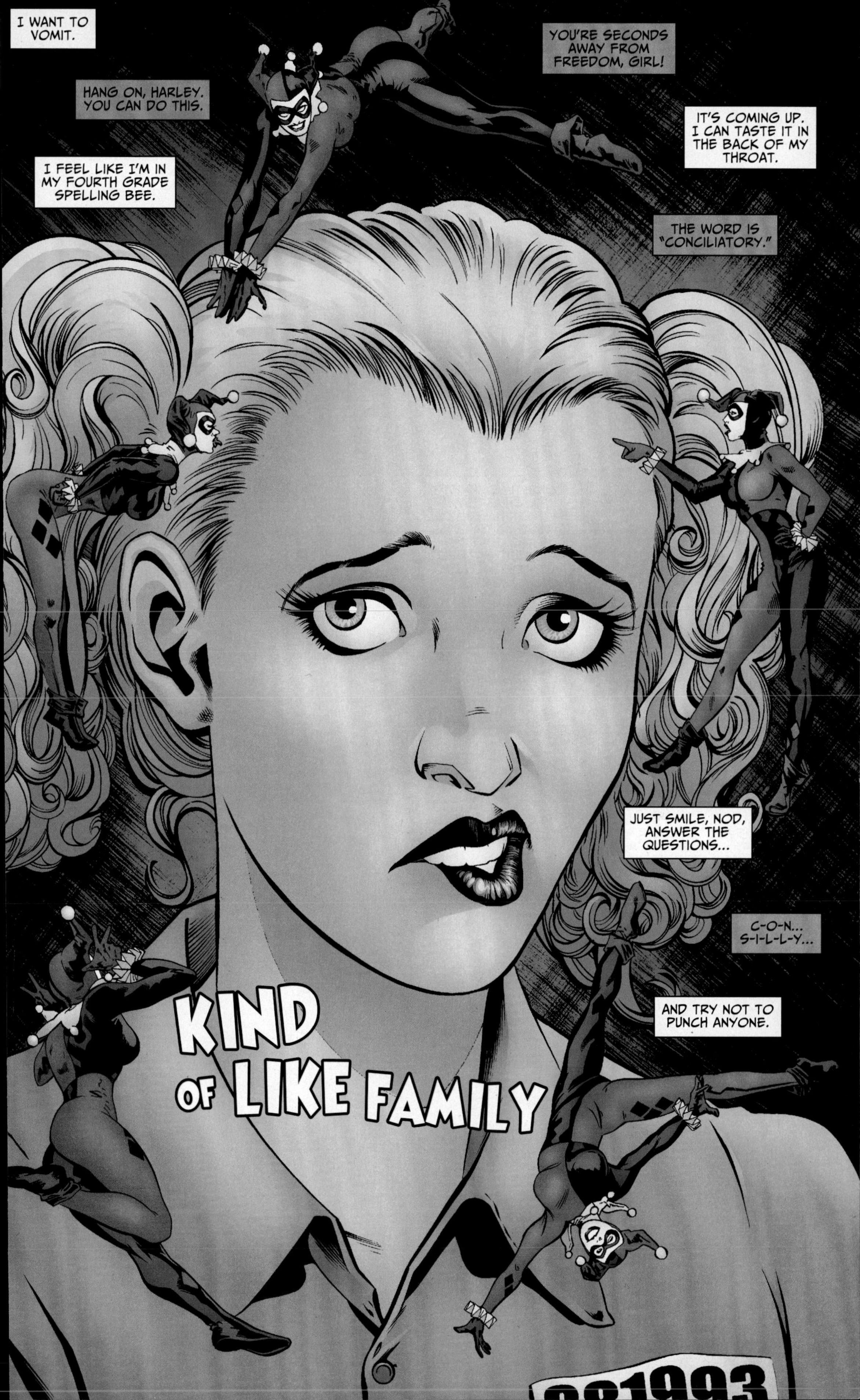

I WANT TO VOMIT.
YOU'RE SECONDS AWAY FROM FREEDOM, GIRL!
HANG ON, HARLEY. YOU CAN DO THIS.
IT'S COMING UP. I CAN TASTE IT IN THE BACK OF MY THROAT.
I FEEL LIKE I'M IN MY FOURTH GRADE SPELLING BEE.
THE WORD IS "CONCILIATORY."
JUST SMILE, NOD, ANSWER THE QUESTIONS...
C-O-N... S-I-L-L-Y...
AND TRY NOT TO PUNCH ANYONE.
KIND OF LIKE FAMILY

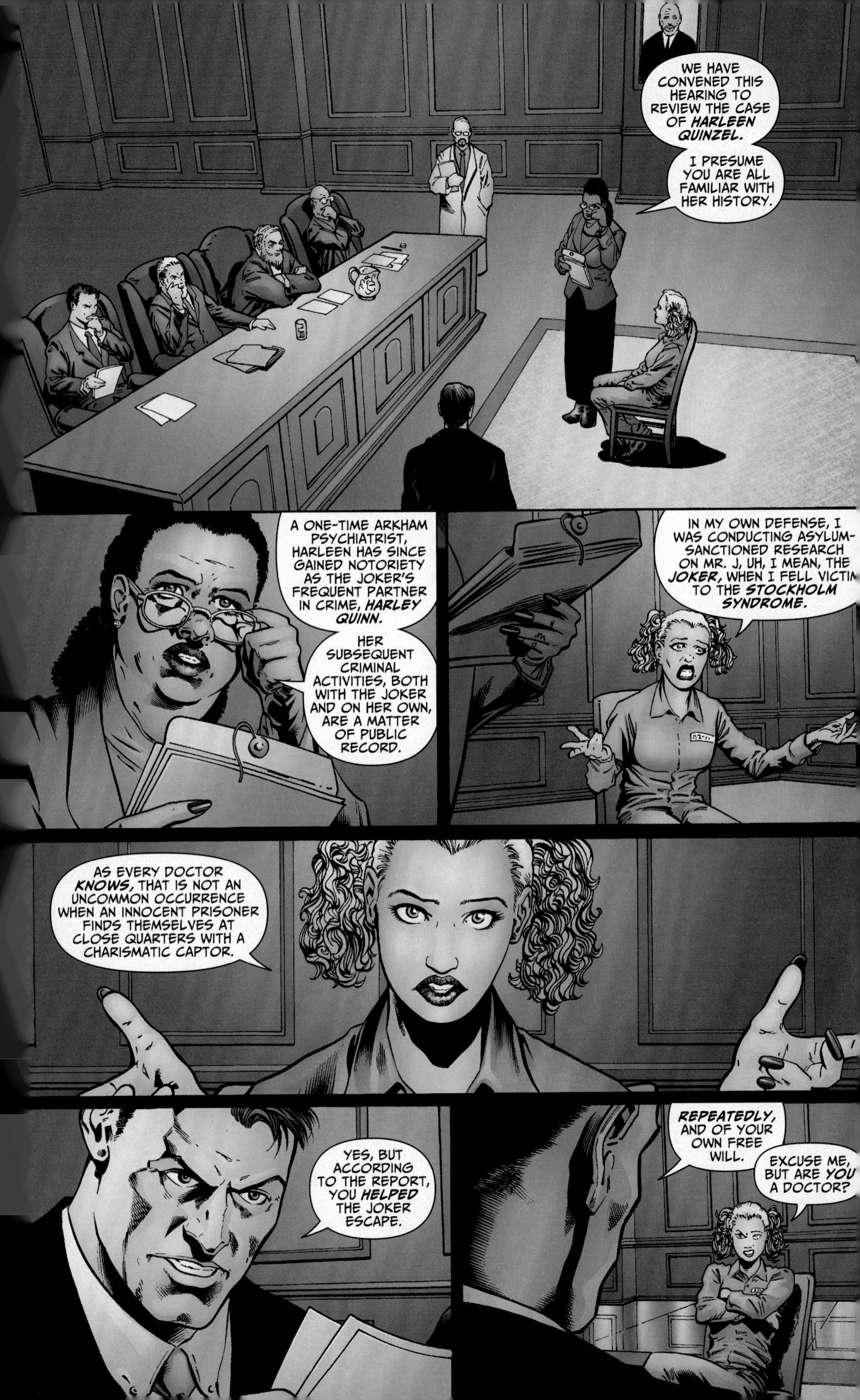

WE HAVE CONVENED THIS HEARING TO REVIEW THE CASE OF HARLEEN QUINZEL.
I PRESUME YOU ARE ALL FAMILIAR WITH HER HISTORY.
A ONE-TIME ARKHAM PSYCHIATRIST, HARLEEN HAS SINCE GAINED NOTORIETY AS THE JOKER'S FREQUENT PARTNER IN CRIME, HARLEY QUINN.
HER SUBSEQUENT CRIMINAL ACTIVITIES, BOTH WITH THE JOKER AND ON HER OWN, ARE A MATTER OF PUBLIC RECORD.
IN MY OWN DEFENSE, I WAS CONDUCTING ASYLUM-SANCTIONED RESEARCH ON MR. J, UH, I MEAN, THE JOKER, WHEN I FELL VICTI
TO THE STOCKHOLM SYNDROME.
AS EVERY DOCTOR KNOWS, THAT IS NOT AN UNCOMMON OCCURRENCE WHEN AN INNOCENT PRISONER FINDS THEMSELVES AT CLOSE QUARTERS WITH A CHARISMATIC CAPTOR.
YES, BUT ACCORDING TO THE REPORT, YOU HELPED THE JOKER ESCAPE.
REPEATEDLY, AND OF YOUR OWN FREE WILL.
EXCUSE ME, BUT ARE YOU A DOCTOR?

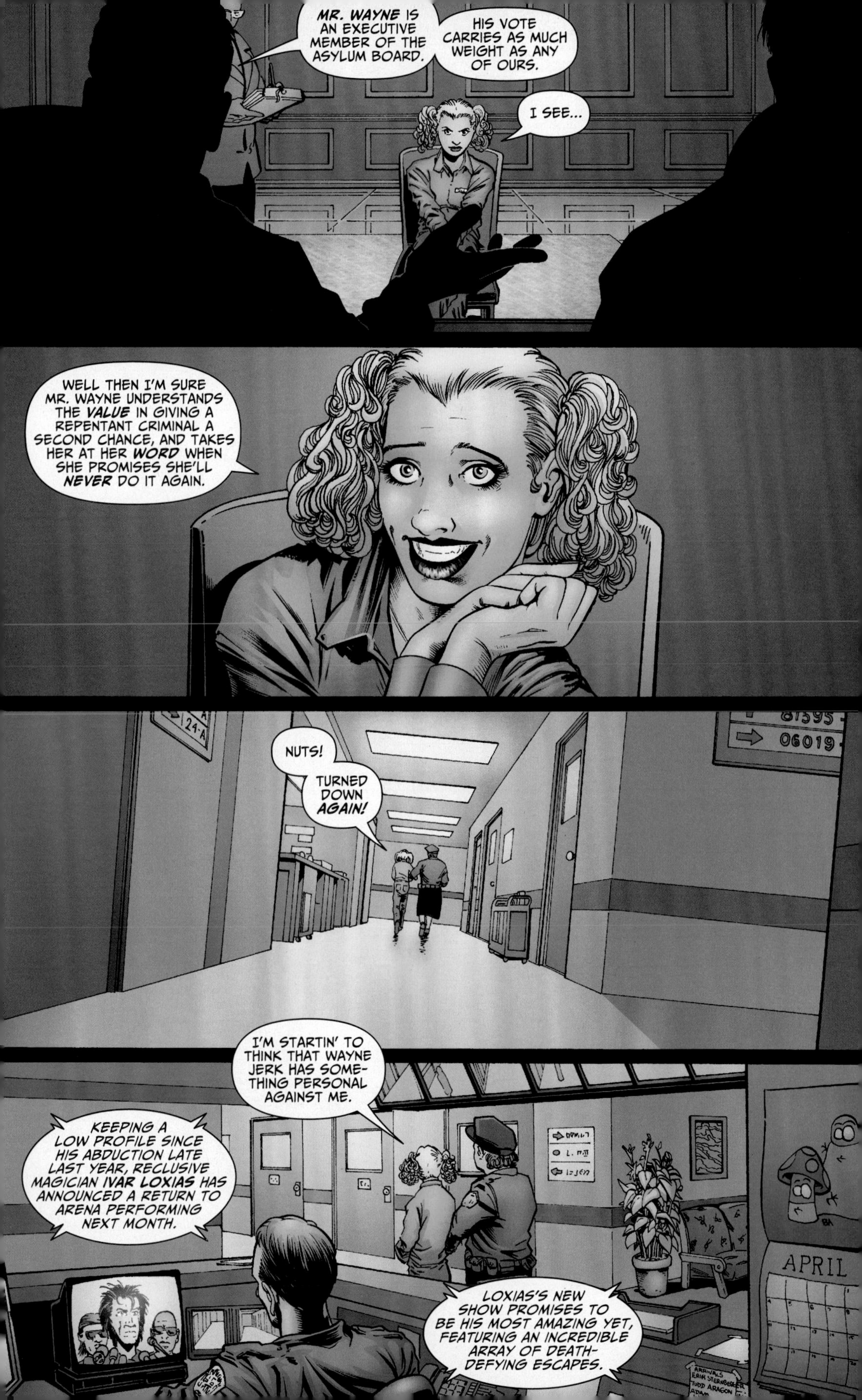

MR. WAYNE IS AN EXECUTIVE MEMBER OF THE ASYLUM BOARD.
HIS VOTE CARRIES AS MUCH WEIGHT AS ANY OF OURS.
I SEE...
WELL THEN I'M SURE MR. WAYNE UNDERSTANDS THE VALUE IN GIVING A REPENTANT CRIMINAL A SECOND CHANCE, AND TAKES HER AT HER WORD WHEN SHE PROMISES SHE'LL NEVER DO IT AGAIN.
NUTS!
TURNED DOWN AGAIN!
I'M STARTIN' TO THINK THAT WAYNE JERK HAS SOME-THING PERSONAL AGAINST ME.
KEEPING A LOW PROFILE SINCE HIS ABDUCTION LATE LAST YEAR, RECLUSIVE MAGICIAN IVAR LOXIAS HAS ANNOUNCED A RETURN TO ARENA PERFORMING NEXT MONTH.
LOXIAS'S NEW SHOW PROMISES TO BE HIS MOST AMAZING YET, FEATURING AN INCREDIBLE ARRAY OF DEATH-DEFYING ESCAPES.
APRIL

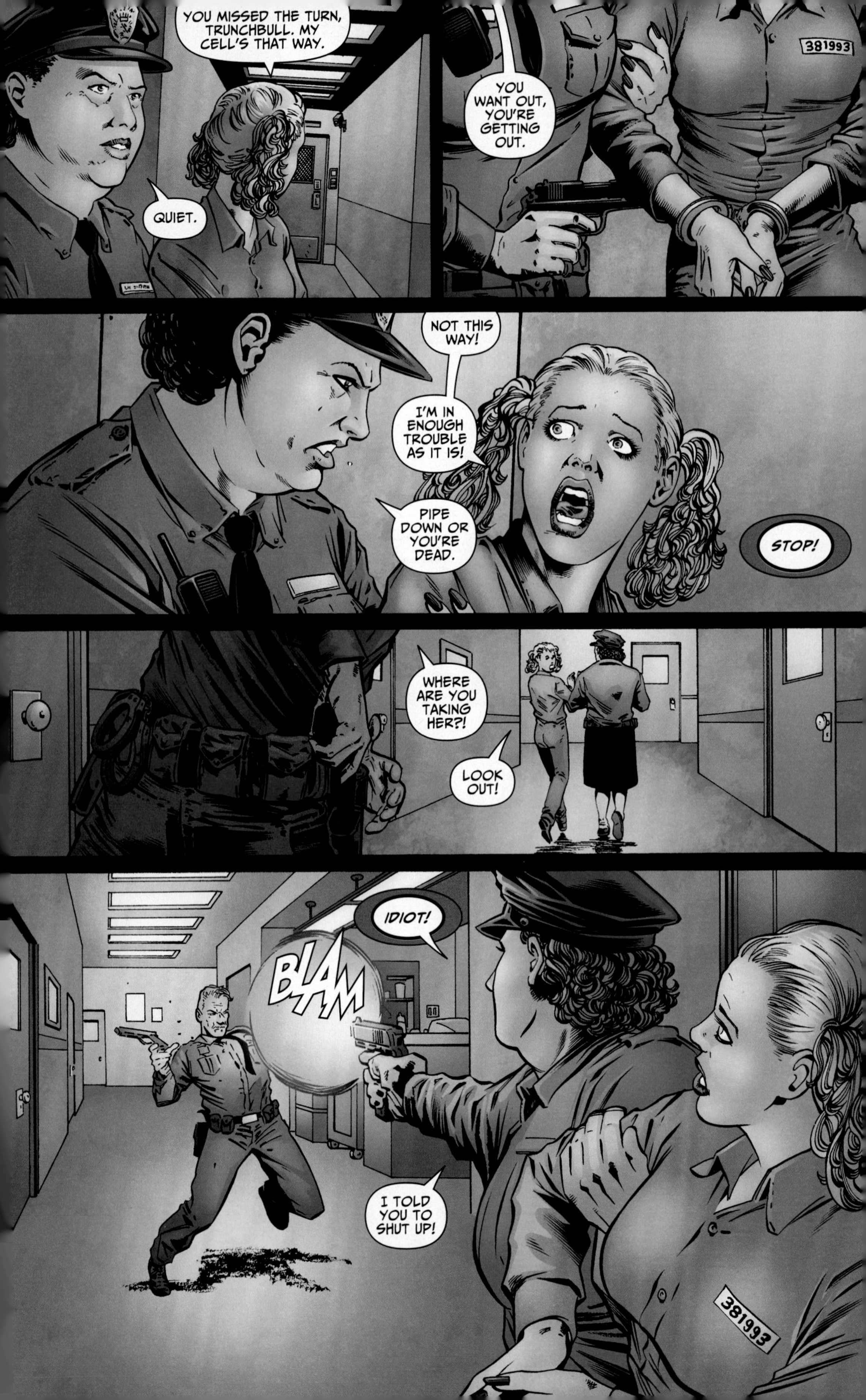
YOU MISSED THE TURN, TRUNCHBULL. MY CELL'S THAT WAY.
QUIET.
381993
YOU WANT OUT, YOU'RE GETTING OUT.
NOT THIS WAY!
I'M IN ENOUGH TROUBLE AS IT IS!
PIPE DOWN OR YOU'RE DEAD.
STOP!
WHERE ARE YOU TAKING HER?!
LOOK OUT!
IDIOT!
BLAM
I TOLD YOU TO SHUT UP!
381993

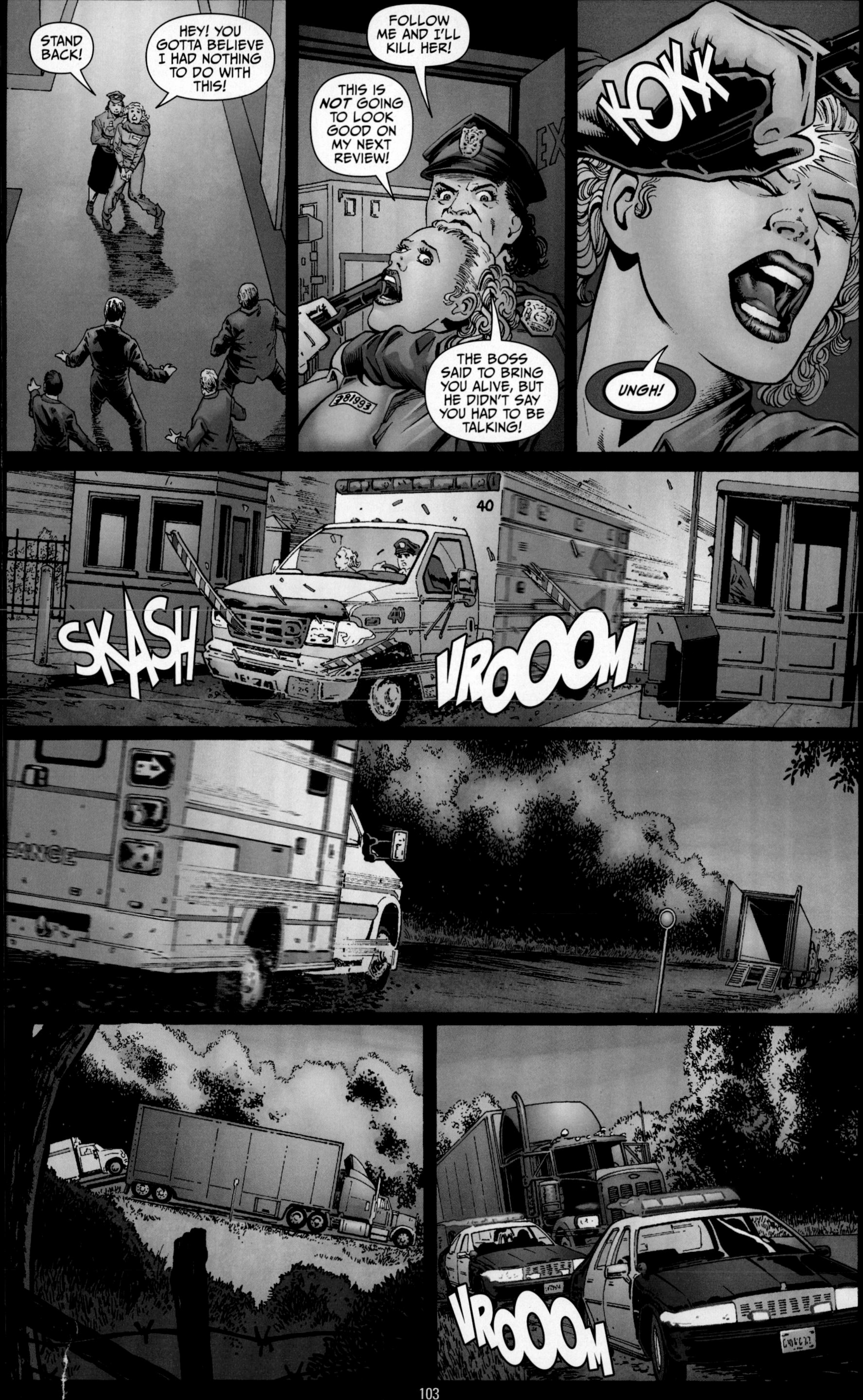
STAND BACK!
HEY! YOU GOTTA BELIEVE I HAD NOTHING TO DO WITH THIS!
FOLLOW ME AND I'LL KILL HER!
THIS IS NOT GOING TO LOOK GOOD ON MY NEXT REVIEW!
THE BOSS SAID TO BRING YOU ALIVE, BUT HE DIDN'T SAY YOU HAD TO BE TALKING!
KOKK
UNGH!
SKASH
VROOOM
VROOOM

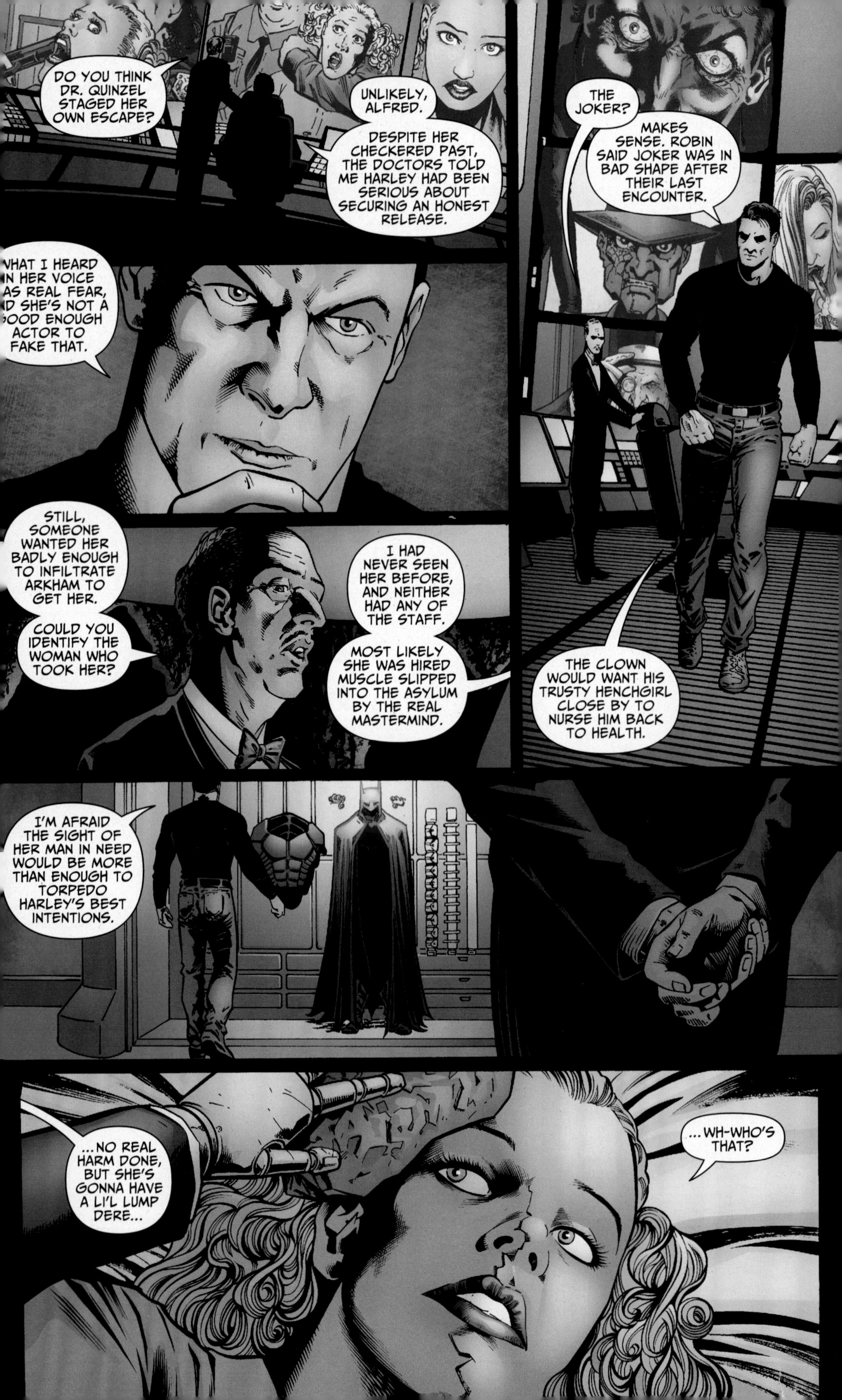
DO YOU THINK DR. QUINZEL STAGED HER OWN ESCAPE?
UNLIKELY, ALFRED.
DESPITE HER CHECKERED PAST, THE DOCTORS TOLD ME HARLEY HAD BEEN SERIOUS ABOUT SECURING AN HONEST RELEASE.
WHAT I HEARD IN HER VOICE WAS REAL FEAR, AND SHE'S NOT A GOOD ENOUGH ACTOR TO FAKE THAT.
STILL, SOMEONE WANTED HER BADLY ENOUGH TO INFILTRATE ARKHAM TO GET HER.
COULD YOU IDENTIFY THE WOMAN WHO TOOK HER?
I HAD NEVER SEEN HER BEFORE, AND NEITHER HAD ANY OF THE STAFF.
MOST LIKELY SHE WAS HIRED MUSCLE SLIPPED INTO THE ASYLUM BY THE REAL MASTERMIND.
THE JOKER?
MAKES SENSE. ROBIN SAID JOKER WAS IN BAD SHAPE AFTER THEIR LAST ENCOUNTER.
THE CLOWN WOULD WANT HIS TRUSTY HENCHGIRL CLOSE BY TO NURSE HIM BACK TO HEALTH.
I'M AFRAID THE SIGHT OF HER MAN IN NEED WOULD BE MORE THAN ENOUGH TO TORPEDO HARLEY'S BEST INTENTIONS.
...NO REAL HARM DONE, BUT SHE'S GONNA HAVE A LI'L LUMP DERE...
...WH-WHO'S THAT?

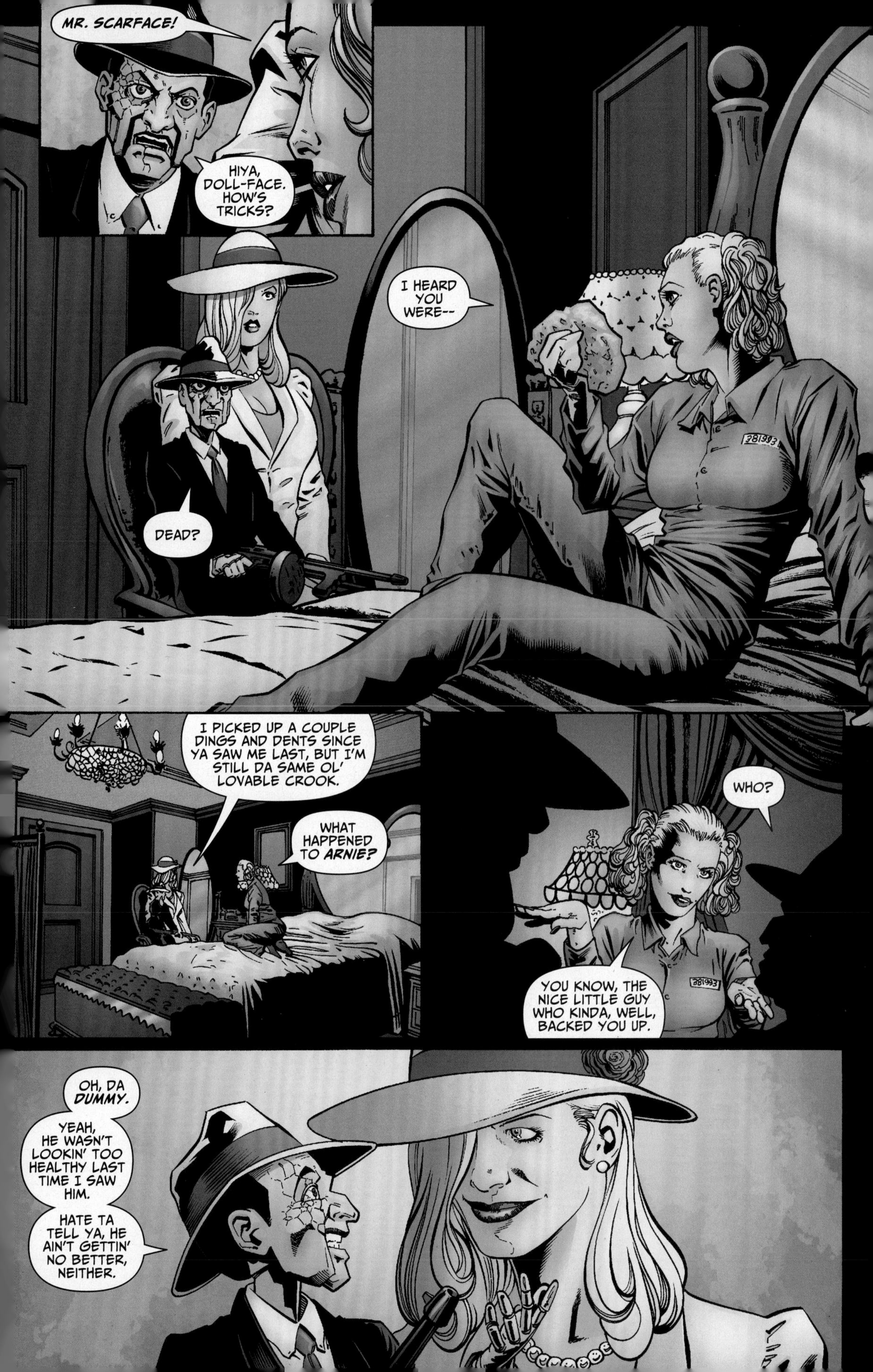
MR. SCARFACE!
HIYA, DOLL-FACE. HOW'S TRICKS?
I HEARD YOU WERE--
DEAD?
I PICKED UP A COUPLE DINGS AND DENTS SINCE YA SAW ME LAST, BUT I'M STILL DA SAME OL' LOVABLE CROOK.
WHAT HAPPENED TO *ARNIE?*
WHO?
YOU KNOW, THE NICE LITTLE GUY WHO KINDA, WELL, BACKED YOU UP.
OH, DA *DUMMY.*
YEAH, HE WASN'T LOOKIN' TOO HEALTHY LAST TIME I SAW HIM.
HATE TA TELL YA, HE AIN'T GETTIN' NO BETTER, NEITHER.

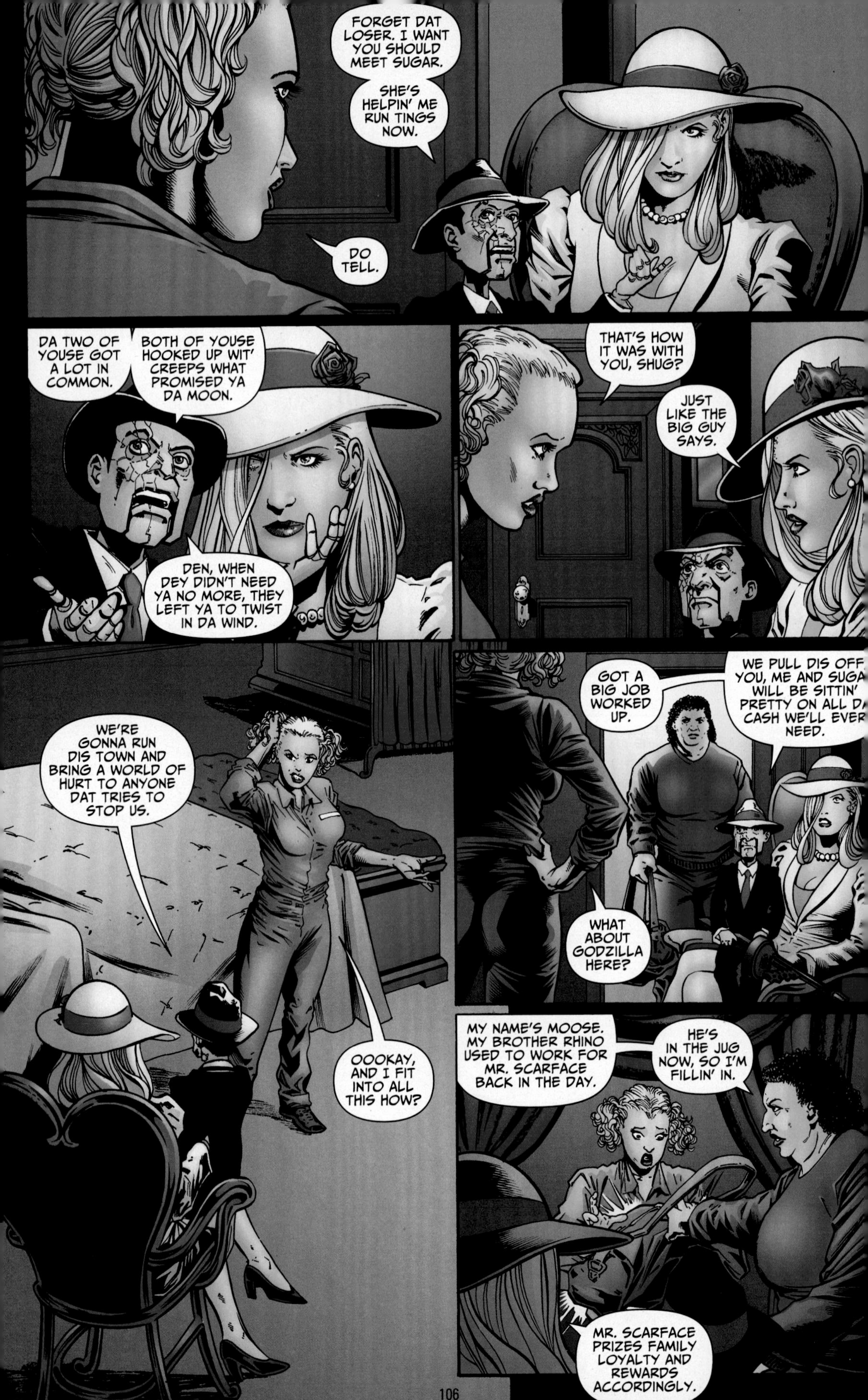
FORGET DAT LOSER. I WANT YOU SHOULD MEET SUGAR.
SHE'S HELPIN' ME RUN TINGS NOW.
DO TELL.
DA TWO OF YOUSE GOT A LOT IN COMMON.
BOTH OF YOUSE HOOKED UP WIT' CREEPS WHAT PROMISED YA DA MOON.
DEN, WHEN DEY DIDN'T NEED YA NO MORE, THEY LEFT YA TO TWIST IN DA WIND.
THAT'S HOW IT WAS WITH YOU, SHUG?
JUST LIKE THE BIG GUY SAYS.
WE'RE GONNA RUN DIS TOWN AND BRING A WORLD OF HURT TO ANYONE DAT TRIES TO STOP US.
OOOKAY, AND I FIT INTO ALL THIS HOW?
GOT A BIG JOB WORKED UP.
WE PULL DIS OFF YOU, ME AND SUGA WILL BE SITTIN' PRETTY ON ALL D CASH WE'LL EVER NEED.
WHAT ABOUT GODZILLA HERE?
MY NAME'S MOOSE. MY BROTHER RHINO USED TO WORK FOR MR. SCARFACE BACK IN THE DAY.
HE'S IN THE JUG NOW, SO I'M FILLIN' IN.
MR. SCARFACE PRIZES FAMILY LOYALTY AND REWARDS ACCORDINGLY.

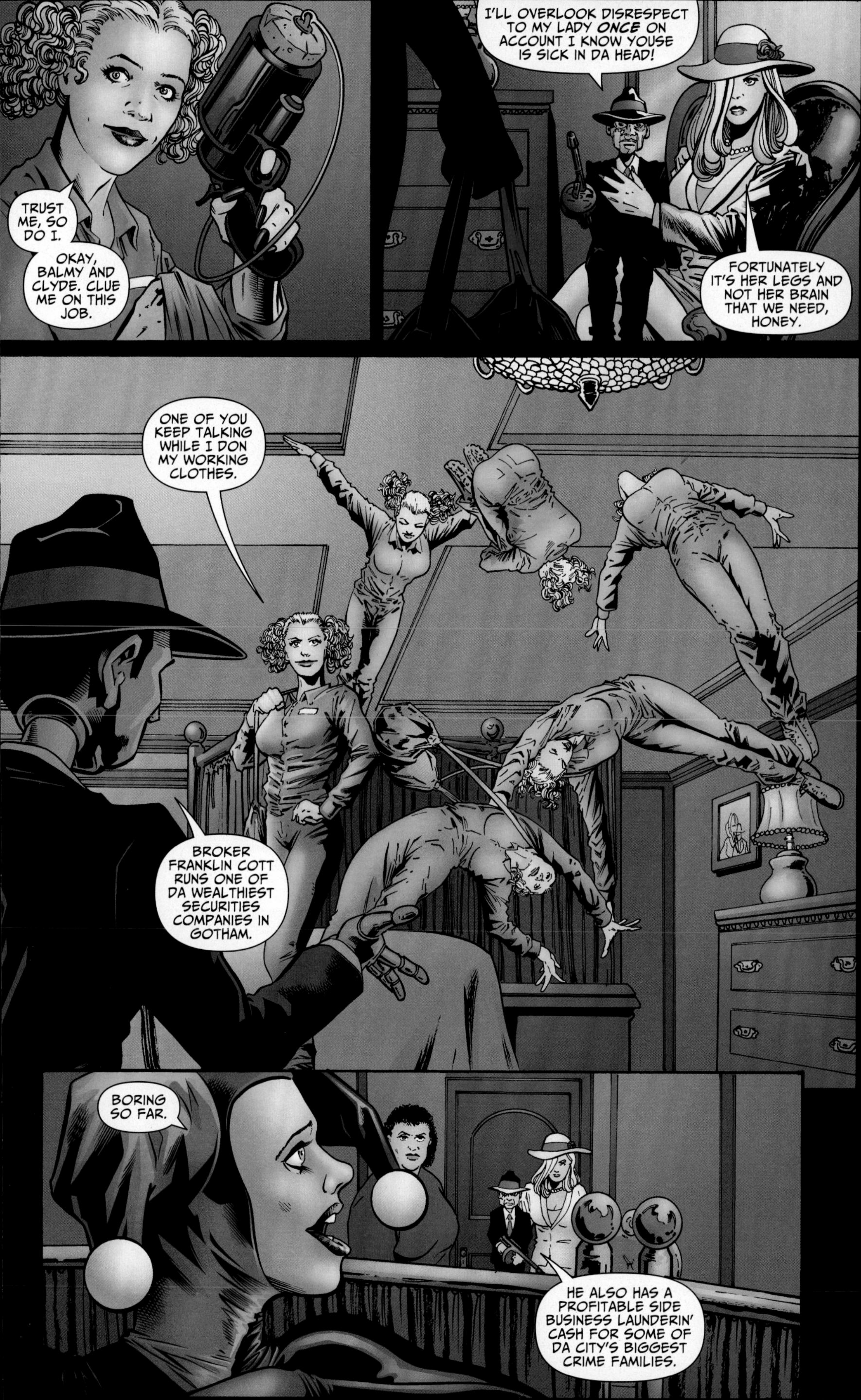
TRUST ME, SO DO I.
OKAY, BALMY AND CLYDE. CLUE ME ON THIS JOB.
I'LL OVERLOOK DISRESPECT TO MY LADY ONCE ON ACCOUNT I KNOW YOUSE IS SICK IN DA HEAD!
FORTUNATELY IT'S HER LEGS AND NOT HER BRAIN THAT WE NEED, HONEY.
ONE OF YOU KEEP TALKING WHILE I DON MY WORKING CLOTHES.
BROKER FRANKLIN COTT RUNS ONE OF DA WEALTHIEST SECURITIES COMPANIES IN GOTHAM.
BORING SO FAR.
HE ALSO HAS A PROFITABLE SIDE BUSINESS LAUNDERIN' CASH FOR SOME OF DA CITY'S BIGGEST CRIME FAMILIES.

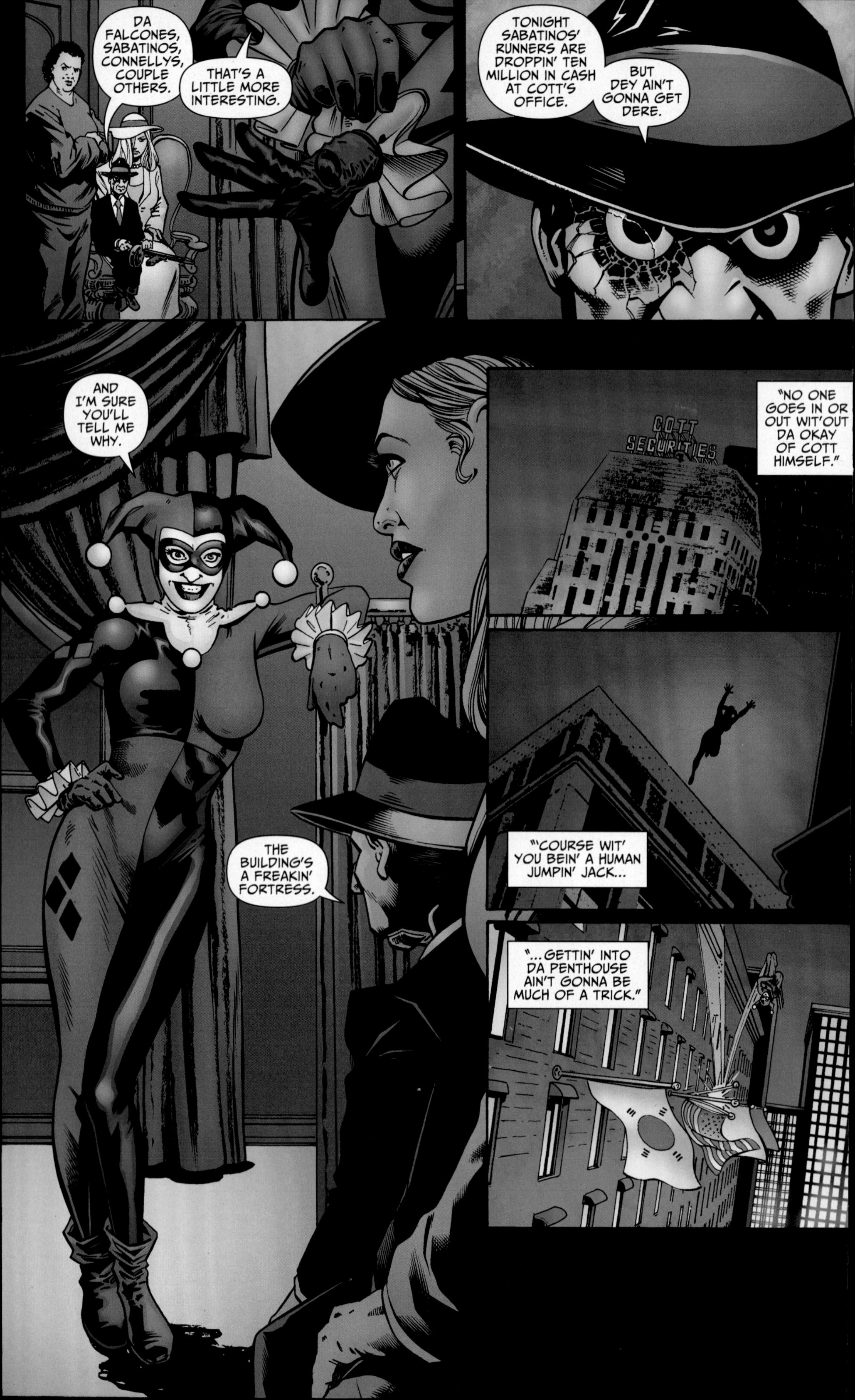
DA FALCONES, SABATINOS, CONNELLYS, COUPLE OTHERS.
THAT'S A LITTLE MORE INTERESTING.
TONIGHT SABATINOS' RUNNERS ARE DROPPIN' TEN MILLION IN CASH AT COTT'S OFFICE.
BUT DEY AIN'T GONNA GET DERE.
AND I'M SURE YOU'LL TELL ME WHY.
THE BUILDING'S A FREAKIN' FORTRESS.
"NO ONE GOES IN OR OUT WIT'OUT DA OKAY OF COTT HIMSELF."
COTT SECURITIES
"'COURSE WIT' YOU BEIN' A HUMAN JUMPIN' JACK...
"...GETTIN' INTO DA PENTHOUSE AIN'T GONNA BE MUCH OF A TRICK."

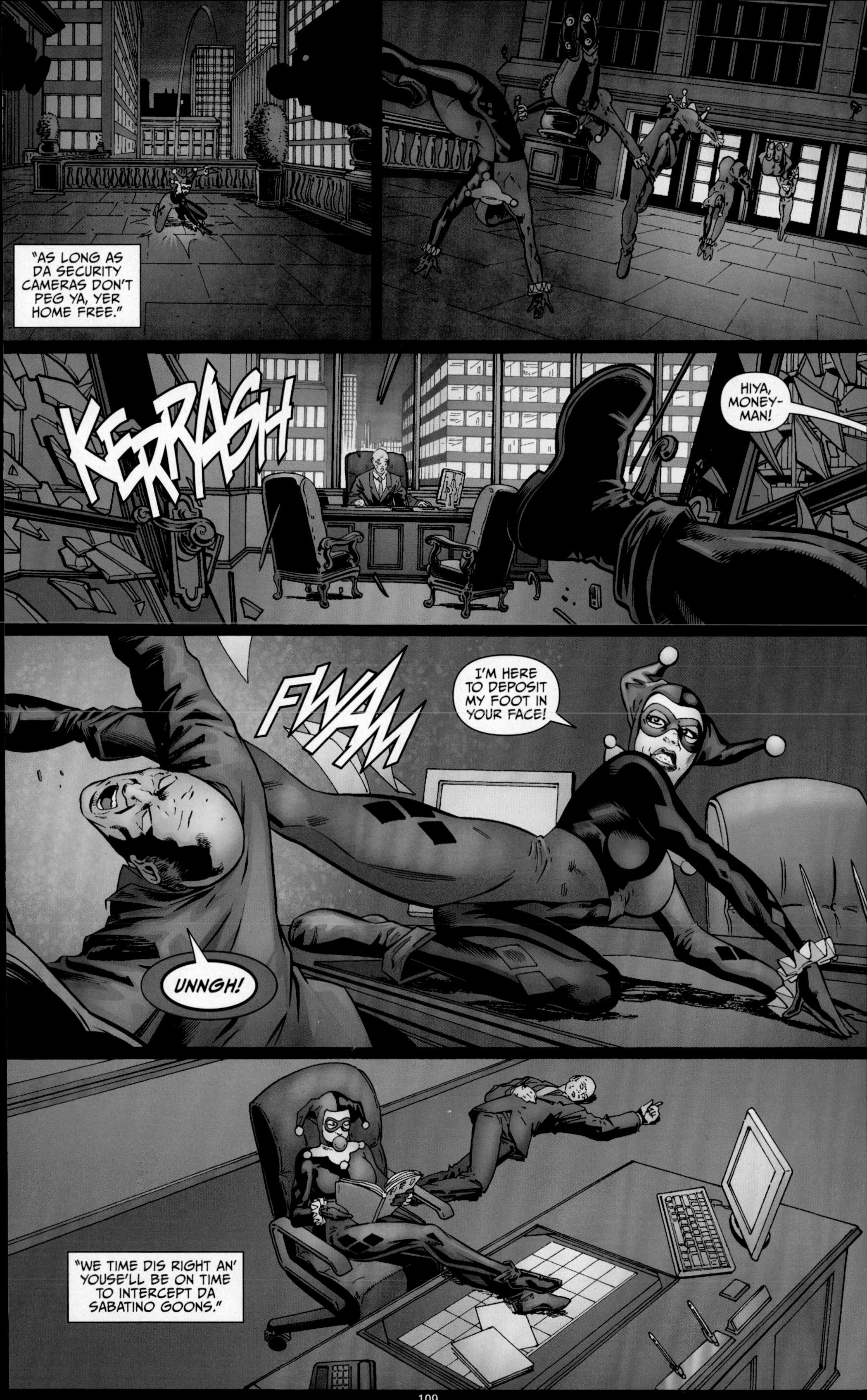
"AS LONG AS DA SECURITY CAMERAS DON'T PEG YA, YER HOME FREE."
KERASH
HIYA, MONEY-MAN!
FWAM
I'M HERE TO DEPOSIT MY FOOT IN YOUR FACE!
UNNGH!
"WE TIME DIS RIGHT AN' YOUSE'LL BE ON TIME TO INTERCEPT DA SABATINO GOONS."

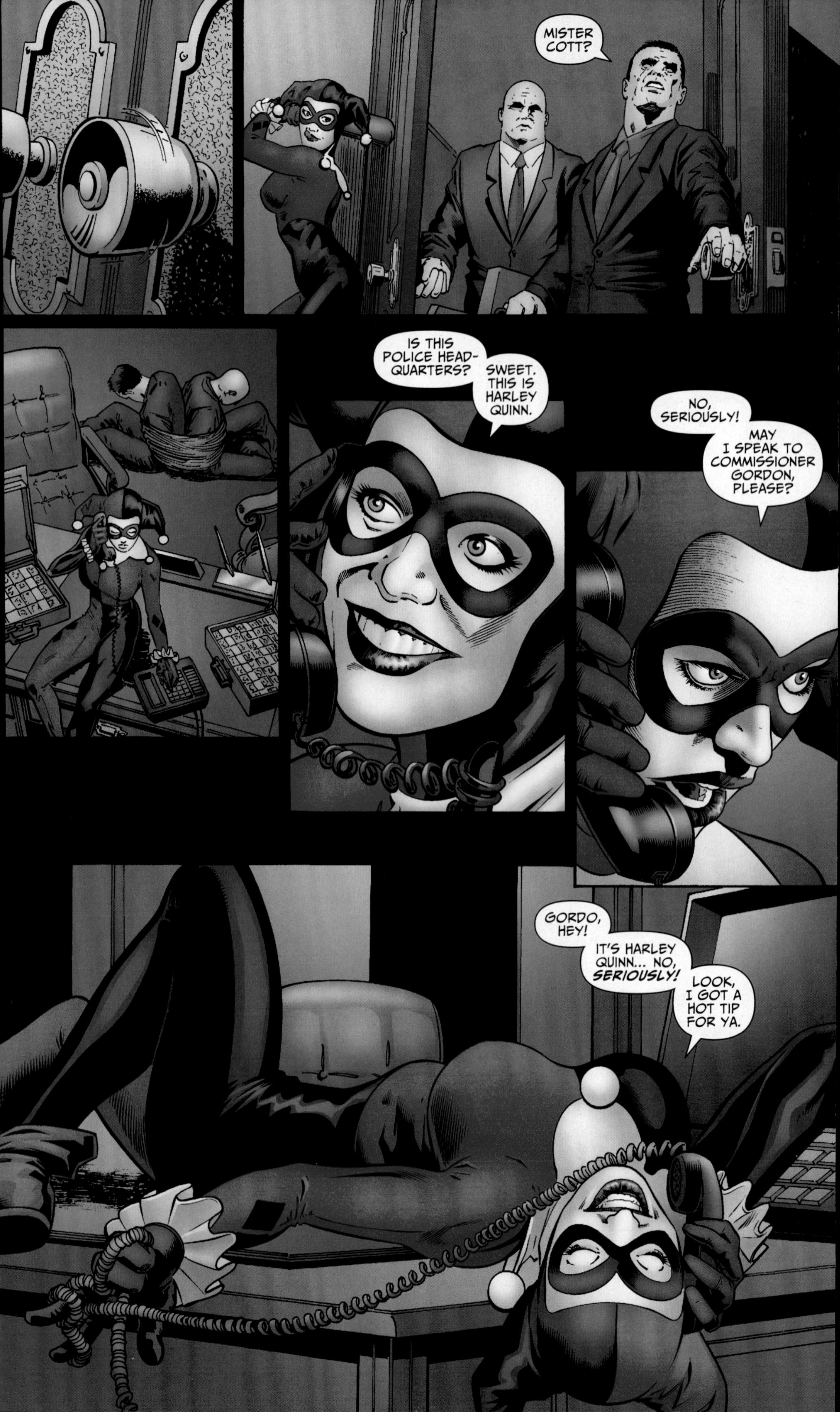
MISTER COTT?
IS THIS POLICE HEAD-QUARTERS?
SWEET. THIS IS HARLEY QUINN.
NO, SERIOUSLY!
MAY I SPEAK TO COMMISSIONER GORDON, PLEASE?
GORDO, HEY!
IT'S HARLEY QUINN... NO, *SERIOUSLY!*
LOOK, I GOT A HOT TIP FOR YA.

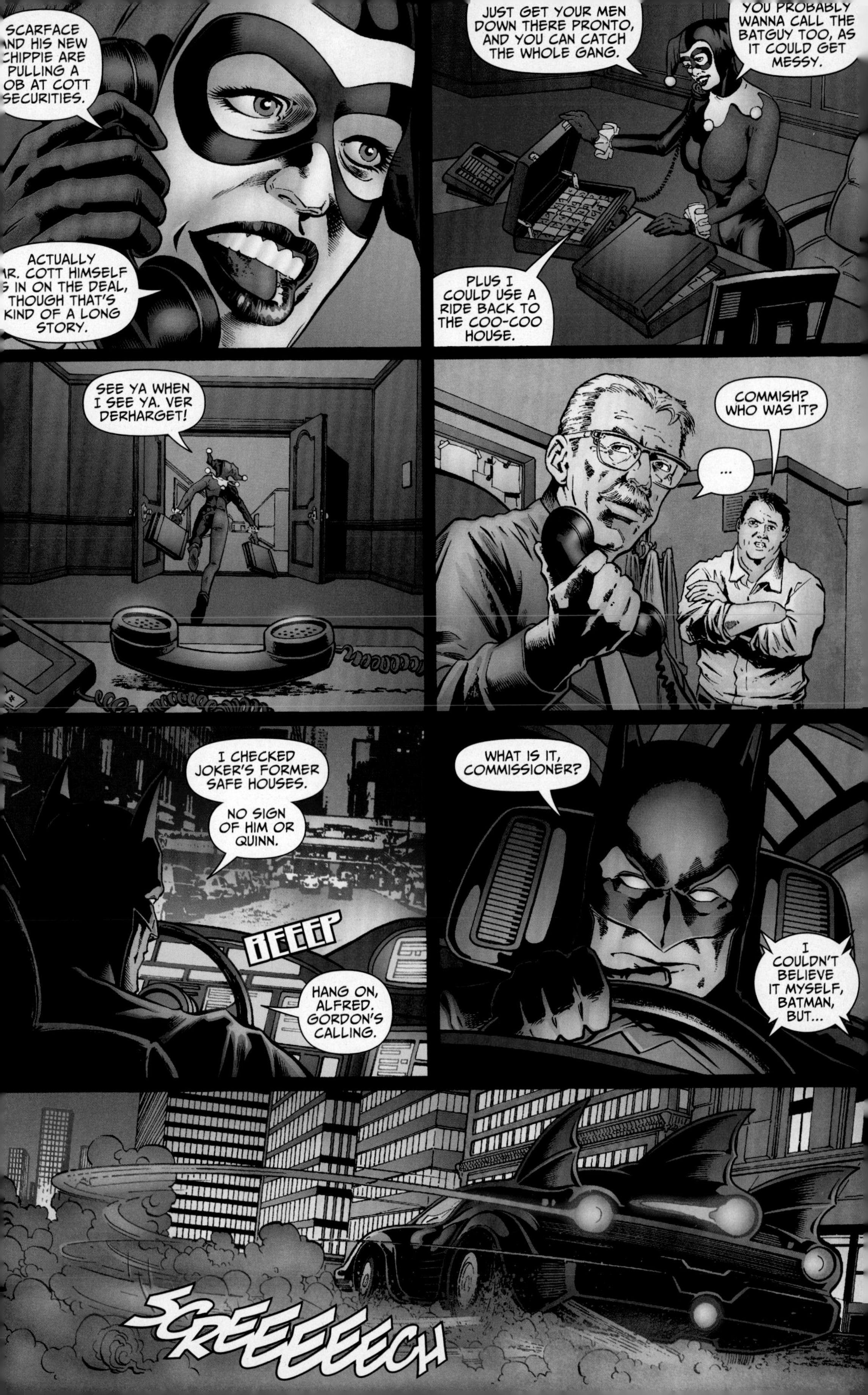
SCARFACE AND HIS NEW CHIPPIE ARE PULLING A JOB AT COTT SECURITIES.
ACTUALLY MR. COTT HIMSELF IS IN ON THE DEAL, THOUGH THAT'S KIND OF A LONG STORY.
JUST GET YOUR MEN DOWN THERE PRONTO, AND YOU CAN CATCH THE WHOLE GANG.
YOU PROBABLY WANNA CALL THE BATGUY TOO, AS IT COULD GET MESSY.
PLUS I COULD USE A RIDE BACK TO THE COO-COO HOUSE.
SEE YA WHEN I SEE YA. VER DERHARGET!
...
COMMISH? WHO WAS IT?
I CHECKED JOKER'S FORMER SAFE HOUSES.
NO SIGN OF HIM OR QUINN.
BEEEP
HANG ON, ALFRED. GORDON'S CALLING.
WHAT IS IT, COMMISSIONER?
I COULDN'T BELIEVE IT MYSELF, BATMAN, BUT...
SCREEEEECH

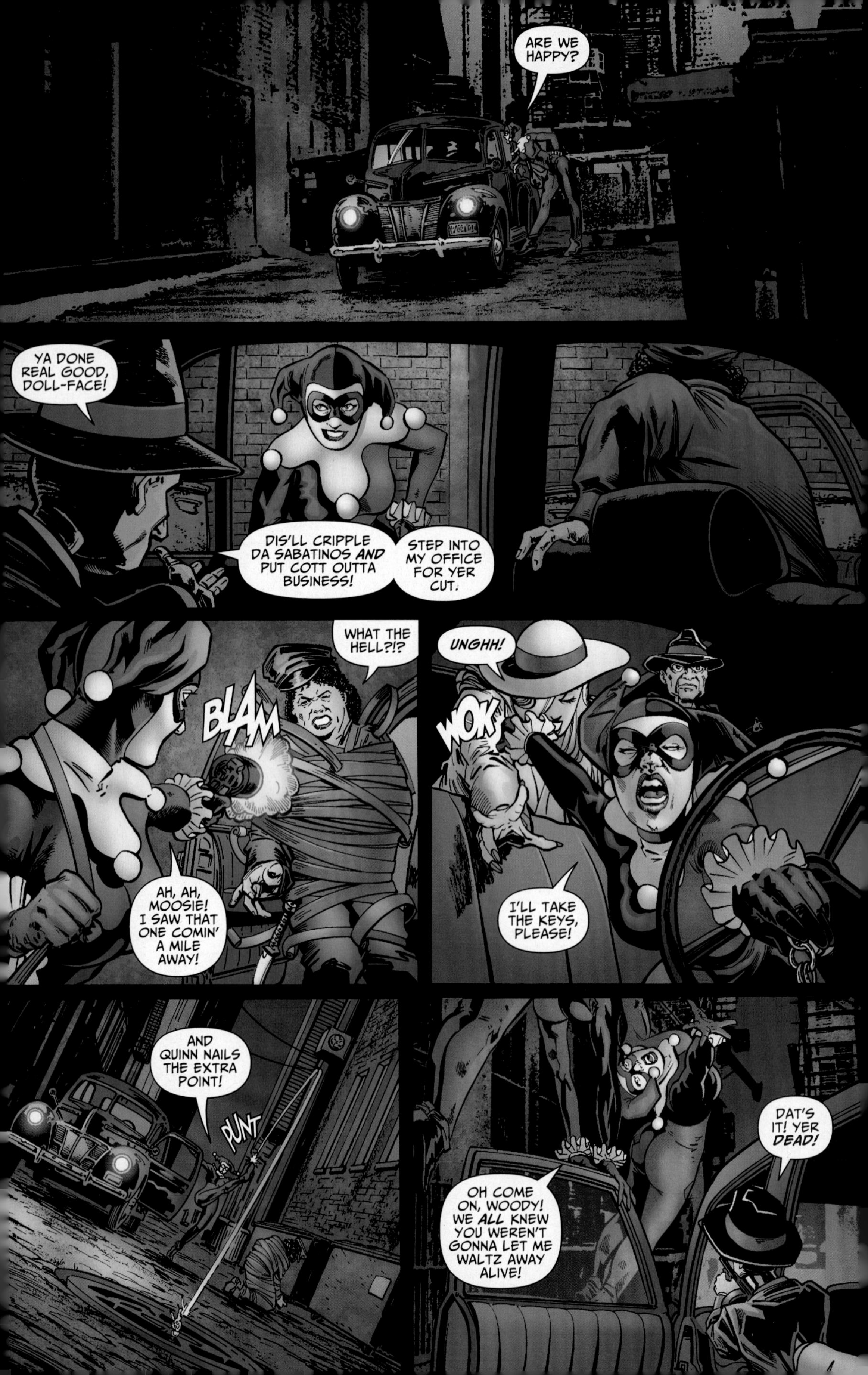

ARE WE HAPPY?
YA DONE REAL GOOD, DOLL-FACE!
DIS'LL CRIPPLE DA SABATINOS *AND* PUT COTT OUTTA BUSINESS!
STEP INTO MY OFFICE FOR YER CUT.
WHAT THE HELL?!?
BLAM
AH, AH, MOOSIE! I SAW THAT ONE COMIN' A MILE AWAY!
UNGHH!
WOK
I'LL TAKE THE KEYS, PLEASE!
AND QUINN NAILS THE EXTRA POINT!
PUNT
DAT'S IT! YER *DEAD!*
OH COME ON, WOODY! WE *ALL* KNEW YOU WEREN'T GONNA LET ME WALTZ AWAY ALIVE!

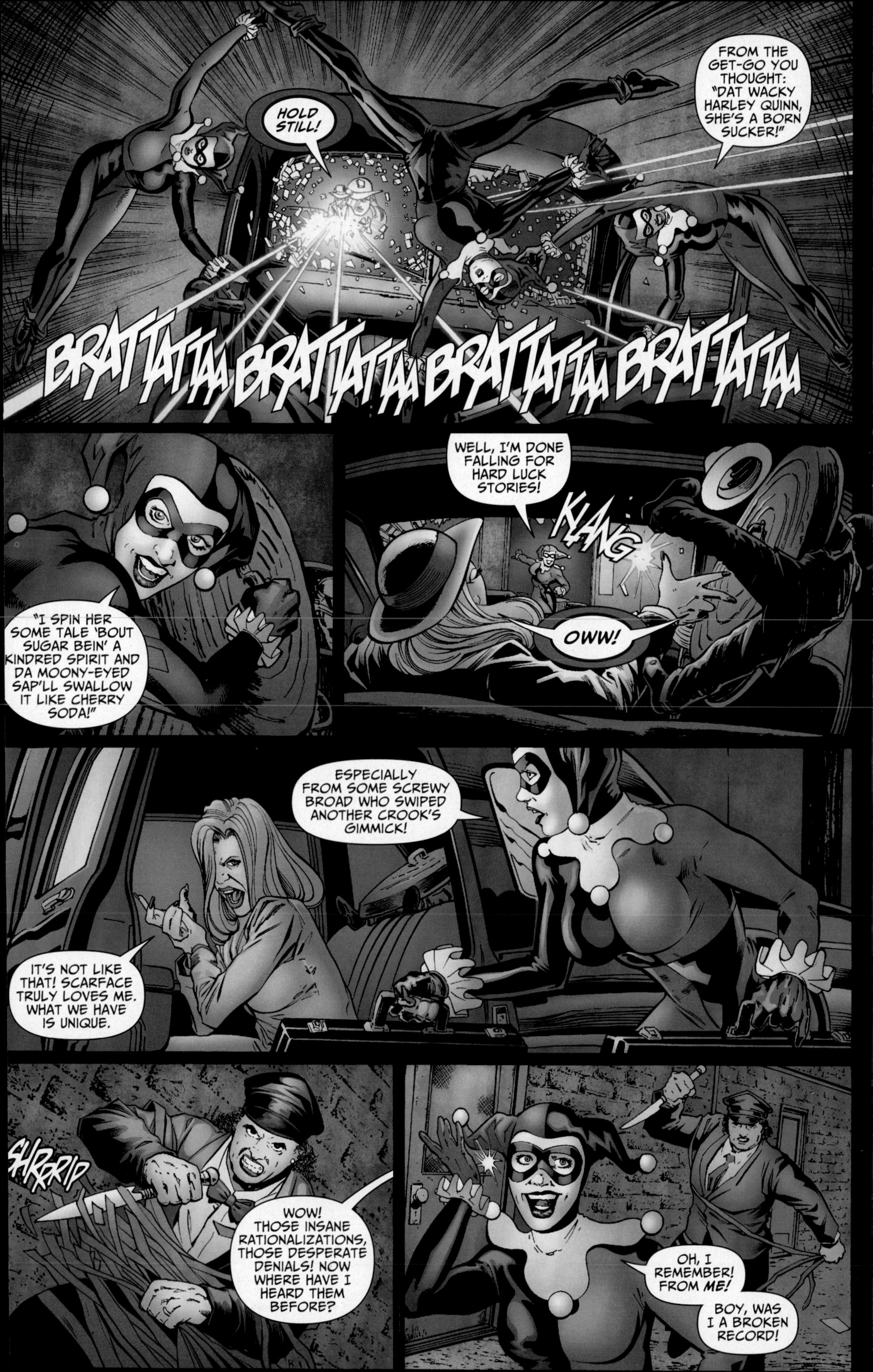
HOLD STILL!
FROM THE GET-GO YOU THOUGHT: "DAT WACKY HARLEY QUINN, SHE'S A BORN SUCKER!"
BRATTATTAA BRATTATTAA BRATTATTAA BRATTATTAA
"I SPIN HER SOME TALE 'BOUT SUGAR BEIN' A KINDRED SPIRIT AND DA MOONY-EYED SAP'LL SWALLOW IT LIKE CHERRY SODA!"
WELL, I'M DONE FALLING FOR HARD LUCK STORIES!
KLANG
OWW!
ESPECIALLY FROM SOME SCREWY BROAD WHO SWIPED ANOTHER CROOK'S GIMMICK!
IT'S NOT LIKE THAT! SCARFACE TRULY LOVES ME. WHAT WE HAVE IS UNIQUE.
SHRRRIP
WOW! THOSE INSANE RATIONALIZATIONS, THOSE DESPERATE DENIALS! NOW WHERE HAVE I HEARD THEM BEFORE?
OH, I REMEMBER! FROM *ME!*
BOY, WAS I A BROKEN RECORD!

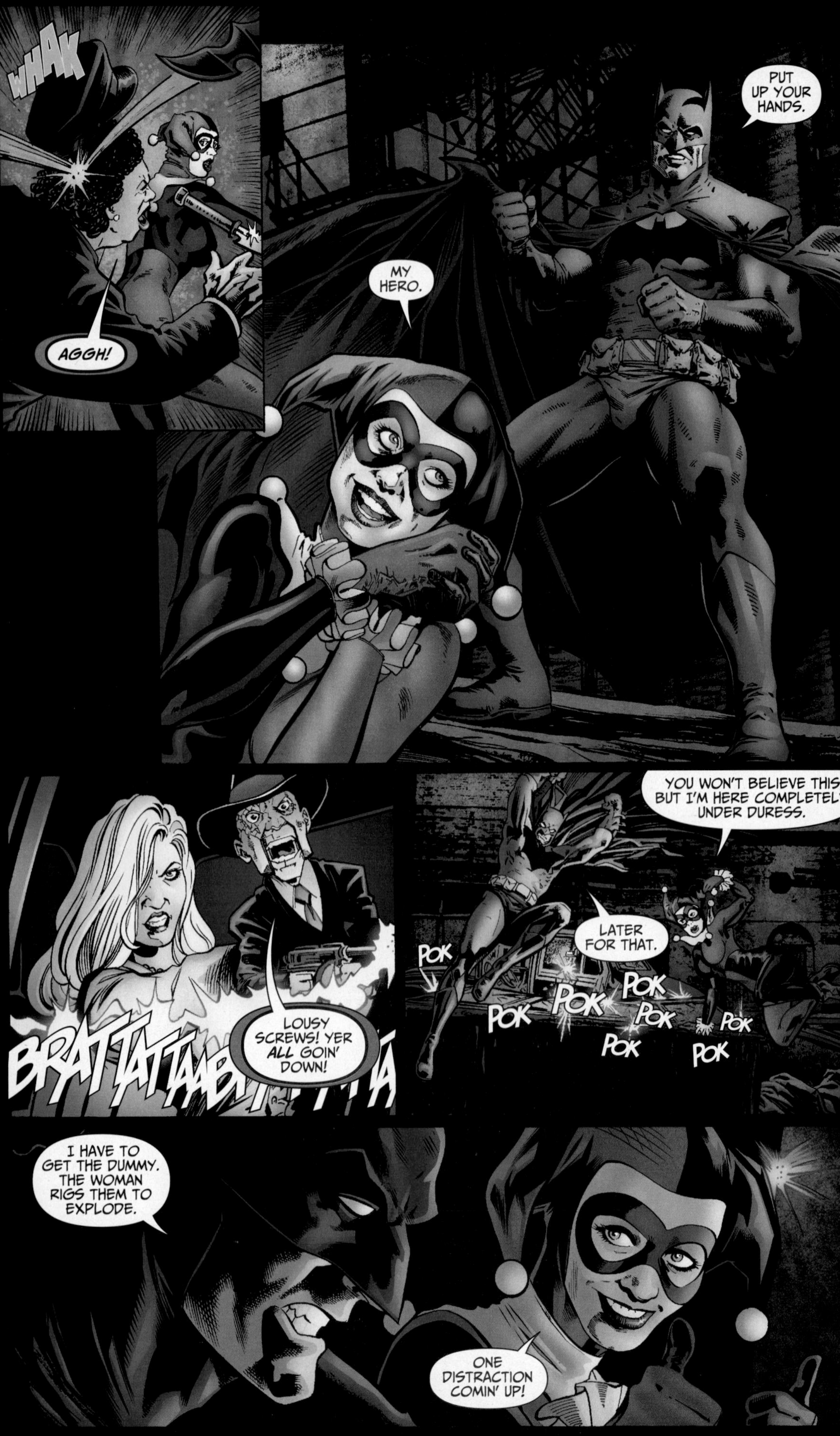
WHAK
AGGH!
PUT UP YOUR HANDS.
MY HERO.
BRATTATTAAB
LOUSY SCREWS! YER ALL GOIN' DOWN!
YOU WON'T BELIEVE THIS, BUT I'M HERE COMPLETELY UNDER DURESS.
LATER FOR THAT.
POK
POK
POK
POK
POK
POK
POK
POK
I HAVE TO GET THE DUMMY. THE WOMAN RIGS THEM TO EXPLODE.
ONE DISTRACTION COMIN' UP!

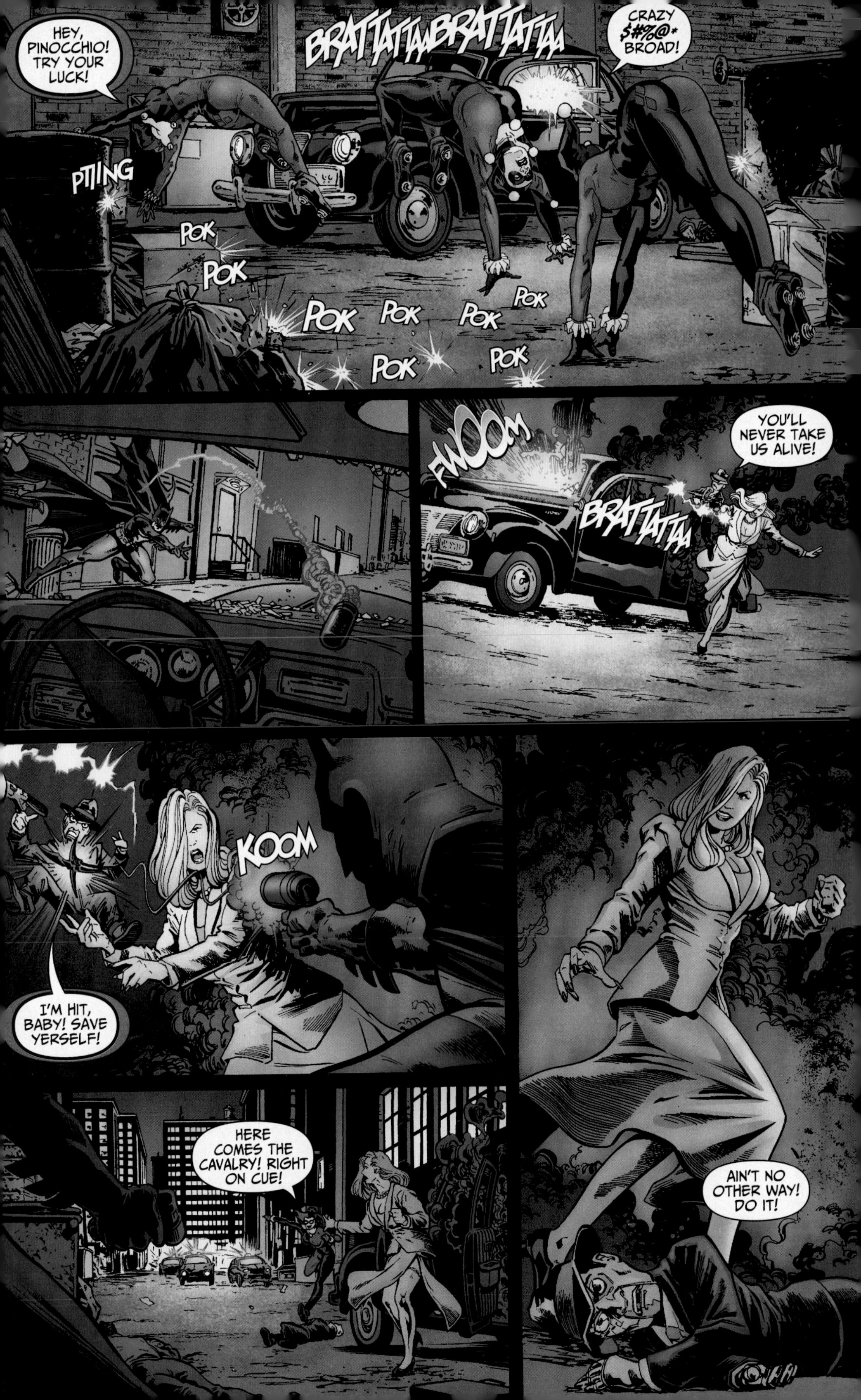
HEY, PINOCCHIO! TRY YOUR LUCK!
BRATTATTAABRATTATTAA
CRAZY $#%@* BROAD!
PTIING
POK
POK
POK
POK
POK
POK
POK
POK
POK
FWOOM
YOU'LL NEVER TAKE US ALIVE!
BRATTATTAA
KOOM
I'M HIT, BABY! SAVE YERSELF!
HERE COMES THE CAVALRY! RIGHT ON CUE!
AIN'T NO OTHER WAY! DO IT!

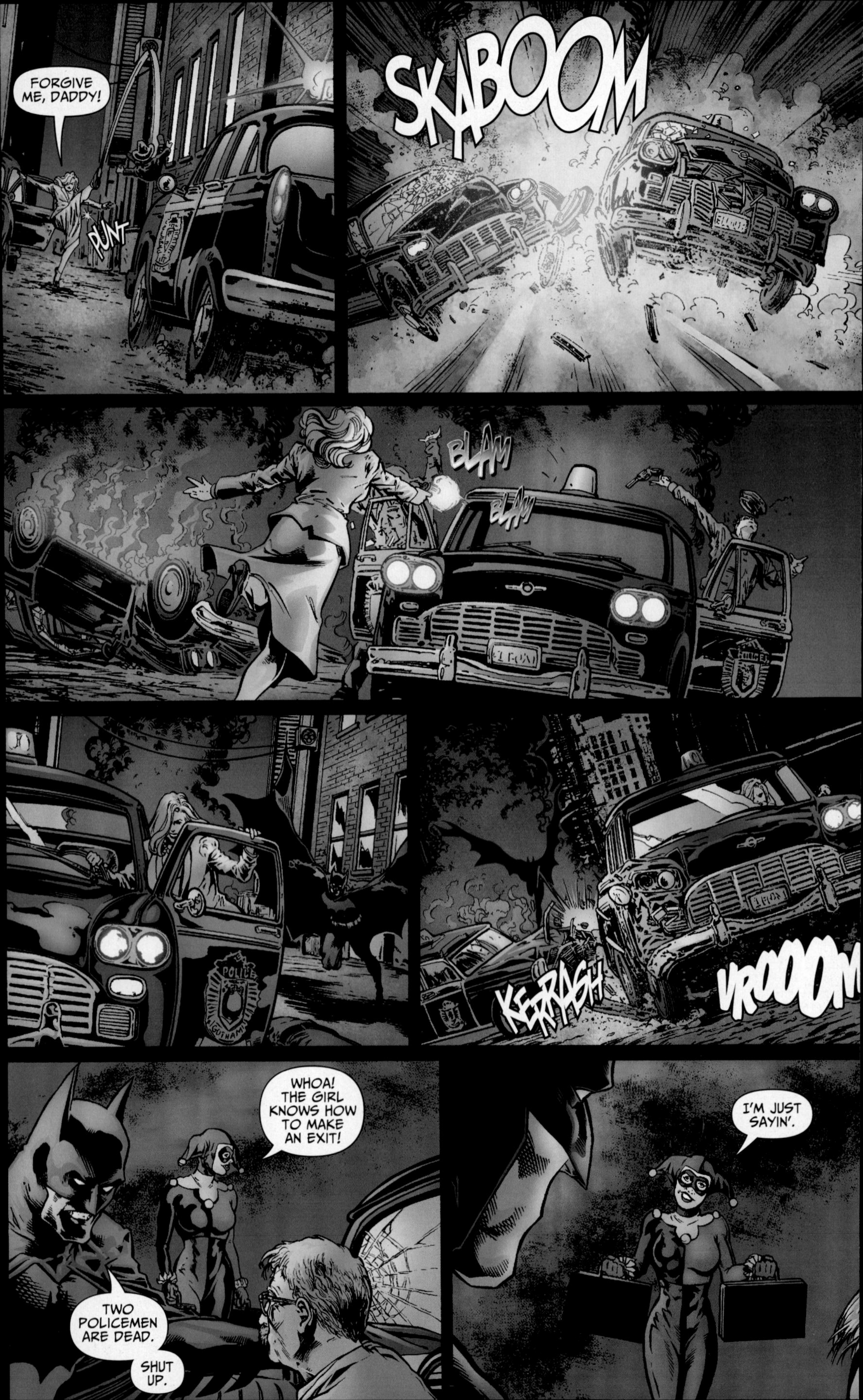
FORGIVE ME, DADDY!
PUNT
SKABOOM
BLAM
BLAM
KERASH
VROOOM
WHOA! THE GIRL KNOWS HOW TO MAKE AN EXIT!
TWO POLICEMEN ARE DEAD.
SHUT UP.
I'M JUST SAYIN'.

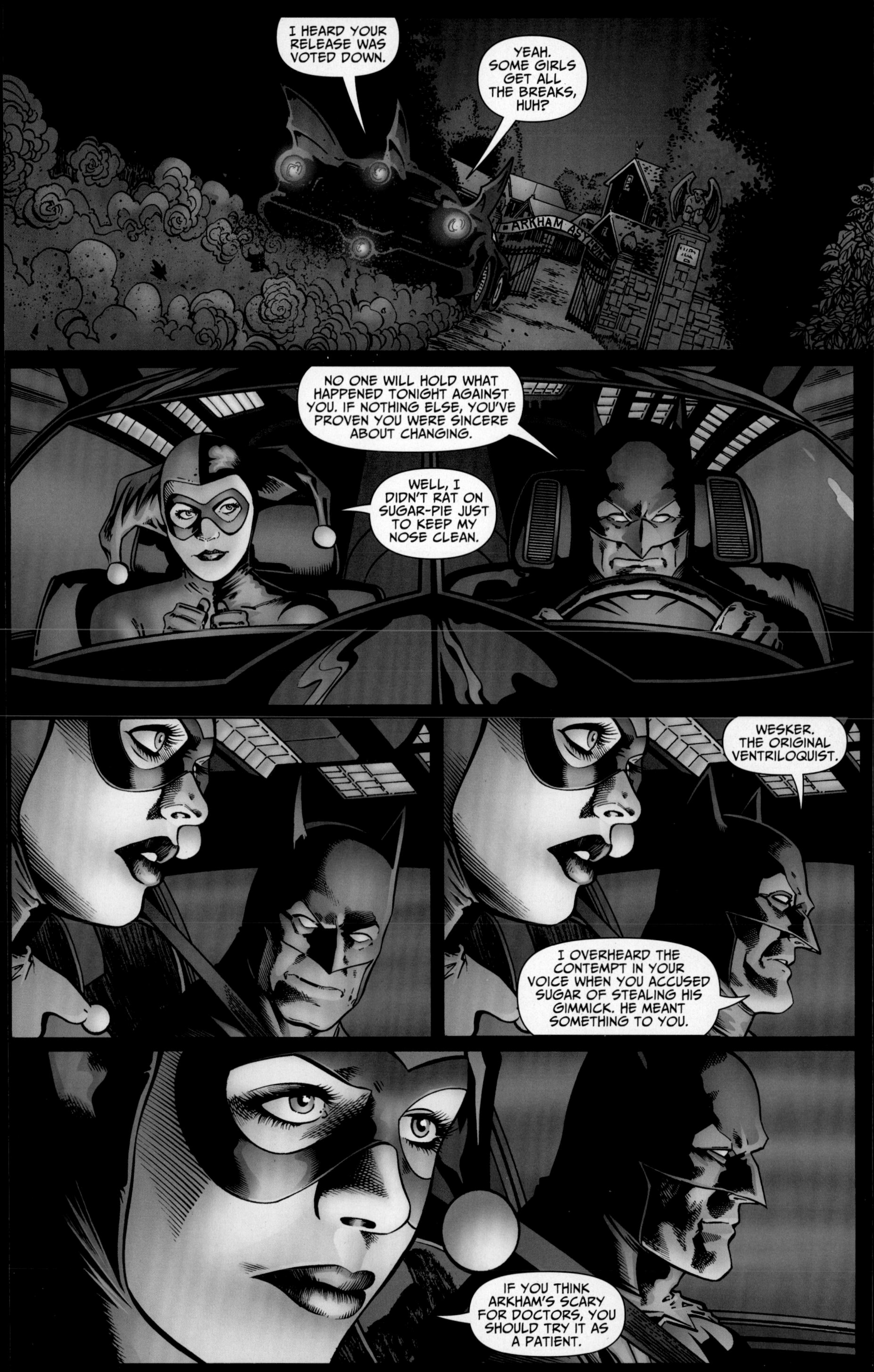
I HEARD YOUR RELEASE WAS VOTED DOWN.
YEAH. SOME GIRLS GET ALL THE BREAKS, HUH?
ARKHAM ASYLUM
NO ONE WILL HOLD WHAT HAPPENED TONIGHT AGAINST YOU. IF NOTHING ELSE, YOU'VE PROVEN YOU WERE SINCERE ABOUT CHANGING.
WELL, I DIDN'T RAT ON SUGAR-PIE JUST TO KEEP MY NOSE CLEAN.
WESKER. THE ORIGINAL VENTRILOQUIST.
I OVERHEARD THE CONTEMPT IN YOUR VOICE WHEN YOU ACCUSED SUGAR OF STEALING HIS GIMMICK. HE MEANT SOMETHING TO YOU.
IF YOU THINK ARKHAM'S SCARY FOR DOCTORS, YOU SHOULD TRY IT AS A PATIENT.

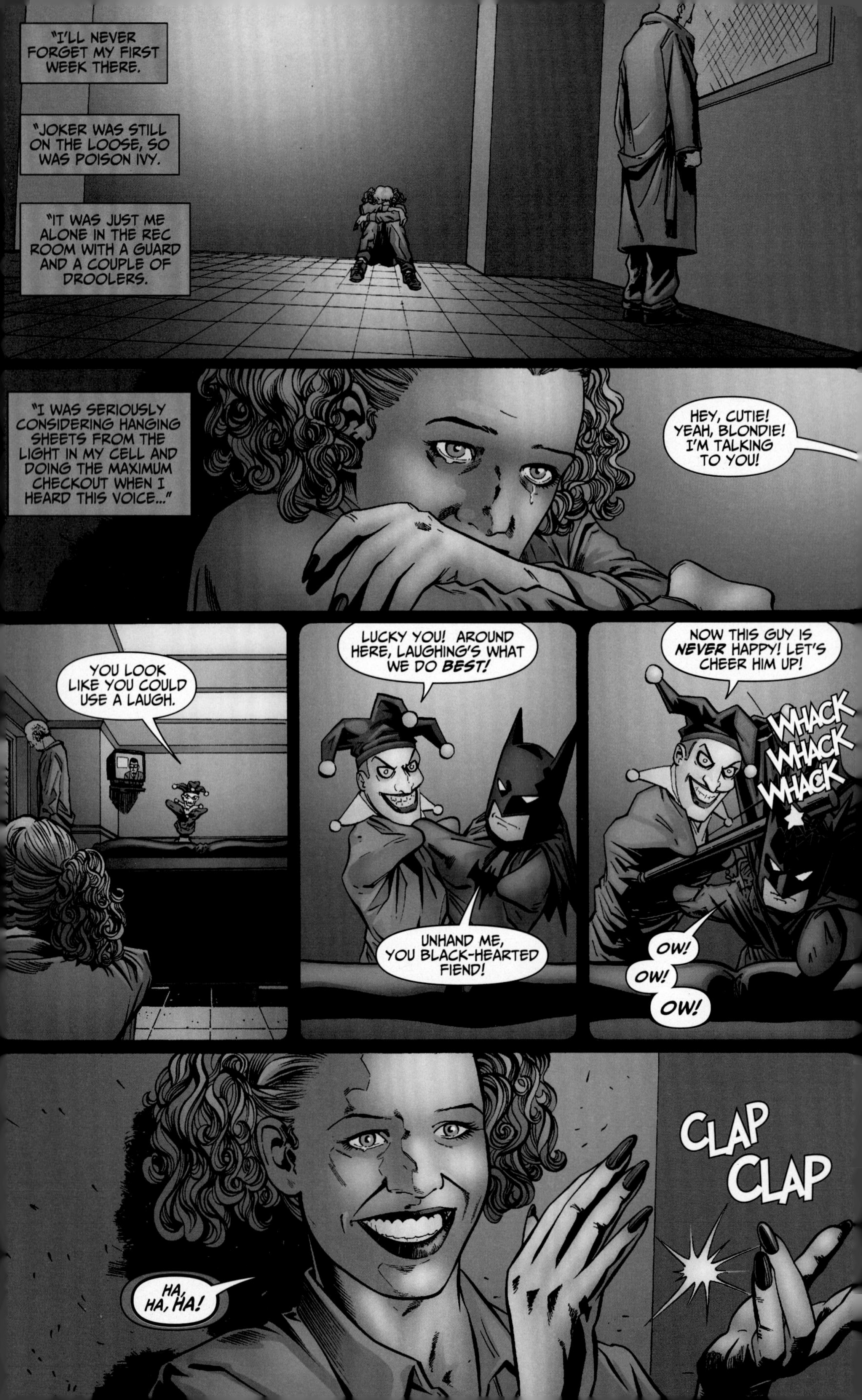
"I'LL NEVER FORGET MY FIRST WEEK THERE.
"JOKER WAS STILL ON THE LOOSE, SO WAS POISON IVY.
"IT WAS JUST ME ALONE IN THE REC ROOM WITH A GUARD AND A COUPLE OF DROOLERS.
"I WAS SERIOUSLY CONSIDERING HANGING SHEETS FROM THE LIGHT IN MY CELL AND DOING THE MAXIMUM CHECKOUT WHEN I HEARD THIS VOICE..."
HEY, CUTIE! YEAH, BLONDIE! I'M TALKING TO YOU!
YOU LOOK LIKE YOU COULD USE A LAUGH.
LUCKY YOU! AROUND HERE, LAUGHING'S WHAT WE DO BEST!
UNHAND ME, YOU BLACK-HEARTED FIEND!
NOW THIS GUY IS NEVER HAPPY! LET'S CHEER HIM UP!
WHACK WHACK WHACK
OW! OW! OW!
CLAP CLAP
HA, HA, HA!

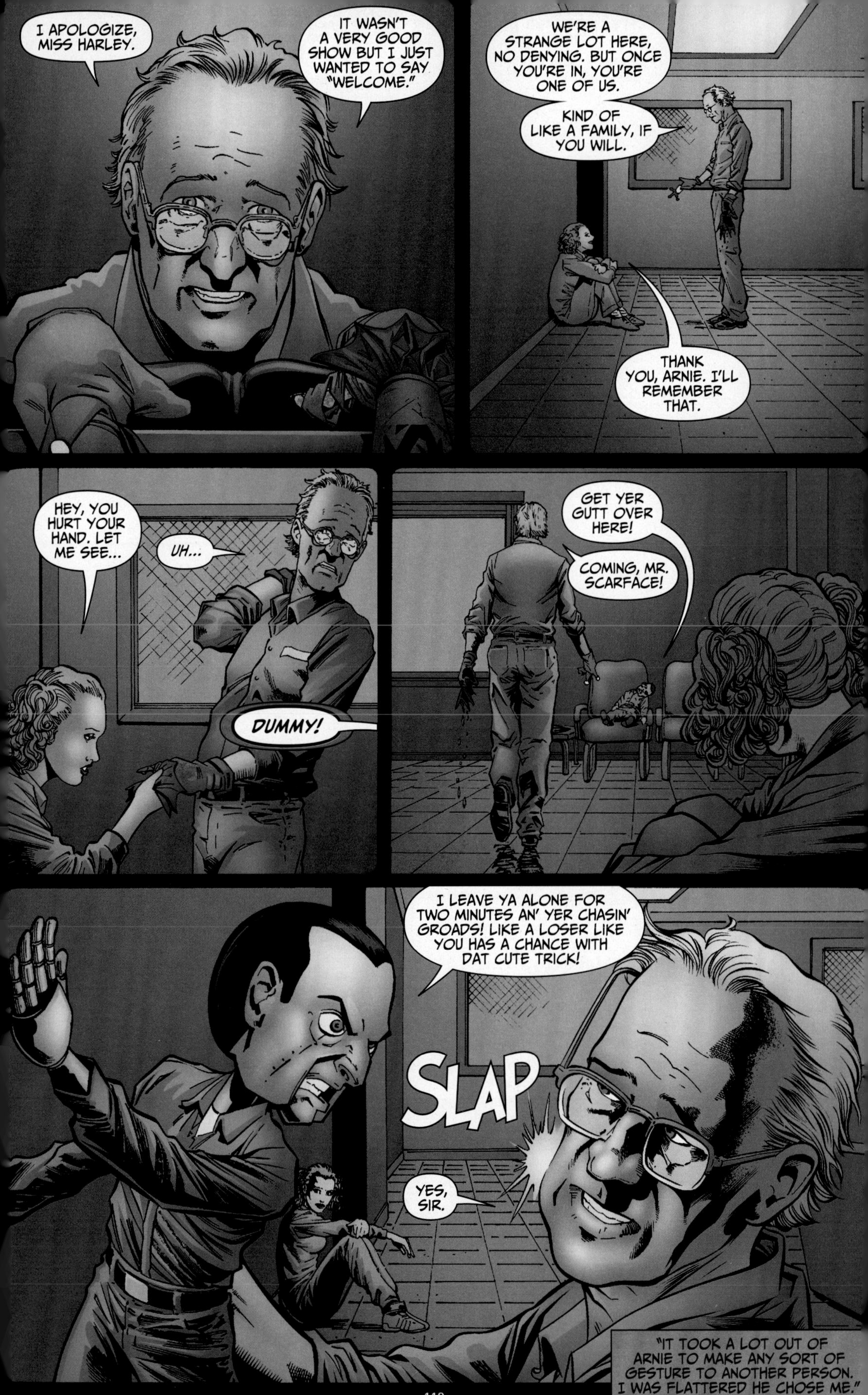

I APOLOGIZE, MISS HARLEY.
IT WASN'T A VERY GOOD SHOW BUT I JUST WANTED TO SAY "WELCOME."
WE'RE A STRANGE LOT HERE, NO DENYING. BUT ONCE YOU'RE IN, YOU'RE ONE OF US.
KIND OF LIKE A FAMILY, IF YOU WILL.
THANK YOU, ARNIE. I'LL REMEMBER THAT.
HEY, YOU HURT YOUR HAND. LET ME SEE...
UH...
DUMMY!
GET YER GUTT OVER HERE!
COMING, MR. SCARFACE!
I LEAVE YA ALONE FOR TWO MINUTES AN' YER CHASIN' GROADS! LIKE A LOSER LIKE YOU HAS A CHANCE WITH DAT CUTE TRICK!
SLAP
YES, SIR.
"IT TOOK A LOT OUT OF ARNIE TO MAKE ANY SORT OF GESTURE TO ANOTHER PERSON. I WAS FLATTERED HE CHOSE ME."

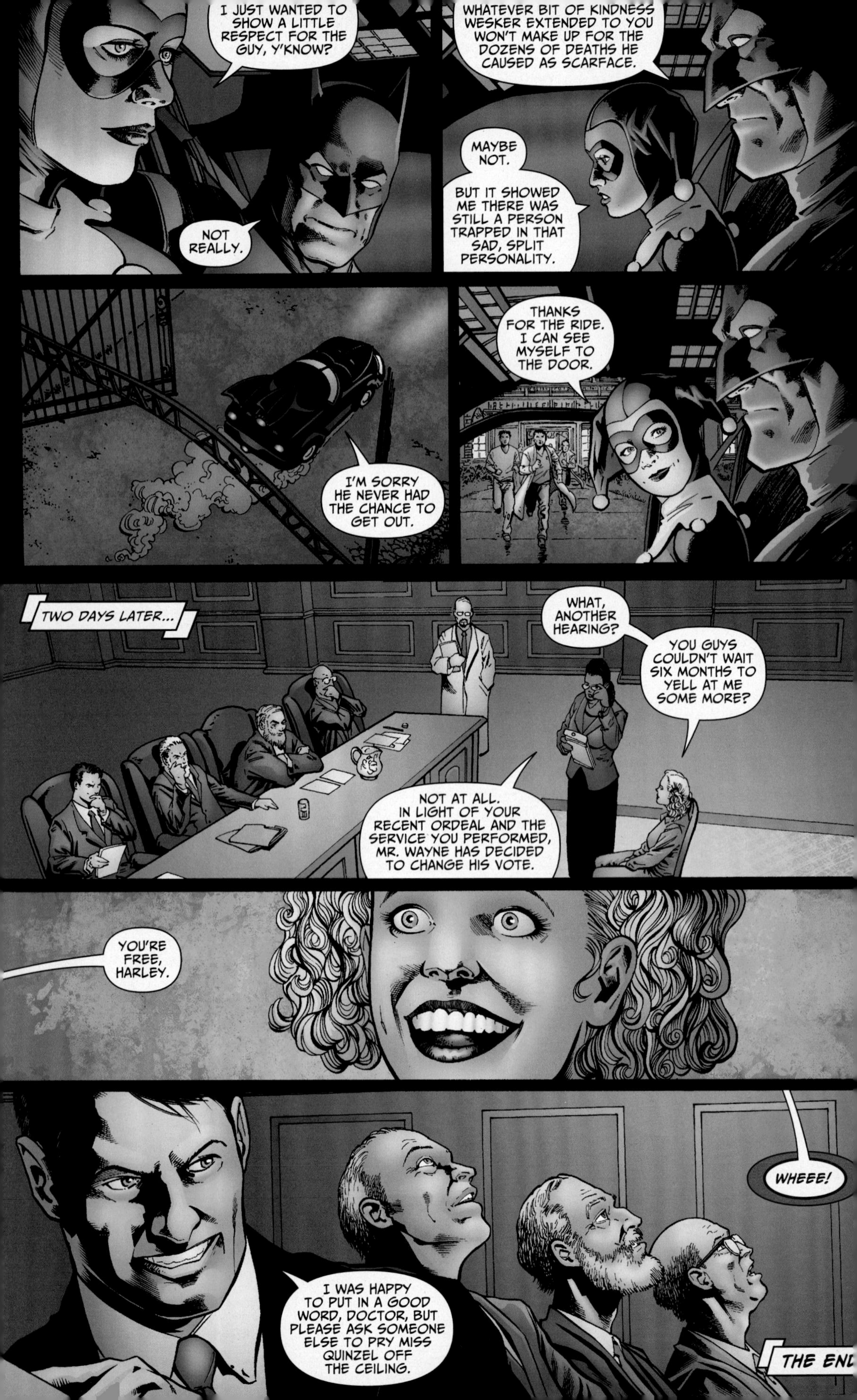

I JUST WANTED TO SHOW A LITTLE RESPECT FOR THE GUY, Y'KNOW?
NOT REALLY.
WHATEVER BIT OF KINDNESS WESKER EXTENDED TO YOU WON'T MAKE UP FOR THE DOZENS OF DEATHS HE CAUSED AS SCARFACE.
MAYBE NOT.
BUT IT SHOWED ME THERE WAS STILL A PERSON TRAPPED IN THAT SAD, SPLIT PERSONALITY.
I'M SORRY HE NEVER HAD THE CHANCE TO GET OUT.
THANKS FOR THE RIDE. I CAN SEE MYSELF TO THE DOOR.
TWO DAYS LATER...
WHAT, ANOTHER HEARING?
YOU GUYS COULDN'T WAIT SIX MONTHS TO YELL AT ME SOME MORE?
NOT AT ALL. IN LIGHT OF YOUR RECENT ORDEAL AND THE SERVICE YOU PERFORMED, MR. WAYNE HAS DECIDED TO CHANGE HIS VOTE.
YOU'RE FREE, HARLEY.
WHEEE!
I WAS HAPPY TO PUT IN A GOOD WORD, DOCTOR, BUT PLEASE ASK SOMEONE ELSE TO PRY MISS QUINZEL OFF THE CEILING.
THE END

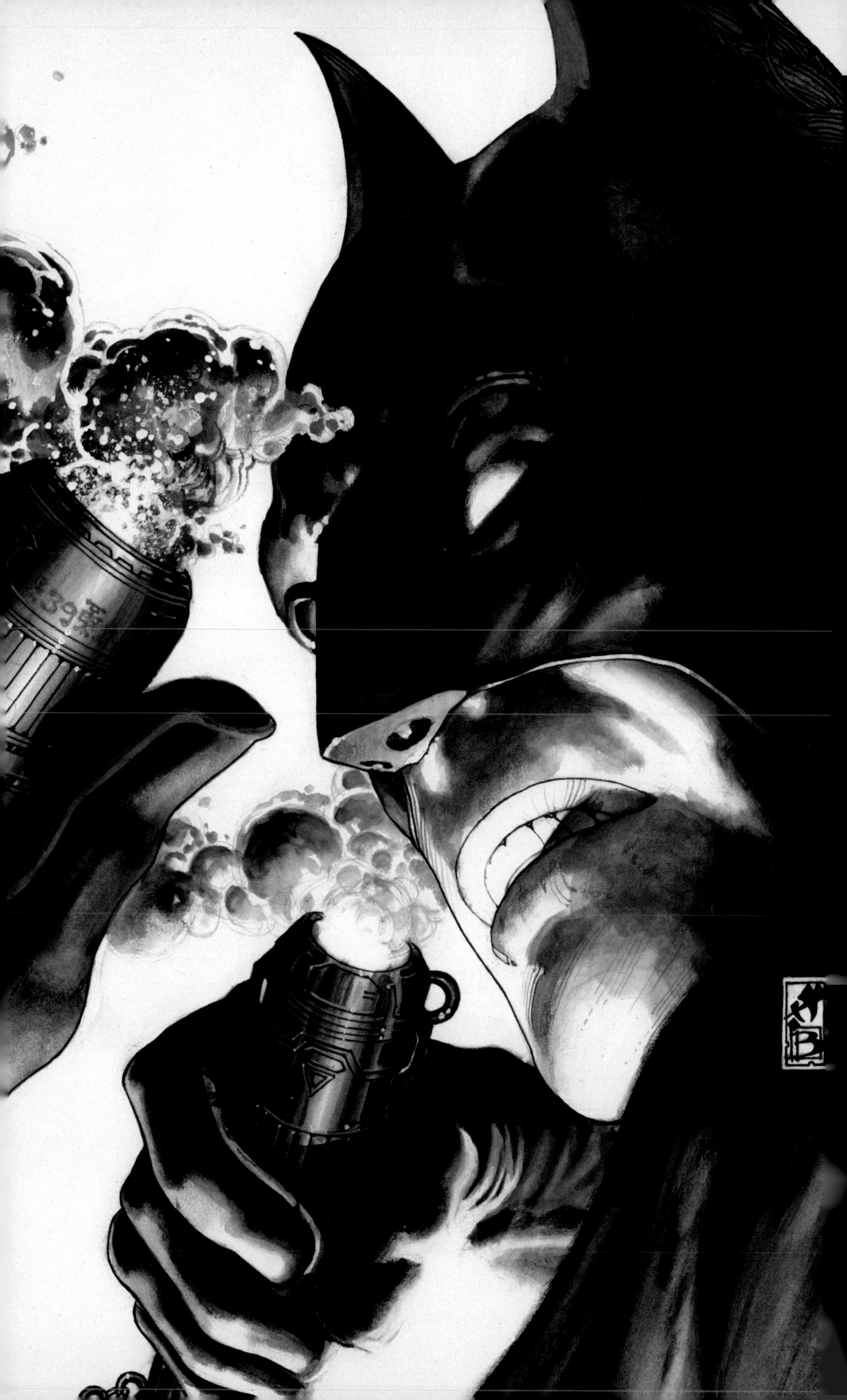

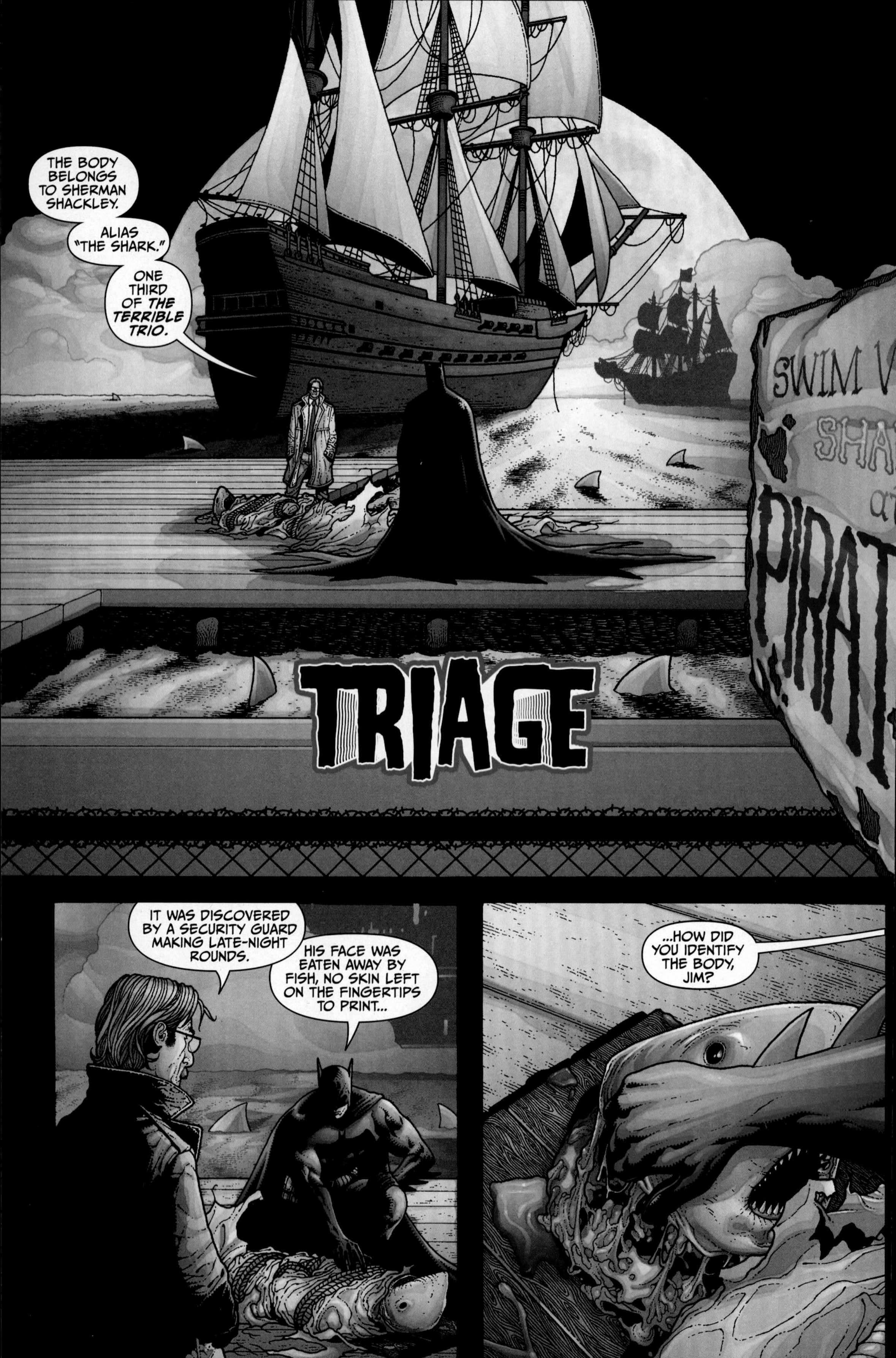
THE BODY BELONGS TO SHERMAN SHACKLEY.
ALIAS "THE SHARK."
ONE THIRD OF THE TERRIBLE TRIO.
SWIM
SHA
at
PIRAT
TRIAGE
IT WAS DISCOVERED BY A SECURITY GUARD MAKING LATE-NIGHT ROUNDS.
HIS FACE WAS EATEN AWAY BY FISH, NO SKIN LEFT ON THE FINGERTIPS TO PRINT...
...HOW DID YOU IDENTIFY THE BODY, JIM?

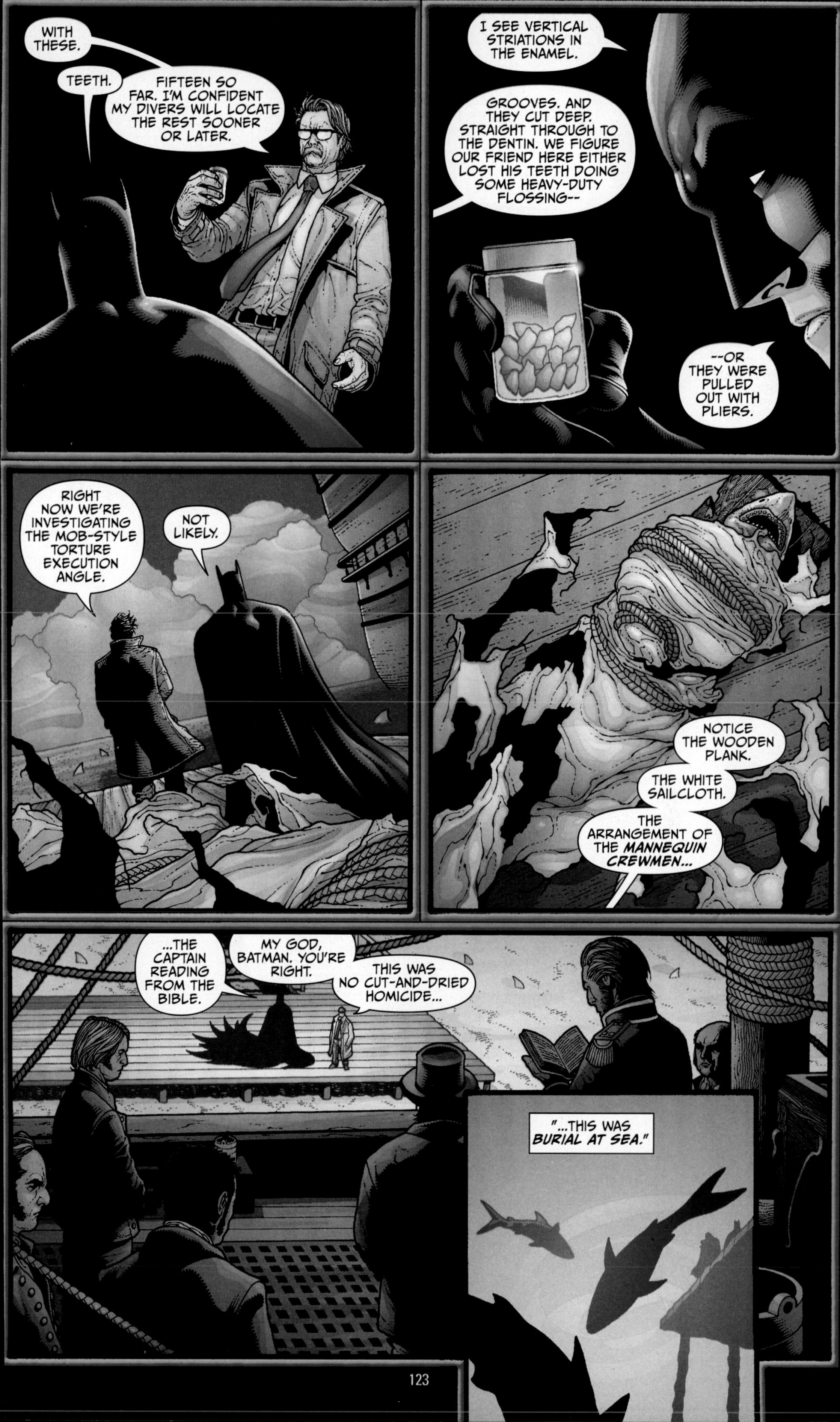
WITH THESE.
TEETH.
FIFTEEN SO FAR. I'M CONFIDENT MY DIVERS WILL LOCATE THE REST SOONER OR LATER.
I SEE VERTICAL STRIATIONS IN THE ENAMEL.
GROOVES. AND THEY CUT DEEP. STRAIGHT THROUGH TO THE DENTIN. WE FIGURE OUR FRIEND HERE EITHER LOST HIS TEETH DOING SOME HEAVY-DUTY FLOSSING--
--OR THEY WERE PULLED OUT WITH PLIERS.
RIGHT NOW WE'RE INVESTIGATING THE MOB-STYLE TORTURE EXECUTION ANGLE.
NOT LIKELY.
NOTICE THE WOODEN PLANK.
THE WHITE SAILCLOTH.
THE ARRANGEMENT OF THE *MANNEQUIN CREWMEN...*
...THE CAPTAIN READING FROM THE BIBLE.
MY GOD, BATMAN. YOU'RE RIGHT.
THIS WAS NO CUT-AND-DRIED HOMICIDE...
"...THIS WAS *BURIAL AT SEA.*"

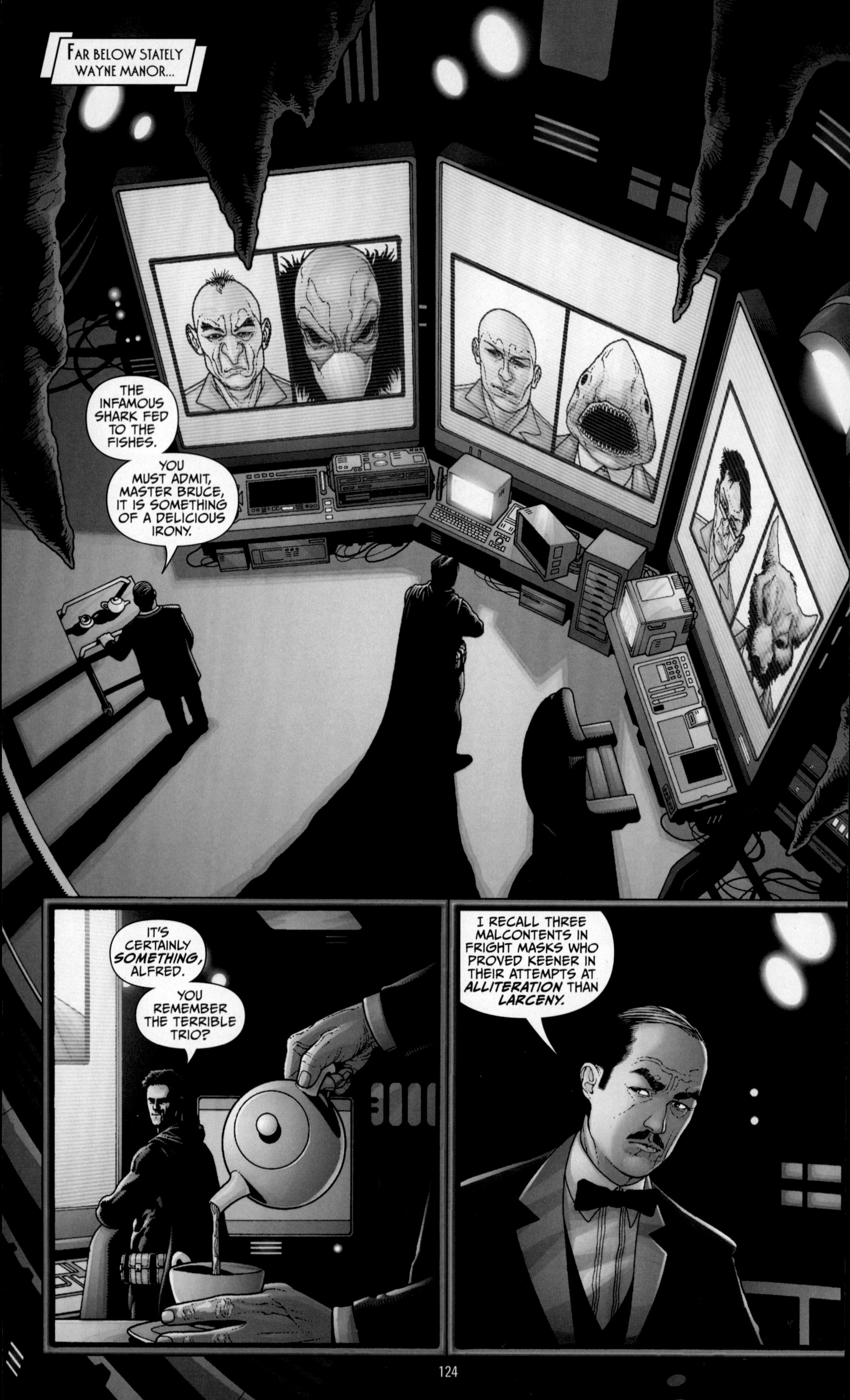

FAR BELOW STATELY WAYNE MANOR...
THE INFAMOUS SHARK FED TO THE FISHES.
YOU MUST ADMIT, MASTER BRUCE, IT IS SOMETHING OF A DELICIOUS IRONY.
IT'S CERTAINLY *SOMETHING,* ALFRED.
YOU REMEMBER THE TERRIBLE TRIO?
I RECALL THREE MALCONTENTS IN FRIGHT MASKS WHO PROVED KEENER IN THEIR ATTEMPTS AT *ALLITERATION* THAN *LARCENY.*

WORD ON THE STREET IS THAT THE TRIO WERE RUNNING SCARED.

THEY'D RETURNED TO GOTHAM HOPING TO CASH IN OLD DEBTS FOR PROTECTION.

WITH GOOD REASON, IT WOULD APPEAR.

AND WHAT OF MESSIEURS VOLPER AND FISK?

COMMISSIONER GORDON APPREHENDED VOLPER TRYING TO BOOK PASSAGE TO SOUTH AMERICA.

AND OUR MAN FISK?

STILL IN GOTHAM SOMEWHERE. SO FAR I HAVEN'T BEEN ABLE TO LOCATE HIM.

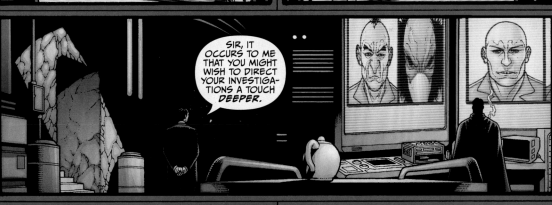

SIR, IT OCCURS TO ME THAT YOU MIGHT WISH TO DIRECT YOUR INVESTIGATIONS A TOUCH *DEEPER.*

YOU KNOW SOMETHING I DON'T, ALFRED?

ONLY WHAT ANY ENGLISH SCHOOLBOY WORTH HIS BLOODING COULD TELL YOU: THAT A FOX PURSUED WILL ALWAYS HEAD TO GROUND.

I WAS TOO CLOSE TO SEE IT...

...EACH MEMBER OF THE TERRIBLE TRIO HAS A PERSONAL AFFECTATION.

SHACKLEY, THE SHARK, FAVORED CRIMES OF A NAUTICAL PERSUASION...

...VOLPER, THE VULTURE, STRUCK FROM THE AIR...

...AND FISK, THE FOX, EXPLOITED THE EARTH.

WORKING IN CONCERT, THEIR MANIAS FOUND EQUILIBRIUM.

BUT NOW, WITH SHACKLEY DEAD...

...THE TRIO DISMANTLED...

...THE INSANITY WILL RETURN...

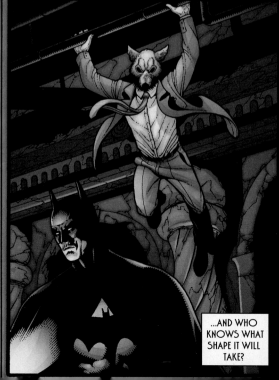

...AND WHO KNOWS WHAT SHAPE IT WILL TAKE?

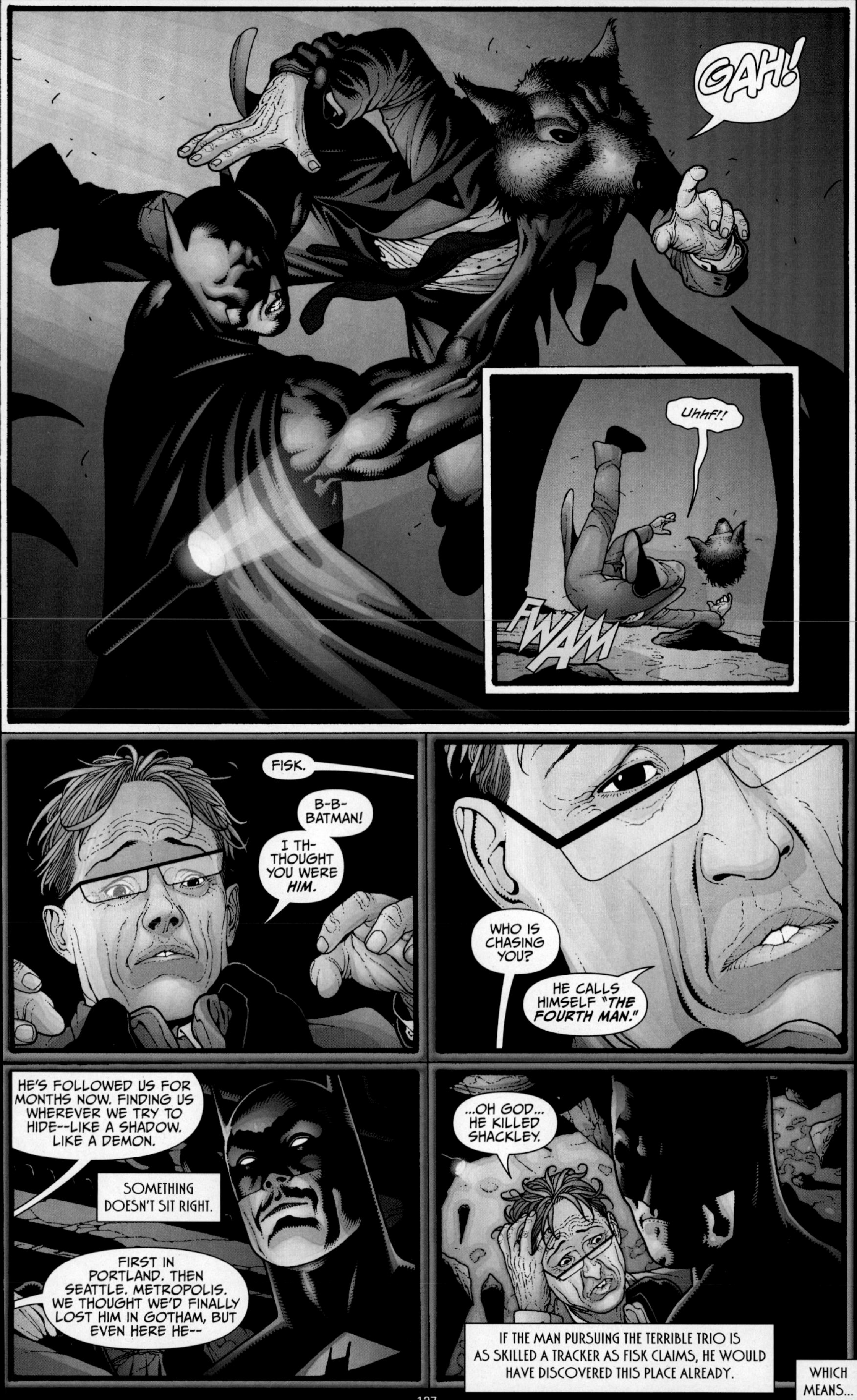
GAH!
Uhhf!!
FWAM
FISK.
B-B-BATMAN!
I TH-THOUGHT YOU WERE *HIM.*
WHO IS CHASING YOU?
HE CALLS HIMSELF "*THE FOURTH MAN.*"
HE'S FOLLOWED US FOR MONTHS NOW. FINDING US WHEREVER WE TRY TO HIDE--LIKE A SHADOW. LIKE A DEMON.
SOMETHING DOESN'T SIT RIGHT.
FIRST IN PORTLAND. THEN SEATTLE. METROPOLIS. WE THOUGHT WE'D FINALLY LOST HIM IN GOTHAM, BUT EVEN HERE HE--
...OH GOD... HE KILLED SHACKLEY.
IF THE MAN PURSUING THE TERRIBLE TRIO IS AS SKILLED A TRACKER AS FISK CLAIMS, HE WOULD HAVE DISCOVERED THIS PLACE ALREADY.
WHICH MEANS...

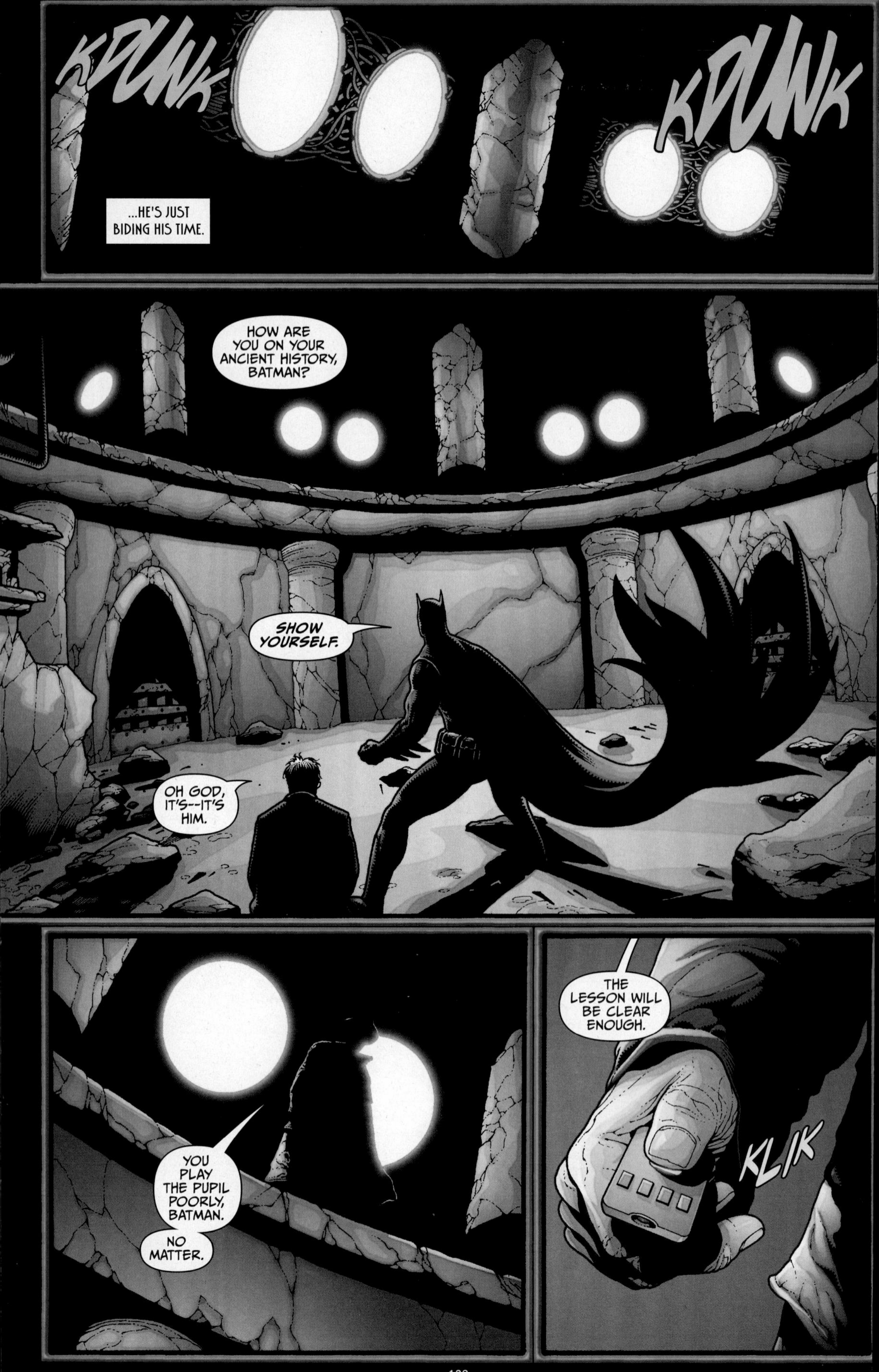
KDUNK
KDUNK
...HE'S JUST BIDING HIS TIME.
HOW ARE YOU ON YOUR ANCIENT HISTORY, BATMAN?
SHOW YOURSELF.
OH GOD, IT'S--IT'S HIM.
YOU PLAY THE PUPIL POORLY, BATMAN.
NO MATTER.
THE LESSON WILL BE CLEAR ENOUGH.
KLIK

KRRNKKRK

THE ANCIENT GREEKS BELIEVED THAT IF A BODY WAS LEFT TO BE SCAVENGED BY WOLVES AND THE BONES WERE DISPERSED, THEN THE SOUL COULD NEVER FIND REST.

TO DENY BURIAL WAS TO DENY *HUMANITY.*

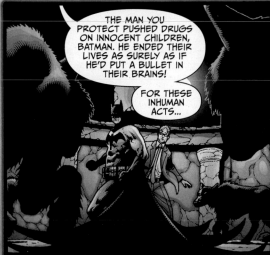

THE MAN YOU PROTECT PUSHED DRUGS ON INNOCENT CHILDREN, BATMAN. HE ENDED THEIR LIVES AS SURELY AS IF HE'D PUT A BULLET IN THEIR BRAINS!

FOR THESE INHUMAN ACTS...

...I SENTENCE YOU BOTH TO DIE LIKE DOGS!

AAIEE!

SHR RIP

SOME CHOOSE TO LIVE AS LAW-ABIDING CITIZENS.

OTHERS CHOOSE THE DARK PATH TOWARDS CRIME.

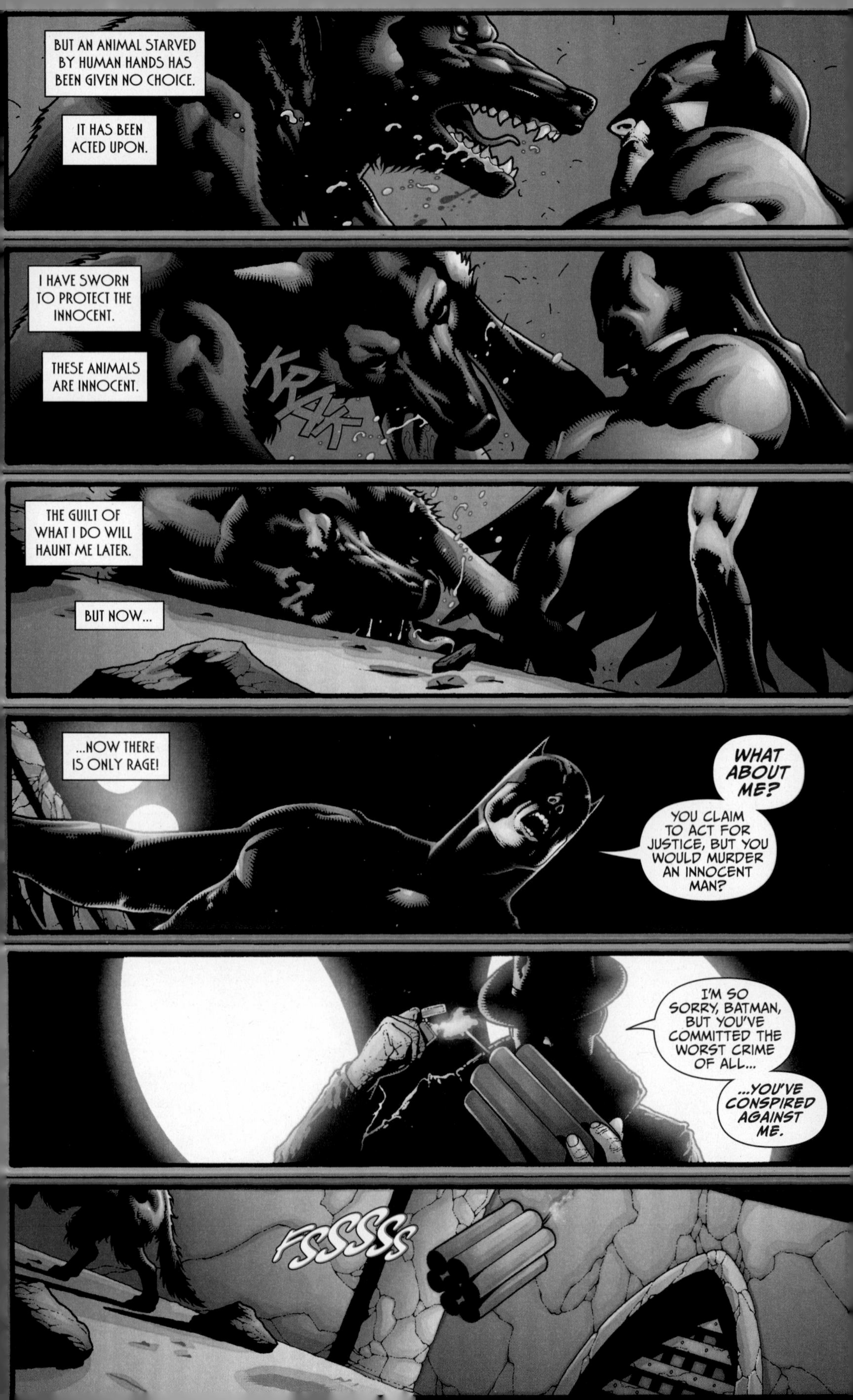

BUT AN ANIMAL STARVED BY HUMAN HANDS HAS BEEN GIVEN NO CHOICE.
IT HAS BEEN ACTED UPON.
I HAVE SWORN TO PROTECT THE INNOCENT.
THESE ANIMALS ARE INNOCENT.
KRAK
THE GUILT OF WHAT I DO WILL HAUNT ME LATER.
BUT NOW...
...NOW THERE IS ONLY RAGE!
WHAT ABOUT ME?
YOU CLAIM TO ACT FOR JUSTICE, BUT YOU WOULD MURDER AN INNOCENT MAN?
I'M SO SORRY, BATMAN, BUT YOU'VE COMMITTED THE WORST CRIME OF ALL...
...YOU'VE CONSPIRED AGAINST ME.
FSSSSs

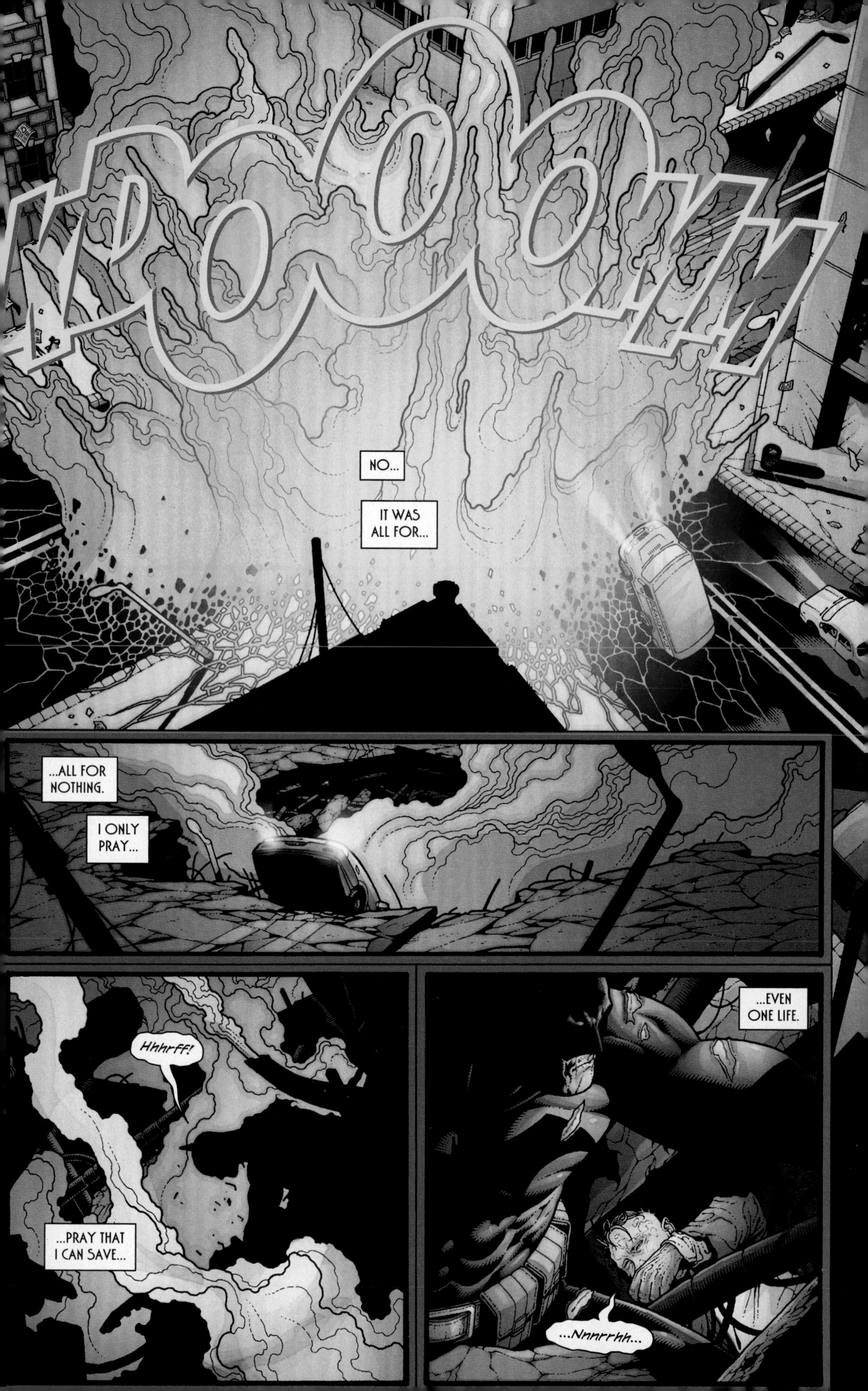
KRDOOOOM
NO...
IT WAS ALL FOR...
...ALL FOR NOTHING.
I ONLY PRAY...
Hhhrff!
...PRAY THAT I CAN SAVE...
...EVEN ONE LIFE.
...Nnnrrhh...

LATER...

HOW IS FISK?

THE E.M.T.'S SAY HIS BLOOD PRESSURE HAS STABILIZED, BUT I DON'T ENVY THE PARADE OF SYRINGES HE'LL BE DROPPING HIS PANTS FOR TOMORROW.

YOU GOT A LINE ON THE CREEP THAT DID THIS?

HE CALLS HIMSELF "THE FOURTH MAN."

"THE FOURTH MAN"?

HE APPEARS TO HAVE HISTORY WITH THE TERRIBLE TRIO.

I SUSPECT HE CHOSE THE MONIKER TO RANKLE THEM.

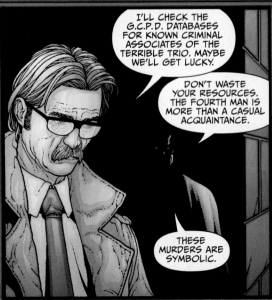

I'LL CHECK THE G.C.P.D. DATABASES FOR KNOWN CRIMINAL ASSOCIATES OF THE TERRIBLE TRIO. MAYBE WE'LL GET LUCKY.

DON'T WASTE YOUR RESOURCES. THE FOURTH MAN IS MORE THAN A CASUAL ACQUAINTANCE.

THESE MURDERS ARE SYMBOLIC.

"SHACKLEY WAS SERVED TO TIGER SHARKS IN A GRIM PARODY OF A BRITISH NAVAL FUNERAL.

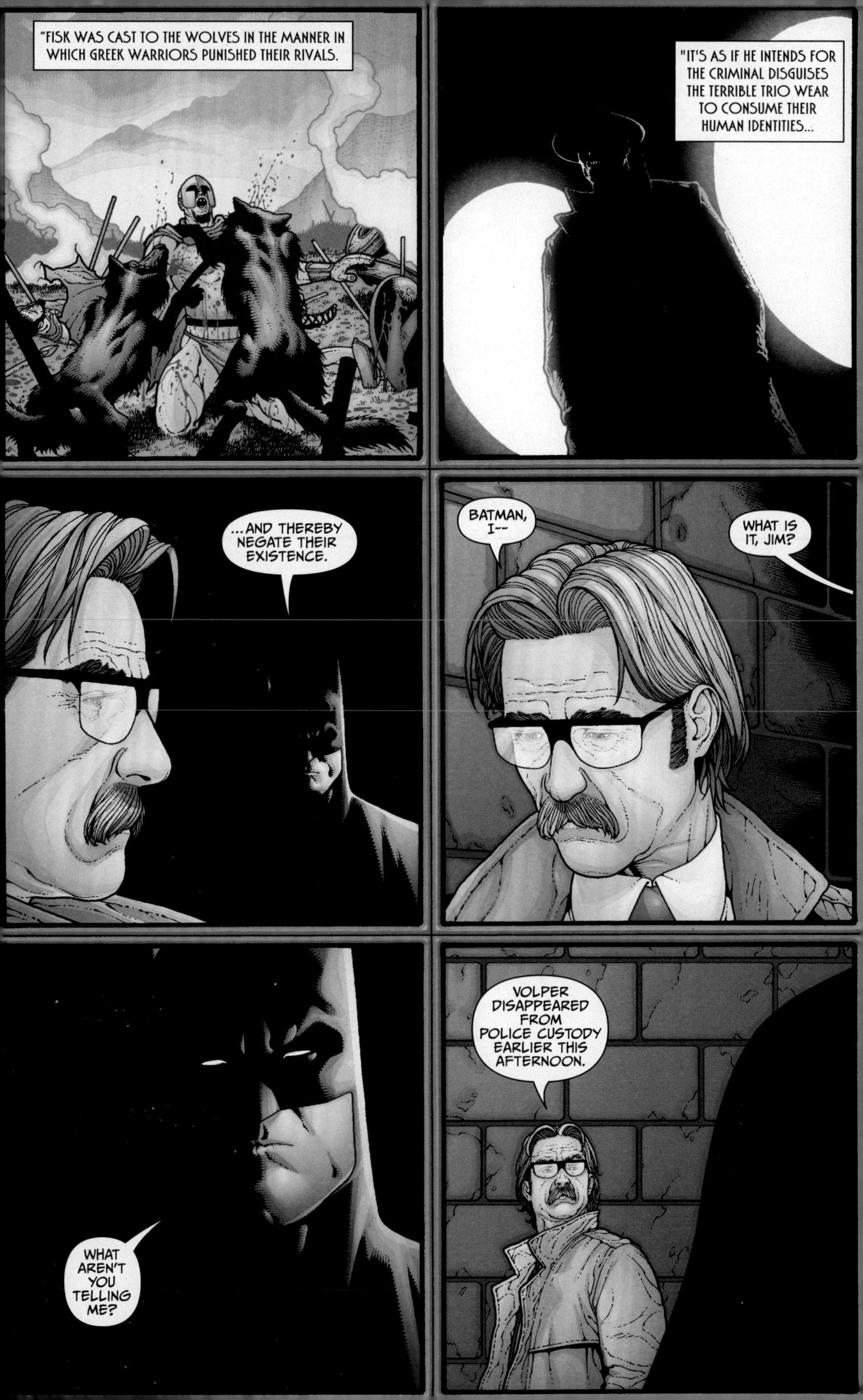
"FISK WAS CAST TO THE WOLVES IN THE MANNER IN WHICH GREEK WARRIORS PUNISHED THEIR RIVALS.
"IT'S AS IF HE INTENDS FOR THE CRIMINAL DISGUISES THE TERRIBLE TRIO WEAR TO CONSUME THEIR HUMAN IDENTITIES...
...AND THEREBY NEGATE THEIR EXISTENCE.
BATMAN, I--
WHAT IS IT, JIM?
WHAT AREN'T YOU TELLING ME?
VOLPER DISAPPEARED FROM POLICE CUSTODY EARLIER THIS AFTERNOON.

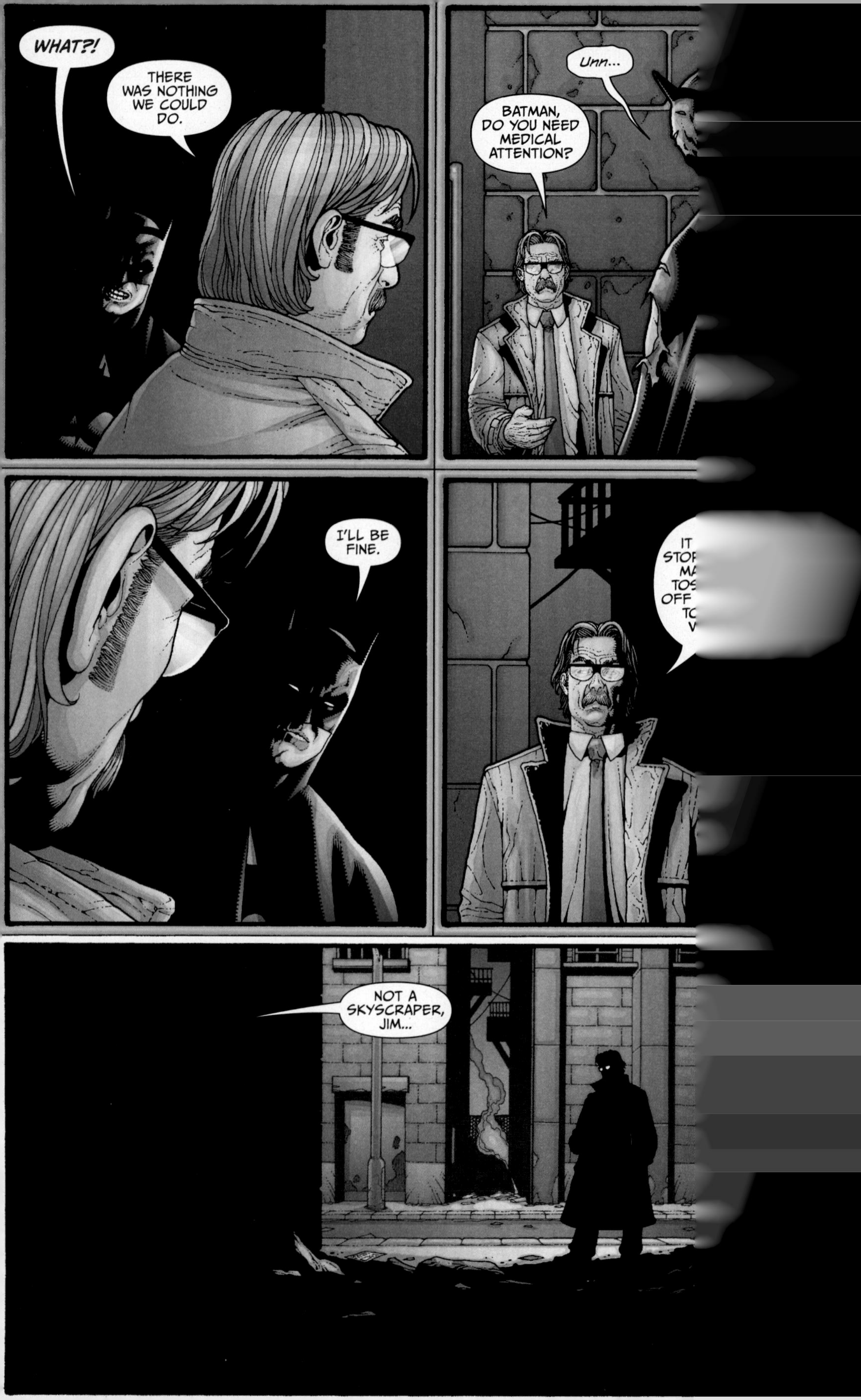
WHAT?!
THERE WAS NOTHING WE COULD DO.
Unn...
BATMAN, DO YOU NEED MEDICAL ATTENTION?
I'LL BE FINE.
NOT A SKYSCRAPER, JIM...

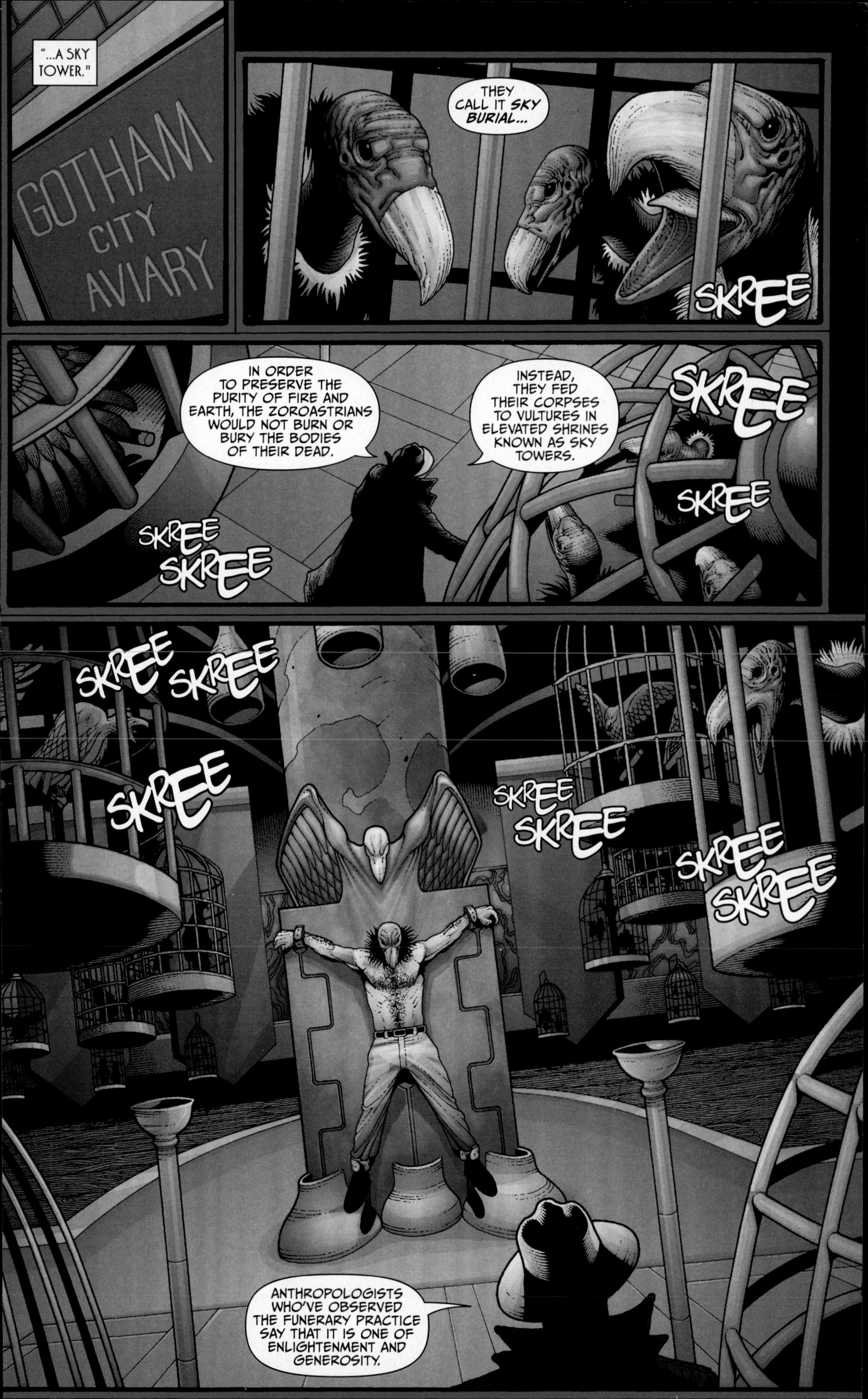

"...A SKY TOWER."
GOTHAM CITY AVIARY
THEY CALL IT SKY BURIAL...
SKREE
IN ORDER TO PRESERVE THE PURITY OF FIRE AND EARTH, THE ZOROASTRIANS WOULD NOT BURN OR BURY THE BODIES OF THEIR DEAD.
INSTEAD, THEY FED THEIR CORPSES TO VULTURES IN ELEVATED SHRINES KNOWN AS SKY TOWERS.
SKREE
SKREE
SKREE SKREE
SKREE SKREE
SKREE
SKREE SKREE
SKREE SKREE
ANTHROPOLOGISTS WHO'VE OBSERVED THE FUNERARY PRACTICE SAY THAT IT IS ONE OF ENLIGHTENMENT AND GENEROSITY.

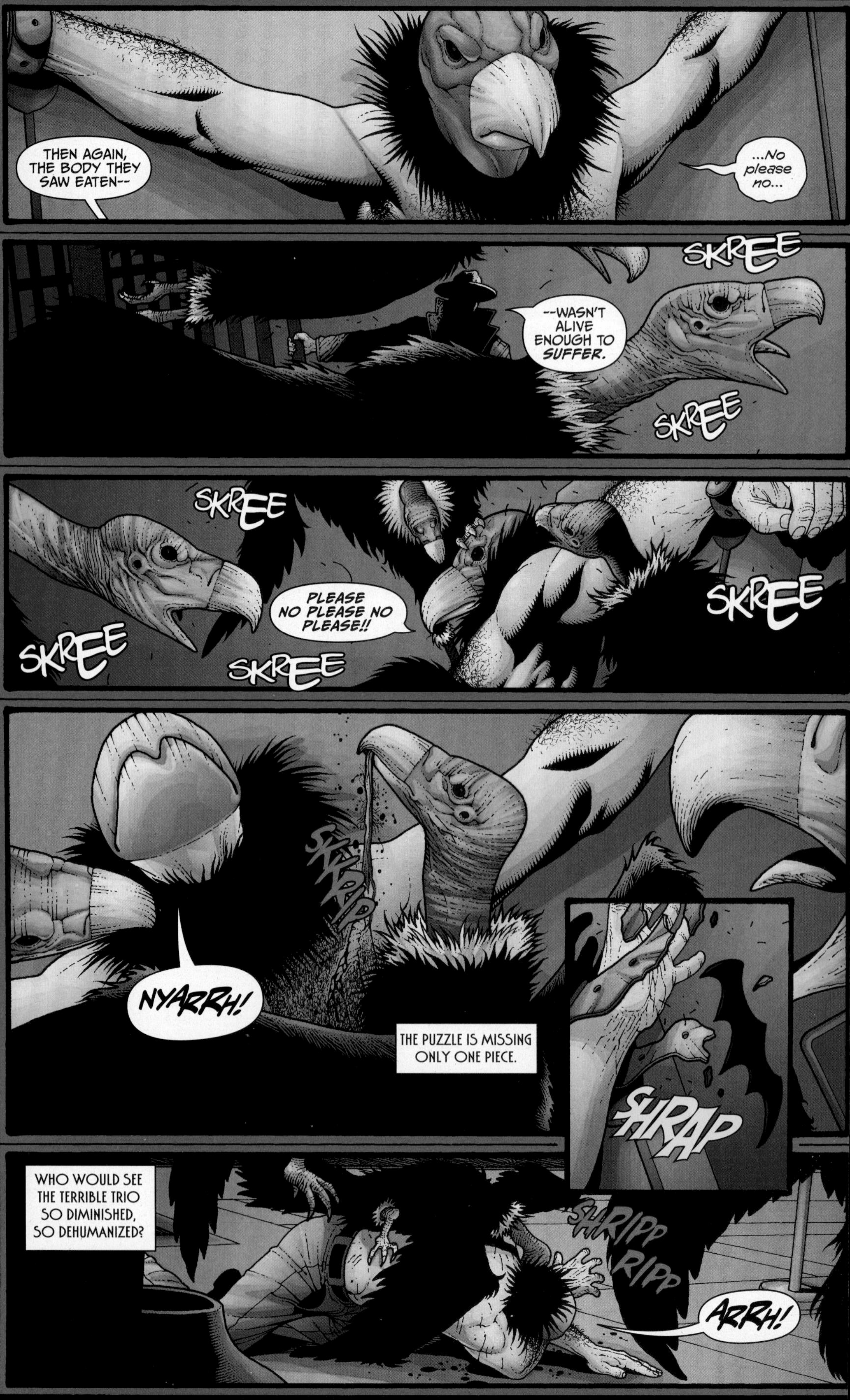
THEN AGAIN, THE BODY THEY SAW EATEN--
...No please no...
SKREE
--WASN'T ALIVE ENOUGH TO *SUFFER.*
SKREE
SKREE
PLEASE NO PLEASE NO PLEASE!!
SKREE
SKREE
SKREE
SHRIP
NYARRH!
THE PUZZLE IS MISSING ONLY ONE PIECE.
SHRAP
WHO WOULD SEE THE TERRIBLE TRIO SO DIMINISHED, SO DEHUMANIZED?
SHRIPP RIPP
ARRH!

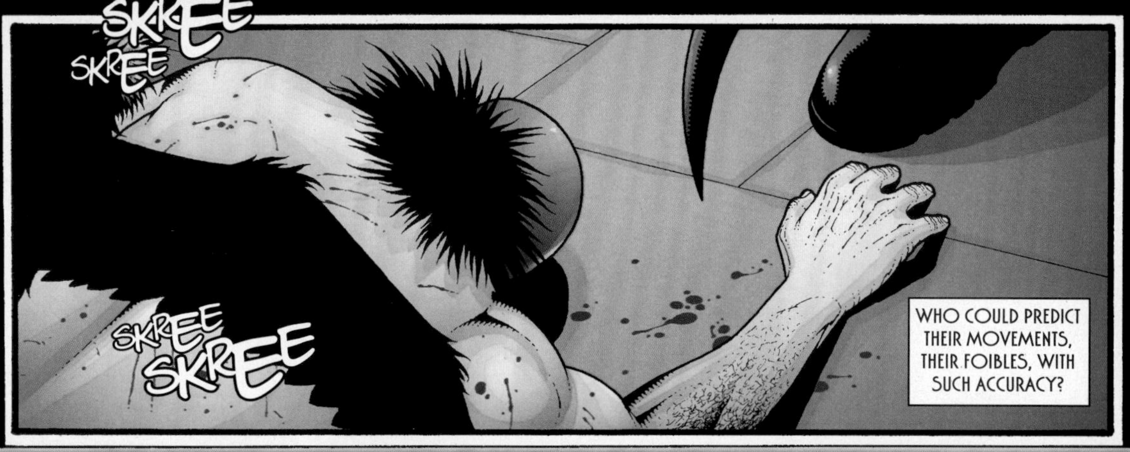
SKREE
SKREE
SKREE
SKREE
WHO COULD PREDICT THEIR MOVEMENTS, THEIR FOIBLES, WITH SUCH ACCURACY?

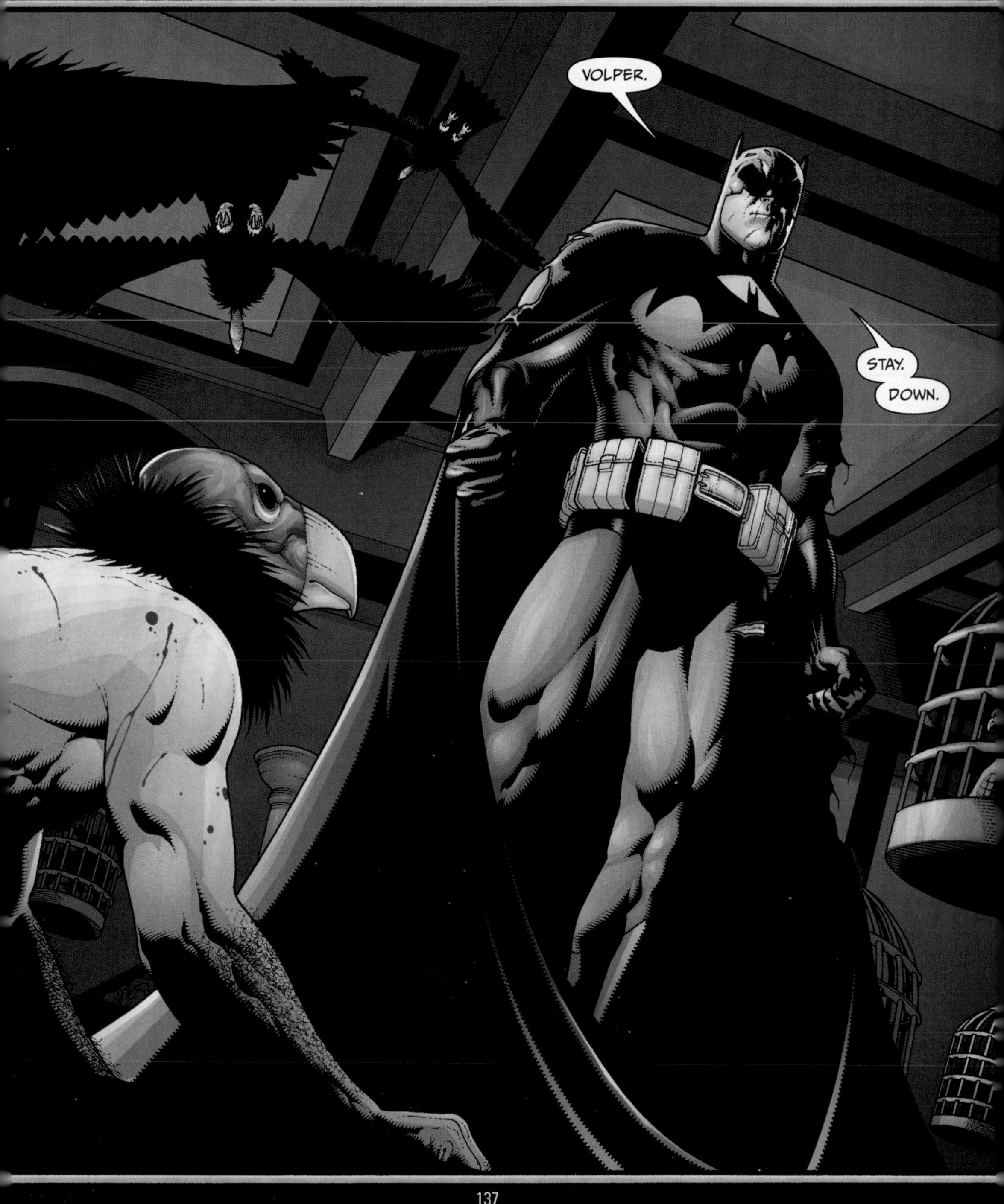
VOLPER.
STAY.
DOWN.

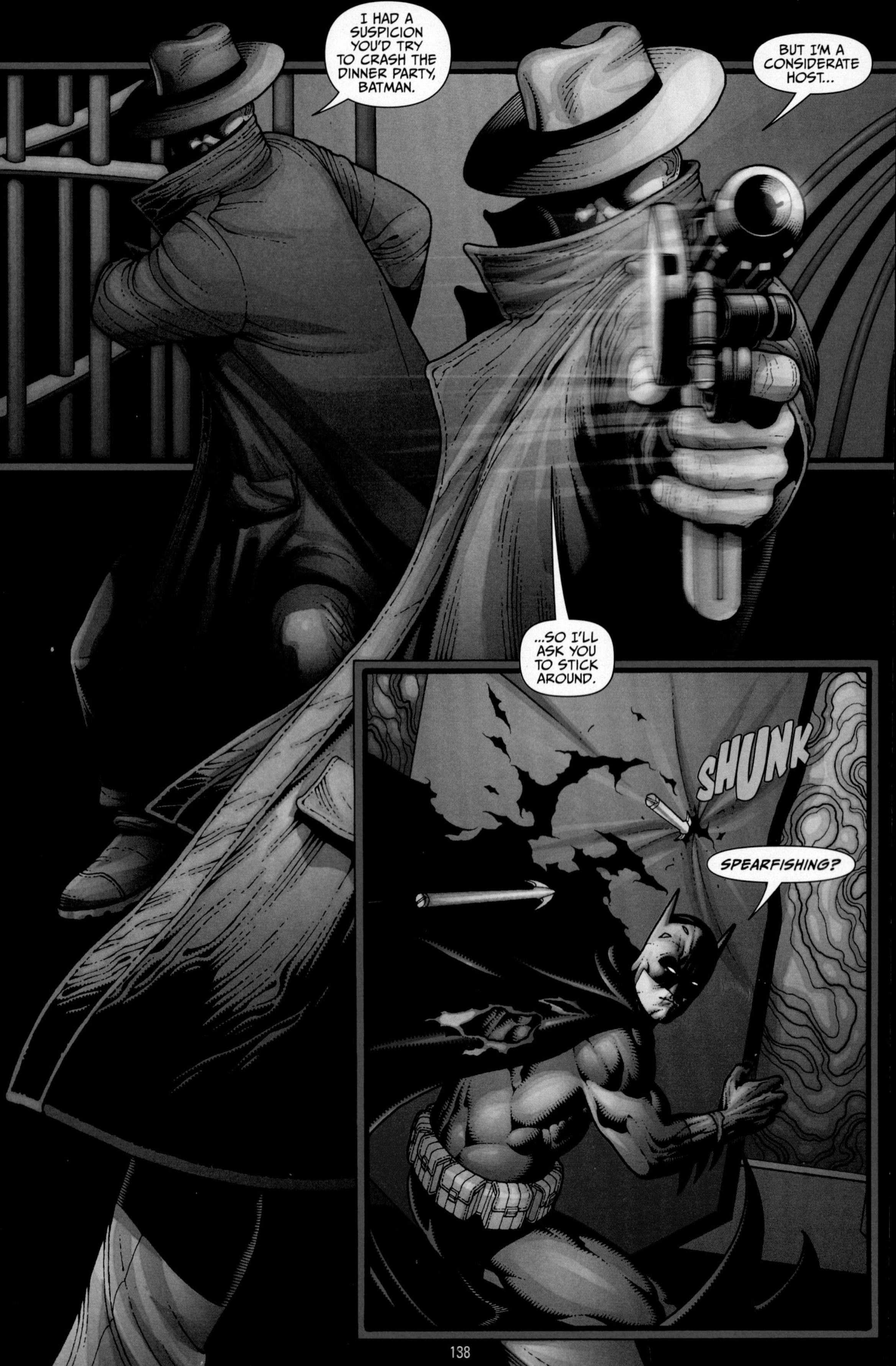
I HAD A SUSPICION YOU'D TRY TO CRASH THE DINNER PARTY, BATMAN.
BUT I'M A CONSIDERATE HOST...
...SO I'LL ASK YOU TO STICK AROUND.
SHUNK
SPEARFISHING?

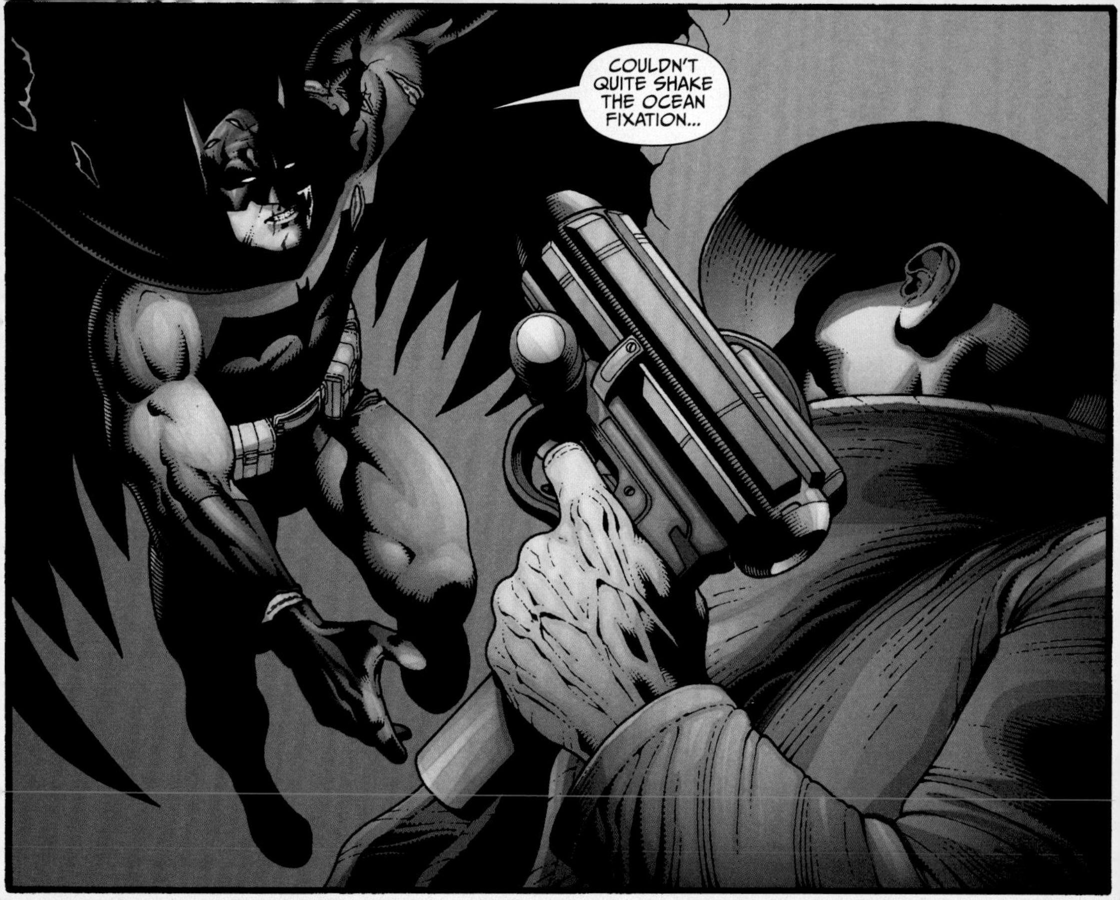
COULDN'T QUITE SHAKE THE OCEAN FIXATION...

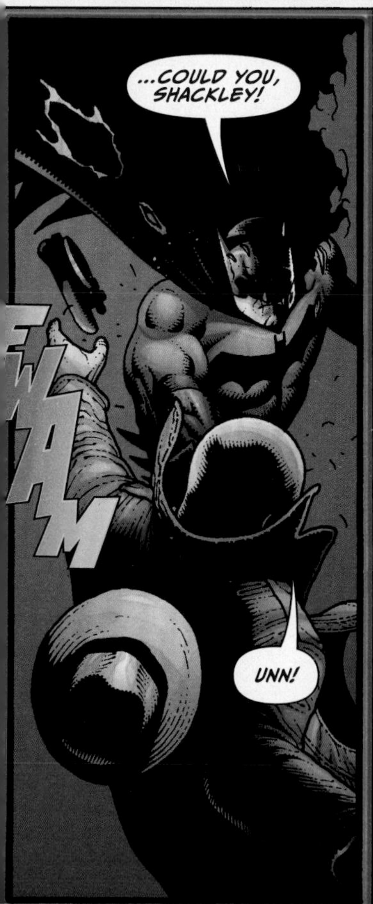
...COULD YOU, SHACKLEY!
FWHAM
UNN!

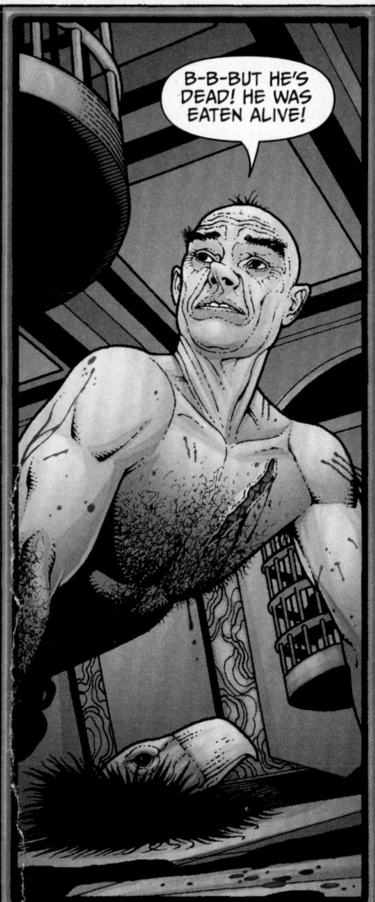
B-B-BUT HE'S DEAD! HE WAS EATEN ALIVE!

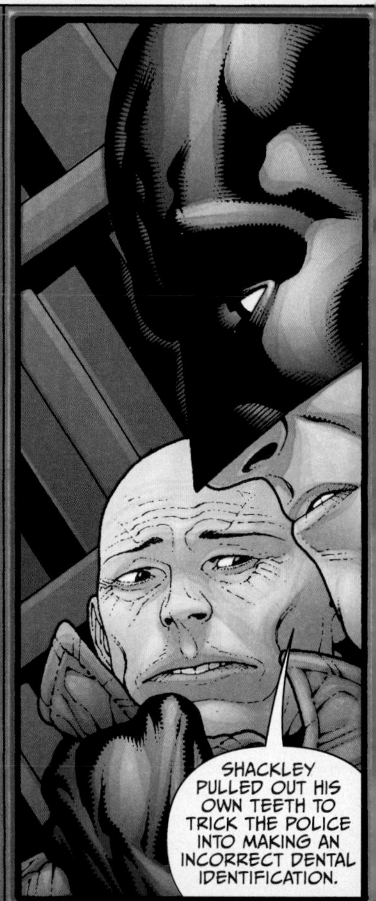
SHACKLEY PULLED OUT HIS OWN TEETH TO TRICK THE POLICE INTO MAKING AN INCORRECT DENTAL IDENTIFICATION.

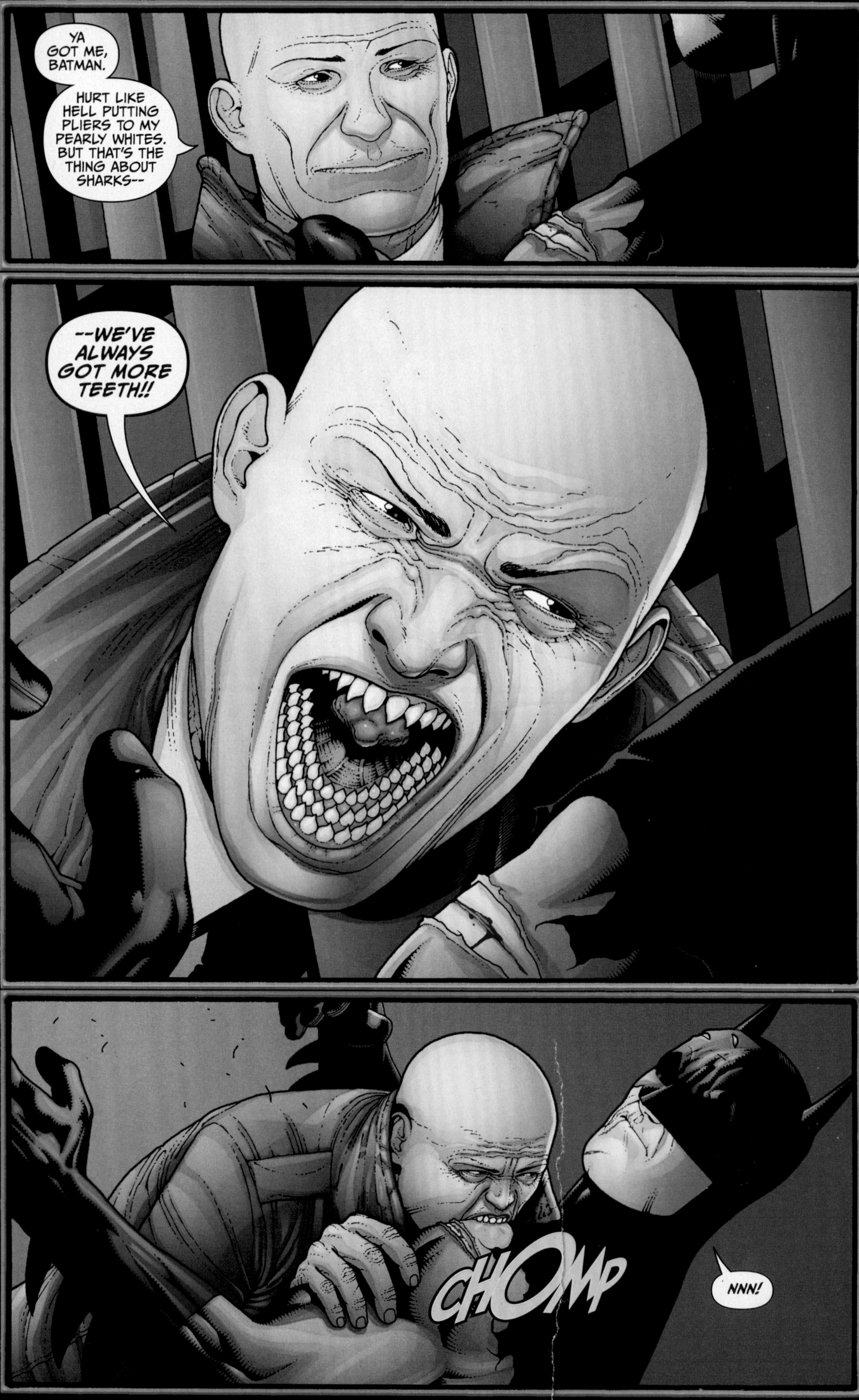
YA GOT ME, BATMAN.
HURT LIKE HELL PUTTING PLIERS TO MY PEARLY WHITES. BUT THAT'S THE THING ABOUT SHARKS--
--WE'VE ALWAYS GOT MORE TEETH!!
CHOMP
NNN!

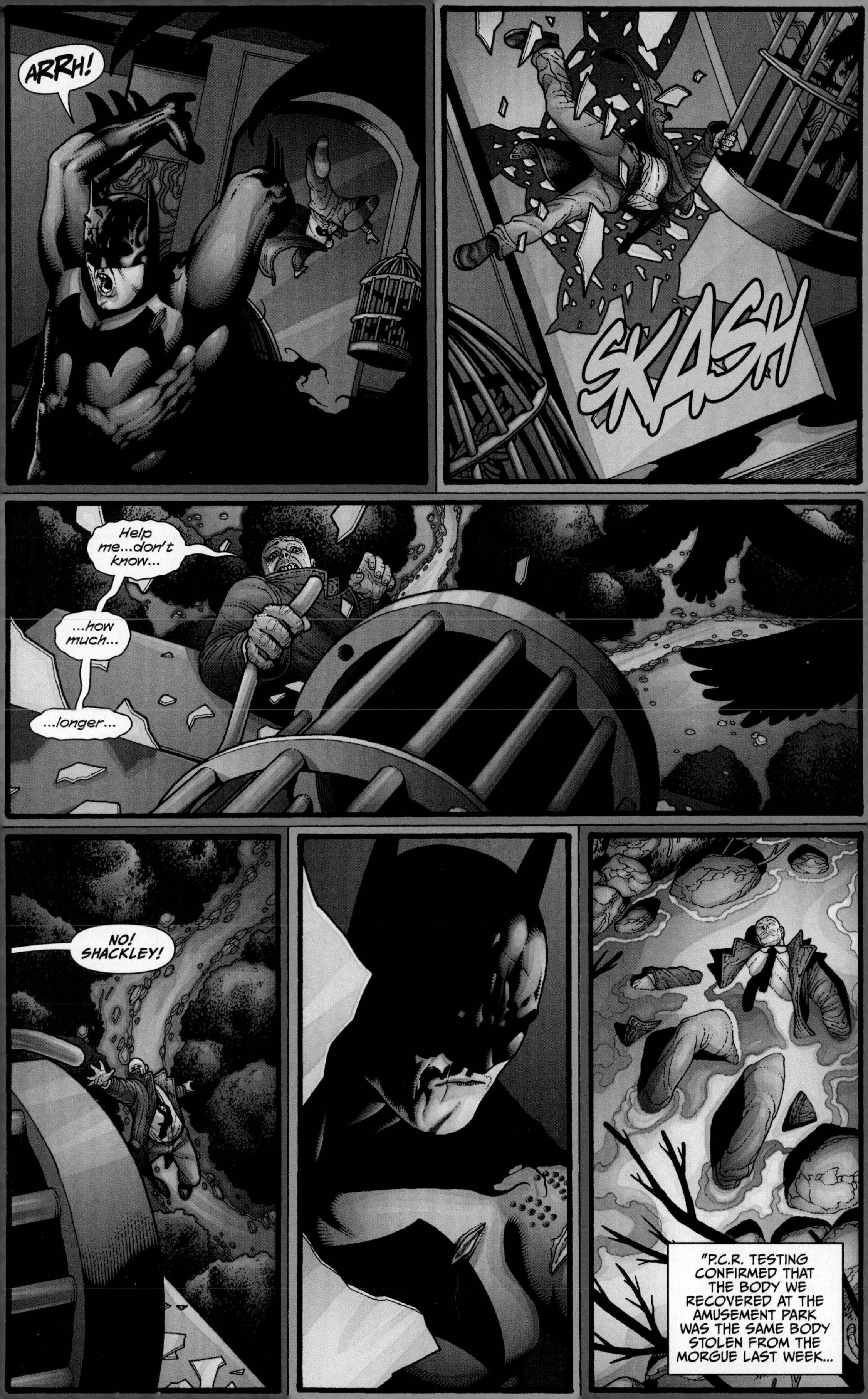
ARRH!
SKASH
Help me...don't know...
...how much...
...longer...
NO! SHACKLEY!
"P.C.R. TESTING CONFIRMED THAT THE BODY WE RECOVERED AT THE AMUSEMENT PARK WAS THE SAME BODY STOLEN FROM THE MORGUE LAST WEEK...

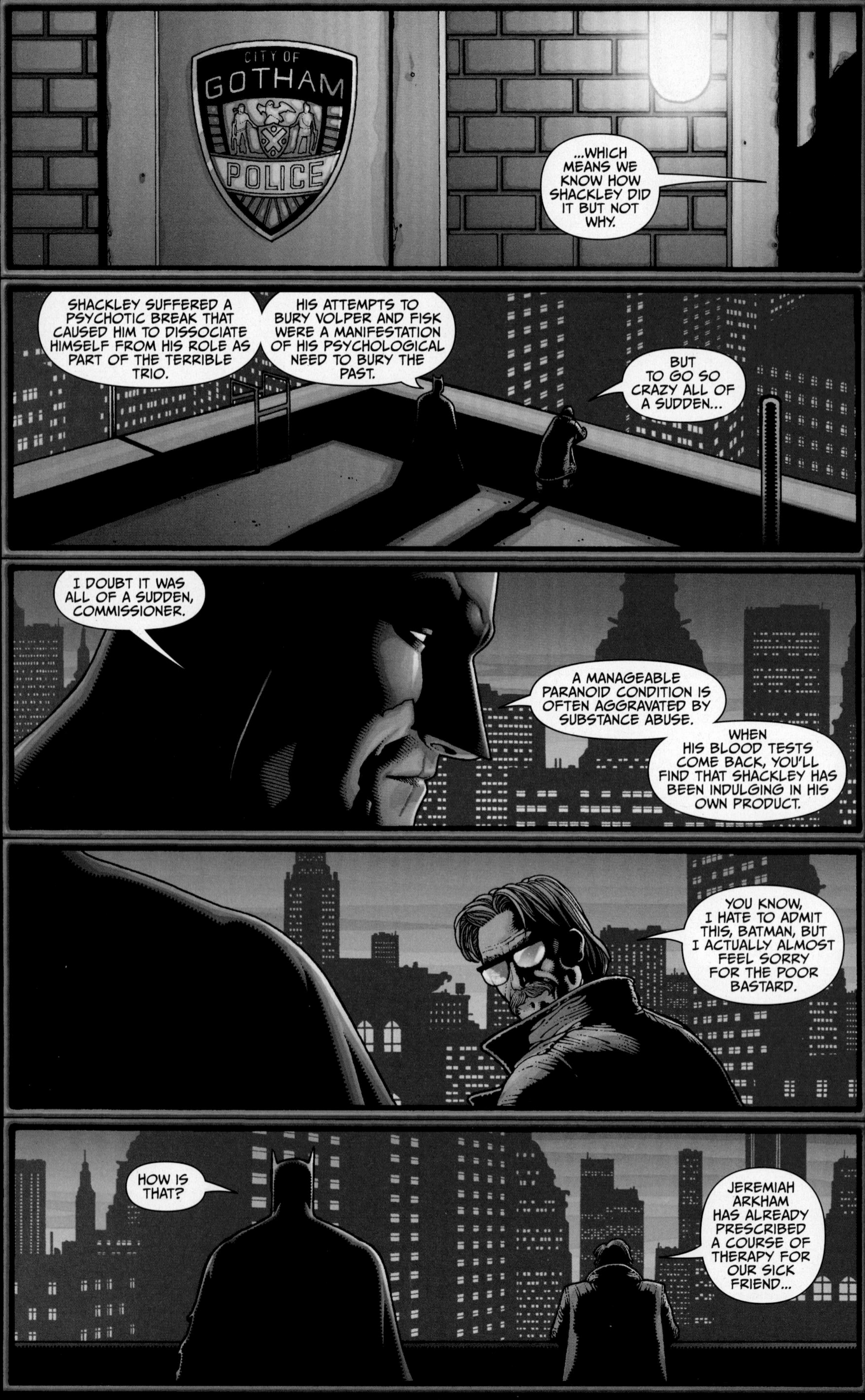
CITY OF GOTHAM
POLICE
...WHICH MEANS WE KNOW HOW SHACKLEY DID IT BUT NOT WHY.
SHACKLEY SUFFERED A PSYCHOTIC BREAK THAT CAUSED HIM TO DISSOCIATE HIMSELF FROM HIS ROLE AS PART OF THE TERRIBLE TRIO.
HIS ATTEMPTS TO BURY VOLPER AND FISK WERE A MANIFESTATION OF HIS PSYCHOLOGICAL NEED TO BURY THE PAST.
BUT TO GO SO CRAZY ALL OF A SUDDEN...
I DOUBT IT WAS ALL OF A SUDDEN, COMMISSIONER.
A MANAGEABLE PARANOID CONDITION IS OFTEN AGGRAVATED BY SUBSTANCE ABUSE.
WHEN HIS BLOOD TESTS COME BACK, YOU'LL FIND THAT SHACKLEY HAS BEEN INDULGING IN HIS OWN PRODUCT.
YOU KNOW, I HATE TO ADMIT THIS, BATMAN, BUT I ACTUALLY ALMOST FEEL SORRY FOR THE POOR BASTARD.
HOW IS THAT?
JEREMIAH ARKHAM HAS ALREADY PRESCRIBED A COURSE OF THERAPY FOR OUR SICK FRIEND...

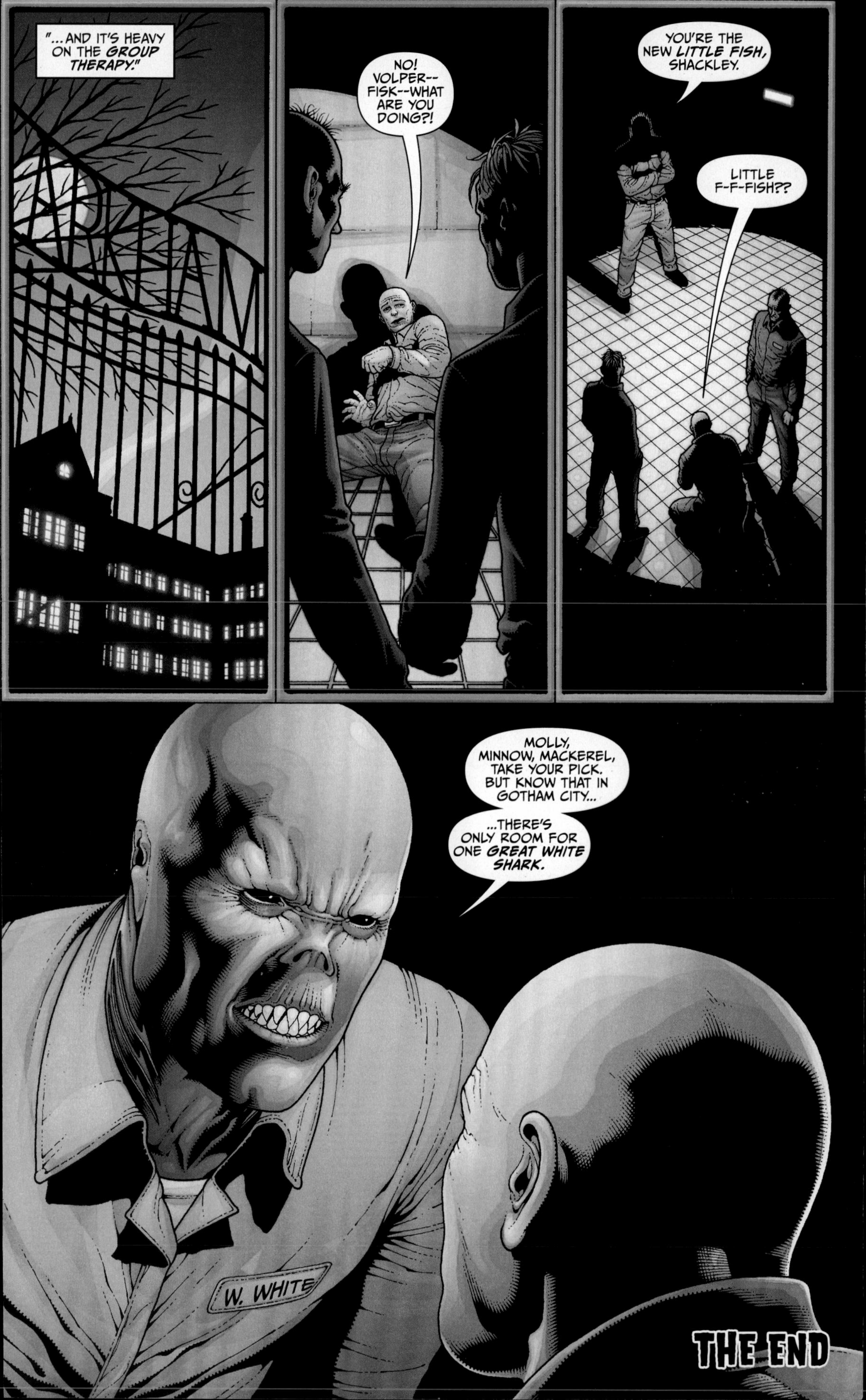
"...AND IT'S HEAVY ON THE GROUP THERAPY."
NO! VOLPER--FISK--WHAT ARE YOU DOING?!
YOU'RE THE NEW LITTLE FISH, SHACKLEY.
LITTLE F-F-FISH??
MOLLY, MINNOW, MACKEREL, TAKE YOUR PICK. BUT KNOW THAT IN GOTHAM CITY...
...THERE'S ONLY ROOM FOR ONE GREAT WHITE SHARK.
W. WHITE
THE END

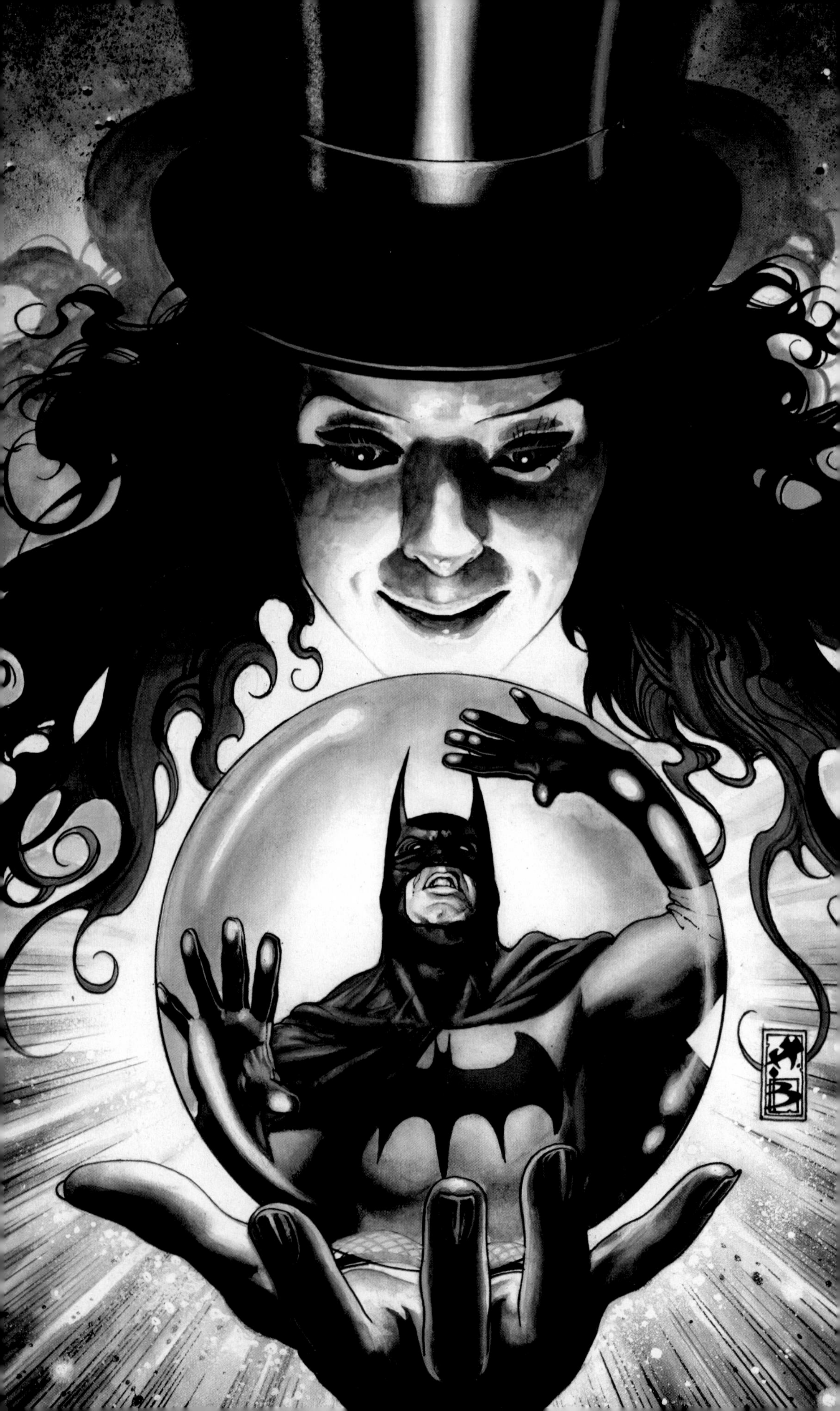

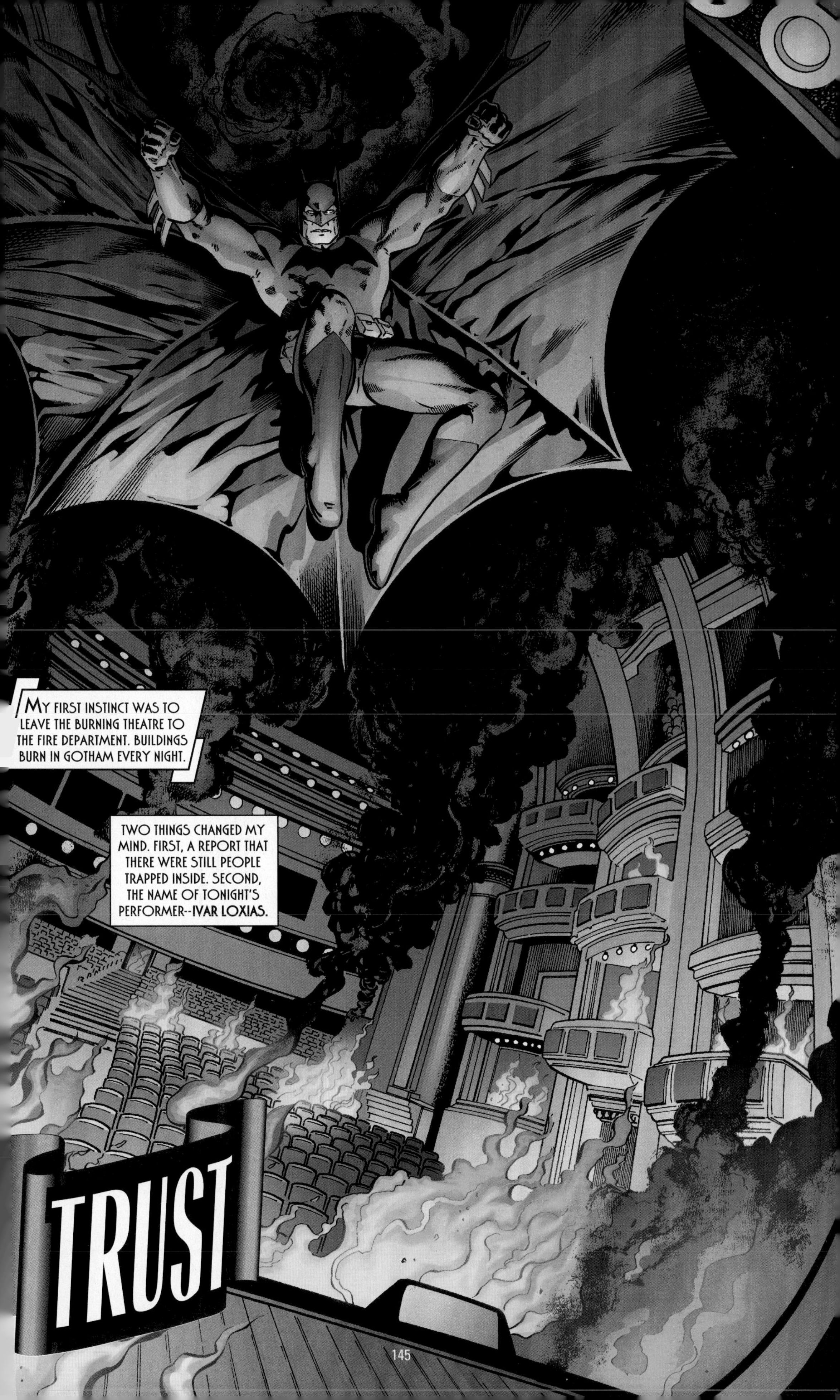
MY FIRST INSTINCT WAS TO LEAVE THE BURNING THEATRE TO THE FIRE DEPARTMENT. BUILDINGS BURN IN GOTHAM EVERY NIGHT.
TWO THINGS CHANGED MY MIND. FIRST, A REPORT THAT THERE WERE STILL PEOPLE TRAPPED INSIDE. SECOND, THE NAME OF TONIGHT'S PERFORMER--IVAR LOXIAS.
TRUST

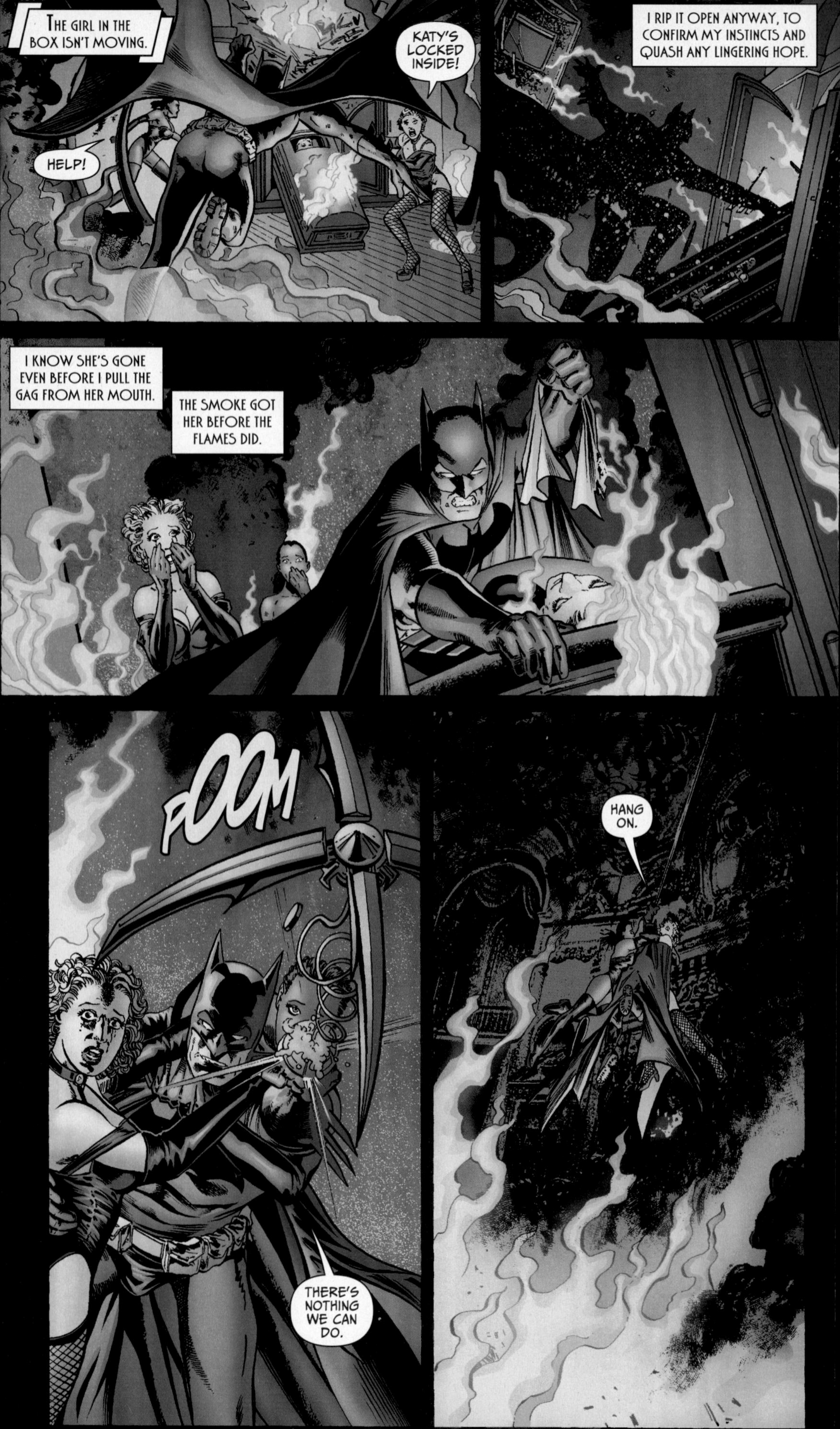
THE GIRL IN THE BOX ISN'T MOVING.
KATY'S LOCKED INSIDE!
HELP!
I RIP IT OPEN ANYWAY, TO CONFIRM MY INSTINCTS AND QUASH ANY LINGERING HOPE.
I KNOW SHE'S GONE EVEN BEFORE I PULL THE GAG FROM HER MOUTH.
THE SMOKE GOT HER BEFORE THE FLAMES DID.
POOM
THERE'S NOTHING WE CAN DO.
HANG ON.

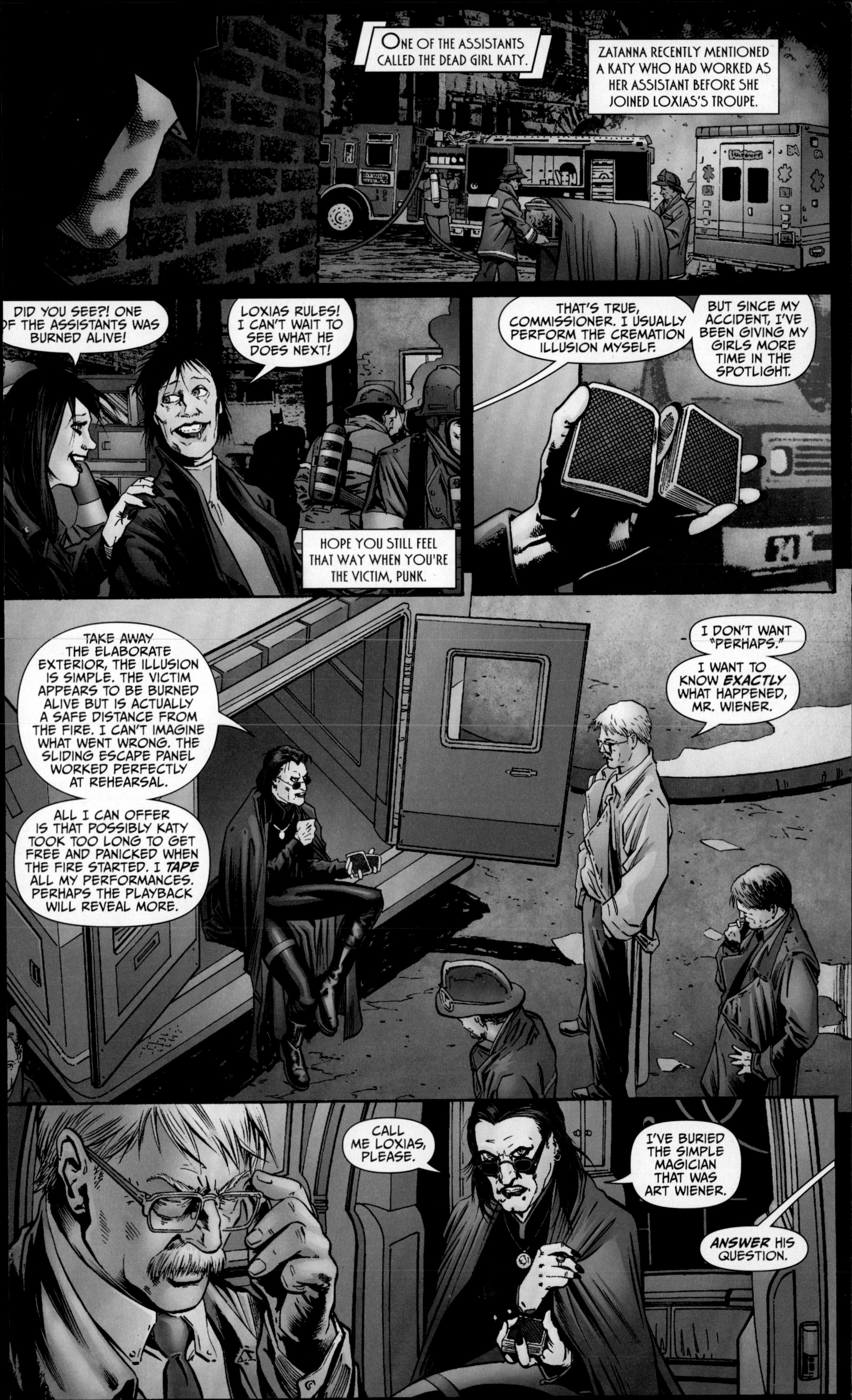
ONE OF THE ASSISTANTS CALLED THE DEAD GIRL KATY.
ZATANNA RECENTLY MENTIONED A KATY WHO HAD WORKED AS HER ASSISTANT BEFORE SHE JOINED LOXIAS'S TROUPE.
DID YOU SEE?! ONE OF THE ASSISTANTS WAS BURNED ALIVE!
LOXIAS RULES! I CAN'T WAIT TO SEE WHAT HE DOES NEXT!
HOPE YOU STILL FEEL THAT WAY WHEN YOU'RE THE VICTIM, PUNK.
THAT'S TRUE, COMMISSIONER. I USUALLY PERFORM THE CREMATION ILLUSION MYSELF.
BUT SINCE MY ACCIDENT, I'VE BEEN GIVING MY GIRLS MORE TIME IN THE SPOTLIGHT.
TAKE AWAY THE ELABORATE EXTERIOR, THE ILLUSION IS SIMPLE. THE VICTIM APPEARS TO BE BURNED ALIVE BUT IS ACTUALLY A SAFE DISTANCE FROM THE FIRE. I CAN'T IMAGINE WHAT WENT WRONG. THE SLIDING ESCAPE PANEL WORKED PERFECTLY AT REHEARSAL.
ALL I CAN OFFER IS THAT POSSIBLY KATY TOOK TOO LONG TO GET FREE AND PANICKED WHEN THE FIRE STARTED. I *TAPE* ALL MY PERFORMANCES. PERHAPS THE PLAYBACK WILL REVEAL MORE.
I DON'T WANT "PERHAPS."
I WANT TO KNOW ***EXACTLY*** WHAT HAPPENED, MR. WIENER.
CALL ME LOXIAS, PLEASE.
I'VE BURIED THE SIMPLE MAGICIAN THAT WAS ART WIENER.
ANSWER HIS QUESTION.

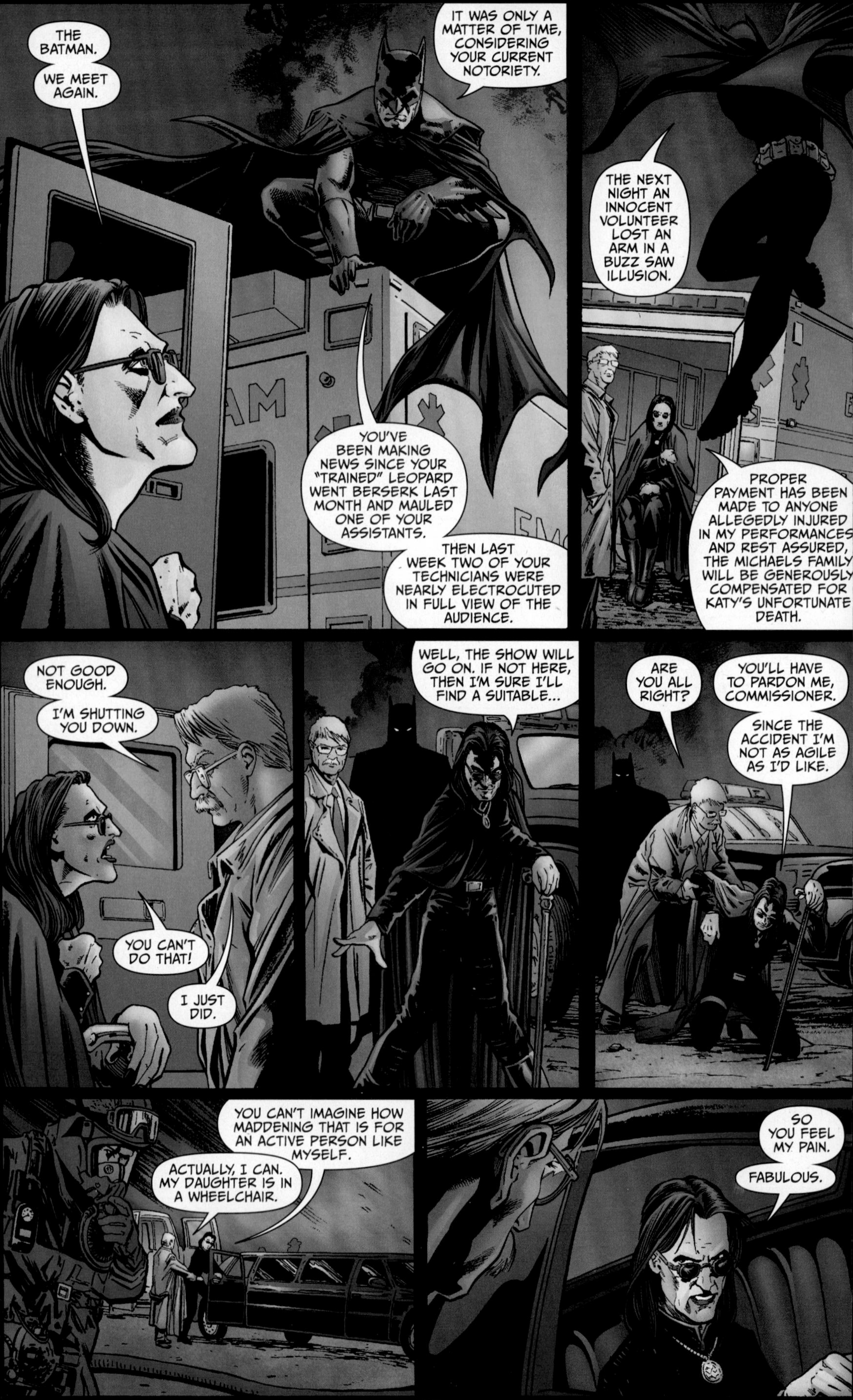
THE BATMAN.
WE MEET AGAIN.
IT WAS ONLY A MATTER OF TIME, CONSIDERING YOUR CURRENT NOTORIETY.
YOU'VE BEEN MAKING NEWS SINCE YOUR "TRAINED" LEOPARD WENT BERSERK LAST MONTH AND MAULED ONE OF YOUR ASSISTANTS.
THEN LAST WEEK TWO OF YOUR TECHNICIANS WERE NEARLY ELECTROCUTED IN FULL VIEW OF THE AUDIENCE.
THE NEXT NIGHT AN INNOCENT VOLUNTEER LOST AN ARM IN A BUZZ SAW ILLUSION.
PROPER PAYMENT HAS BEEN MADE TO ANYONE ALLEGEDLY INJURED IN MY PERFORMANCES AND REST ASSURED, THE MICHAELS FAMILY WILL BE GENEROUSLY COMPENSATED FOR KATY'S UNFORTUNATE DEATH.
NOT GOOD ENOUGH.
I'M SHUTTING YOU DOWN.
YOU CAN'T DO THAT!
I JUST DID.
WELL, THE SHOW WILL GO ON. IF NOT HERE, THEN I'M SURE I'LL FIND A SUITABLE...
ARE YOU ALL RIGHT?
YOU'LL HAVE TO PARDON ME, COMMISSIONER.
SINCE THE ACCIDENT I'M NOT AS AGILE AS I'D LIKE.
YOU CAN'T IMAGINE HOW MADDENING THAT IS FOR AN ACTIVE PERSON LIKE MYSELF.
ACTUALLY, I CAN. MY DAUGHTER IS IN A WHEELCHAIR.
SO YOU FEEL MY PAIN.
FABULOUS.

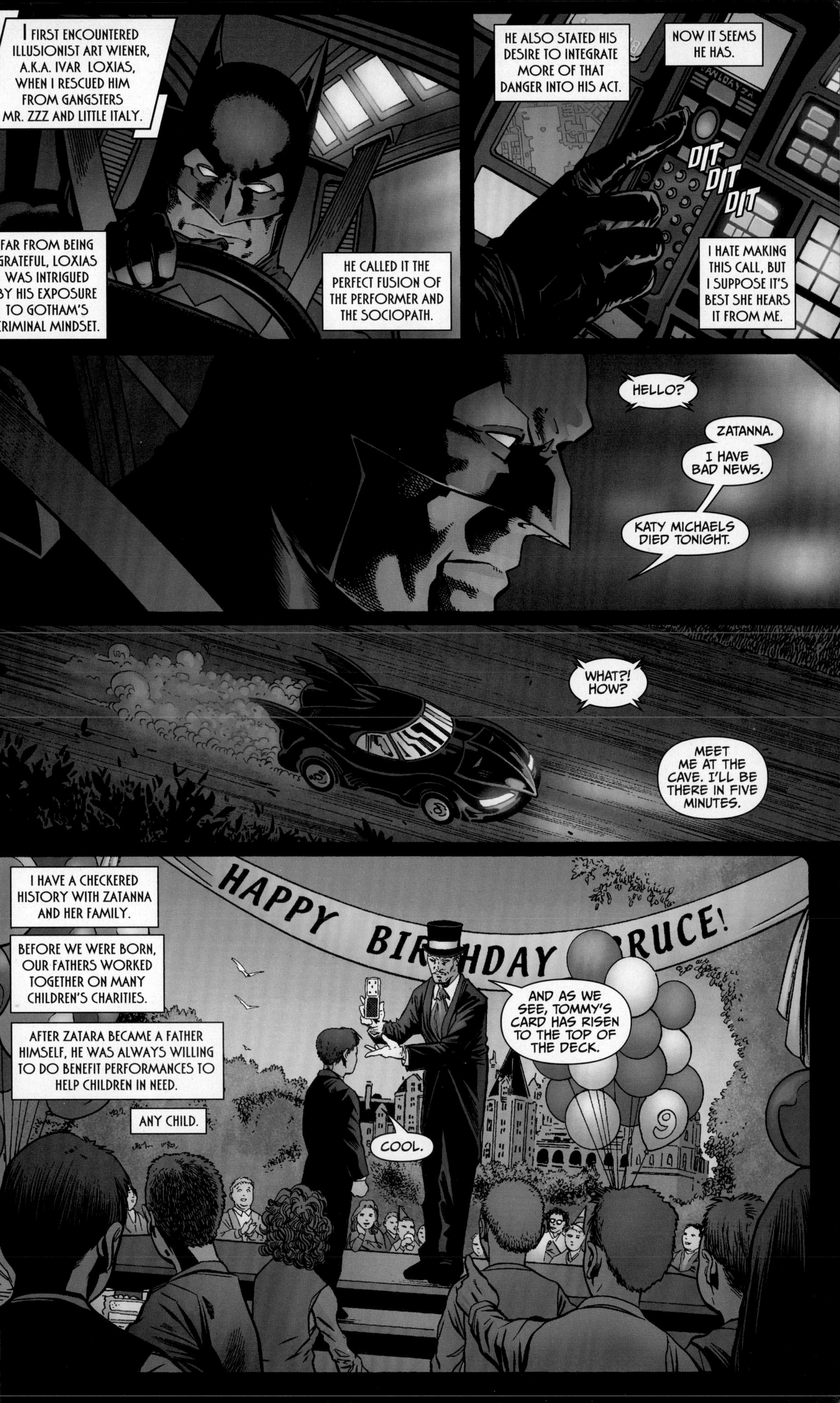
I FIRST ENCOUNTERED ILLUSIONIST ART WIENER, A.K.A. IVAR LOXIAS, WHEN I RESCUED HIM FROM GANGSTERS MR. ZZZ AND LITTLE ITALY.
FAR FROM BEING GRATEFUL, LOXIAS WAS INTRIGUED BY HIS EXPOSURE TO GOTHAM'S CRIMINAL MINDSET.
HE CALLED IT THE PERFECT FUSION OF THE PERFORMER AND THE SOCIOPATH.
HE ALSO STATED HIS DESIRE TO INTEGRATE MORE OF THAT DANGER INTO HIS ACT.
NOW IT SEEMS HE HAS.
DIT DIT DIT
I HATE MAKING THIS CALL, BUT I SUPPOSE IT'S BEST SHE HEARS IT FROM ME.
HELLO?
ZATANNA.
I HAVE BAD NEWS.
KATY MICHAELS DIED TONIGHT.
WHAT?! HOW?
MEET ME AT THE CAVE. I'LL BE THERE IN FIVE MINUTES.
HAPPY BIRTHDAY BRUCE!
I HAVE A CHECKERED HISTORY WITH ZATANNA AND HER FAMILY.
BEFORE WE WERE BORN, OUR FATHERS WORKED TOGETHER ON MANY CHILDREN'S CHARITIES.
AFTER ZATARA BECAME A FATHER HIMSELF, HE WAS ALWAYS WILLING TO DO BENEFIT PERFORMANCES TO HELP CHILDREN IN NEED.
ANY CHILD.
AND AS WE SEE, TOMMY'S CARD HAS RISEN TO THE TOP OF THE DECK.
COOL.

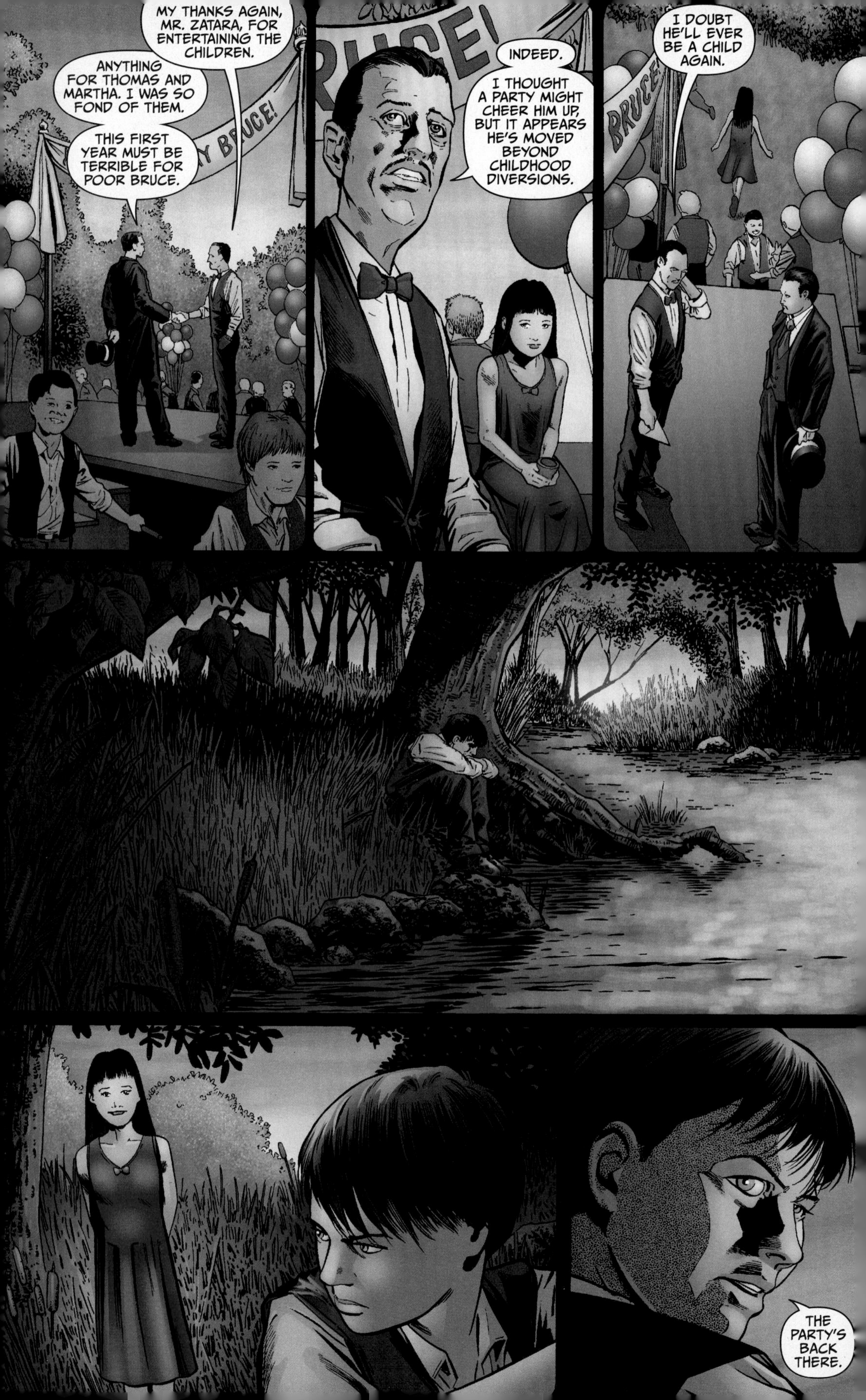

MY THANKS AGAIN, MR. ZATARA, FOR ENTERTAINING THE CHILDREN.
ANYTHING FOR THOMAS AND MARTHA. I WAS SO FOND OF THEM.
THIS FIRST YEAR MUST BE TERRIBLE FOR POOR BRUCE.
INDEED.
I THOUGHT A PARTY MIGHT CHEER HIM UP, BUT IT APPEARS HE'S MOVED BEYOND CHILDHOOD DIVERSIONS.
I DOUBT HE'LL EVER BE A CHILD AGAIN.
THE PARTY'S BACK THERE.

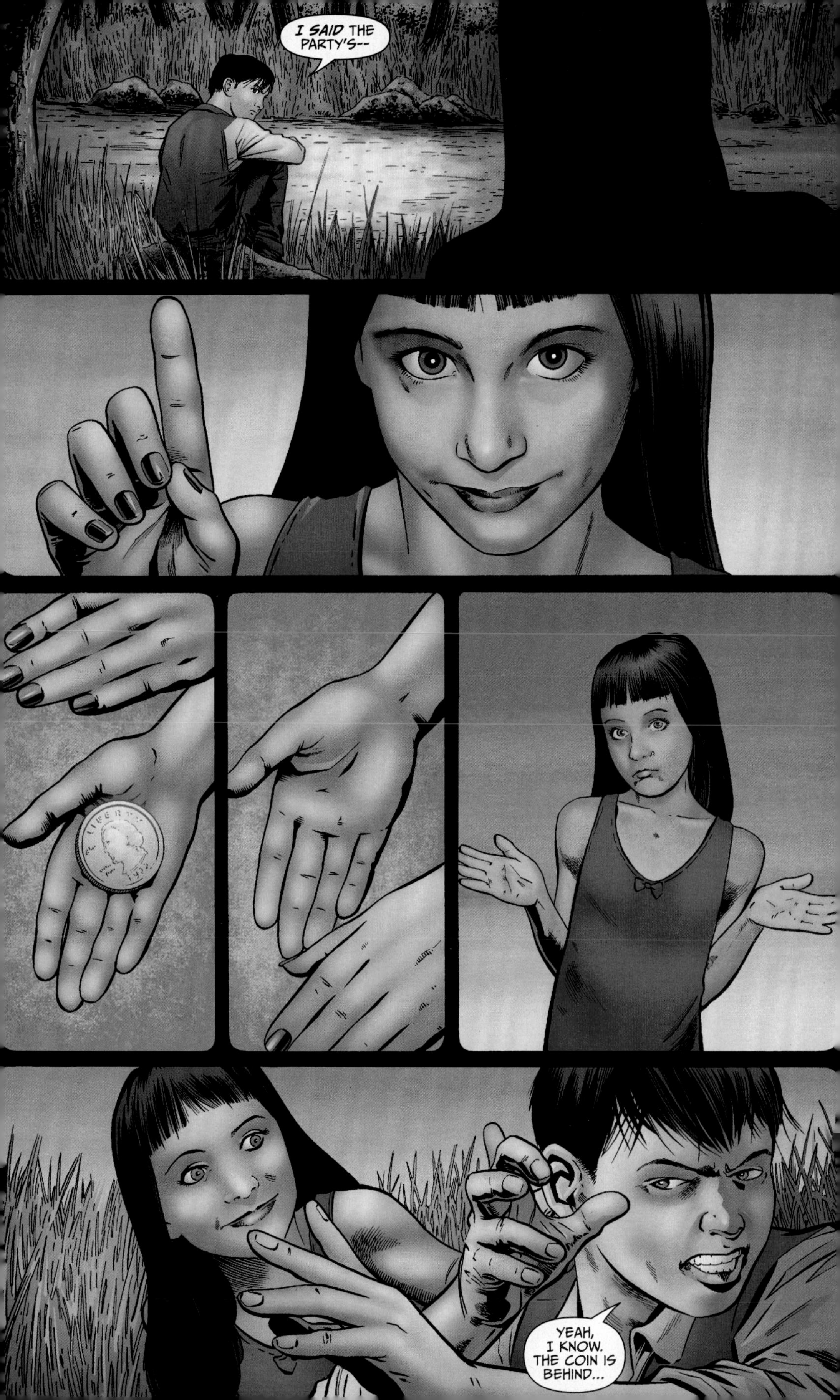
I *SAID* THE PARTY'S--
YEAH, I KNOW. THE COIN IS BEHIND...

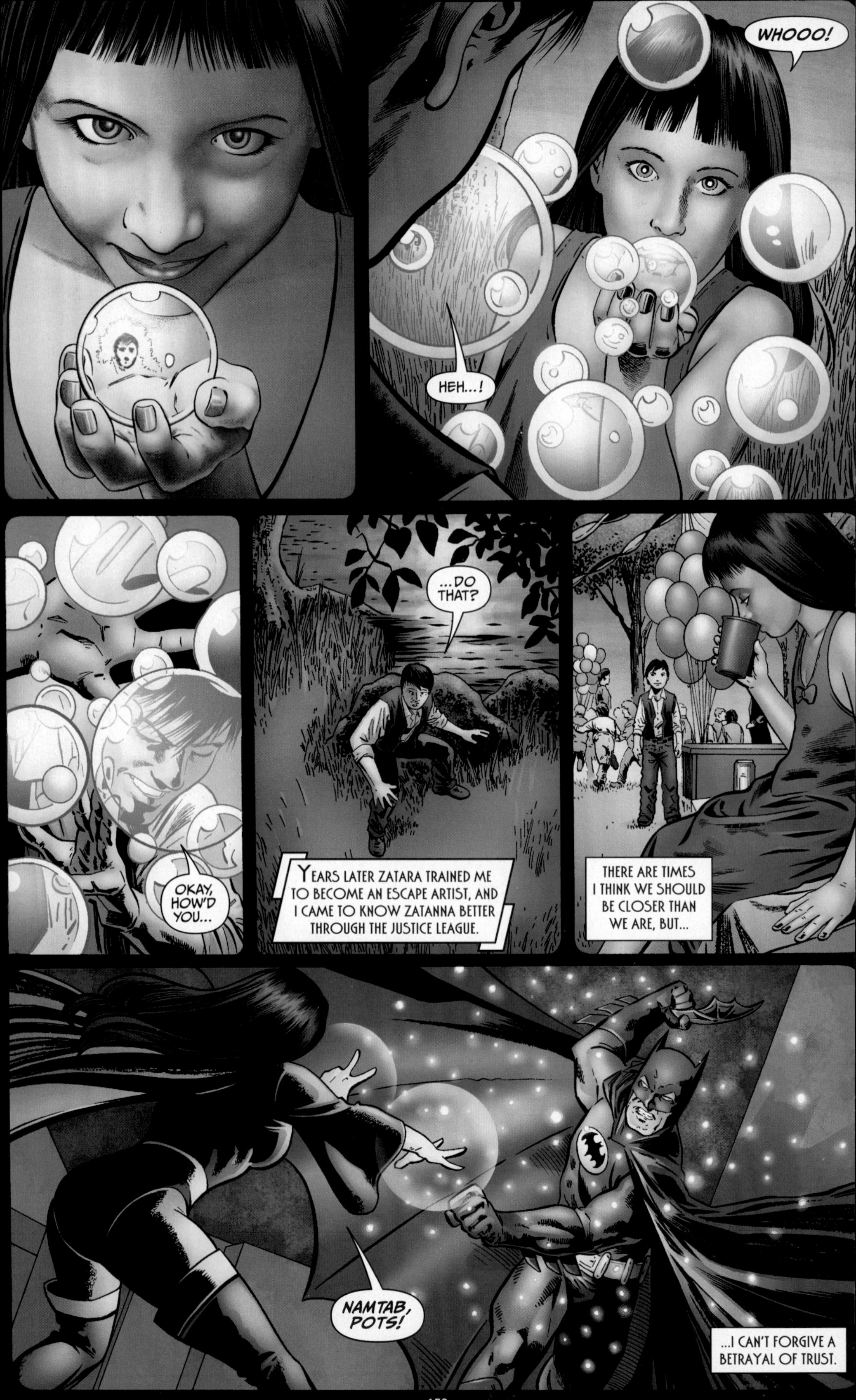

WHOOO!
HEH...!
OKAY, HOW'D YOU...
...DO THAT?
YEARS LATER ZATARA TRAINED ME TO BECOME AN ESCAPE ARTIST, AND I CAME TO KNOW ZATANNA BETTER THROUGH THE JUSTICE LEAGUE.
THERE ARE TIMES I THINK WE SHOULD BE CLOSER THAN WE ARE, BUT...
NAMTAB, POTS!
...I CAN'T FORGIVE A BETRAYAL OF TRUST.

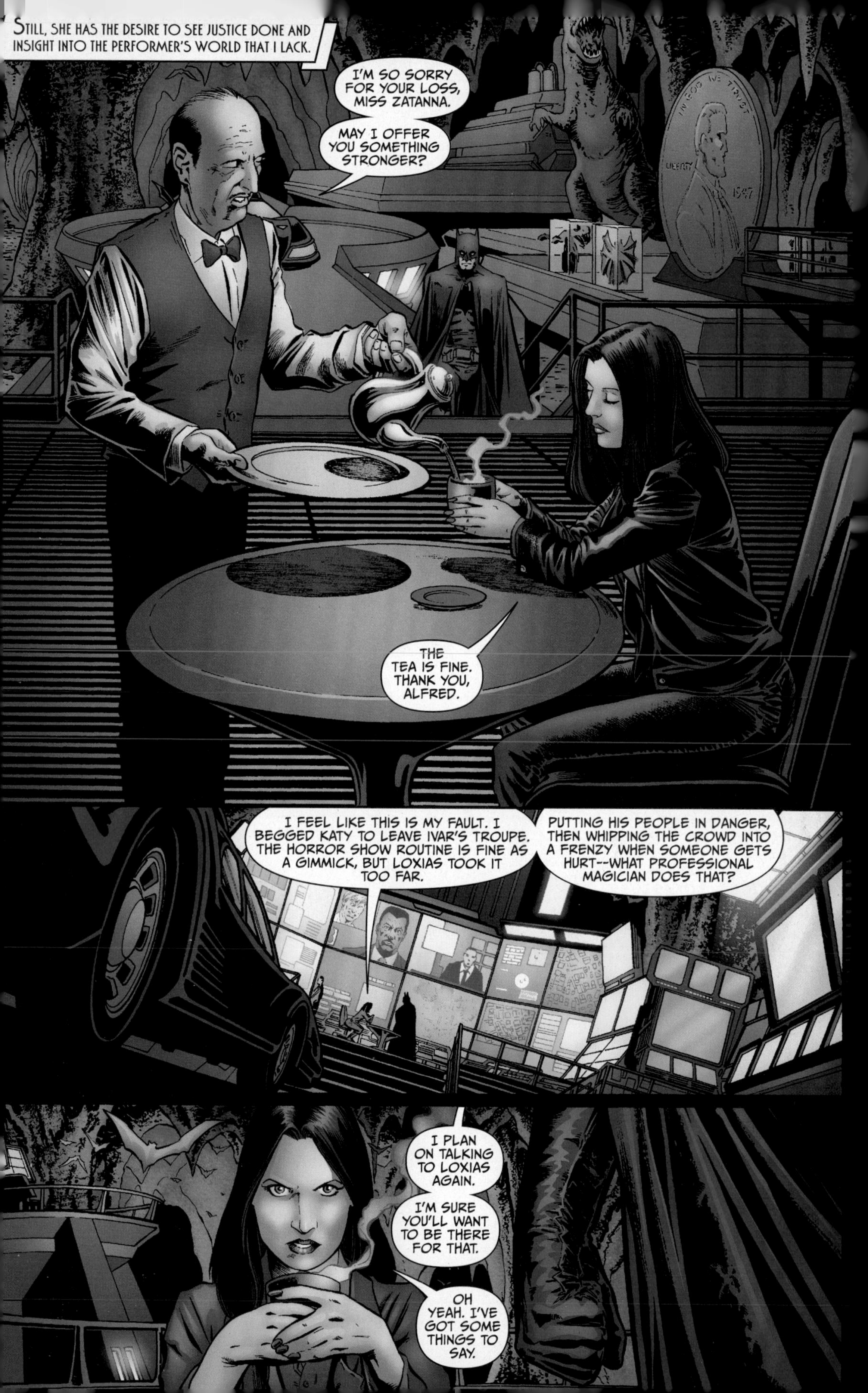

STILL, SHE HAS THE DESIRE TO SEE JUSTICE DONE AND INSIGHT INTO THE PERFORMER'S WORLD THAT I LACK.
I'M SO SORRY FOR YOUR LOSS, MISS ZATANNA.
MAY I OFFER YOU SOMETHING STRONGER?
THE TEA IS FINE. THANK YOU, ALFRED.
I FEEL LIKE THIS IS MY FAULT. I BEGGED KATY TO LEAVE IVAR'S TROUPE. THE HORROR SHOW ROUTINE IS FINE AS A GIMMICK, BUT LOXIAS TOOK IT TOO FAR.
PUTTING HIS PEOPLE IN DANGER, THEN WHIPPING THE CROWD INTO A FRENZY WHEN SOMEONE GETS HURT--WHAT PROFESSIONAL MAGICIAN DOES THAT?
I PLAN ON TALKING TO LOXIAS AGAIN.
I'M SURE YOU'LL WANT TO BE THERE FOR THAT.
OH YEAH. I'VE GOT SOME THINGS TO SAY.

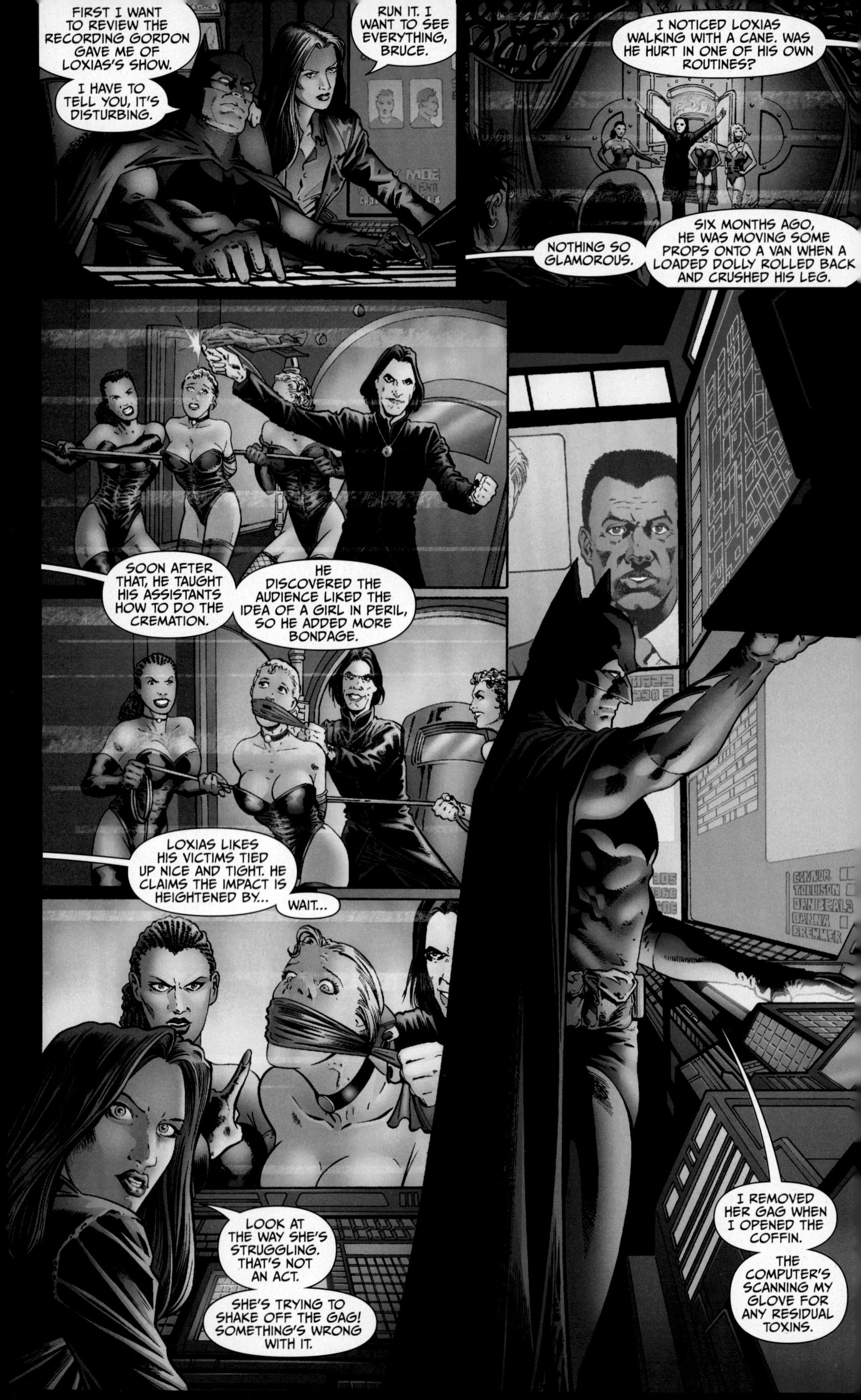
FIRST I WANT TO REVIEW THE RECORDING GORDON GAVE ME OF LOXIAS'S SHOW.
I HAVE TO TELL YOU, IT'S DISTURBING.
RUN IT. I WANT TO SEE EVERYTHING, BRUCE.
I NOTICED LOXIAS WALKING WITH A CANE. WAS HE HURT IN ONE OF HIS OWN ROUTINES?
NOTHING SO GLAMOROUS.
SIX MONTHS AGO, HE WAS MOVING SOME PROPS ONTO A VAN WHEN A LOADED DOLLY ROLLED BACK AND CRUSHED HIS LEG.
SOON AFTER THAT, HE TAUGHT HIS ASSISTANTS HOW TO DO THE CREMATION.
HE DISCOVERED THE AUDIENCE LIKED THE IDEA OF A GIRL IN PERIL, SO HE ADDED MORE BONDAGE.
LOXIAS LIKES HIS VICTIMS TIED UP NICE AND TIGHT. HE CLAIMS THE IMPACT IS HEIGHTENED BY...
WAIT...
LOOK AT THE WAY SHE'S STRUGGLING. THAT'S NOT AN ACT.
SHE'S TRYING TO SHAKE OFF THE GAG! SOMETHING'S WRONG WITH IT.
I REMOVED HER GAG WHEN I OPENED THE COFFIN.
THE COMPUTER'S SCANNING MY GLOVE FOR ANY RESIDUAL TOXINS.

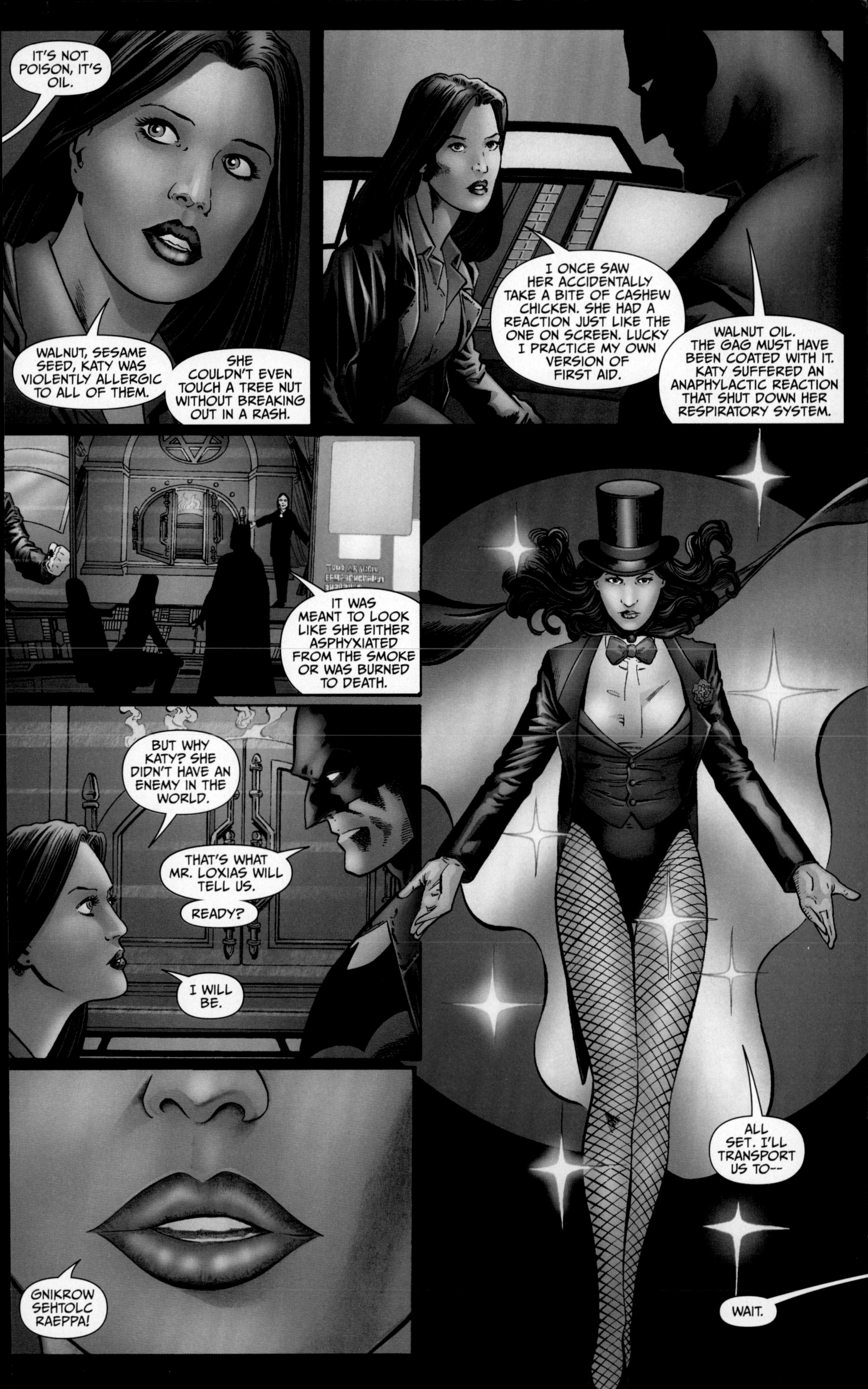
IT'S NOT POISON, IT'S OIL.
WALNUT, SESAME SEED, KATY WAS VIOLENTLY ALLERGIC TO ALL OF THEM.
SHE COULDN'T EVEN TOUCH A TREE NUT WITHOUT BREAKING OUT IN A RASH.
I ONCE SAW HER ACCIDENTALLY TAKE A BITE OF CASHEW CHICKEN. SHE HAD A REACTION JUST LIKE THE ONE ON SCREEN. LUCKY I PRACTICE MY OWN VERSION OF FIRST AID.
WALNUT OIL. THE GAG MUST HAVE BEEN COATED WITH IT. KATY SUFFERED AN ANAPHYLACTIC REACTION THAT SHUT DOWN HER RESPIRATORY SYSTEM.
IT WAS MEANT TO LOOK LIKE SHE EITHER ASPHYXIATED FROM THE SMOKE OR WAS BURNED TO DEATH.
BUT WHY KATY? SHE DIDN'T HAVE AN ENEMY IN THE WORLD.
THAT'S WHAT MR. LOXIAS WILL TELL US.
READY?
I WILL BE.
GNIKROW SEHTOLC RAEPPA!
ALL SET. I'LL TRANSPORT US TO--
WAIT.

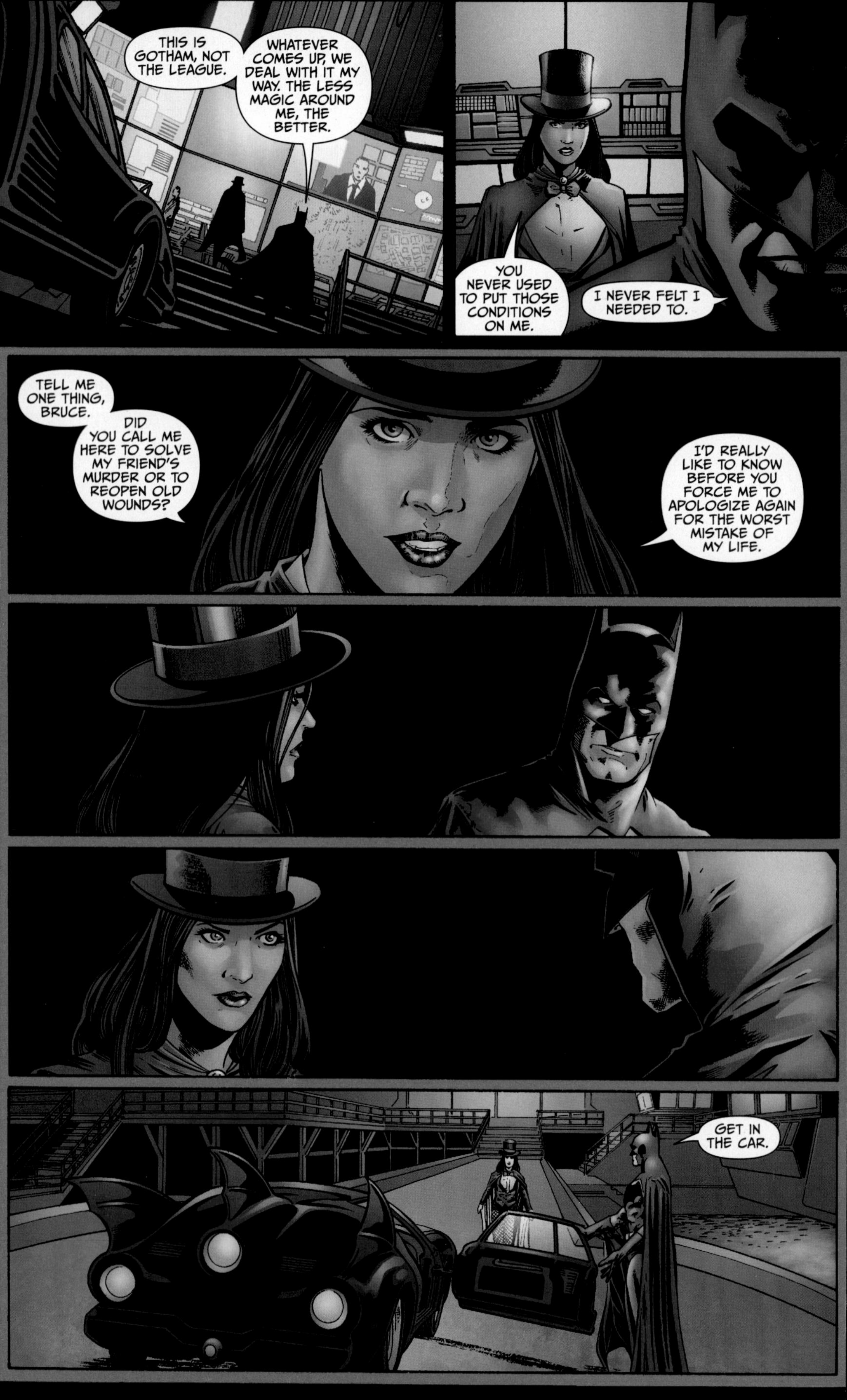
THIS IS GOTHAM, NOT THE LEAGUE.
WHATEVER COMES UP, WE DEAL WITH IT MY WAY. THE LESS MAGIC AROUND ME, THE BETTER.
YOU NEVER USED TO PUT THOSE CONDITIONS ON ME.
I NEVER FELT I NEEDED TO.
TELL ME ONE THING, BRUCE.
DID YOU CALL ME HERE TO SOLVE MY FRIEND'S MURDER OR TO REOPEN OLD WOUNDS?
I'D REALLY LIKE TO KNOW BEFORE YOU FORCE ME TO APOLOGIZE AGAIN FOR THE WORST MISTAKE OF MY LIFE.
GET IN THE CAR.

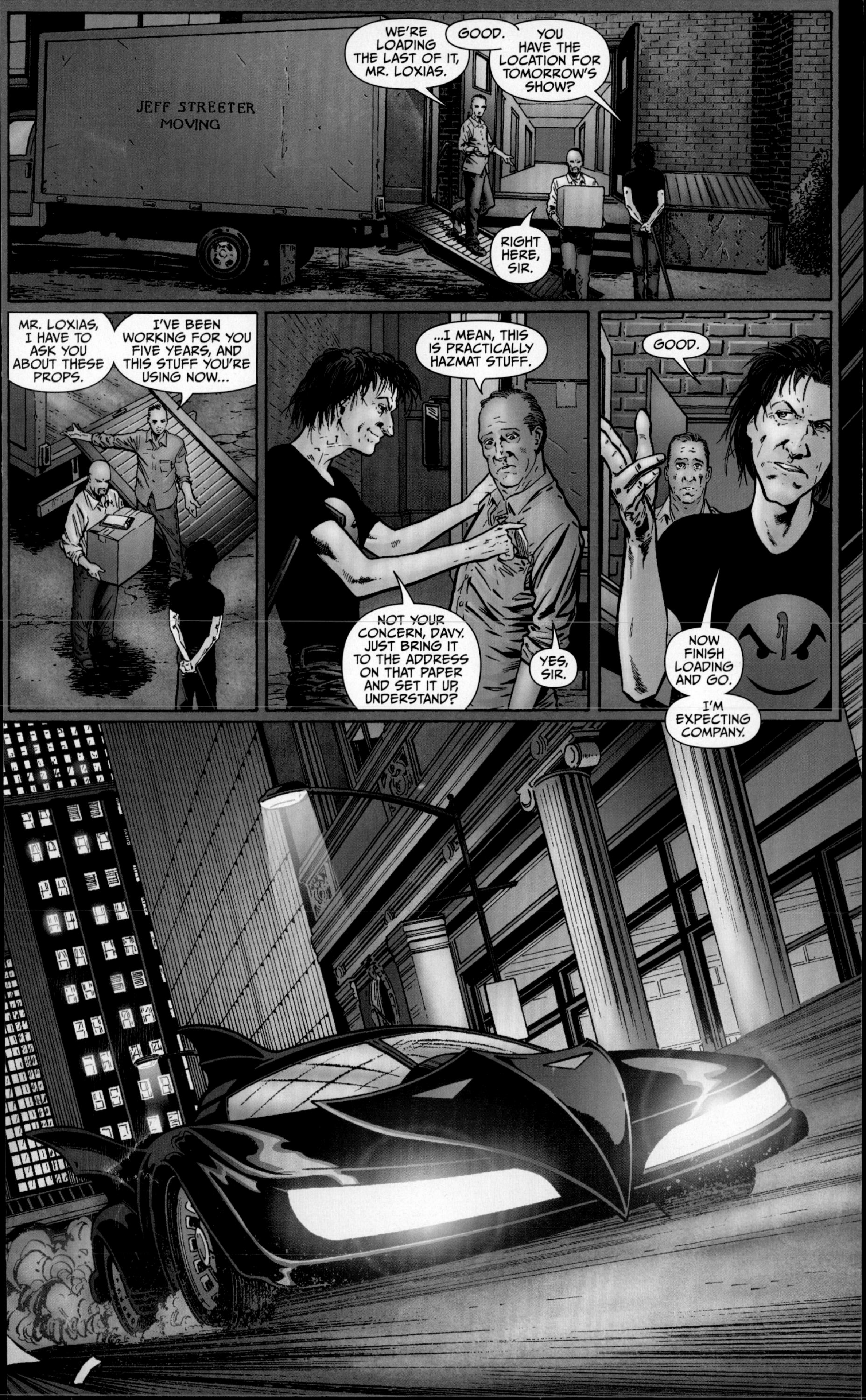
JEFF STREETER
MOVING
WE'RE LOADING THE LAST OF IT, MR. LOXIAS.
GOOD.
YOU HAVE THE LOCATION FOR TOMORROW'S SHOW?
RIGHT HERE, SIR.
MR. LOXIAS, I HAVE TO ASK YOU ABOUT THESE PROPS.
I'VE BEEN WORKING FOR YOU FIVE YEARS, AND THIS STUFF YOU'RE USING NOW...
...I MEAN, THIS IS PRACTICALLY HAZMAT STUFF.
NOT YOUR CONCERN, DAVY. JUST BRING IT TO THE ADDRESS ON THAT PAPER AND SET IT UP, UNDERSTAND?
YES, SIR.
GOOD.
NOW FINISH LOADING AND GO.
I'M EXPECTING COMPANY.

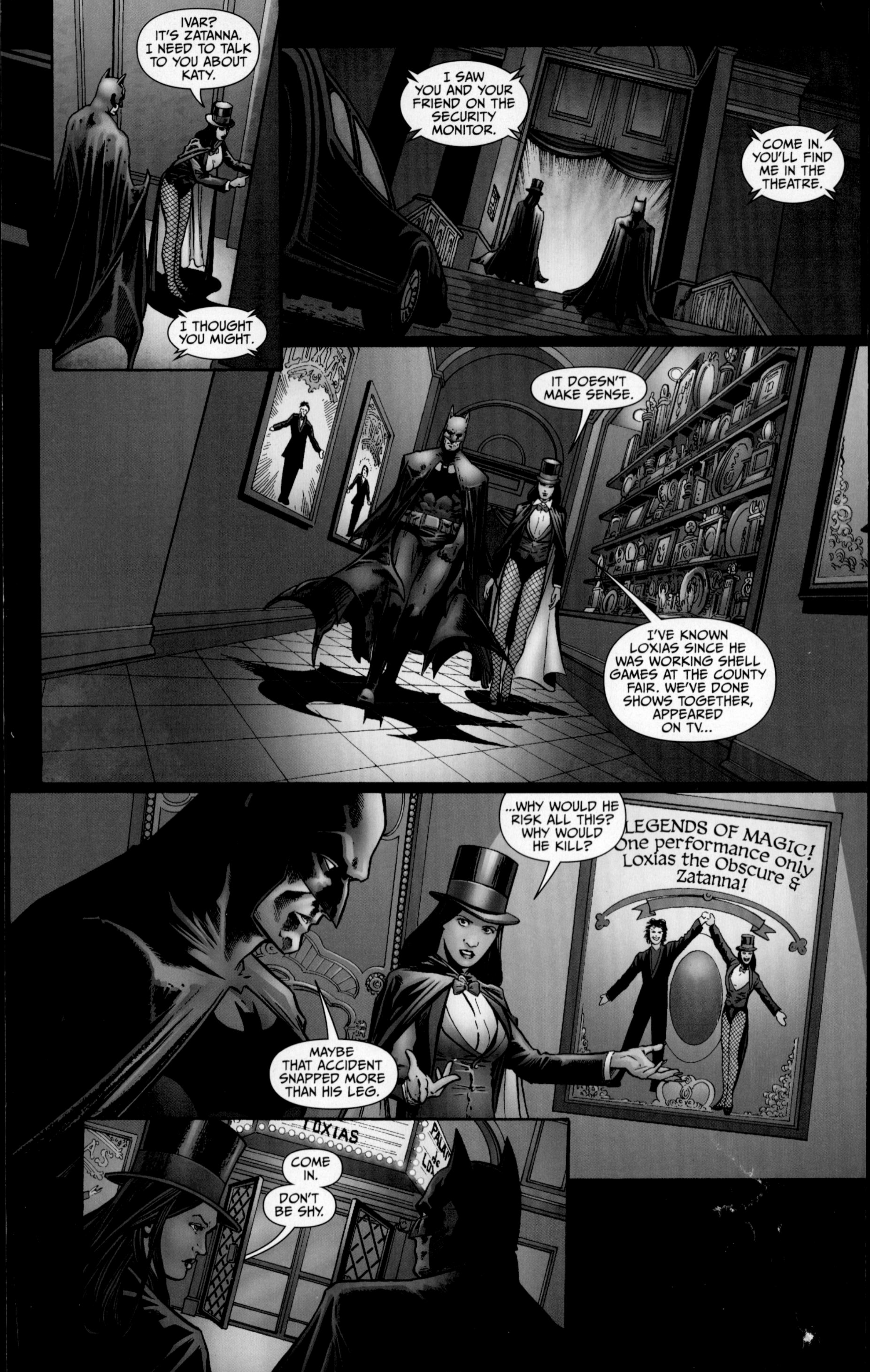
IVAR? IT'S ZATANNA. I NEED TO TALK TO YOU ABOUT KATY.
I THOUGHT YOU MIGHT.
I SAW YOU AND YOUR FRIEND ON THE SECURITY MONITOR.
COME IN. YOU'LL FIND ME IN THE THEATRE.
LOXIAS
IT DOESN'T MAKE SENSE.
I'VE KNOWN LOXIAS SINCE HE WAS WORKING SHELL GAMES AT THE COUNTY FAIR. WE'VE DONE SHOWS TOGETHER, APPEARED ON TV...
...WHY WOULD HE RISK ALL THIS? WHY WOULD HE KILL?
LEGENDS OF MAGIC! One performance only Loxias the Obscure & Zatanna!
MAYBE THAT ACCIDENT SNAPPED MORE THAN HIS LEG.
LOXIAS
COME IN.
DON'T BE SHY.

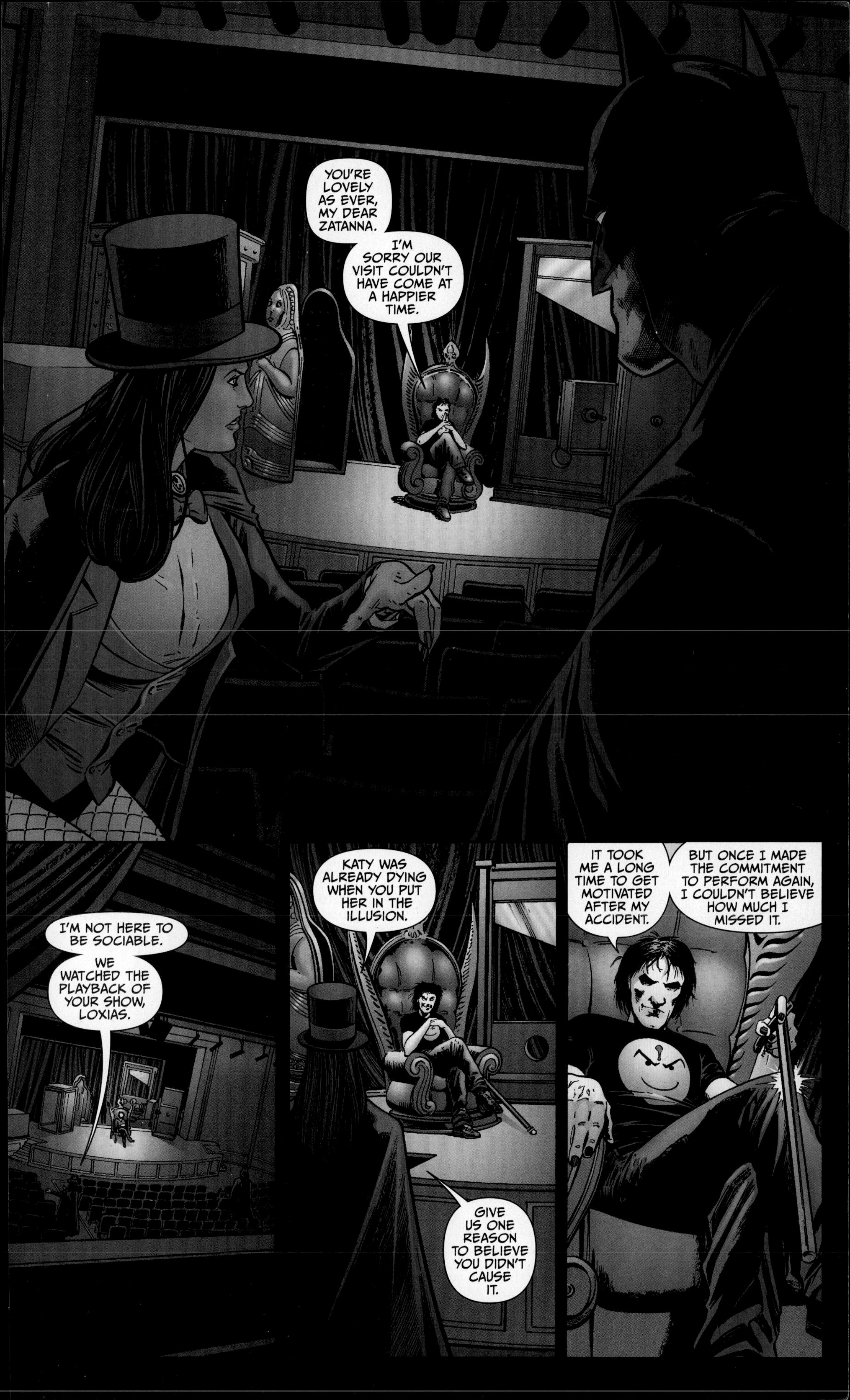
YOU'RE LOVELY AS EVER, MY DEAR ZATANNA.
I'M SORRY OUR VISIT COULDN'T HAVE COME AT A HAPPIER TIME.
I'M NOT HERE TO BE SOCIABLE.
WE WATCHED THE PLAYBACK OF YOUR SHOW, LOXIAS.
KATY WAS ALREADY DYING WHEN YOU PUT HER IN THE ILLUSION.
GIVE US ONE REASON TO BELIEVE YOU DIDN'T CAUSE IT.
IT TOOK ME A LONG TIME TO GET MOTIVATED AFTER MY ACCIDENT.
BUT ONCE I MADE THE COMMITMENT TO PERFORM AGAIN, I COULDN'T BELIEVE HOW MUCH I MISSED IT.

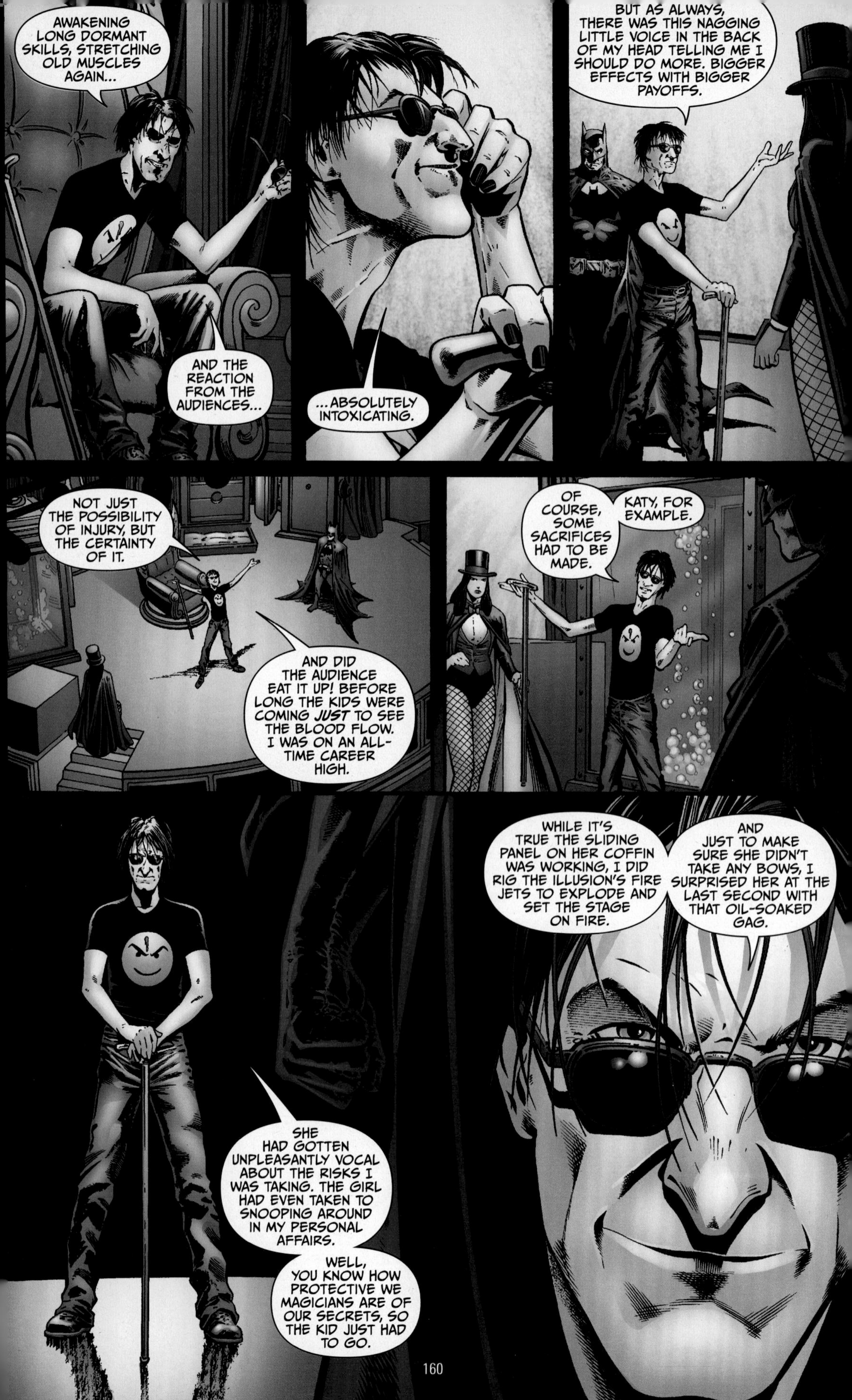
AWAKENING LONG DORMANT SKILLS, STRETCHING OLD MUSCLES AGAIN...
AND THE REACTION FROM THE AUDIENCES...
...ABSOLUTELY INTOXICATING.
BUT AS ALWAYS, THERE WAS THIS NAGGING LITTLE VOICE IN THE BACK OF MY HEAD TELLING ME I SHOULD DO MORE. BIGGER EFFECTS WITH BIGGER PAYOFFS.
NOT JUST THE POSSIBILITY OF INJURY, BUT THE CERTAINTY OF IT.
AND DID THE AUDIENCE EAT IT UP! BEFORE LONG THE KIDS WERE COMING *JUST* TO SEE THE BLOOD FLOW. I WAS ON AN ALL-TIME CAREER HIGH.
OF COURSE, SOME SACRIFICES HAD TO BE MADE.
KATY, FOR EXAMPLE.
SHE HAD GOTTEN UNPLEASANTLY VOCAL ABOUT THE RISKS I WAS TAKING. THE GIRL HAD EVEN TAKEN TO SNOOPING AROUND IN MY PERSONAL AFFAIRS.
WELL, YOU KNOW HOW PROTECTIVE WE MAGICIANS ARE OF OUR SECRETS, SO THE KID JUST HAD TO GO.
WHILE IT'S TRUE THE SLIDING PANEL ON HER COFFIN WAS WORKING, I DID RIG THE ILLUSION'S FIRE JETS TO EXPLODE AND SET THE STAGE ON FIRE.
AND JUST TO MAKE SURE SHE DIDN'T TAKE ANY BOWS, I SURPRISED HER AT THE LAST SECOND WITH THAT OIL-SOAKED GAG.

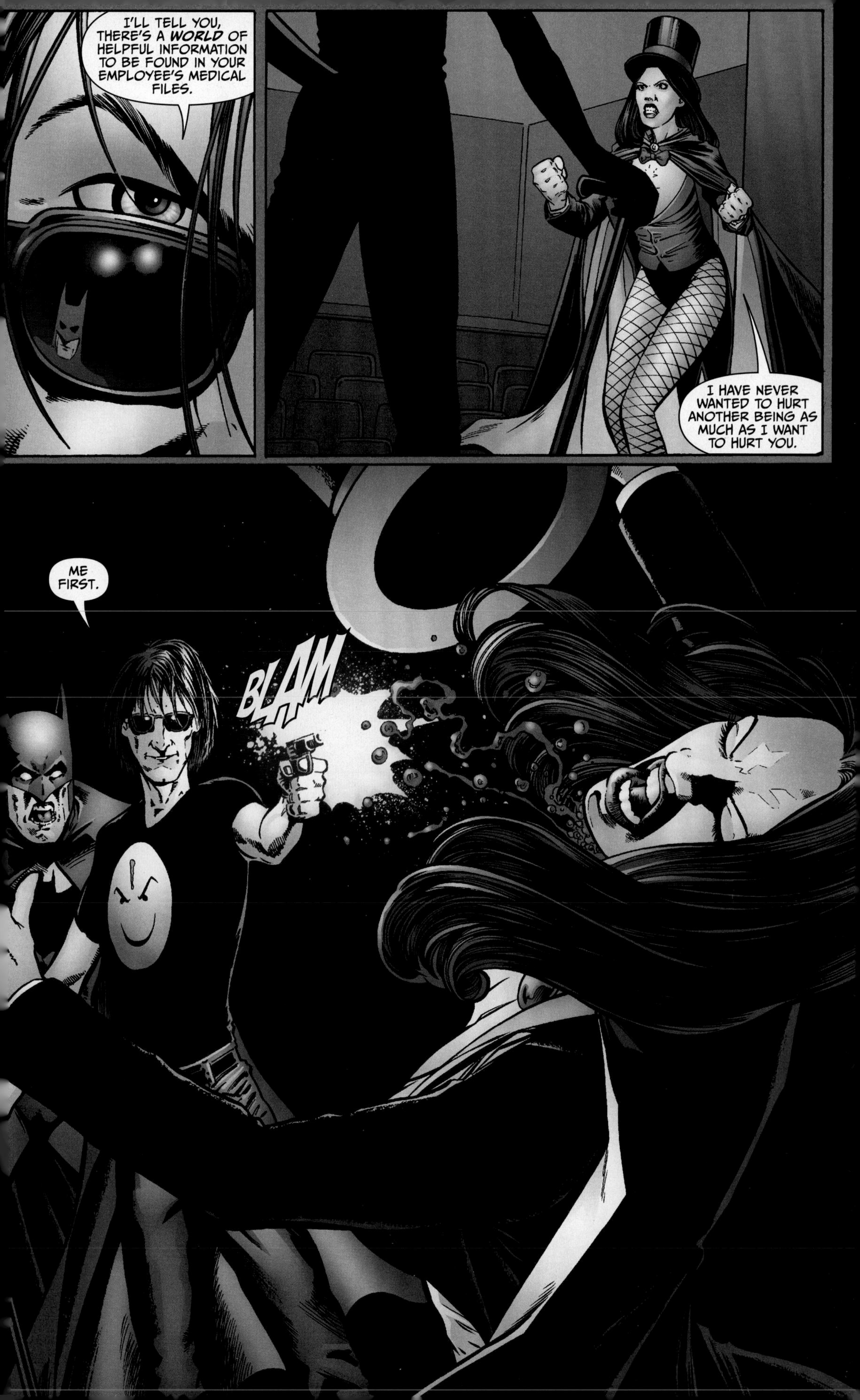
I'LL TELL YOU, THERE'S A WORLD OF HELPFUL INFORMATION TO BE FOUND IN YOUR EMPLOYEE'S MEDICAL FILES.
I HAVE NEVER WANTED TO HURT ANOTHER BEING AS MUCH AS I WANT TO HURT YOU.
ME FIRST.
BLAM

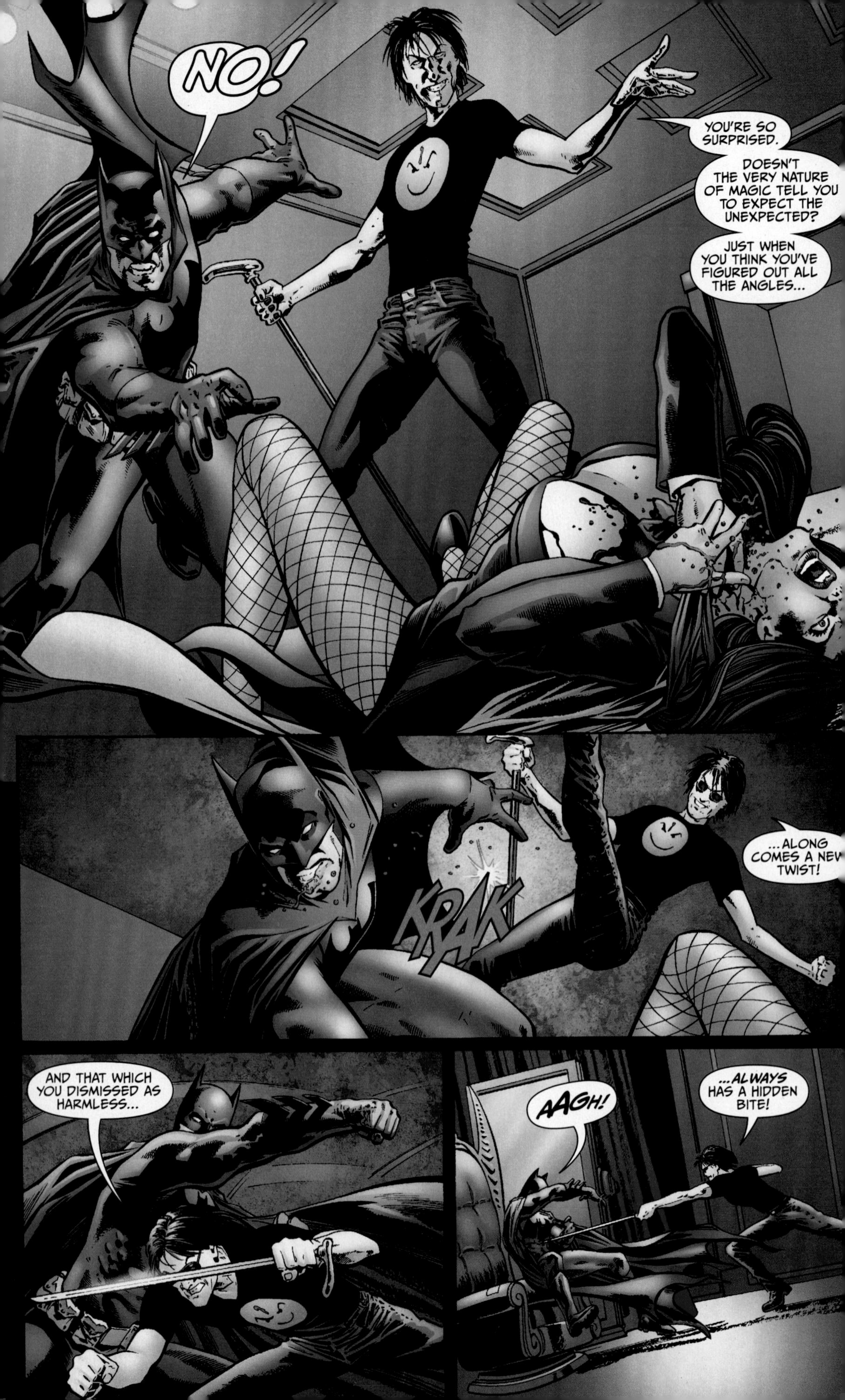
NO!
YOU'RE SO SURPRISED.
DOESN'T THE VERY NATURE OF MAGIC TELL YOU TO EXPECT THE UNEXPECTED?
JUST WHEN YOU THINK YOU'VE FIGURED OUT ALL THE ANGLES...
...ALONG COMES A NEW TWIST!
KRAK
AND THAT WHICH YOU DISMISSED AS HARMLESS...
AAGH!
...ALWAYS HAS A HIDDEN BITE!

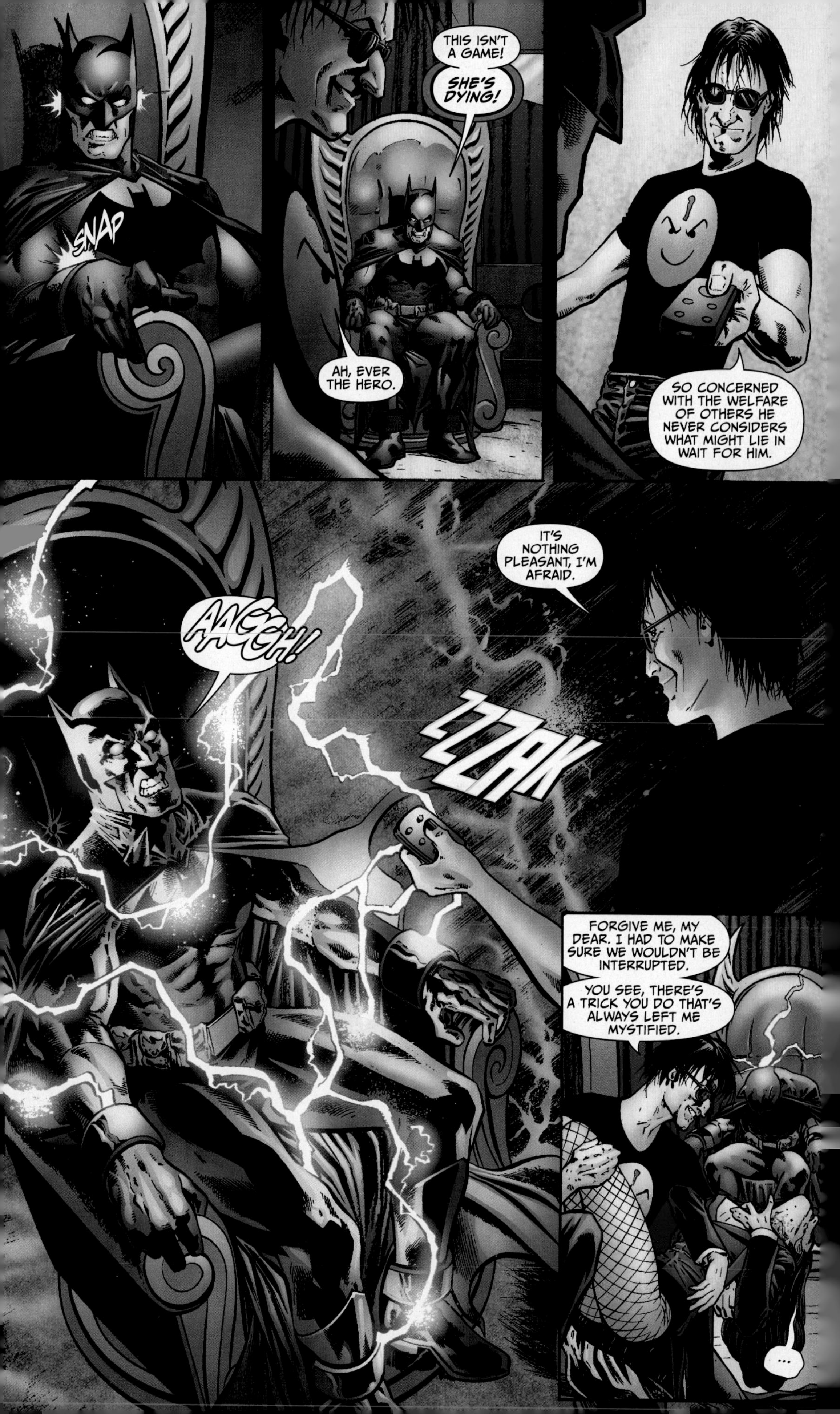
SNAP
THIS ISN'T A GAME!
SHE'S DYING!
AH, EVER THE HERO.
SO CONCERNED WITH THE WELFARE OF OTHERS HE NEVER CONSIDERS WHAT MIGHT LIE IN WAIT FOR HIM.
IT'S NOTHING PLEASANT, I'M AFRAID.
AAGGH!
ZZZAK
FORGIVE ME, MY DEAR. I HAD TO MAKE SURE WE WOULDN'T BE INTERRUPTED.
YOU SEE, THERE'S A TRICK YOU DO THAT'S ALWAYS LEFT ME MYSTIFIED.
...

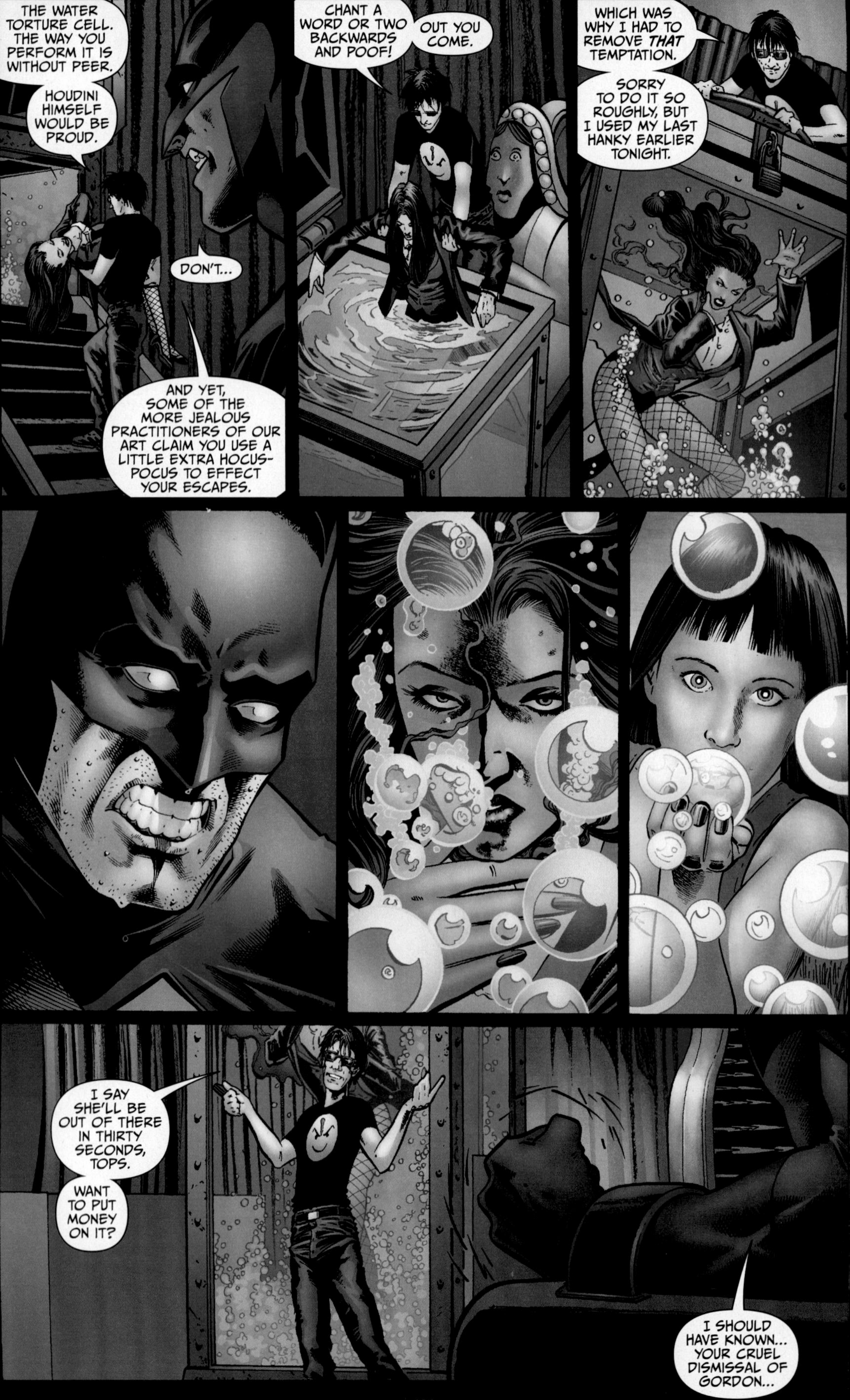
THE WATER TORTURE CELL. THE WAY YOU PERFORM IT IS WITHOUT PEER.
HOUDINI HIMSELF WOULD BE PROUD.
DON'T...
AND YET, SOME OF THE MORE JEALOUS PRACTITIONERS OF OUR ART CLAIM YOU USE A LITTLE EXTRA HOCUS-POCUS TO EFFECT YOUR ESCAPES.
CHANT A WORD OR TWO BACKWARDS AND POOF!
OUT YOU COME.
WHICH WAS WHY I HAD TO REMOVE *THAT* TEMPTATION.
SORRY TO DO IT SO ROUGHLY, BUT I USED MY LAST HANKY EARLIER TONIGHT.
I SAY SHE'LL BE OUT OF THERE IN THIRTY SECONDS, TOPS.
WANT TO PUT MONEY ON IT?
I SHOULD HAVE KNOWN... YOUR CRUEL DISMISSAL OF GORDON...

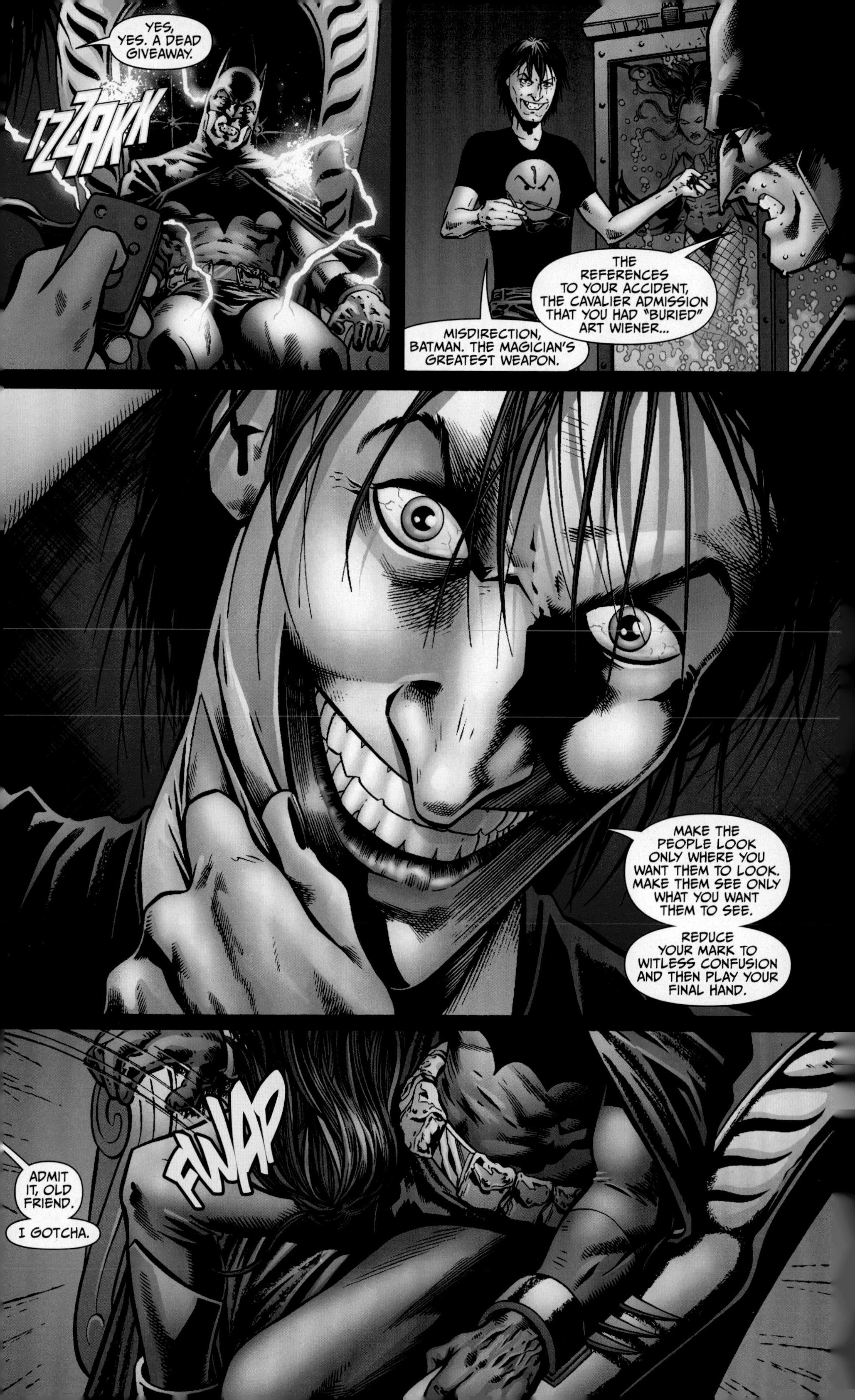
YES, YES. A DEAD GIVEAWAY.
TZZAKK
THE REFERENCES TO YOUR ACCIDENT, THE CAVALIER ADMISSION THAT YOU HAD "BURIED" ART WIENER...
MISDIRECTION, BATMAN. THE MAGICIAN'S GREATEST WEAPON.
MAKE THE PEOPLE LOOK ONLY WHERE YOU WANT THEM TO LOOK. MAKE THEM SEE ONLY WHAT YOU WANT THEM TO SEE.
REDUCE YOUR MARK TO WITLESS CONFUSION AND THEN PLAY YOUR FINAL HAND.
FWAP
ADMIT IT, OLD FRIEND.
I GOTCHA.

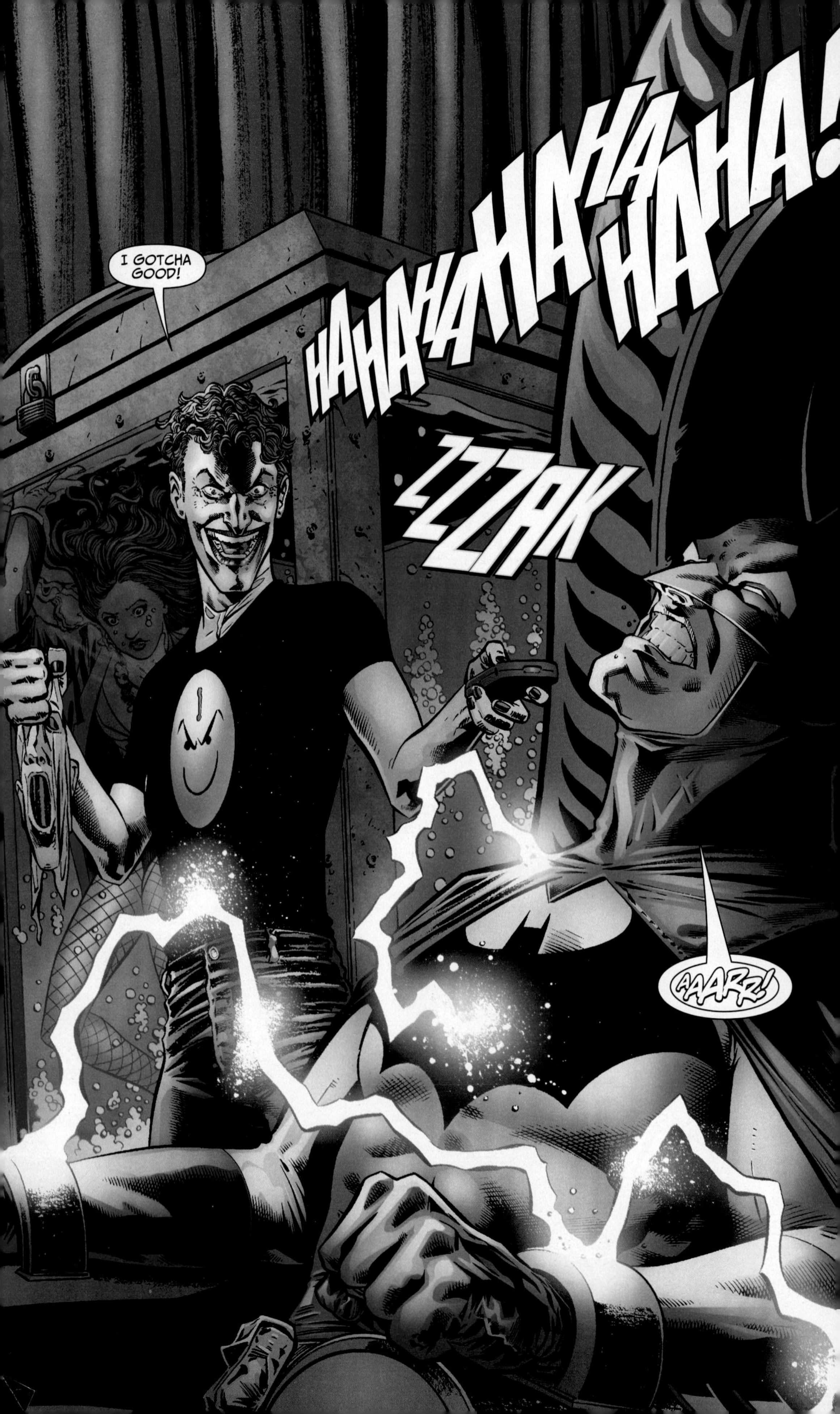
I GOTCHA GOOD!
HAHAHAHAHAHA HAHAHA!
ZZZAK
AAARR!

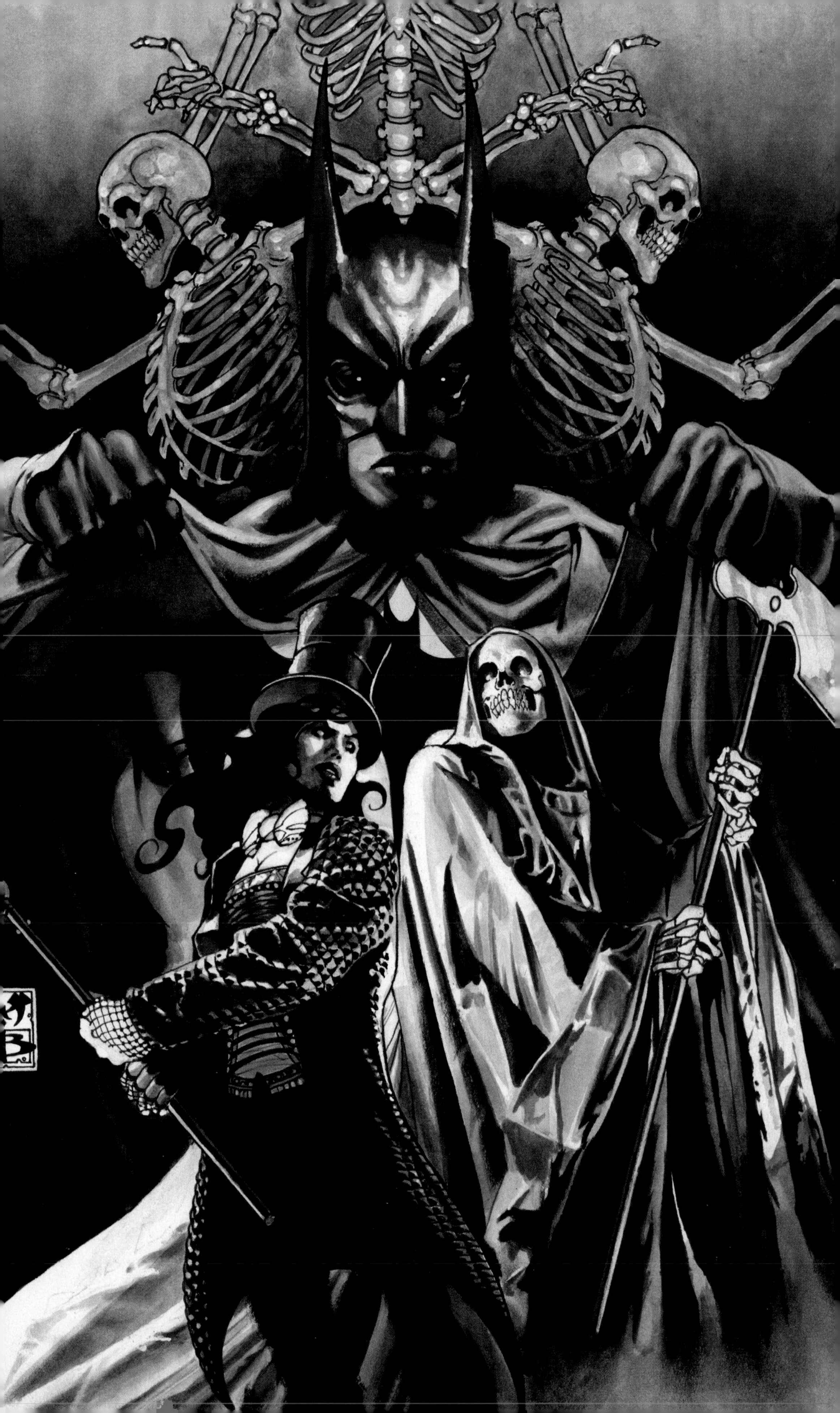

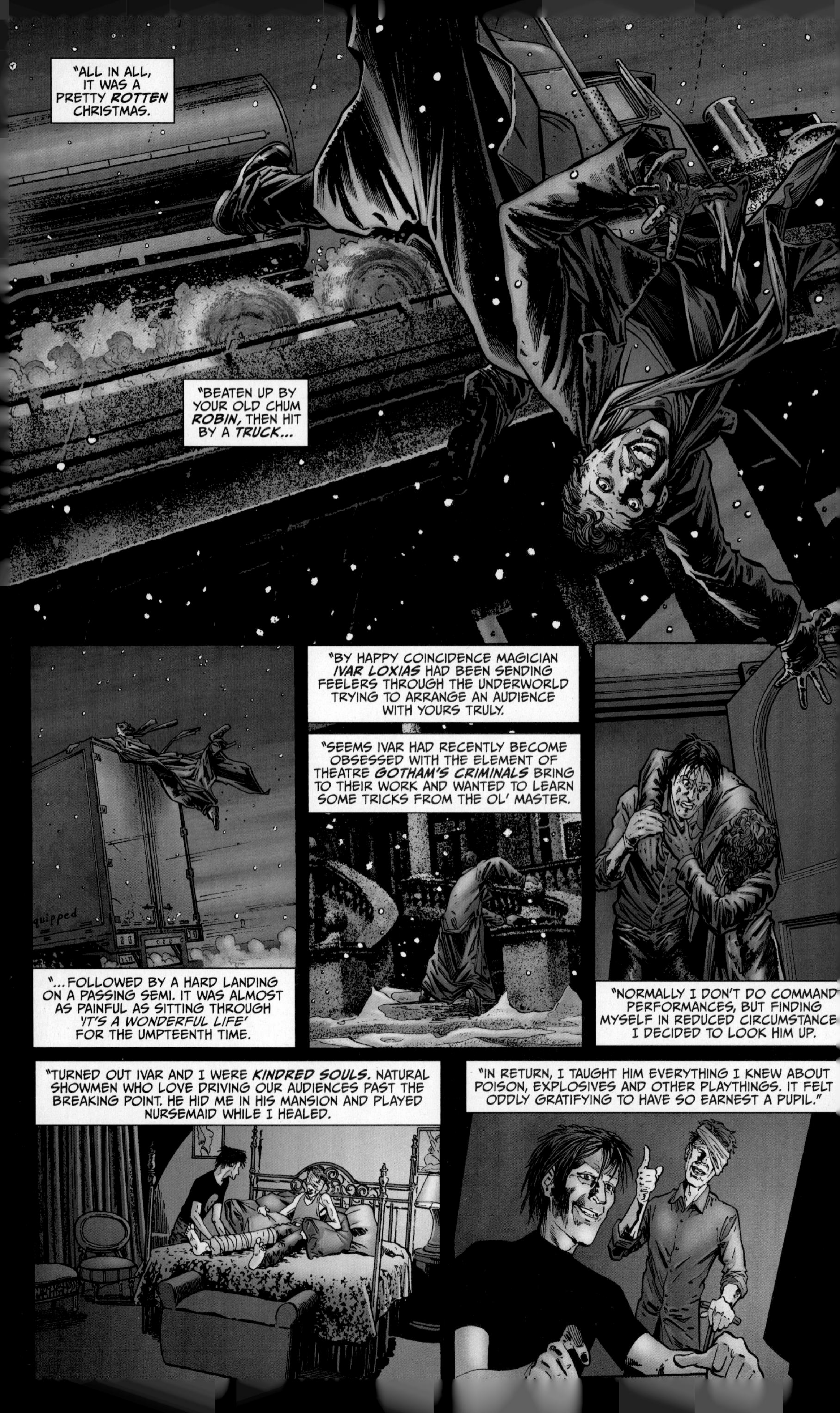
"ALL IN ALL, IT WAS A PRETTY ROTTEN CHRISTMAS.
"BEATEN UP BY YOUR OLD CHUM ROBIN, THEN HIT BY A TRUCK...
"...FOLLOWED BY A HARD LANDING ON A PASSING SEMI. IT WAS ALMOST AS PAINFUL AS SITTING THROUGH 'IT'S A WONDERFUL LIFE' FOR THE UMPTEENTH TIME.
"BY HAPPY COINCIDENCE MAGICIAN IVAR LOXIAS HAD BEEN SENDING FEELERS THROUGH THE UNDERWORLD TRYING TO ARRANGE AN AUDIENCE WITH YOURS TRULY.
"SEEMS IVAR HAD RECENTLY BECOME OBSESSED WITH THE ELEMENT OF THEATRE GOTHAM'S CRIMINALS BRING TO THEIR WORK AND WANTED TO LEARN SOME TRICKS FROM THE OL' MASTER.
"NORMALLY I DON'T DO COMMAND PERFORMANCES, BUT FINDING MYSELF IN REDUCED CIRCUMSTANCE I DECIDED TO LOOK HIM UP.
"TURNED OUT IVAR AND I WERE KINDRED SOULS. NATURAL SHOWMEN WHO LOVE DRIVING OUR AUDIENCES PAST THE BREAKING POINT. HE HID ME IN HIS MANSION AND PLAYED NURSEMAID WHILE I HEALED.
"IN RETURN, I TAUGHT HIM EVERYTHING I KNEW ABOUT POISON, EXPLOSIVES AND OTHER PLAYTHINGS. IT FELT ODDLY GRATIFYING TO HAVE SO EARNEST A PUPIL."

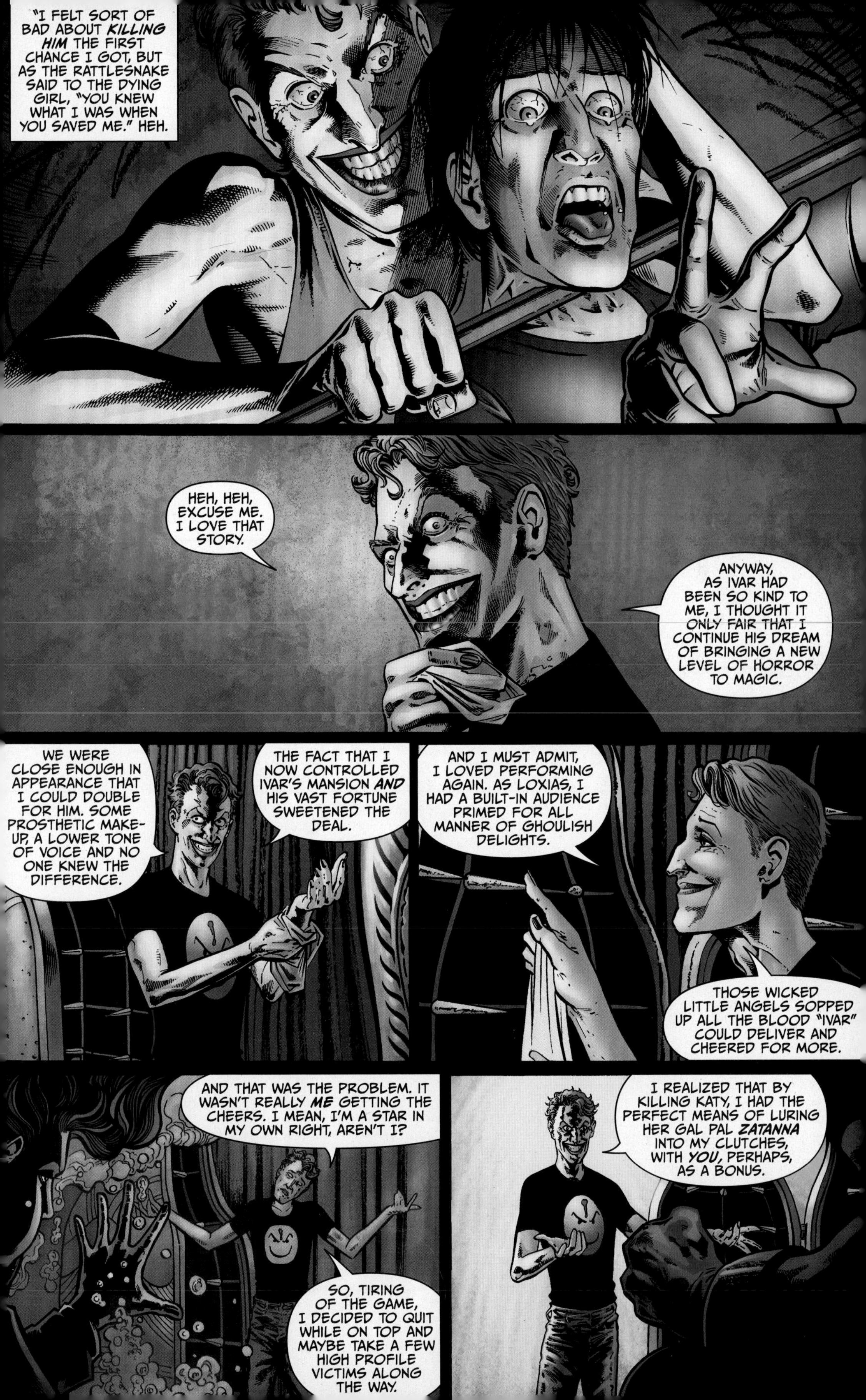
"I FELT SORT OF BAD ABOUT KILLING HIM THE FIRST CHANCE I GOT, BUT AS THE RATTLESNAKE SAID TO THE DYING GIRL, "YOU KNEW WHAT I WAS WHEN YOU SAVED ME." HEH.
HEH, HEH, EXCUSE ME. I LOVE THAT STORY.
ANYWAY, AS IVAR HAD BEEN SO KIND TO ME, I THOUGHT IT ONLY FAIR THAT I CONTINUE HIS DREAM OF BRINGING A NEW LEVEL OF HORROR TO MAGIC.
WE WERE CLOSE ENOUGH IN APPEARANCE THAT I COULD DOUBLE FOR HIM. SOME PROSTHETIC MAKE-UP, A LOWER TONE OF VOICE AND NO ONE KNEW THE DIFFERENCE.
THE FACT THAT I NOW CONTROLLED IVAR'S MANSION AND HIS VAST FORTUNE SWEETENED THE DEAL.
AND I MUST ADMIT, I LOVED PERFORMING AGAIN. AS LOXIAS, I HAD A BUILT-IN AUDIENCE PRIMED FOR ALL MANNER OF GHOULISH DELIGHTS.
THOSE WICKED LITTLE ANGELS SOPPED UP ALL THE BLOOD "IVAR" COULD DELIVER AND CHEERED FOR MORE.
AND THAT WAS THE PROBLEM. IT WASN'T REALLY ME GETTING THE CHEERS. I MEAN, I'M A STAR IN MY OWN RIGHT, AREN'T I?
SO, TIRING OF THE GAME, I DECIDED TO QUIT WHILE ON TOP AND MAYBE TAKE A FEW HIGH PROFILE VICTIMS ALONG THE WAY.
I REALIZED THAT BY KILLING KATY, I HAD THE PERFECT MEANS OF LURING HER GAL PAL ZATANNA INTO MY CLUTCHES, WITH YOU, PERHAPS, AS A BONUS.

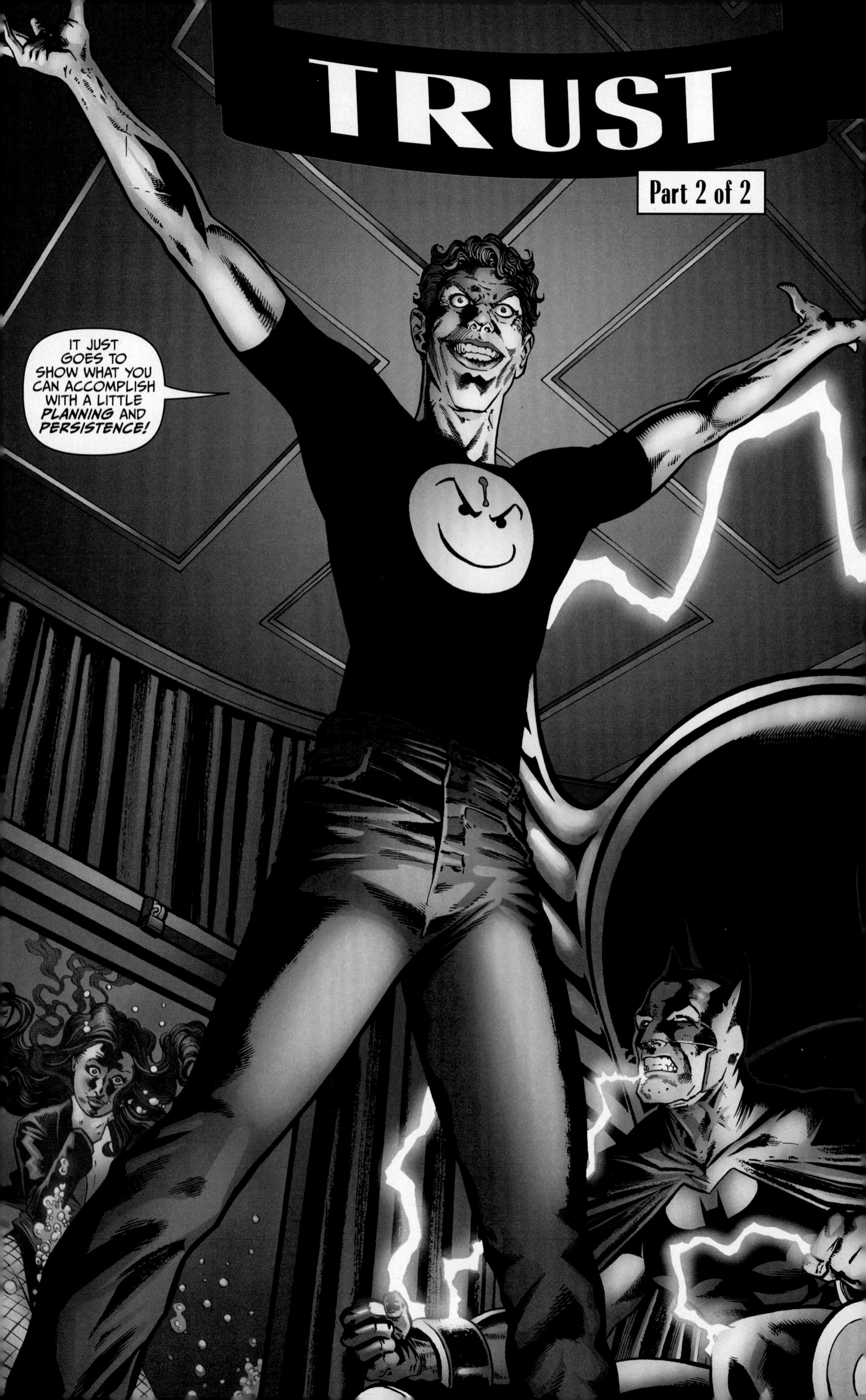
TRUST
Part 2 of 2
IT JUST GOES TO SHOW WHAT YOU CAN ACCOMPLISH WITH A LITTLE PLANNING AND PERSISTENCE!

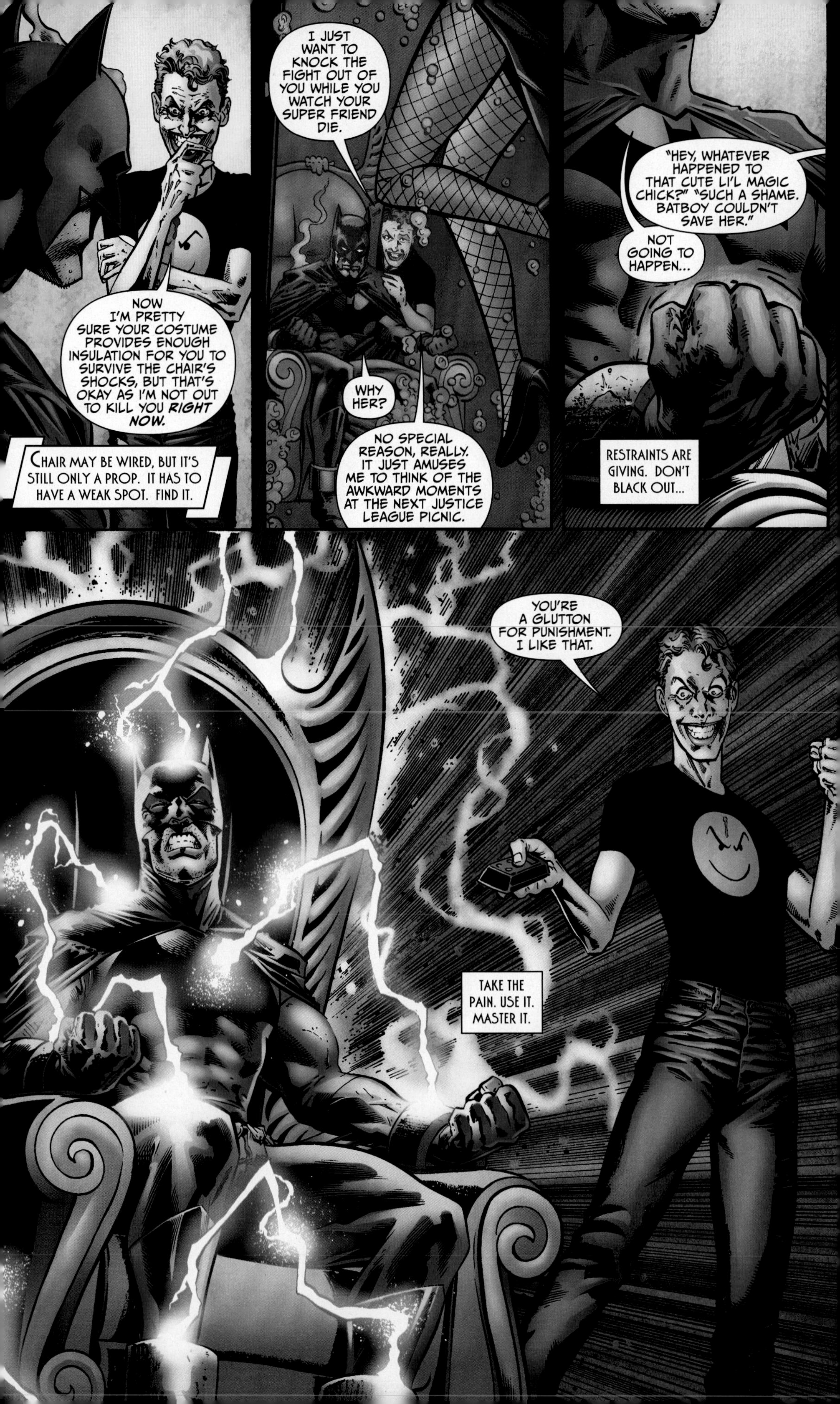
NOW I'M PRETTY SURE YOUR COSTUME PROVIDES ENOUGH INSULATION FOR YOU TO SURVIVE THE CHAIR'S SHOCKS, BUT THAT'S OKAY AS I'M NOT OUT TO KILL YOU *RIGHT NOW.*
CHAIR MAY BE WIRED, BUT IT'S STILL ONLY A PROP. IT HAS TO HAVE A WEAK SPOT. FIND IT.
I JUST WANT TO KNOCK THE FIGHT OUT OF YOU WHILE YOU WATCH YOUR SUPER FRIEND DIE.
WHY HER?
NO SPECIAL REASON, REALLY. IT JUST AMUSES ME TO THINK OF THE AWKWARD MOMENTS AT THE NEXT JUSTICE LEAGUE PICNIC.
"HEY, WHATEVER HAPPENED TO THAT CUTE LI'L MAGIC CHICK?" "SUCH A SHAME. BATBOY COULDN'T SAVE HER."
NOT GOING TO HAPPEN...
RESTRAINTS ARE GIVING. DON'T BLACK OUT...
YOU'RE A GLUTTON FOR PUNISHMENT. I LIKE THAT.
TAKE THE PAIN. USE IT. MASTER IT.

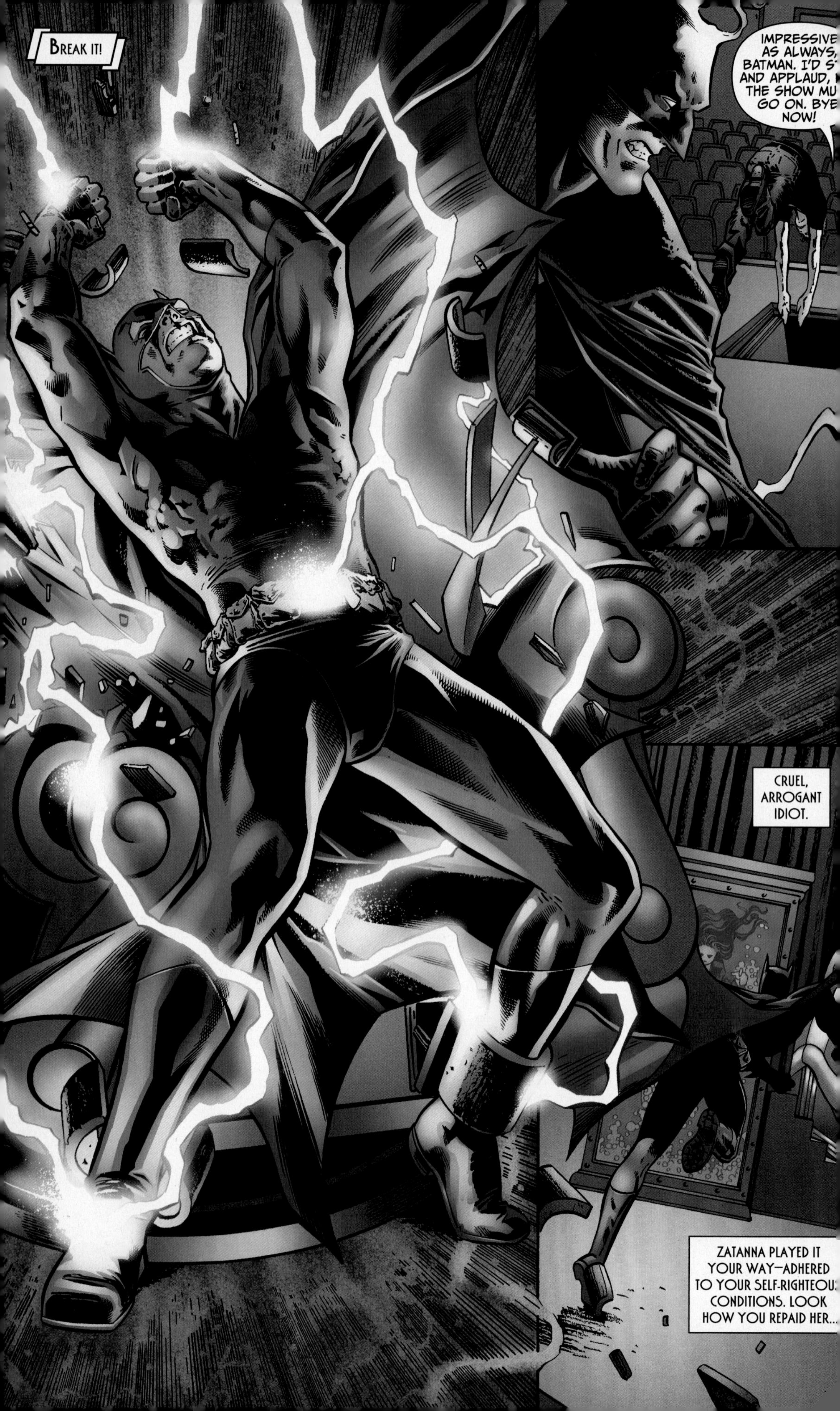

BREAK IT!
IMPRESSIVE AS ALWAYS, BATMAN. I'D S AND APPLAUD, THE SHOW MU GO ON. BYE NOW!
CRUEL, ARROGANT IDIOT.
ZATANNA PLAYED IT YOUR WAY—ADHERED TO YOUR SELF-RIGHTEOU CONDITIONS. LOOK HOW YOU REPAID HER...

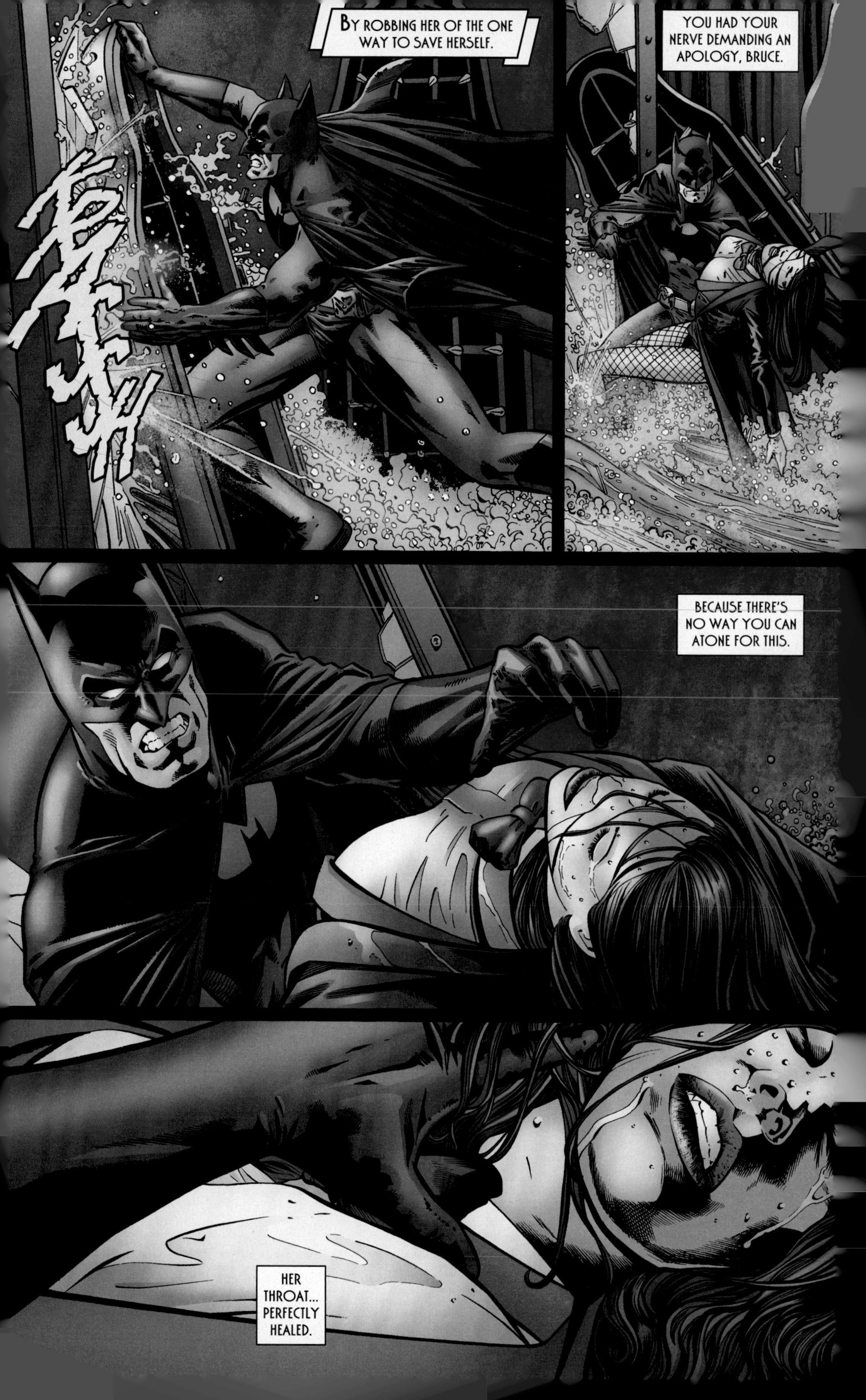

By robbing her of the one way to save herself.
You had your nerve demanding an apology, Bruce.
Because there's no way you can atone for this.
Her throat... perfectly healed.

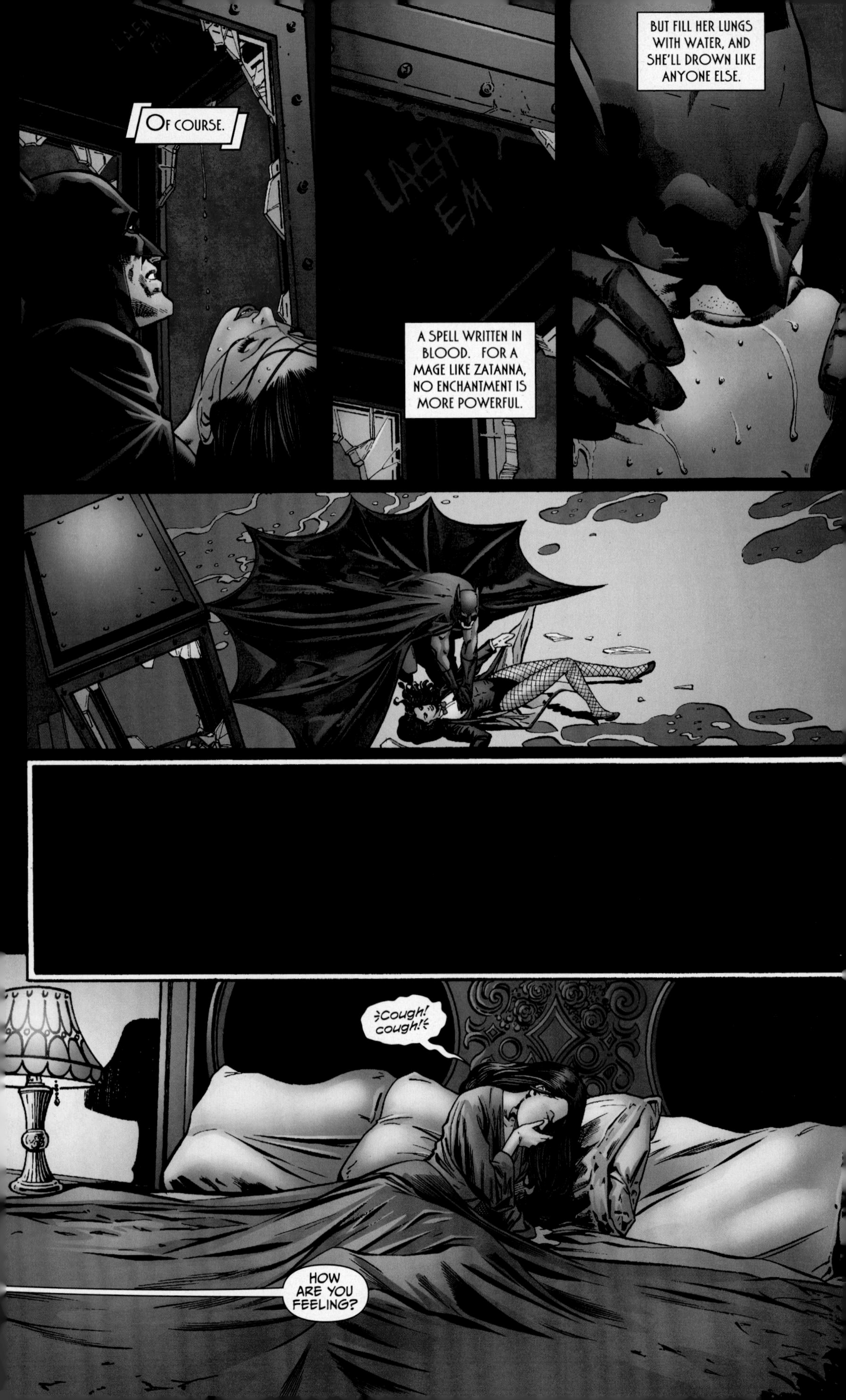
OF COURSE.
LAEH EM
A SPELL WRITTEN IN BLOOD. FOR A MAGE LIKE ZATANNA, NO ENCHANTMENT IS MORE POWERFUL.
BUT FILL HER LUNGS WITH WATER, AND SHE'LL DROWN LIKE ANYONE ELSE.
Cough! cough!
HOW ARE YOU FEELING?

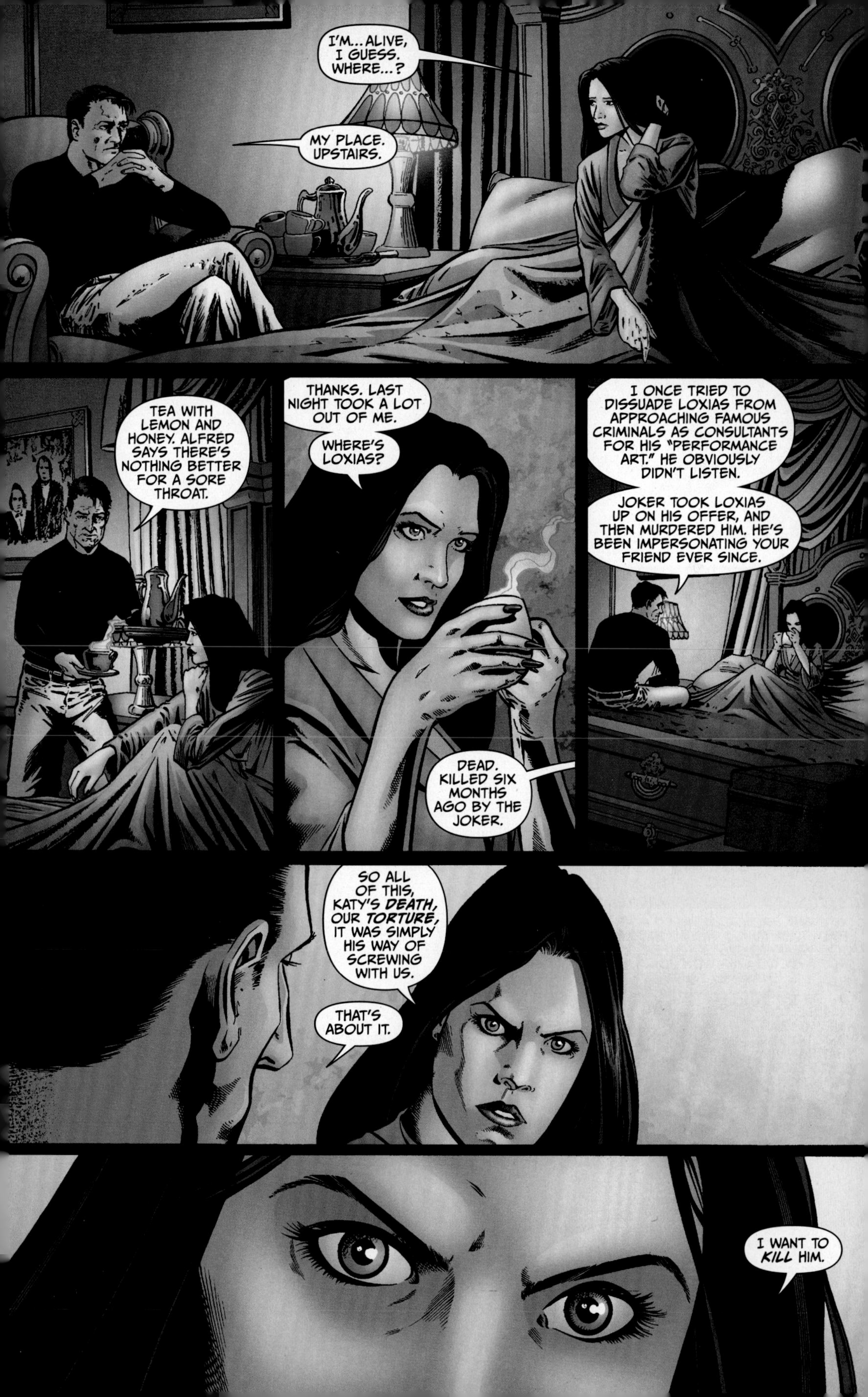
I'M... ALIVE, I GUESS. WHERE...?
MY PLACE. UPSTAIRS.
TEA WITH LEMON AND HONEY. ALFRED SAYS THERE'S NOTHING BETTER FOR A SORE THROAT.
THANKS. LAST NIGHT TOOK A LOT OUT OF ME.
WHERE'S LOXIAS?
DEAD. KILLED SIX MONTHS AGO BY THE JOKER.
I ONCE TRIED TO DISSUADE LOXIAS FROM APPROACHING FAMOUS CRIMINALS AS CONSULTANTS FOR HIS "PERFORMANCE ART." HE OBVIOUSLY DIDN'T LISTEN.
JOKER TOOK LOXIAS UP ON HIS OFFER, AND THEN MURDERED HIM. HE'S BEEN IMPERSONATING YOUR FRIEND EVER SINCE.
SO ALL OF THIS, KATY'S *DEATH*, OUR *TORTURE*, IT WAS SIMPLY HIS WAY OF SCREWING WITH US.
THAT'S ABOUT IT.
I WANT TO *KILL* HIM.

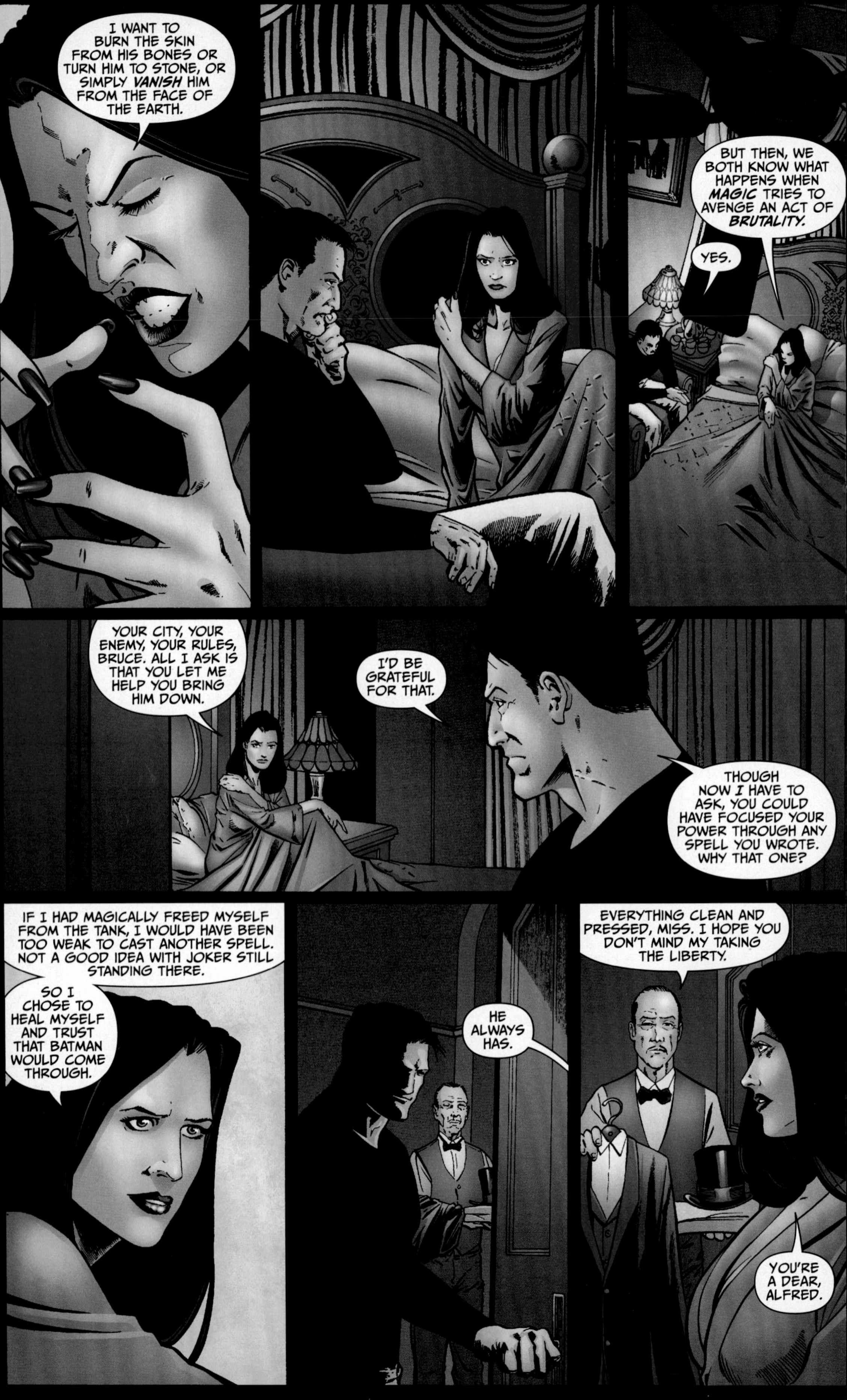
I WANT TO BURN THE SKIN FROM HIS BONES OR TURN HIM TO STONE, OR SIMPLY VANISH HIM FROM THE FACE OF THE EARTH.
BUT THEN, WE BOTH KNOW WHAT HAPPENS WHEN MAGIC TRIES TO AVENGE AN ACT OF BRUTALITY.
YES.
YOUR CITY, YOUR ENEMY, YOUR RULES, BRUCE. ALL I ASK IS THAT YOU LET ME HELP YOU BRING HIM DOWN.
I'D BE GRATEFUL FOR THAT.
THOUGH NOW I HAVE TO ASK, YOU COULD HAVE FOCUSED YOUR POWER THROUGH ANY SPELL YOU WROTE. WHY THAT ONE?
IF I HAD MAGICALLY FREED MYSELF FROM THE TANK, I WOULD HAVE BEEN TOO WEAK TO CAST ANOTHER SPELL. NOT A GOOD IDEA WITH JOKER STILL STANDING THERE.
SO I CHOSE TO HEAL MYSELF AND TRUST THAT BATMAN WOULD COME THROUGH.
HE ALWAYS HAS.
EVERYTHING CLEAN AND PRESSED, MISS. I HOPE YOU DON'T MIND MY TAKING THE LIBERTY.
YOU'RE A DEAR, ALFRED.

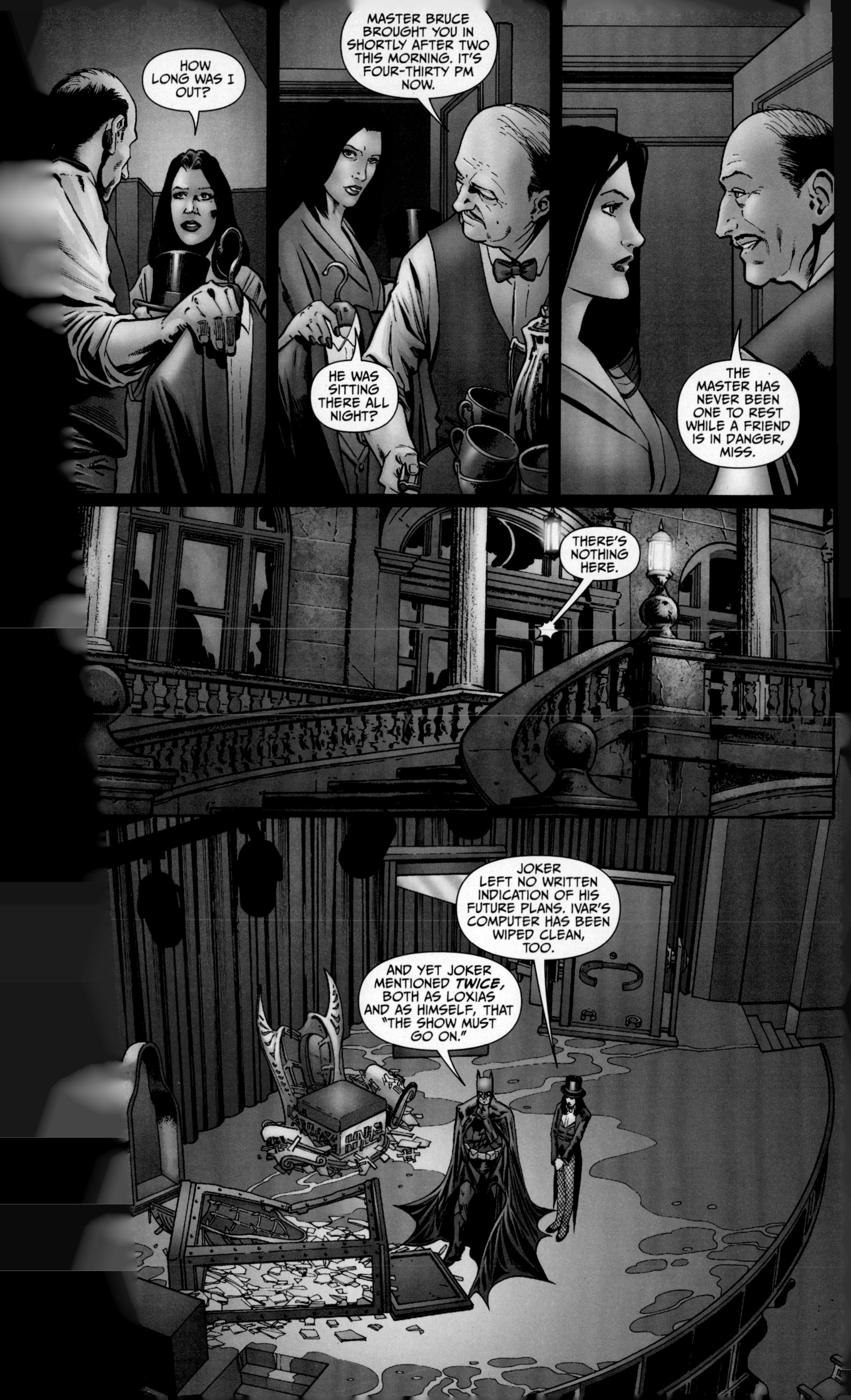
HOW LONG WAS I OUT?
MASTER BRUCE BROUGHT YOU IN SHORTLY AFTER TWO THIS MORNING. IT'S FOUR-THIRTY PM NOW.
HE WAS SITTING THERE ALL NIGHT?
THE MASTER HAS NEVER BEEN ONE TO REST WHILE A FRIEND IS IN DANGER, MISS.
THERE'S NOTHING HERE.
JOKER LEFT NO WRITTEN INDICATION OF HIS FUTURE PLANS. IVAR'S COMPUTER HAS BEEN WIPED CLEAN, TOO.
AND YET JOKER MENTIONED **TWICE,** BOTH AS LOXIAS AND AS HIMSELF, THAT "THE SHOW MUST GO ON."

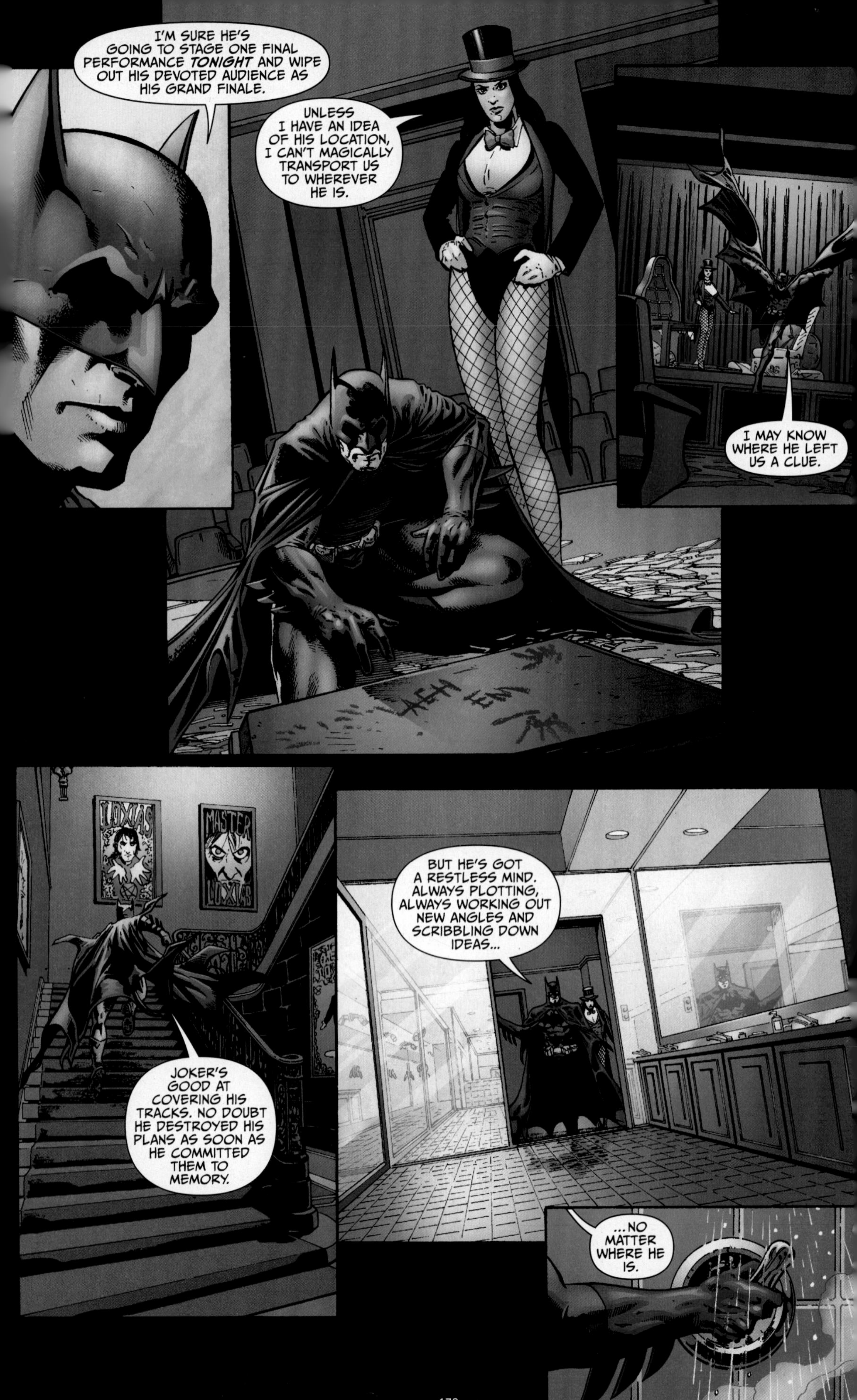
I'M SURE HE'S GOING TO STAGE ONE FINAL PERFORMANCE TONIGHT AND WIPE OUT HIS DEVOTED AUDIENCE AS HIS GRAND FINALE.
UNLESS I HAVE AN IDEA OF HIS LOCATION, I CAN'T MAGICALLY TRANSPORT US TO WHEREVER HE IS.
I MAY KNOW WHERE HE LEFT US A CLUE.
LUXIAS
MASTER LUXIAS
JOKER'S GOOD AT COVERING HIS TRACKS. NO DOUBT HE DESTROYED HIS PLANS AS SOON AS HE COMMITTED THEM TO MEMORY.
BUT HE'S GOT A RESTLESS MIND. ALWAYS PLOTTING, ALWAYS WORKING OUT NEW ANGLES AND SCRIBBLING DOWN IDEAS...
...NO MATTER WHERE HE IS.

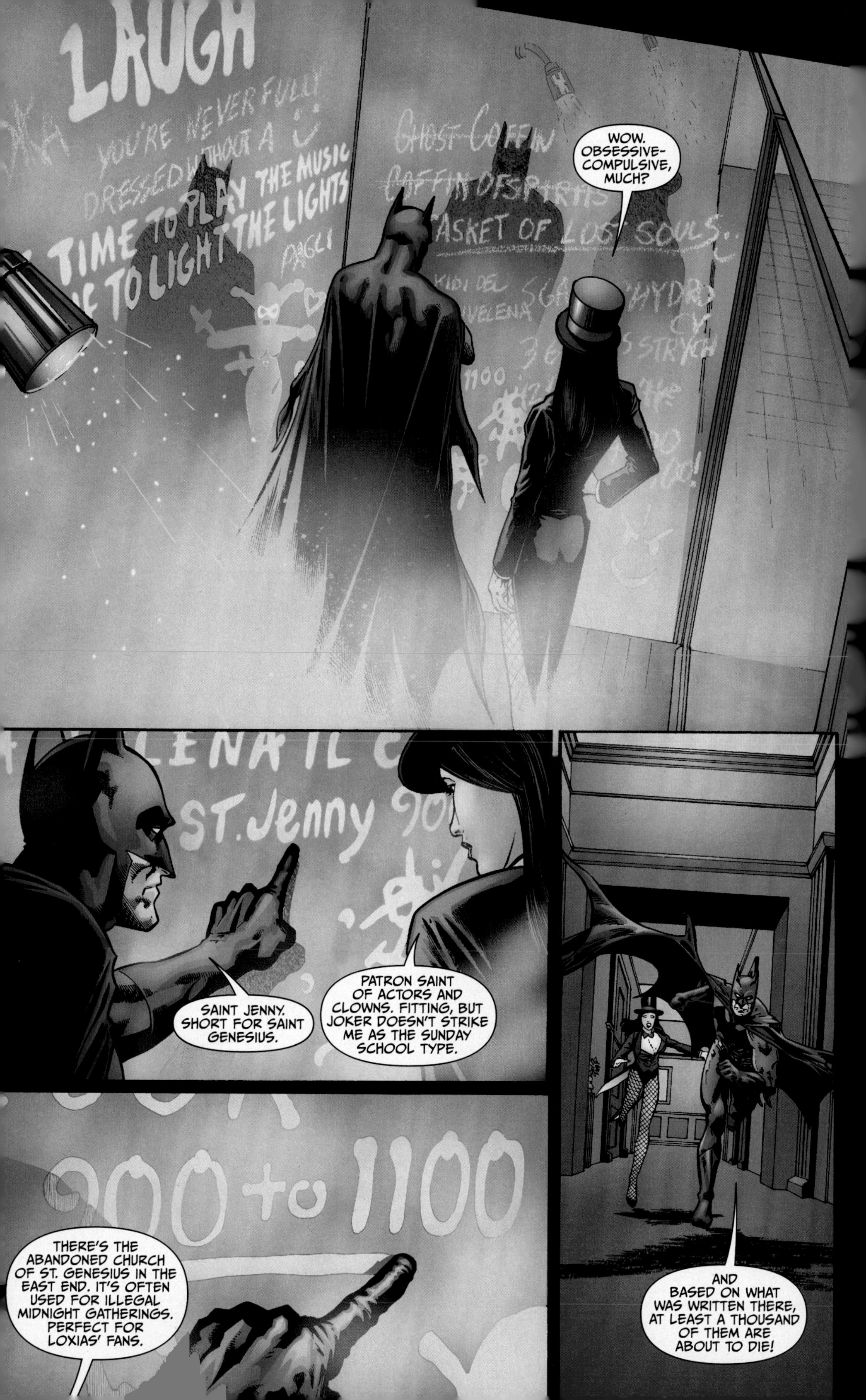

LAUGH
TIME TO PLAY THE MUSIC
TIME TO LIGHT THE LIGHTS
CASKET OF LOST SOULS.
WOW. OBSESSIVE-COMPULSIVE, MUCH?
ST. Jenny
SAINT JENNY. SHORT FOR SAINT GENESIUS.
PATRON SAINT OF ACTORS AND CLOWNS. FITTING, BUT JOKER DOESN'T STRIKE ME AS THE SUNDAY SCHOOL TYPE.
900 to 1100
THERE'S THE ABANDONED CHURCH OF ST. GENESIUS IN THE EAST END. IT'S OFTEN USED FOR ILLEGAL MIDNIGHT GATHERINGS. PERFECT FOR LOXIAS' FANS.
AND BASED ON WHAT WAS WRITTEN THERE, AT LEAST A THOUSAND OF THEM ARE ABOUT TO DIE!

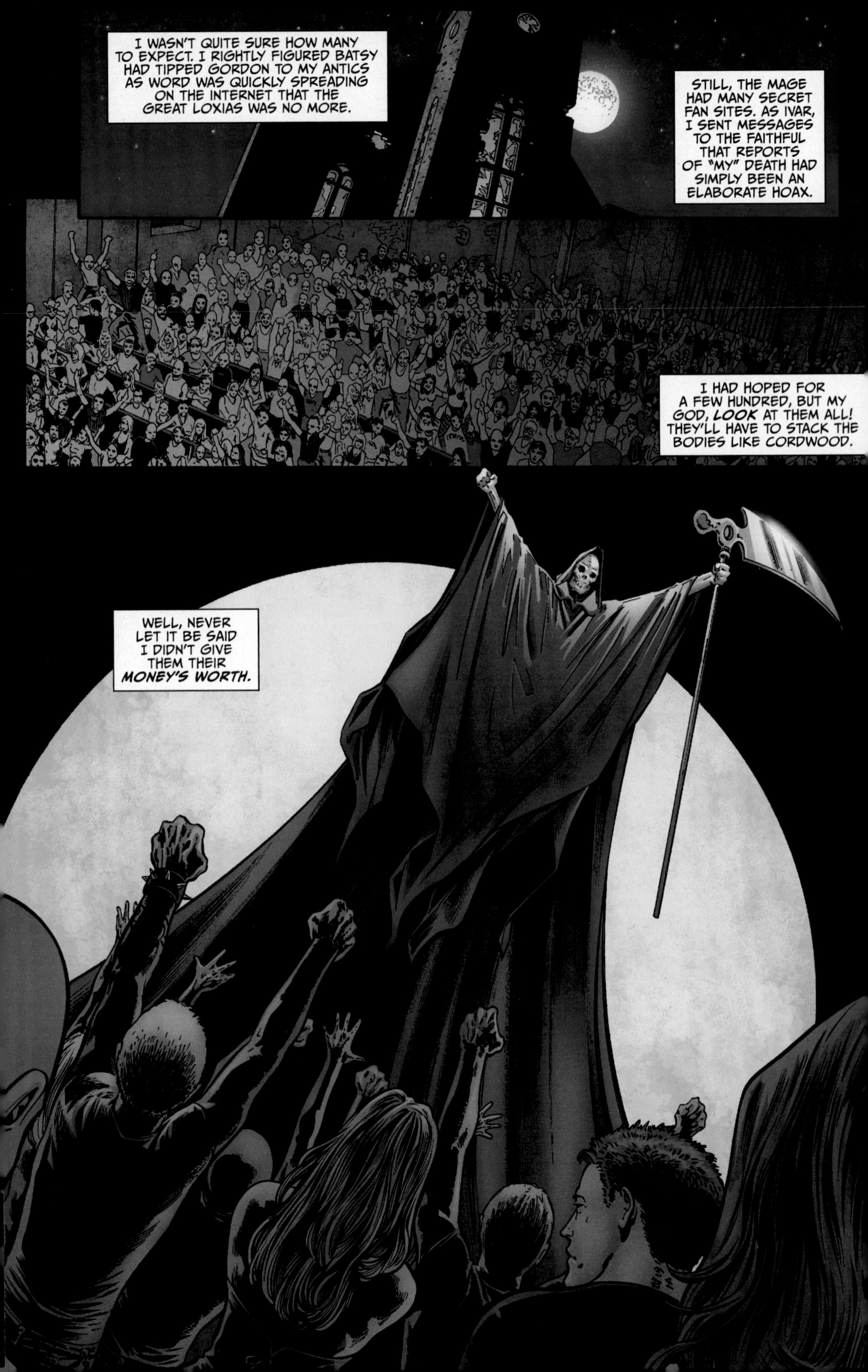
I WASN'T QUITE SURE HOW MANY TO EXPECT. I RIGHTLY FIGURED BATSY HAD TIPPED GORDON TO MY ANTICS AS WORD WAS QUICKLY SPREADING ON THE INTERNET THAT THE GREAT LOXIAS WAS NO MORE.
STILL, THE MAGE HAD MANY SECRET FAN SITES. AS IVAR, I SENT MESSAGES TO THE FAITHFUL THAT REPORTS OF "MY" DEATH HAD SIMPLY BEEN AN ELABORATE HOAX.
I HAD HOPED FOR A FEW HUNDRED, BUT MY GOD, ***LOOK*** AT THEM ALL! THEY'LL HAVE TO STACK THE BODIES LIKE CORDWOOD.
WELL, NEVER LET IT BE SAID I DIDN'T GIVE THEM THEIR ***MONEY'S WORTH.***

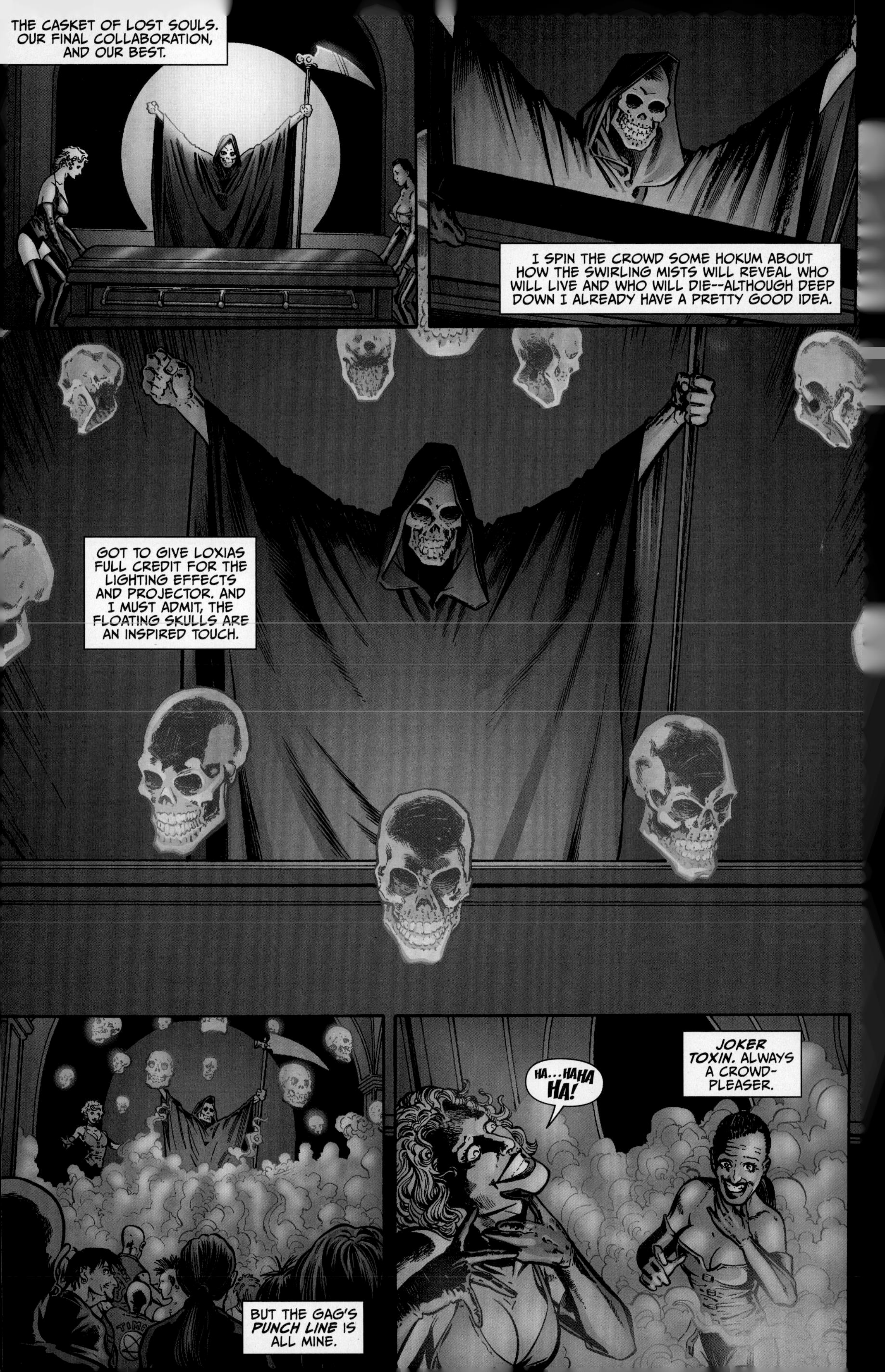
THE CASKET OF LOST SOULS. OUR FINAL COLLABORATION, AND OUR BEST.
I SPIN THE CROWD SOME HOKUM ABOUT HOW THE SWIRLING MISTS WILL REVEAL WHO WILL LIVE AND WHO WILL DIE--ALTHOUGH DEEP DOWN I ALREADY HAVE A PRETTY GOOD IDEA.
GOT TO GIVE LOXIAS FULL CREDIT FOR THE LIGHTING EFFECTS AND PROJECTOR. AND I MUST ADMIT, THE FLOATING SKULLS ARE AN INSPIRED TOUCH.
BUT THE GAG'S *PUNCH LINE* IS ALL MINE.
HA...HAHA HA!
JOKER TOXIN. ALWAYS A CROWD-PLEASER.

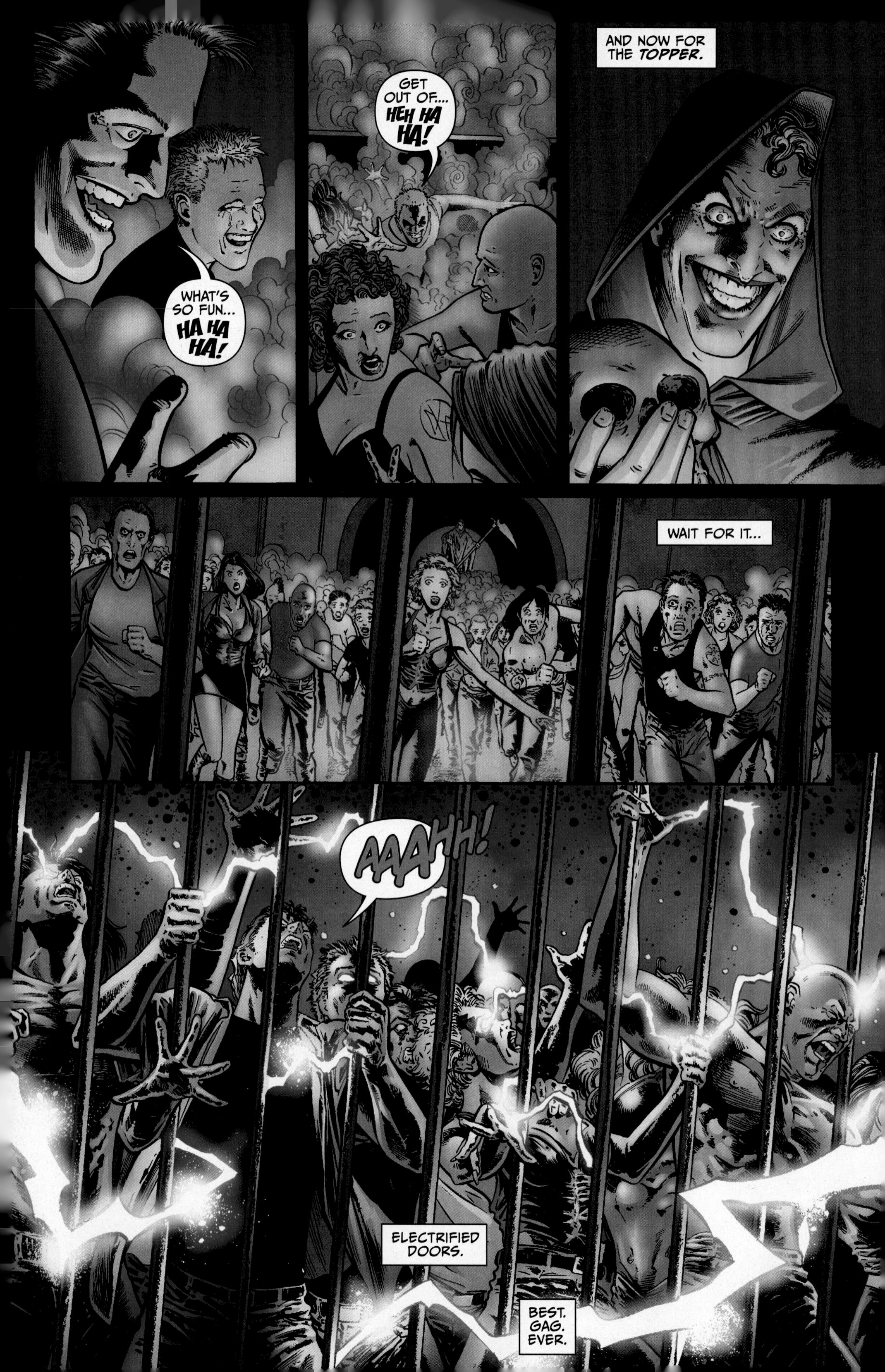
WHAT'S SO FUN... HA HA HA!
GET OUT OF... HEH HA HA!
AND NOW FOR THE *TOPPER*.
WAIT FOR IT...
AAAHH!
ELECTRIFIED DOORS.
BEST. GAG. EVER.

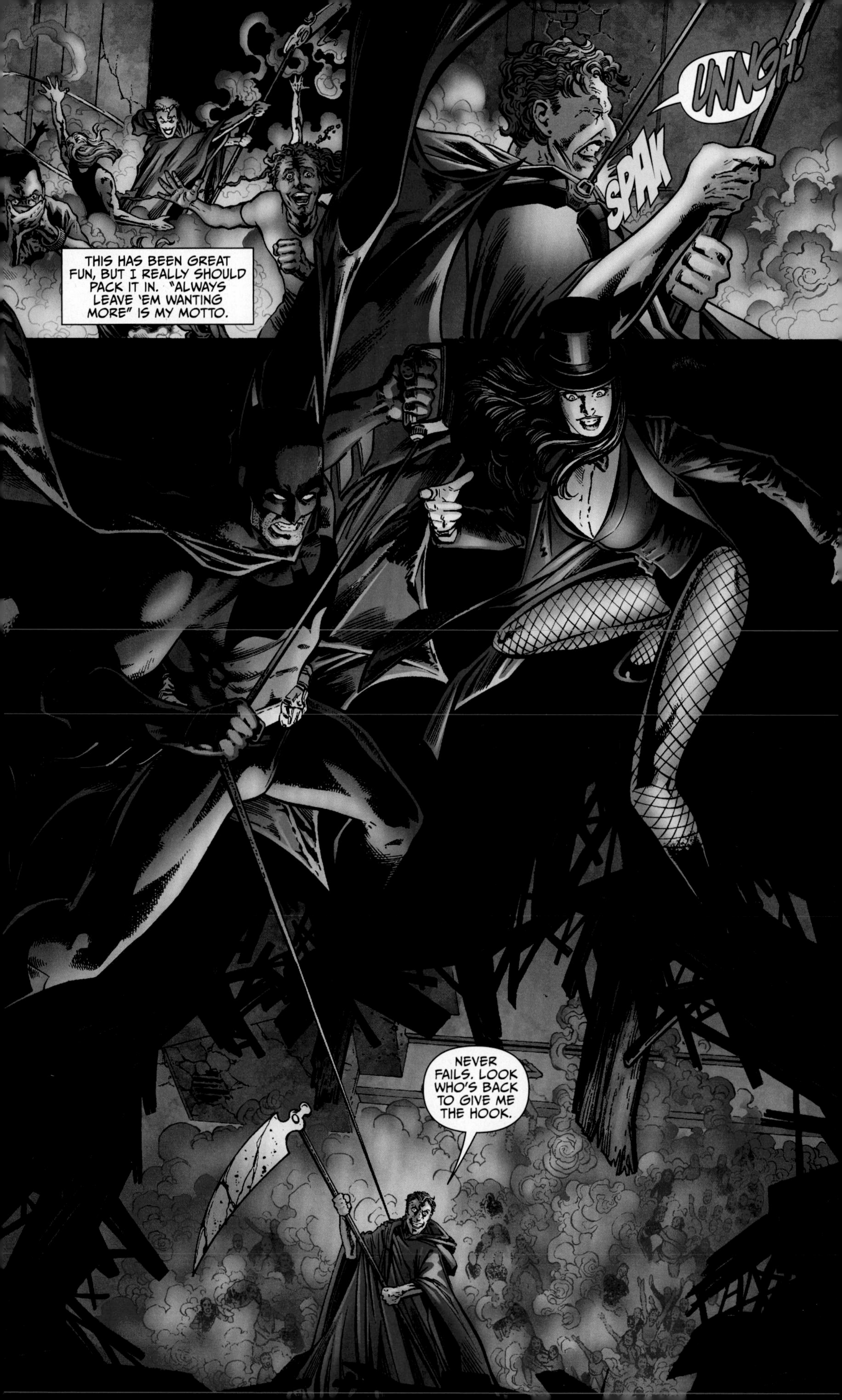
UNNGH!
SPAK
THIS HAS BEEN GREAT FUN, BUT I REALLY SHOULD PACK IT IN. "ALWAYS LEAVE 'EM WANTING MORE" IS MY MOTTO.
NEVER FAILS. LOOK WHO'S BACK TO GIVE ME THE HOOK.

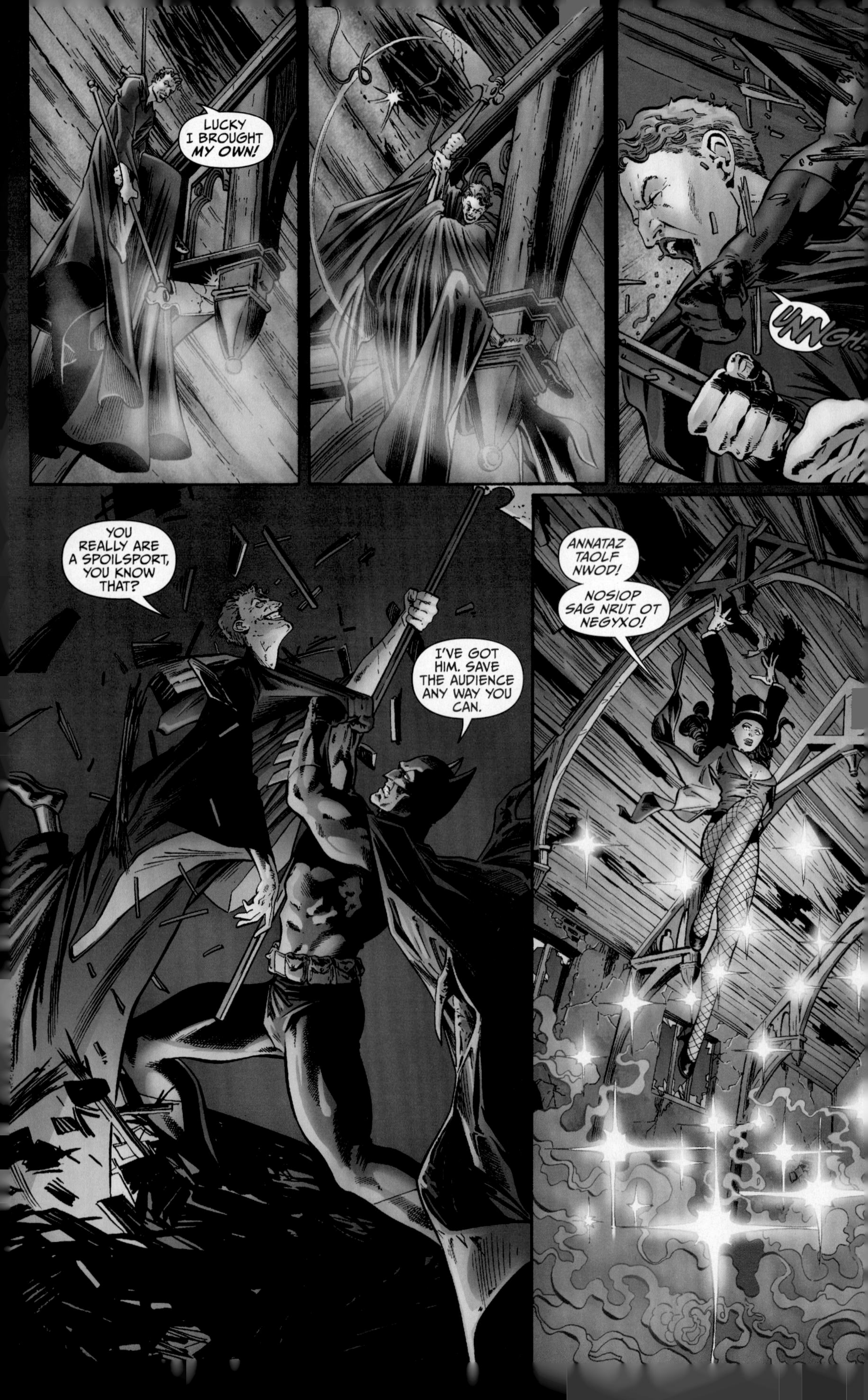
LUCKY I BROUGHT MY OWN!
UNNGH
YOU REALLY ARE A SPOILSPORT, YOU KNOW THAT?
I'VE GOT HIM. SAVE THE AUDIENCE ANY WAY YOU CAN.
ANNATAZ TAOLF NWOD!
NOSIOP SAG NRUT OT NEGYXO!

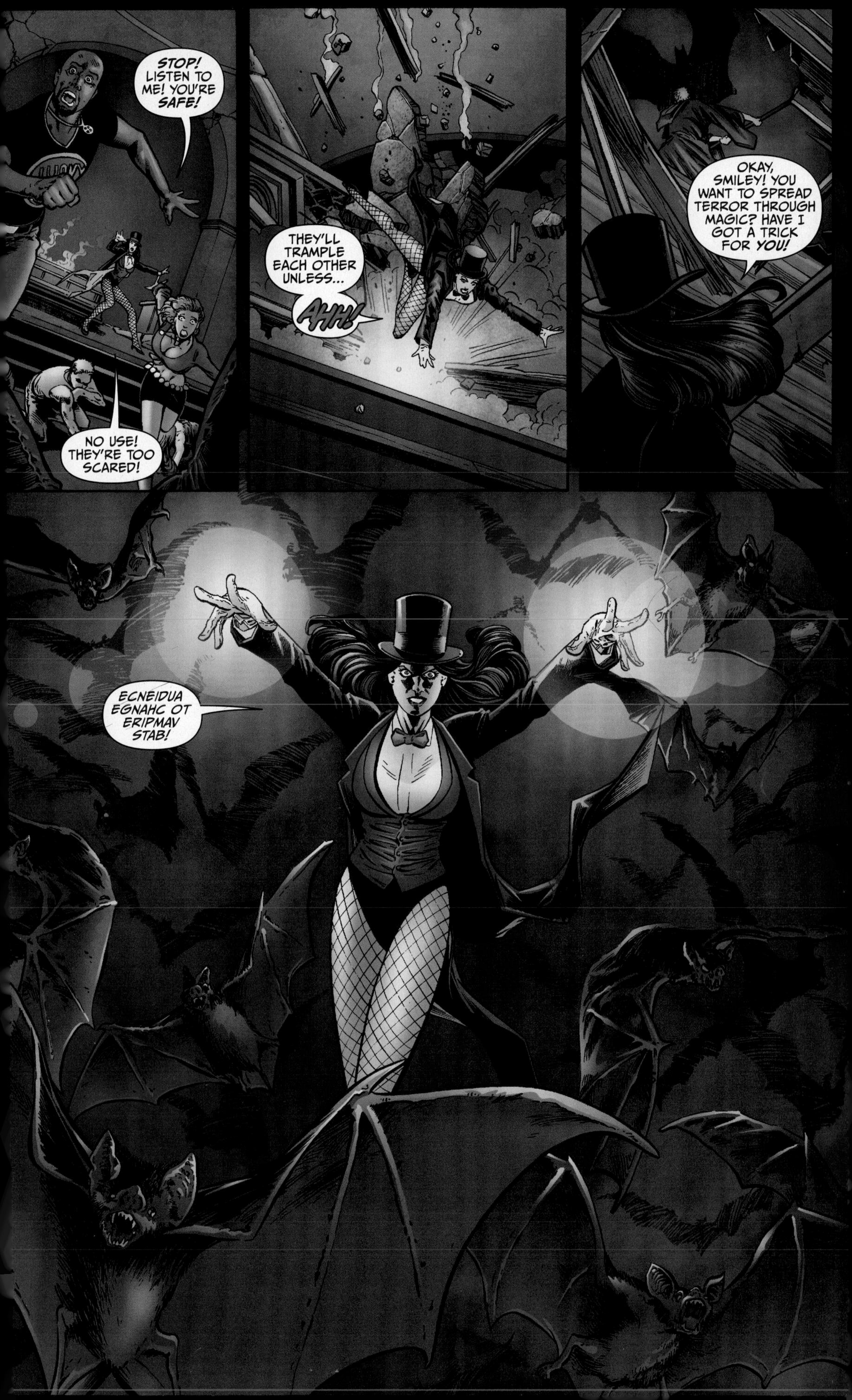
STOP! LISTEN TO ME! YOU'RE SAFE!
NO USE! THEY'RE TOO SCARED!
THEY'LL TRAMPLE EACH OTHER UNLESS...
AHH!
OKAY, SMILEY! YOU WANT TO SPREAD TERROR THROUGH MAGIC? HAVE I GOT A TRICK FOR YOU!
ECNEIDUA EGNAHC OT ERIPMAV STAB!

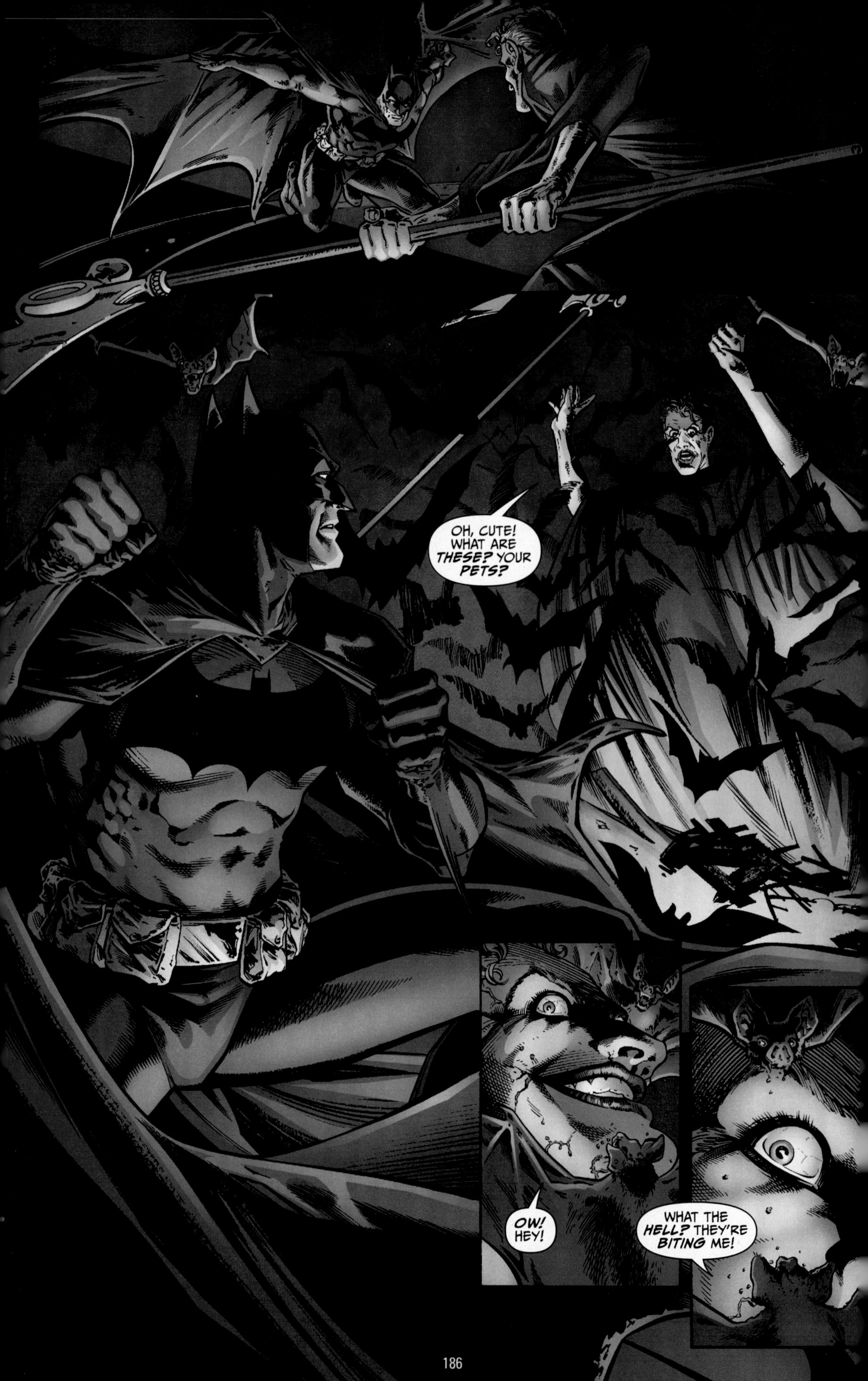
OH, CUTE! WHAT ARE THESE? YOUR PETS?
OW! HEY!
WHAT THE HELL? THEY'RE BITING ME!

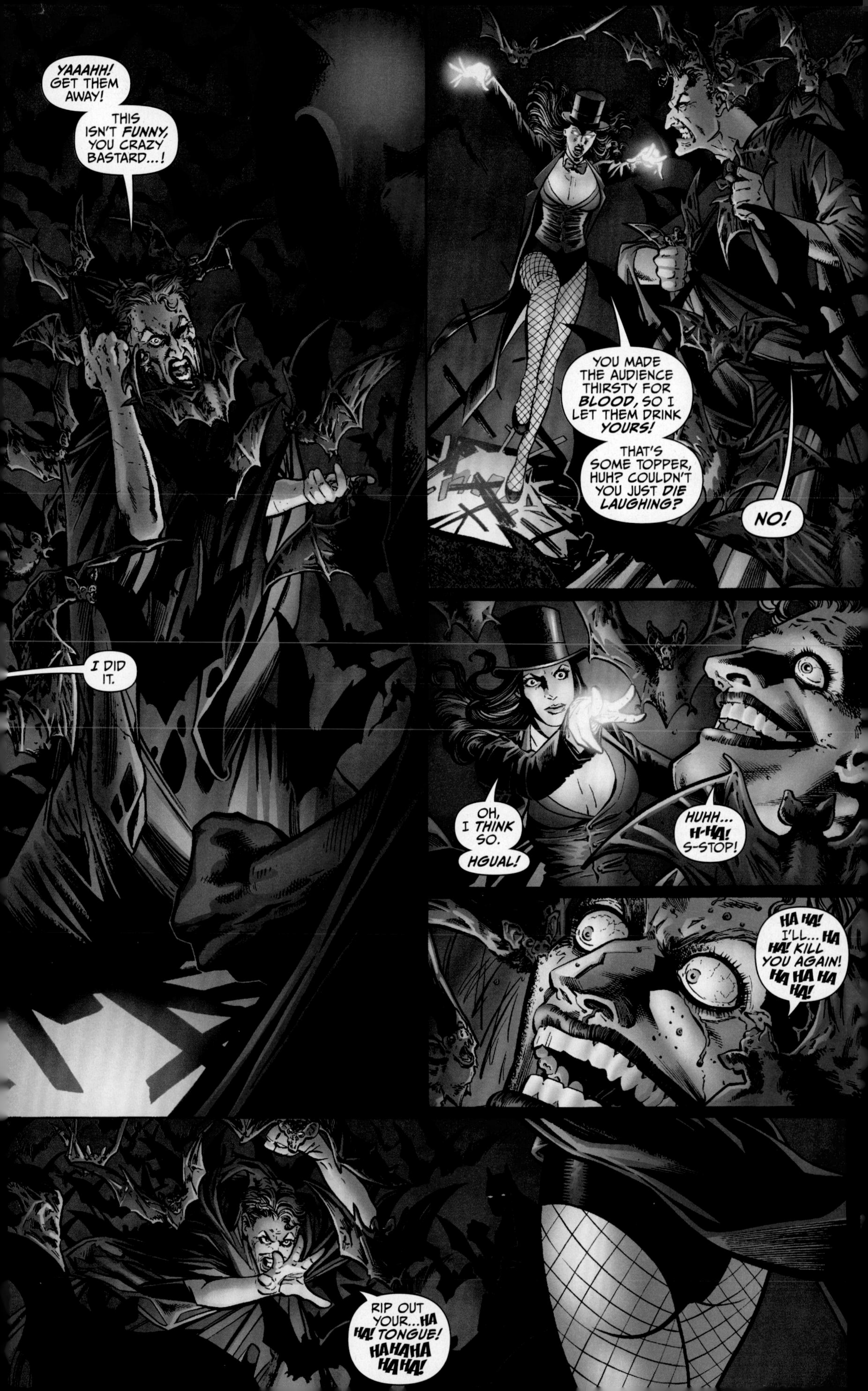

YAAAHH! GET THEM AWAY!
THIS ISN'T FUNNY, YOU CRAZY BASTARD...!
YOU MADE THE AUDIENCE THIRSTY FOR BLOOD, SO I LET THEM DRINK YOURS!
THAT'S SOME TOPPER, HUH? COULDN'T YOU JUST DIE LAUGHING?
NO!
I DID IT.
OH, I THINK SO. HGUAL!
HUHH... H-HA! S-STOP!
HA HA! I'LL... HA HA! KILL YOU AGAIN! HA HA HA HA!
RIP OUT YOUR...HA HA! TONGUE! HAHAHA HAHA!

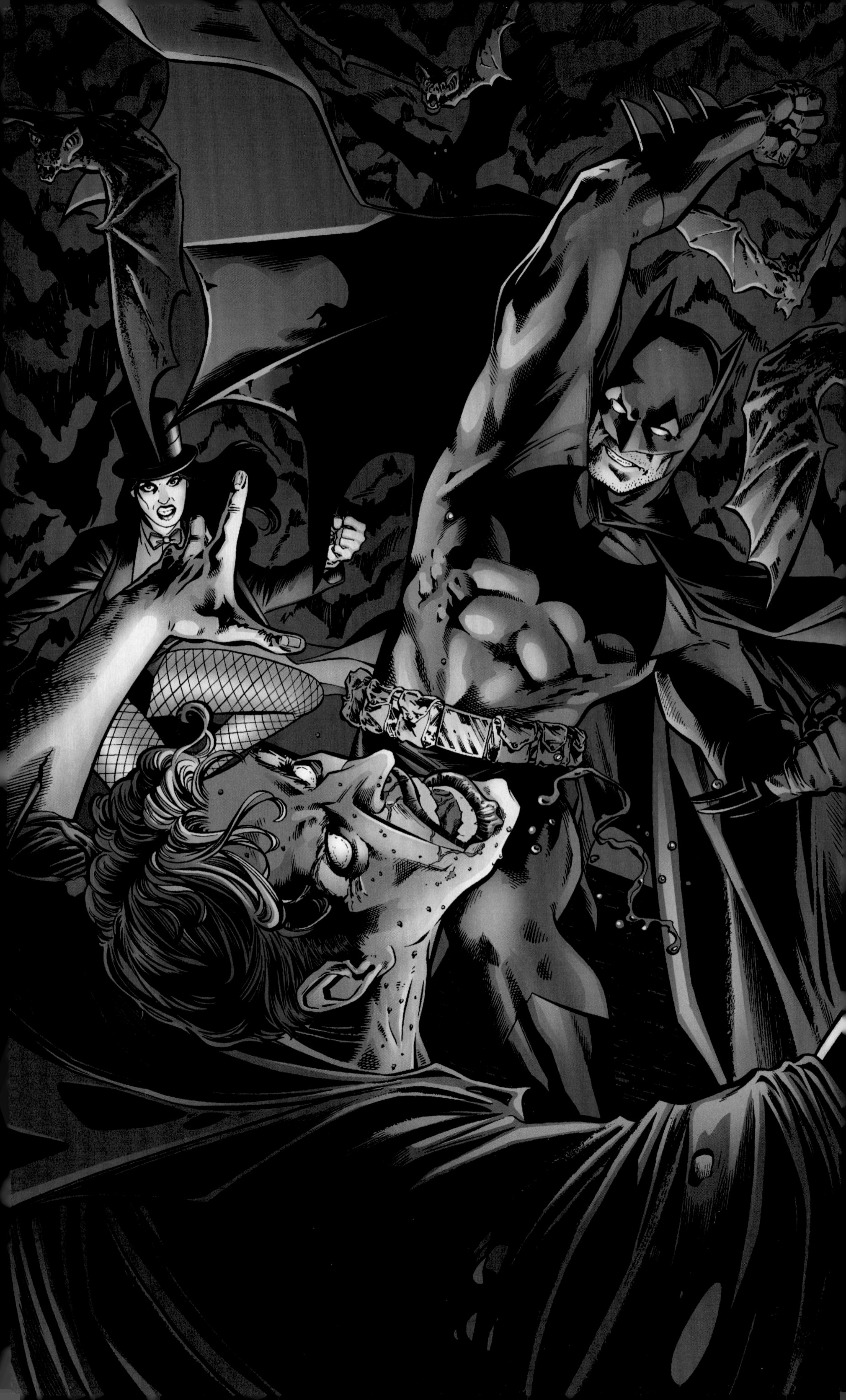

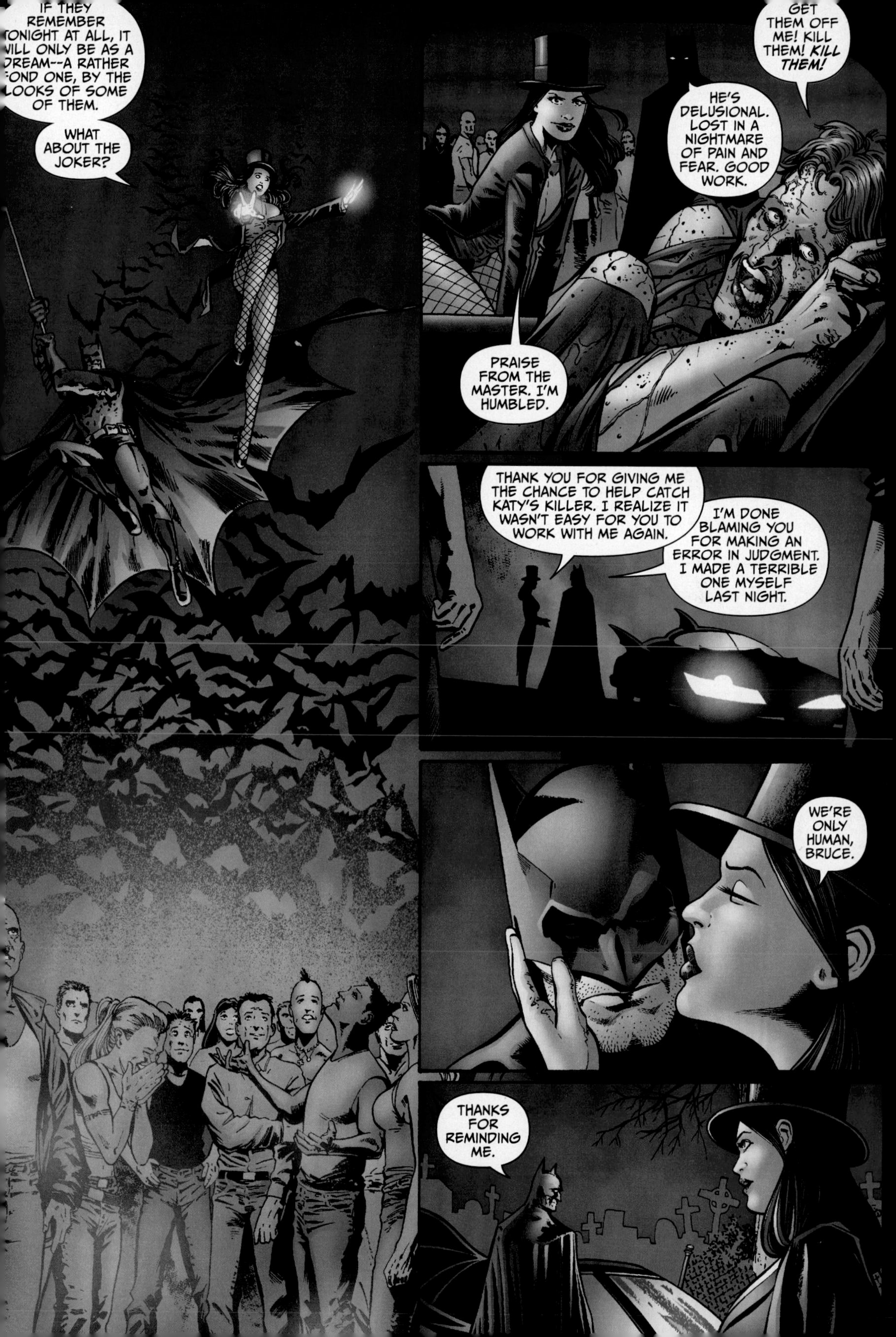
IF THEY REMEMBER TONIGHT AT ALL, IT WILL ONLY BE AS A DREAM--A RATHER FOND ONE, BY THE LOOKS OF SOME OF THEM.
WHAT ABOUT THE JOKER?
GET THEM OFF ME! KILL THEM! *KILL THEM!*
HE'S DELUSIONAL. LOST IN A NIGHTMARE OF PAIN AND FEAR. GOOD WORK.
PRAISE FROM THE MASTER. I'M HUMBLED.
THANK YOU FOR GIVING ME THE CHANCE TO HELP CATCH KATY'S KILLER. I REALIZE IT WASN'T EASY FOR YOU TO WORK WITH ME AGAIN.
I'M DONE BLAMING YOU FOR MAKING AN ERROR IN JUDGMENT. I MADE A TERRIBLE ONE MYSELF LAST NIGHT.
WE'RE ONLY HUMAN, BRUCE.
THANKS FOR REMINDING ME.

READ MORE OF THE DARK KNIGHT DETECTIVE'S ADVENTURES IN THESE COLLECTIONS FROM DC COMICS:

BATMAN

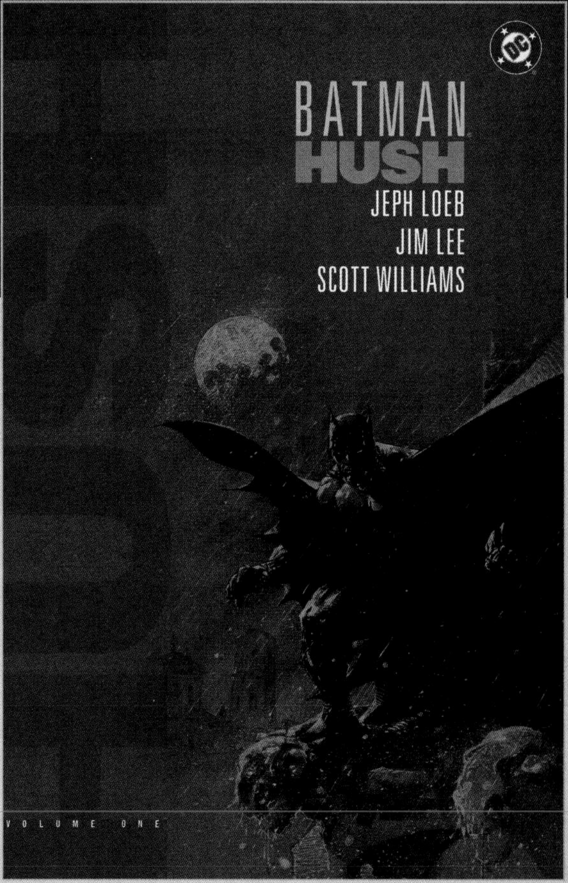
BATMAN
HUSH
JEPH LOEB
JIM LEE
SCOTT WILLIAMS
VOLUME ONE

BATMAN: HUSH VOLUME 1

Jeph Loeb, Jim Lee and **Scott Williams** tell an epic tale of friendship, trust and betrayal, in the first volume of a tale that spans a lifetime of the Dark Knight.

"THE ACTION IS EXCITING AND THE DETAIL IS METICULOUS."
— CRITIQUES ON INFINITE EARTHS

BATMAN:
THE DARK KNIGHT RETURNS

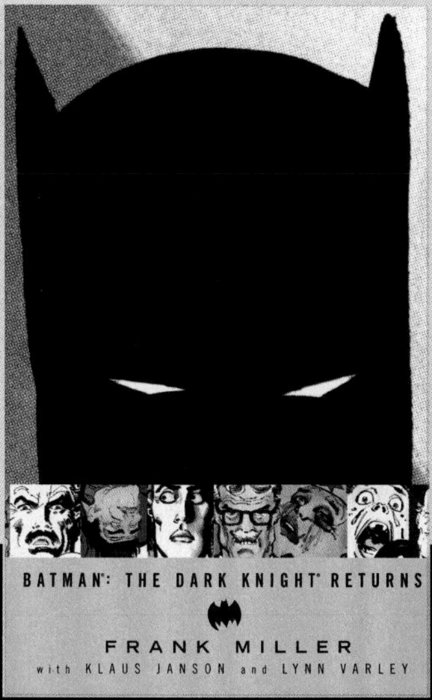
BATMAN: THE DARK KNIGHT RETURNS
FRANK MILLER
with KLAUS JANSON and LYNN VARLEY

FRANK MILLER
KLAUS JANSON
LYNN VARLEY

BATMAN:
THE LONG HALLOWEEN

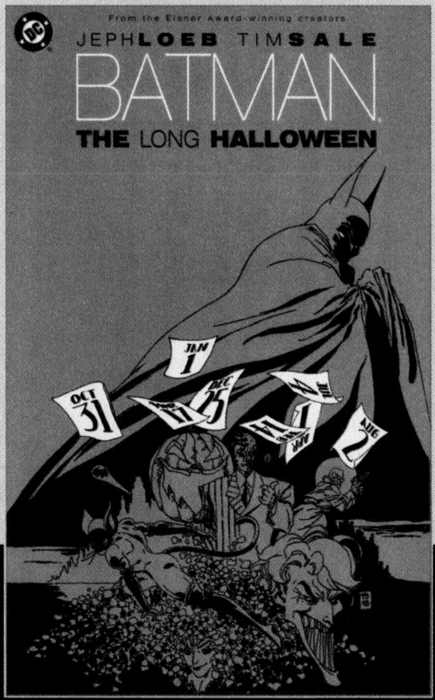
From the Eisner Award-winning creators
JEPH LOEB TIM SALE
BATMAN
THE LONG HALLOWEEN

JEPH LOEB
TIM SALE

BATMAN:
YEAR ONE

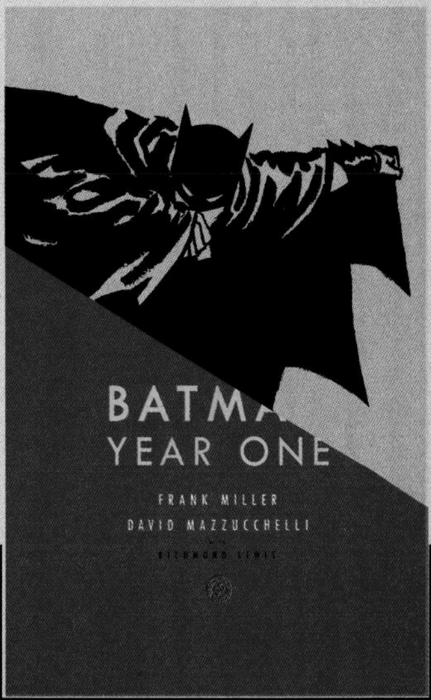
YEAR ONE
FRANK MILLER
DAVID MAZZUCCHELLI

FRANK MILLER
DAVID MAZZUCCHELLI